Rethinking Disney

RETHINKING
Disney

PRIVATE CONTROL, PUBLIC DIMENSIONS

EDITED BY Mike Budd and Max H. Kirsch

Wesleyan University Press MIDDLETOWN, CONNECTICUT

2005

Published by Wesleyan University Press, Middletown, CT 06459
© 2005 by Wesleyan University Press
All rights reserved
Printed in the United States of America
5 4 3 2 1

LIBRARY OF CONGRESS CATALOGING-IN-PUBLICATION DATA

Rethinking Disney : private control, public dimensions / edited by Mike Budd and Max H. Kirsch.

p. cm.

Selected papers from the international conference "Rethinking Disney" held in Nov. 2000 at Florida Atlantic University.

Includes bibliographical references and index.

ISBN-10: 0-8195-6789-2 (alk. paper)

ISBN-13: 978-0-8195-6789-5 (alk. paper)

ISBN-10: 0-8195-6790-6 (pbk. : alk. paper)

ISBN-13: 978-0-8195-6790-1 (pbk. : alk. paper)

1. Walt Disney Company—Congresses.

I. Budd, Mike, 1944–

II. Kirsch, Max H., 1953–

PN1999.W27R48 2005

384'.8'0979494—dc22   2005012229

Chapter 1, Dick Hebdige, "Dis-gnosis: Disney and the Re-tooling of Knowledge, Art, Culture, Life, Etcetera," originally appeared in Cultural Studies <http://www.tandf.co.uk/journals>.

For Caleb Blackmon and Dashiell Budd

CONTENTS

PREFACE

This book originated with an international conference on Disney in November 2000 sponsored by the new interdisciplinary Public Intellectuals Ph.D. Program at Florida Atlantic University. "Rethinking Disney: Private Control and Public Dimensions" attracted more than a hundred scholars from around the world to Fort Lauderdale, Florida, to present papers and workshops probing the history, products, activities, influence, and global reach of the Walt Disney Company. This volume collects several of the outstanding papers presented in connection with the conference, in most cases extensively revised.

The theme of the conference was inspired and supported by the beginning of the Ph.D. Program in Comparative Studies: The Public Intellectuals Program, in the Dorothy F. Schmidt College of Arts and Letters at Florida Atlantic University. For several of the faculty and students involved in starting this groundbreaking program, it seemed entirely appropriate to begin by thinking about the public life of one of the dominant private institutions in our own state of Florida. Our students' and colleagues' commitment to exploring publicness and to expanding the public role of scholars and intellectuals in struggles for social justice has been a constant inspiration in every phase of this project.

For their contributions to the conference, the editors thank Stefanie Gapinski, Rod Faulds, and the late Teresa Brennan, as well as James Lamare, then-dean of the Dorothy F. Schmidt College of Arts and Letters at Florida Atlantic University, whose financial support was crucial. Many thanks for advice and encouragement at key points go to William Covino, Susan Willis, Janet Wasko, Eileen Meehan, Eric Smoodin, Clay Steinman, Lynn Appleton, Joan Budd, and other friends, family members, and colleagues.

Suzanna Tamminen and the friendly and professional folks at Wesleyan University Press gave this project just the home it needed and understood it from the beginning.

Finally, Mike Budd thanks Suzanne Sheber, who counseled, challenged, and supported in countless ways for five years, and then at a crucial moment provided invaluable editorial assistance.

Rethinking Disney

Introduction: Private Disney, Public Disney

Mike Budd

The Disney Aura

Virtually since they became famous in the 1930s, the products and practices of the Walt Disney Company have had about them a distinctive aura. Compounded of the company's shrewdly constructed imaginary personalities, stories, themed fantasy spaces, and merchandise that tap into transcultural myths of magic and childhood innocence, its general reputation for quality goods and services, and the ingenuous responses of millions of children and adults all over the world, all tied together with highly professional image, brand, and infrastructural management, this aura, this trusted reputation, is the envy of many another multinational corporation. Considering the highly developed corporate synergy in which every Disney product is both a commodity and an ad for every other Disney commodity, it is scarcely an exaggeration to say that each story the company tells, each theme the company deploys builds the Disney brand.

But as the corporation has grown beyond its classic animated films into live-action features, theme parks, television, radio, publishing, sports, new media, and even urban planning and development, both its internal practices and its attempts to control its increasingly complex, now global public environment have generated multiplying conflicts that begin to contradict the classic Disney

1

publicity image. Many on the left were aware of these contradictions as early as the late thirties, even before Walt Disney's paternalistic and exploitative labor practices led to the bitter Disney cartoonists' strike of 1941 and Walt's reactionary anti-Communism was expressed in his angry testimony to the House Un-American Activities Committee in 1947.[1] In recent years, however, the sheer size and global reach of the Walt Disney Company, increasing public awareness of its corporate culture of obsessive control, and its institutional compulsion to transform more and more of the world's stories, images, and cultures into products for sale have produced a small but growing gap between the public image of the company and its carefully constructed aura of sweet innocence, nostalgia, magic, happiness, and fun. With the family audience for its wholesome "Classic Disney" films, theme parks, and merchandise never growing as rapidly as the company's relentless demand for greater profits, Disney has been forced to move into areas that contrast with its G-rated image, which are, in corporate parlance, "outside the brand," including network and cable television (ABC, ESPN), R-rated films and warning-labeled music, and urban development (the New Urbanist town of Celebration, Florida).

On the one hand, anyone who has reflected critically on the company or its ubiquitous products has likely discovered quite concretely the power of the Disney aura. Few texts or brands enjoy the relative immunity of Disney products from criticism within mainstream U.S. opinion; compare, for example, Warner Brothers' Looney Tune characters such as Bugs Bunny and Daffy Duck, which are marketed in multiple media, theme parks, and merchandise like the familiar Disney characters but which do not benefit from the quasi-sacred status of Disney icons.[2] At an international conference on Disney in 2000, many professors and teachers reported special difficulties in getting students to develop critical approaches in the face of the distinctive Disney mystique.[3] Summarizing the results of the Global Disney Audiences Project, which studied the reception of Disney products internationally through 1,250 respondents in eighteen countries, Janet Wasko and Eileen R. Meehan point out that "the multitude not only favors Disney but also often considers as taboo any serious examination—never mind any criticism—of Disney's meaning and impact."[4] As many commentators have suggested, this power derives in large part from Disney's close association with and appropriation of childhood innocence as a personal and cultural memory for several generations of parents and children in many countries. The intensity of this taboo for many people, the often deeply felt resistance to questioning the assumptions of an intensely pleasurable and reassuring mass cultural experience to which they became uncritically attached as children, contributes to the Disney aura and suggests denial, even repression.

On the other hand, growing public attention to Disney's less savory aspects and activities suggests the return of the repressed, the difficulties of image control even for Disney's formidable publicity and marketing apparatus. While the aura continues in most quarters to protect the pseudosacred exchange value of the brand, and to bring tangible bottom-line benefits such as a generally pliant and enthusiastic low-wage workforce at the theme parks, more and more people are becoming aware of problems and contradictions in Disney's behavior. Janet Wasko summarizes:

> During the last decade, there has been a definite backlash to Disney's intense expansion, as some consumers have come to view the Disney Company as behaving in an overtly greedy and overly materialistic manner. The Disney cynics are typically still involved as consumers of Disney products, but are critical of the increases in theme park prices and the intense marketing and merchandising efforts.[5]

Concerns about commercialization, consumerism, U.S. cultural imperialism, and feminine and romantic stereotypes in Disney products erode the aura for some, and increasingly generate perceptions of corporate hypocrisy when measured against the company's squeaky-clean image.

In the United States this small but significant shift in attitudes about Disney, likely concentrated in segments of the college-educated professional class, is both cause and effect of a shift in print-media coverage of Disney in newspapers, magazines, and books read by this class. Along with the usual plethora of pro-Disney stories, many of these print media now occasionally carry stories about Disney's problems, misdeeds, and greedy or controlling corporate behavior, presented in a way that often suggests that it is the contrast with Disney's innocent, family-values image that makes these stories newsworthy or important. Disney has become a big and inviting media target, and draws special attention to its corporate behavior because writers, artists, editors, and segments of the public are increasingly aware that behind all those cute characters, that family fun, and that nearly impenetrable aura is another avaricious multinational corporation. This is not to suggest that such negative perceptions and publicity are significantly hurting Disney's profits yet. However, the company has become so large and multifaceted that its aggressive drive to control, privatize, and commodify everything in its environment constantly generates conflicts both large and small with public institutions, interest groups, and expectations.

The following are among the kinds of stories that are problematic for the Disney aura.

Problems: Excessive Executive Pay, a Docile Board of Directors, and Exploited Workers

Although the company, and CEO Michael Eisner as the successor to Walt Disney himself, has received lots of good publicity for its successful products and expansion since the mid-eighties, attention in the business press and elsewhere has also sometimes focused on Eisner's remuneration, which reached grotesque heights in the nineties. In 1993 he became the highest-paid executive in the country, receiving more than $203 million in salary and stock options. While many undoubtedly thought Eisner deserving for bringing Disney back after the stagnation that followed Walt's death in 1966, press coverage now increasingly invited people to think of the home of Mickey Mouse in a more complicated way than they had before, as a corporation that charged what the market would bear and used its power to enrich its leaders. By June 2000, after several years of lackluster performance by the company, during which Eisner was paid more than $636.9 million over three years, he was called the CEO who "gave the least relative to his paycheck."[6] In 1997 *Business Week* suggested the reasons for this disparity between performance and reward: Disney had the worst board of directors in the country, "a meek, handpicked group, many of whom have long ties to Eisner or the company."[7] Widespread media attention also accrued to the golden parachutes of executives Michael Ovitz (over $200 million) and Jeffrey Katzenberg (around $100 million).[8] Since these figures were hardly atypical for U.S. executives, Disney was becoming an emblem of excessive executive pay during a period of widespread layoffs and stagnant stock prices.

Less visible in the mainstream U.S. press, however, and unlikely to change with new corporate leadership, was the enormous disparity between this executive compensation for top Disney bosses and the minimum wage paid to many of the thousands of "cast members" and other workers at the theme parks; as a union comparison showed, in 1997 a U.S. minimum-wage earner made $4.75 an hour, an average worker $11.88, the president of the United States $96, and Michael Eisner $98,191.[9]

However, the mainstream press largely missed or trivialized one of the most important parts of the story—sweatshops. Like other global corporations, Disney licenses its merchandise manufacturing to those who search the world for the lowest possible production costs, leading the "race to the bottom" in wages and working conditions. While these corporations draw first-world consumers more tightly within the world of commodity fetishism and wasteful consumption, their licensees force former peasants and rural dwellers into the maw of globalized capitalist production. Hence the pitiful wages and sweatshop working conditions of the mostly young women in Haiti, Vietnam, China, Macau, Honduras, Bangladesh, and many other developing countries as well as the United States who make the Winnie the Pooh and Pocahontas shirts, the Lion King outfits, the Sleeping Beauty and Little Mermaid tiaras and wands that Disney sells at auratically inflated prices. When in 1996 a spasm of media attention focused briefly on Kathie Lee Gifford's clothing line amid revelations that some of it was produced by sweatshop labor, Disney, the owner of Gifford's successful television show on ABC, largely escaped attention despite its own practice of buying sweatshop-produced garments for more than twenty years, a practice that continues today.[10] As James F. Tracy points out, Disney plays a significant role in the exploitative global division of labor.[11]

Problems: Obsessive Control of Copyright, Employees, and Clients

Disney has a well-deserved reputation for being arrogant with competitors and public institutions, cheap with employees, and aggressively litigious with possible copyright violators.[12] This last trait has been well publicized through recent events. In 1989 the company threatened to sue three Florida day-care centers for using Disney characters in murals without authorization. Universal and Hanna-Barbera quickly granted permission for use of their characters without charge, and their figures were substituted. That same year, Disney sued the Academy of Motion Picture Arts and Sciences after Snow White characters appeared at the Oscar ceremony without Disney's permission. In the nineties the company forced a French AIDS association to stop using versions of Disney cartoon characters in a public education campaign. And in 1997, after proposing a series of stamps based on Disney characters, the company demanded payment from the U.S. Postal Service for their use. Of course the USPS refused, and so Warner Brothers rather than Disney figures appeared on U.S. stamps.[13]

Problems: Disney's America

In November 1993 Disney announced plans to build a historical theme park to be located on three thousand acres in Prince William County, Virginia, thirty-five miles west of Washington, D.C., and five miles from the Manassas National Battlefield Park, which memorializes one of the bloodier battles of the Civil War. The $625 million project was to include a one-hundred-acre theme park, twenty-five hundred homes, two million square feet of office space, hotels, a golf course, and a campground. And, following the precedent of Disney World in Orlando and other private projects like sports stadiums, it was to be subsidized by $200 million from the state and $75 million from county taxpayers. Reporting on his discussions with Disney lawyers in terms that evoked the experiences of other public officials in Florida, California, and elsewhere, Prince William County executive Jim Mullen wrote that they made it clear that the public subsidy was nonnegotiable: "It was not a request, it was not respectful, and it was confidently stated."[14] As Stacy Warren shows in her essay in this volume, organized opposition developed quickly on two fronts: Protect Historic America fought the Disneyfication of U.S. history, while the Piedmont Environmental Council, a regional environmental preservation group, opposed the destructive sprawl that would accompany the development. The latter group enjoyed the financial backing and national political clout of its residents, "Virginia gentry, suburban squires, and Washington power brokers."[15] Finding itself by mid-1994 in a public battle it could not control, Disney tried to cast itself in a populist mold and the opposition as elitist historians and fox-hunting gentry who cared little about jobs for ordinary people. But the opposition began to slow down Disney's public relations machine and its expedited development timetable with lawsuits, congressional resolutions, and administrative procedures. Absorbing major losses from Euro-Disney and distracted by the death of president Frank Wells, the departure of film executive Jeffrey Katzenberg, and the quadruple-bypass surgery of Michael Eisner, Disney withdrew from the project in September 1994.[16]

There are many such problems, and this collection will examine others. But the point is that they are more than just headaches for Disney public relations, or occasions for glee or head shaking at the missteps of a very distinctive multinational corporation. They are symptoms of a larger phenomenon, skirmish lines in an uncoordinated hegemonic war over the boundaries and definitions of public and private, in which the Walt Disney Company in all its myriad forms and activities around the globe acts as a leading force in capitalist globalization, appropriating and privatizing public spaces, activities, and spheres, while various labor, community, public interest, human rights, religious, and other nongovernmental organizations (NGOs) and citizens work to hold the company publicly accountable. As Disney has developed into a global leader in the transformation of people into consumers and low-wage workers, these scattered skirmishes assume significance as parts of larger struggles and movements, as they help reconstruct a publicness that might provide new alternatives and opposition to the constantly morphing ways in which capital turns social relations into private property.

As Disney has grown into a more significant and integral place within globalizing political and cultural economies at various levels, responses to Disney within educated and other circles have changed as well. In addition to the emergent, more complex sense of Disney's contradictions among limited publics discussed above, intellectual and academic analysis of Disney has undergone numerous changes since the thirties. Many artists, intellectuals, and critics praised the early Disney cartoons with their flat, antirealist style (as in the first Mickey Mouse short, *Plane Crazy,* in 1928), celebrating the anarchic energy and carnivalesque rudeness still valued today. But as commercial pressures forced Disney films to become more conventional during the thirties, many elite critics and intellectuals rejected Disney.[17] While the popular press continued to celebrate almost everything Disney produced at least until Walt's death in 1966, the formulaic quality of the company's products became evident to some from the late thirties on. Mostly lacking an analysis of the economic or institutional reasons for the change, the high-culture criticism of this period in the United States often focused on the mass-cultural blandness and aesthetic banalities introduced into Disney's adaptations of fairy tales such as *Snow White and the Seven Dwarfs* (1937) and literary classics such as *Alice in Wonderland* (1951) and *Peter Pan* (1953). Indeed, the term "Disneyfication" arose in this period to describe the studio's sanitization, homogenization, and Americanization of its literary and artistic sources in folk and fairy tales and classic, mostly European children's literature and illustrations.[18] The broadening of the scope of this term in recent academic analysis responds not only to the enormous growth in Disney's size and power but also to larger socioeconomic changes that give the name of Disney to broad historical transformations far beyond the direct activity or even influence of the Walt Disney Company itself. For example, Greg Siegel in chapter 11 of this volume analyzes the Disneyfication of the contemporary sports stadium. And Alan Bryman, in *The Disneyization of Society,* in analogy to George Ritzer's *The McDonaldization of Society,* argues that the newer term "Disneyization" describes many of the leading developments in the contemporary social landscape: themed environments; combinations of various forms of consumption; intensive brand merchandising; emotional and performative labor; and control and surveillance of consumers and workers.[19]

Bringing the early period of Disney criticism to a culmination, and looking forward to the next, was *The Disney Version: The Life, Times, Art and Commerce of Walt Disney,* by Richard Schickel. First published in 1968, two years after Walt Disney's death, then in new editions in 1985 and 1997, this influential book updated an older tradition of cultural criticism in the United States practiced by writers such as Van Wyck Brooks, Gilbert Seldes, and John Dewey, based in aesthetic and moral judgment but attempting to reach out beyond the traditional class snobbery and narrow moralism of the genteel tradition in American letters to create a more inclusive and democratic public culture based in an expanding and educated middle class. By 1968, however, it was implicitly clear to Schickel that the older standards of morality and aesthetic discrimination were inadequate if not entirely impossible bases on which to build a critical understanding of Disney. Mixing a critical, psychoanalytically inflected biography of Walt the founder with film analyses, studio history, and social history, Schickel explored the debilitating effects of the hypocritical hierarchy of high and low culture that deformed and misunderstood Disney's work, though he neglected the class roots of that hierarchy. In his foreword Schickel blamed many of the ills of modernity on the failures of the "intellectual community" to deal with popular culture. It is worth quoting these words at length, since they evoke so strongly the by then residual hope for a more democratically responsive society in which public intellectuals might affect the course of rapidly growing culture industries.

> I undertook this work precisely because the period of Disney's greatest economic success, his greatest personal power, coincided with the decline of active interest in him in the intellectual community. As usual, the people who claim to concern themselves the most with popular culture missed the point. When Disney ceased to make any claims as an artist they dropped him, as if only the artist is capable of influencing the shape and direction of our culture. In America, that seems to me a preposterous proposition. Our environment, our sensibilities, the very quality of both our waking and sleeping hours are all formed largely by people with no more artistic conscience or intelligence than a cumquat. If the happy few do not study them at least as seriously as they study Andy Warhol, then they will lose their grip on the American reality and, with it, whatever chance they might have of remaking it in a more pleasing style. To me it seems clear that the destruction of our old sense of community, the irrational and unrationalized growth of our "electronic" culture, the familiar modern diseases of fragmentation and alienation, are in large measure the results of the failure of the intellectual community to deal realistically—and on the basis of solid, even practical knowledge—with the purveyors of popular culture.[20]

The invocation of Andy Warhol here is key, for with Warhol the "intellectual community," at least the culturally powerful arbiters of taste within it, were confronted with a phenomenon they helped to create but could barely understand at the time: an artist who embraced, not just the popular, mass-produced images of Disney and others, but the overt commercialism of the commodity form itself. Warhol celebrated all those things that had made Disney financially successful but déclassé—the banal, the mechanically reproduced, the commercial sellout, and the advertising aesthetic. He called his studio "The Factory" and produced high art that simulated mass-produced imagery; as Walter Benjamin had described, the aura of the commodity fetish supplanted the aura of the artistic original.21 The "intellectual community," or at least an influential part of it, had ceased to treat modern art as a refuge from or even an alternative to commodified mass culture, making it instead an exclusive part of commodified culture, a niche market, a boutique. The high modernist view was giving way in some quarters to what would later be called postmodernism, including the pseudopopulist embrace of the commercial.22 Schickel rightly ridiculed the ineffectual snobbism of isolated aesthetes who dreamed of keeping mass culture in its place, who still assumed some proper correlation between the good, the beautiful, and the privileged. Pointing to the irrelevance of aesthetic standards to much of U.S. life ("no more artistic conscience or intelligence than a cumquat"), he tried to recuperate a moral criticism with some appreciation of Disney's power to construct public cultural formations. But as he was writing, the very basis of a public morality of criticism was being challenged even in elite intellectual circles by (among others) Susan Sontag's attack on the interpretation of any public meaning as revenge against the "erotics" of art.23

On a much larger scale, the social movements and cultural transformations of the sixties and seventies radically problematized the social and economic exclusions that constituted "the public" and "public morality" while making laughable the claims of aesthetic discrimination, distinction, and taste as the basis of public judgment. Young people rejected the cultural hierarchy of high and low art, embracing them both with seeming equanimity, though they could not erase the persistent social and economic inequalities that continually regenerated the conditions for cultural inequalities.24 The young, educated, and affluent thus had even more choices, and could move more easily, with less guilt or snobbery, among cultural levels; although cultural hierarchies did not disappear, the boundaries became more porous for many privileged baby boomers as their market power generated the simulation of cultural egalitarianism. Many did not see that cultural hierarchies of taste rested on social and economic stratifications: the problem with Disney and other cultural oligopolists was never primarily one of aesthetics or morality but of power. Much of U.S. cultural studies continues to revel in the supposedly powerful transgressions of taste in parody, irony, and performance, forgetting that contemporary corporate elites, unlike their bourgeois predecessors, have few commitments to high culture and good taste. Schickel's *Disney Version* was written at a historical moment when an older tradition of U.S. cultural criticism aspiring to publicness was largely exhausted, while a newer, narrower, and more radical academic cultural studies had yet to develop.

Whereas Disney during this period was a frequent target of countercultural parodies and critiques as the straight antithesis to radical social change, these critiques waned in the late seventies as a new sensibility made the studio's sentimentalism and conformity more acceptable to many educated tastes.25 By the eighties, professional-managerial boomers with cosmopolitan tastes and lots of disposable income, more socially liberal than their parents and now, with children of their own, becoming Disney's core consumers, could enjoy both Disney and elite culture. And by the late eighties Disney was responding to the upward redistribution of wealth and income throughout the U.S. economy as well as the inflation of its own aura with higher theme park admission prices and other ways of targeting the more affluent. Such consumers were less moralistic and more comfortable crossing boundaries between high and low culture than their parents had been, and this made it easier in the eighties and nineties for Disney, now in full acquisitions mode, to move "outside the brand" with new film studios such as Touchstone and Hollywood Pictures, record labels, and radio, television, and cable networks that brought revenues beyond the boundaries of the profitable but limiting Disney label. Whereas the founder, Walt Disney, was a relatively uneducated, middlebrow midwestern WASP, the new era in Disney history was led by a Hollywood insider, Michael Eisner, cosmopolitan, Jewish, from an upper-class New York family.

Though religious fundamentalists and social conservatives protested the violation of what they took to be Disney's promise of family-values morality, the economic pressures for "stockholder value" and high levels of profit were too strong and the moralizers' threats too feeble. A boycott called by Southern Baptists and the American Family Association beginning in 1996 to protest Disney-owned ABC's lesbian-themed sitcom *Ellen* and other similar transgressions was ineffectual. Newspaper columnists and editorial cartoonists enjoyed pointing out, given Disney's surprisingly vast holdings, all the consumer deprivations boycotters would visit on themselves, thus suggesting provisional mainstream social acceptance of a diversified corporate Disney that could circulate both G- and R-rated culture. The pervasive influence of commercial culture and ties to the corporate right had long since caused leaders of the religious right to downplay their critiques of market idolatry, and few of the faithful wanted to do without Disney. For its part, Disney had learned to play the shifting wants and needs of its core audience for G-rated entertainment, to treat those wants and needs not as demands to be supplied, or human aspirations to be respected and articulated, but as raw materials to be extracted and reconstructed, with the most profitable selected, hyperinflated, packaged, and sold back to the customers in an incomplete but adequately efficient process. As a successful conglomerate within the increasingly concentrated global culture industries, Disney also learned to rationalize the processes whereby it promoted synergy among the multiplying units of its commercial empire while minimizing public perceptions of contradiction in the values articulated by those different units. Most of the time the corporation seemed to be good at figuring out how to maximize profits while staying just below the threshold where some products or policies would prompt too much bad publicity or effective boycotts.

Contemporary Disney Studies

With continuing political and cultural polarization making it difficult to claim either morality or aesthetics as the basis of a public criticism of mass culture, the conditions among some U.S. intellectuals developed for a more usable focus on power. This was especially the province of the left, and during the seventies and eighties, while progressive forces were in retreat in the larger society, the small but growing academic left developed a new interest in mass culture and a wide range of new theoretical paradigms and analytical tools to understand it. Much of this work came to be called cultural studies, and too much of it celebrated "popular culture" uncritically, largely ignoring its conditions of production and overstating its occasional subversive potential and the market freedom of consumers to make their own meanings. But in more socially critical traditions, grounded in social history, institutional analysis, and the political economy of culture, the focus on the politics of culture began to produce sophisticated interdisciplinary syntheses more adequate to the complexities of contemporary cultural production, circulation, and reception.

Among these were a new generation of Disney studies, beginning in the late eighties, most of which owed little to Schickel or other previous work on Disney. Like other Disney critics of his generation and earlier, Richard Schickel wrote for the educated general reader, a category some observers argued was in decline in the last decades of the twentieth century. In contrast the new Disney critics were usually university professors who wrote for smaller audiences mostly composed of other professors and students, and who often used more specialized discourses. The same conditions that made it possible for their work to be more precise and rigorous, with extended and detailed analyses and arguments, and to introduce new, unfamiliar, and often radical ideas and approaches, also limited their readership and perhaps thereby the public resonance of their work. But something else made their work deeper and richer: growing up in the fifties and sixties, they had experienced Disney not just as part of their childhoods but as ubiquitous. Their political commitments meant that they often understood Disney as both ordinary and alarming, as part of the texture of everyday life at the center of a U.S.-based empire that covered its brutalities both at home and abroad with endless pop-cultural distractions. There was little room for polemics in this work, however. Gone was the time when intellectuals could pretend that Disney was an invading force against which lines could be drawn, the purity of children's culture protected, a public consensus rallied. We were all Walt's children now; we were not just in the belly of the beast; perhaps the beast was part of us. The new Disney critics implicitly had to try to understand why people, perhaps including at least part of themselves, actually liked, even needed Disney—without attacking, demonizing, or condescending to those people. This sobering task has informed all the best recent work on Disney, unifying it as a collective project, as it has informed much other critical work on mass culture. In a world in which Disney is almost everywhere, and so nearly universally admired, constructing a credible place of dissent is a task not lightly assumed. The repression built into Disney's aura, the destructive apparatus of control that constitutes its fantasy machine, cannot be assaulted directly; it must be understood and opposed not just by reasoned analysis but also by an approach that itself evokes the anti-Disney, conjures into being an antidote and antithesis to the whole naturalized commonsensical Disney embrace. Dialectically, successful critique can emerge only from immersion in the Disney experience, including its very real and often valuable pleasures.

Another way of saying this is to suggest that contemporary Disney critics, like so many others essaying the invisible lines of power structuring ordinary lives in consumer capitalism, struggle to write their way out of an academic ghetto and to construct a public where none existed before. They do this not necessarily by writing more accessibly, since it is not just the transparency of the language but the political possibilities inherent in the ideas that make writing difficult. Writing clearly often means not writing about ideas that are too radical, since access is easier when conceptual frames are "realistic," already familiar, even redundant. As part of a general tendency to refuse disciplinary boundaries in the pursuit of knowledge, especially knowledge of power, studies of Disney participate in struggles to construct theoretically informed left academic writing as a limited but generative and critical counterpublic.[26]

If Disney studies are contributing to the reconstruction of a new kind of public criticism of mass culture, the sources for these studies are many. The Critical Theory of Walter Benjamin and Theodor Adorno, along with the contemporary work of Susan Buck-Morss, Miriam Hansen and others working in the Frankfurt School tradition, provide one source.[27] The critical cultural studies tradition of Raymond Williams and Stuart Hall provides another.[28] Analytical attention to the politics of gender construction, especially in relation to race, class, sexuality, the family, and nation, is particularly germane to Disney, and has been developed in a number of critiques of the films, most prominently in *From Mouse to Mermaid: The Politics of Film, Gender, and Culture,* edited by Elizabeth Bell, Lynda Haas, and Laura Sells.[29] And Guy DeBord, Henri Lefebvre, Michel de Certeau, and others have constructed a powerful tradition of analysis of everyday life in consumer capitalism.[30] As Disney became more prominent in a metastasizing commercial culture, several critics in this broad international tradition analyzed the company's products, among them Ariel Dorfman and Armand Mattelart, Umberto Eco, Louis Marin, Alexander Wilson, and Sharon Zukin.[31] In the seventies the first of the studies in this tradition came from European and Latin American intellectuals and provided the foundation for the development of a new, more sophisticated approach to Disney in the United States. Here the work of Susan Willis has been key in developing the terms for contemporary critical analysis of Disney, especially in the volume *Inside the Mouse: Work and Play at Disney World.*[32] With Karen Klugman, Jane Kuenz, and Shelton Waldrep, Willis formed The Project on Disney, juxtaposing their perspectives in alternating chapters to form a multifaceted understanding and critique of various experiences of Walt Disney World. Informed by a left feminist politics of the family, consumption, and the interplay of public and private spheres, by Karen Klugman's obliquely revealing photographs of people and attractions at Disney World that cut against the grain of "photo opportunities," and by a constant movement between the banalities of everyday play and work and the largely invisible structures of power that form the material conditions for those banalities, the book is an entirely successful model of how to do socially critical cultural studies. The whole complex portrait of life at Disney World is given radical new dimensions by Jane Kuenz's extensive exploration, in "Working at the Rat," of the complexities of labor at the theme park. If one of the central mechanisms of consumer capitalism is concealing the work that goes into producing the goods and services that form the smooth surface of consumption, this essay unpacks that process of concealment in the uncanny mixture of self-surveillance and subversion, enforced familiarity and isolation, enjoyment in the work and dislike of the Disney Company that is the contradictory daily reality of many "cast members" and other low-paid Disney employees. And if that concealing of labor is usually experienced by consumers and producers alike as a congealing, a reification of the relations among humans into relations among things, *Inside the Mouse* explodes that smoothly themed sheen into its constituent social relations in conflict.

Disney's theme parks, usually reliable profit centers and densely compacted spaces of totalizing consumption, have become the site of major studies of the Disney phenomenon. While "animation is clearly the heart and soul of Disney, and it drives the whole content machine and ancillary sales,"[33] the parks bring all the elements together in the experience of walking or riding through a narrativized space, a theme-in-motion so successful at promoting sales that it has become the model for shopping malls, sports stadiums, and the gentrified urban bubbles of North American "fantasy cities."[34] It's the dream project for the designers of the "experience economy": Disney World is a mall you pay to get into. Beyond the films and other media, and always pushing the merchandise, this is the strangely distracting and pleasurable new permutation of *flânerie* being adapted and exported to the world, wherever enough people have enough money to become a new market. Steve Fjellman calls this experience "commodity Zen," and in *Vinyl Leaves: Walt Disney World and America* he makes it central to his argument that Disney World is a key to understanding the contemporary United States. Whereas the writers of *Inside the Mouse* are literature professors who have combined a textual reading of postmodern experience with a sociological imagination, Fjellman is a critical anthropologist who seeks to understand his own culture through one of its central institutions. His nearly exhaustive description and analysis of several of Disney's Orlando parks is, like *Inside the Mouse,* refreshingly candid about the pleasures of Disney World: in a characteristic outburst, he exclaims, "I love it! I could live there. I love its infinitude, its theater, its dadaism. I love its food, its craft, its simulations. It gets me to think, to remember, and to make up new fantasies. I appreciate its civility and its safety. I crave its contradictions."[35] Yet he also gives us a critical account of the social implications of the institution, which is the more disturbing for his disarmingly modest tone.

> At all the parks we are overwhelmed by the number and velocity of messages. Images speed past us, disconnected from each other save for their tone. Disparate elements of design jumble our minds as we pass from theme to theme. Normal relations between buildings and façade do not hold. All tales seem the same size; difference is obliterated, overwhelmed. WDW is the postmodern sublime, and before it, lest we swoon, we enter a strange, hyperactive mental zone.

This buzz is precisely the state the purveyors of commodification would have us enter. The world of commodities presents itself in an onslaught of discrete, disconnected packages, and the pursuit of these packages—each designed to fill some artificially constructed need—leaves minimal space in our lives for coherent critical thought about what we are doing. We are encouraged to pay attention only to those things that are amusing and fun and to get through our other activities as expeditiously as possible.

At WDW we enter this state of commodity satori.[36]

Joining *Vinyl Leaves* (1992), *Inside the Mouse* (1995), and *From Mouse to Mermaid* (1995) in the new Disney studies were two other books. *Disney Discourse: Producing the Magic Kingdom,* edited by Eric Smoodin,[37] was more wide ranging than the other volumes in its attention to films, theme parks, global marketing, and popular history. It shared with them, however, not only the theoretical apparatus of film, media, and cultural studies but also an increased awareness of the interconnections among the parts of the Disney empire that has become crucial to understanding the subsumption of aesthetic autonomy and individual experience within the dictates of brand synergy. The other book, Alan Bryman's *Disney and His Worlds,*[38] though less critical, brought the concepts of organizational sociology to bear on the business history and the theme parks, and laid the groundwork for his more significant synthesis of issues in *The Disneyization of Society.*

This Volume

The essays in this volume develop and extend the recent lines in critical scholarship on Disney, and focus on new or previously unexamined aspects of the Disney phenomenon. The essays are divided into five parts, reflecting many of the current concerns of critical cultural and political-economic studies. Part I, on "Alternative Histories," contributes to independent histories of Disney activities and practices only recently developing. Disney will not usually allow researchers into its archives unless it can control or approve what they publish. In addition, as part of brand management, it produces and promotes a constant barrage of books, articles, DVDs, new media, and other materials that promulgate the company's version of its own history. Liberally sprinkled with pixie dust, these authorized publications make the history of the Walt Disney Company into a variation on a Disney fantasy narrative. The dominant model is Great Man history, centering on Walt Disney as creative genius and Michael Eisner as genial heir to and savior of the magic. These great men head an organization made up of happy and creative people, centered on the Imagineers, Engineers of the Imagination. Another version of history is technological determinism. Here technology is divorced from its grounding in social and economic conditions, so that questions about the importance of cheap labor by women or foreign workers for the profitability of Disney animation, or the role of the multiplane camera in developing a naturalistic and consumable narrative space in Disney animation of the thirties, for example, are not likely to be addressed. This ideological version of a self-acting technology[39] is intertwined with a formalist art-historical approach that equally divorces art from social histories.

But Disney histories are being rewritten by Janet Wasko, Norman M. Klein, Esther Leslie, Steven Watts, Richard E. Foglesong, and others[40] and part I in this volume continues this revisionist tradition. In chapter 1, Dick Hebdige opens the collection with a wide-ranging retrospective titled "Disgnosis: Disney and the Re-tooling of Knowledge, Art, Culture, Life, Etcetera." Hebdige's distinctive style playfully weaves together a nuanced mix of voices in difference and combination, parody and endorsement, quotation and imitation ("Here, for instance, in the style of Gore Vidal is a huffy read of what Disney did to the Mediterranean Hercules myth . . ."), juxtaposing the incompatibilities of a corporation that has efficiently rationalized and industrialized human subjectivity, leisure, and fantasy. Many popular and academic treatments of Disney begin with the by now familiar litany of the company's holdings, constantly growing; as I have suggested above, the contradiction (or is it yin/yang?) of greedy multinational conglomerate and precious childhood innocence is becoming conventional wisdom. In Hebdige's hands, however, this list is recontextualized and refunctioned within critical and oppositional histories: a history of elite, popular, and left attitudes toward Disney since the thirties, tracing how these attitudes are framed by the vicissitudes of status and class; a history of art world fashions since midcentury, showing how Pop's accommodation with the domination of corporate culture in the sixties gave way to the performances of Karen Finley or Paul McCarthy later on, a deliberately "infantile response to an aggressively normative and expansionist corporate culture" epitomized by Disney; and, linking these and other heterogeneous fragments, a constant focus on the complex relations of historical modernity, artistic modernism, the avant-garde, and mass culture, organized around the dialectics of domination and subordination.

Where Hebdige takes an expansive overview of Disney history, in chapter 2 Susan Willis focuses on the historical implications of one theme park. In "Disney's Bestiary," she extends her critical exploration of Disney's packaged and themed experience, best known through her work with The Project on

Disney in *Inside the Mouse*. Again in juxtaposition with the unsettling photographs of Karen Klugman, Willis here thoroughly defamiliarizes Animal Kingdom, one of the newest of the theme parks at Disney World, which opened in 1998. Willis constructs alternative histories and analytic frameworks to the preferred stories embedded in the park. The essay is a critical counter-tour through several of the imaginary geographies of Animal Kingdom, with each region as a themed environment "defined by a particular dominant narrative genre": a generic Africa as safari adventure, India as history (as of 1948), the Tree of Life as fable of the triumph of technology, and DinoLand as tale of species extinction. With an irony that is gentler than Hebdige's but no less pointed, Willis organizes her tour around the movement from life to death, from real animals as actors in a narrative of wildness constructed by "hidden technologies" to the story of dinosaurs, whose fate suggests the future of the living animals we see. And she compares Disney as corporate zookeeper with the fictional Rosen Corporation in Philip K. Dick's novel *Do Androids Dream of Electric Sheep?* (adapted into the film *Blade Runner*). "With so many imaginative variations on the theme of animals, do we really need real ones?"

It has become increasingly difficult to think of media and entertainment corporations as epiphenomena of leisure, mere purveyors of popular culture peripheral to the global political economy centered on work. Disney's historical trajectory from a cartoon maker on the margins of the Hollywood oligopoly in the thirties to today, a major multinational entertainment conglomerate and one of the Fortune 400, is perhaps only the most dramatic evidence of the integration of the culture industries into consumer capitalism. It is significant that perhaps the most important analysis of Disney as global purveyor of capitalist ideology came from a developing country far from the centers of power. In 1971 the socialist struggles of Salvador Allende's Chile helped to produce *How to Read Donald Duck: Imperialist Ideology in the Disney Comic* by Ariel Dorfman and Armand Mattelart, the English translation of which was seized by the U.S. Customs Bureau in 1975 (then released a year later) for alleged infringement on Disney copyrights. Developing an underground reputation in left circles and beyond as what John Berger called "a handbook of decolonisation," the book pioneered the demystification of "popular" culture for many and was translated into many languages. More recently, and in a less militant vein, Janet Wasko has analyzed the Walt Disney Company as capitalist enterprise in *Understanding Disney*, concentrating on political economy, how the company works, its classic products and theme parks, as well as audience reception. And with Mark Phillips and Eileen R. Meehan, along with other contributors and researchers in eighteen countries in the Global Disney Audiences Project, Wasko has explored the reception of Disney around the world.[41]

Part II, "Capitalism, Commodification, Globalization," develops this research tradition by linking political-economic analysis with cultural studies, seeing Disney as part of the "shock troops" of capitalist ideology and commodification. As in part I, we have an extensive, wide-ranging overview followed by a specific case study that resonates with the more general essay. In chapter 3, "Monarchs, Monsters, and Multiculturalism: Disney's Menu for Global Hierarchy," Lee Artz argues strongly that Disney's animated features not only drive the company's bottom line but are also central to its ideological themes. Enumerating the advantages of Disney's realist style of animation for persuasive and pedagogical purposes, he analyzes the themes and values embedded in structural patterns of social hierarchy in five of Disney's most financially successful films of the nineties, *Aladdin* (1992), *The Lion King* (1994), *Pocahontas* (1995), *Mulan* (1998), and *Tarzan* (1999), as well as those in films made by the company's (now former) partner Pixar for distribution and marketing by Disney, *Toy Story* (1995), *A Bug's Life* (1998), *Toy Story II* (1999), *Monsters, Inc.* (2001), and *Finding Nemo* (2003). "The distinguishing themes in Disney animated features include (1) the naturalization of hierarchy; (2) the defense of elite coercion and power; (3) the promotion of hyperindividualism; (4) the denigration of democratic solidarity." Unlike most critiques of representations of class, gender, race, and sexuality, however, this one links ideology to its possible economic functions. "Disney's dream world of individual heroes and royalty rests on cultural privilege, social inequality, and human alienation—the same ingredients obtained and produced by the socioeconomic practices of Disney and other capitalist enterprises—validating the observations of Dorfman and Mattelart nearly three decades ago that Disney's representations promote capitalist hegemony and political quiescence." There is no capitalist conspiracy here, since the ideology is obvious and pervasive. And Artz's broad, even blunt critique is followed by a call for action: "Rather than searching for the occasional instance of tweaking by resistive animators or hoping that individual subversive readings may prompt a social movement, those who oppose Disney's autocratic production model and generic content should replace them with cooperative creations and narratives."

In the fourth chapter, "*The Lion King*, Mimesis, and Disney's Magical Capitalism," Maurya Wickstrom takes us to the very heart of the contemporary commodification process, developing the Marxist theory of commodity fetishism through the work of Walter Benjamin and Michael Taussig[42]on mimesis as well as her own wide-ranging meditation on Disney experiences. During the nineties, with Disney as a key real estate player, a "New Times Square" emerged in New York to replace the seedy peep shows and porn theaters of the seventies and eighties. "Entertainment retail," exemplified by

Disney's renovation of the New Amsterdam Theatre on Forty-second Street with a Disney Store next door, became part of a larger trend in "global cities" such as New York, London, and Tokyo, combining theatrical and commercial activity.43 With twenty million visitors a year, Times Square was increasingly treated by corporations as a "key global advertising site," a "global image format" for postindustrial tourists, its sense of place eroded for an abstractly themed no-where dominated by corporate logos, giant advertising spaces, and copyrighted cartoon characters.

As part of this historical transformation, Disney hired experimental theater artist Julie Taymor to direct the stage version of *The Lion King,* opening at the New Amsterdam in November 1997. The show was not only a huge financial success but a critical one as well, adding greatly, like Michael Eisner's patronage of major contemporary architects,44 to Disney's cultural capital, revaluing the company's image upward among tastemakers of the professional-managerial class by demonstrating that a definitively middlebrow culture producer could impress with conspicuous displays of aesthetic distinction. This happens because Taymor's *Lion King* departs sharply from the film in its production design to use the materials of live theater:

> Humans, whose own bodies are molded into service, animate full-body carapaces to bring these characters "to life." For instance, the giraffes are people walking on all fours on stilts, with their faces just visible below the giraffe's neck and head, which is worn like an enormously elongated hat. The gazelles are mounted, in units of three, on the head and both arms of actors who are camouflaged in their shades and patterns.

The "magic" of this production comes from the simulated return to theater's premodern origins in ritual, the "primitive mimesis" of actor becoming but not disappearing into animal, insect, moving savannah. Yet this potentially liberatory use of mimesis is subsumed within a larger spatial and social context that refetishizes the puppets as commodities, remystifies the labor involved and congeals the theatrical experience as part of shopping:

> The first glimpse of the puppets/performers is when they process from the back of the house and onto the stage. Because there is a Disney store directly adjacent to the theater lobby, just steps away from the doors into the theater itself, and because before the show the doors to the store were open onto the lobby, the animals/actors appear to be coming from the store, which is filled with various reproductions of Mufasa and the animals in his kingdom, from playsuits to stuffed animals to toys that can help children "become like" the characters. The

puppet/human characters seem to be their commodity parents translated, come to life and flowing down the aisle. . . .

An ad from the program places the bodies of the audience inside the fiction of the musical and simultaneously directs them to the consumption that will enable even "more" absorption: "Enjoy your audience with the King [Mufasa]. And remember, even in the jungle, American Express helps you do more." And, indeed, after intermission, the theater is full of shopping bags.

This phenomenon extends Disney's historical leadership in the commodification of entertainment, beginning with the company's pioneering licensing of playsuits in the 1930s so that children could enact the stories they had just seen in Disney films. And Wickstrom argues that the attacks in 2004 by Roy E. Disney, Walt's nephew, on CEO Michael Eisner (as of 2004, deposed as chairman of the board) over the alleged loss of the traditional Disney "magic" are symptomatic of alternative strategies for corporate commodification: "Roy Disney, protesting his faith in the 'magic kingdom' but all the while heavily invested in the company's profits, fears that magical capitalism, built on the mimetic desire diverted to commodity fetishism, is the only way those profits can be sustained." Complementing Lee Artz's broader argument about the uses of animation for ideology, Wickstrom shows how, in the convergence of primitive mimesis and commodity fetishism, the consumer performs and becomes the commodity to a greater extent than before. As Susan Willis would ask, "With so many imaginative variations on the theme of animals, do we really need real ones?"

Part III, titled "Hierarchies: Race, Class, Gender, Sexuality," focuses on hierarchies. This is the area of Disney scholarship—and of studies of mass culture generally—that has attracted the most attention because of the culture industries' power to frame and organize social understandings of difference. Public critiques of Disney's representations of African-Americans and other racial groups are almost as old as the company's habit of caricaturing such groups, and similar critiques have emerged in recent decades around Disney's representations of women and lesbian/gay/bisexual/transgendered people. An extensive scholarly literature has emerged. Whereas the essays in part II tend to see various social and economic inequalities organized or subsumed by global consumer capitalism, those in this section and this line of research are more likely to see the social hierarchies of identity as incompletely integrated or articulated, as at least somewhat independent of one another.

Sean Griffin's book *Tinker Belles and Evil Queens: The Walt Disney Company from the Inside Out*[45] is a valuable study of the complex interactions between Disney and various lesbian and gay communities both in and outside the company from the thirties to the nineties. In chapter 5, "Curiouser and

Curiouser: Gay Days at the Disney Theme Parks," Griffin extends the analysis to trace the history of these gatherings at Disneyland and Walt Disney World, and explores their cultural, political, and economic implications. Although begun in 1978 on the occasion of a kind of invasion or "guerrilla raid" of Disneyland in the spirit of seventies gay activism, Gay Days was always in large part an expression of the desire to assimilate, bringing together what seemed to be a quintessentially heteronormative entertainment experience with an emergent sexual minority now in public self-definition. While it was about queering Disney, transforming conservative, family-values culture, it was also about fitting in, having fun in one of the most conformist places imaginable. In the eighties, in response to the AIDS crisis, Gay Days became a respectable charity event, and in the nineties a rapidly growing vacation date. By 2002 there were six days of parties in and around Disney World, and Gay Days attracted 125,000 people, one of the busiest days of the year at the park. Gay Days parties became part of a global gay party "circuit" promoted by the travel and tourism industries, in which affluent gays jetted to different cities every weekend for "extravagant blowouts for thousands of revelers, most of them no longer organized as AIDS benefits." As more and more lesbians and gays appeared at the Disney theme parks in their red shirts on the designated day in the first week of June, they mixed with sometimes surprised (and occasionally hostile) heterosexual guests to create public problems for an entertainment corporation too big to avoid such issues.

From its beginnings Disney has grown by turning public spaces, institutions, and resources to its private ends. But the corporation has expanded to the point where the dimensions of publicness it has privatized, the commons it has enclosed, are large, heterogeneous, complex, and occasionally democratic enough to become difficult to control. As Disney, like other large corporations, usurps many of the powers and functions of both the state and civil society, it is more and more often faced with public problems associated with these sectors.[46] Compounding this situation was the semiorganized wrath of Christian fundamentalists at Disney's gay-friendly policies, which resulted in a failed boycott of Disney, attempts to fly over the park (nixed post-9/11) with banners exhorting Gay Day visitors to choose Jesus over sodomy, and unconfirmed reports of "God squads" seeking converts from among the red-shirted crowds. Presented with an unruly mixture of out gays and straights in a private, proprietary space simulating and/or replacing public space, Disney responded like the quasi- or pseudopublic entity that it was becoming. As Griffin describes, the company constantly disavowed any sponsorship of Gay Day, put up innocuous signs at the entrance to the park alerting straights to possible unauthorized but unpreventable expressions of same-sex affection, gave free tickets to other parks, and increased security. There was the occasional video of simulated sex acts by gay men dancing at Disney's Pleasure Island or other transgressions, which shocked mainly the puritans who could not stop showing them. But lesbian and gay park-goers generally policed themselves and each other more than adequately.

In a larger sense we might see this phenomenon as a tacit renegotiation of a hegemonic social contract, including newly public groups within the mainstream as long as they behave themselves. Of course this applies primarily to affluent gay men, much more visible to marketers than lesbians because of their relatively large disposable incomes; lesbians, like other women, still earn significantly less than men. In a struggle over who gets to be publicly visible in Disney World, as in so many other marketplaces of ideas, the ideas (or humans) with the highest exchange value as commodities are victorious. Updating a principle operative in eighteenth-century bourgeois public debates, a capitalism of flexible accumulation allows gays and lesbians within public spaces as long as they have sufficient property and focus on consuming Disney products and services.[47] Contemporary lesbian/gay and Christian evangelical identities, like others, are in major part, and in different ways, mediated by commercial culture; few in either of these very different movements would question the conventional wisdom of the market or of consumer capitalism.

Whereas Sean Griffin considers the history of lesbians and gays becoming visible in the Disney theme parks, in chapter 6, "Anglophilia and the Discreet Charm of the English Voice in Disney's *Pocahontas* Films," Radha Jhappan and Daiva Stasiulis look at and listen closely to *Pocahontas* (1995) and the home video sequel *Pocahontas II: Journey to a New World* (1998). Building on and arguing with a wide range of popular and scholarly sources on the politics of Disney representations, and drawing particularly on Ella Shohat and Robert Stam's attention to voice within a historical analysis of film and media discourses of Eurocentrism and colonialism, Jhappan and Stasiulis focus on constructions of whiteness and Britishness, especially through an ambivalent American Anglophilia and love of the English voice. Giving due credit to Disney's "attempt to offer a sympathetic and respectful portrayal of the 'Indians,'" they consider four textual strategies decentering whiteness in the *Pocahontas* films. While acknowledging gains made, and despite critical praise for the films' supposed political correctness, Jhappan and Stasiulis identify multiple ways the films recuperate English (and white American) superiority and justify colonialism:

> The impression left at the end of each film, that British imperialism was called off, is indeed one of the most fanciful yet serious departures from reality committed

by Disney's narratives. . . . Although the "Indians" are "more human-looking, if nippleless, and are indeed more human or humane than the nasty, brutish colonists who stem yet from cartoon's native domain—caricature," the physical and linguistic diversity of the English serves as a device to distinguish them as individuals, and ultimately, as more "human.". . . Most important, within a narrative of colonization, the interracial love story between Smith and Pocahontas serves to legitimize that colonization. . . . Unlike Disney's other animated features that are based on fairy tales and have no claims to truth, the *Pocahontas* films engage the Euro-American imagination in a tissue of deceits that end up redeeming the colonization project as a love story between two different worlds, rather than depicting it as the holocaust it was for the Native Americans.

The approach weaves together extended analyses of discursive strategies and a nonreductive comparison of the films with the historical figures and events they represent, acknowledging limited textual autonomy while holding Disney accountable.

The essays in part IV, "Representation, Simulation, Appropriation," address related issues. And just as Radha Jhappan and Daiva Stasiulis explicate Disney's *Pocahontas* films as discursive recolonizations of the story of British imperialism and European genocide in the Americas, Aaron Taylor sees Disney's transformation of the public character and narratives of Winnie the Pooh as acts of expropriation and colonization. In chapter 7, "Everybody Wants a Piece of Pooh: Winnie, from Adaptation to Market Saturation," Taylor analyzes the history of Disney's appropriation of the A. A. Milne stories and accompanying Ernest A. Shepard drawings, from the two Disney films *Winnie the Pooh and the Honey Tree* (1966) and *Winnie the Pooh and the Blustery Day* (1968) to the recent proliferation of Disneyfied Winnie the Pooh merchandise. With the successful video rerelease of *The Many Adventures of Winnie the Pooh* in 1996 Disney launched a worldwide marketing campaign for product tie-ins, and by 1998 Pooh eclipsed even Mickey Mouse, earning an estimated $3.4 to $4 billion, and by 2001 the bear was accounting for around "one-fifth of the company's $25 billion gross globally."

Though he evinces a genuine affection for Milne's characters and stories, with their whimsical and beloved phrasings, Taylor does not fetishize them as sacred originals but critiques the "fidelity approach" to adaptation studies. He traces the intertwining of finance and cultural capital. "British neocolonial anxieties" at the appropriation of a national treasure are juxtaposed with nationalist claims of cultural origin by Canada and the United States, while a Disney publicist claims that "Pooh belongs to everybody. He can be anything you want him to be." This commercial interest in multiplying the meanings and identities of a character is part of a larger decontextualization and reification, traced here through a variety of texts and situations. It appears most prominently in the splitting of Pooh into two product lines, the familiar bright yellow Disney Pooh and associated figures, and the newer "Classic Pooh," based closely on Shepard's drawings: "By ostensibly returning to the character's origins in its development of a new line of merchandise, the company extends its reach over an alternative version of the character, colonizing the work at its very source and tightening the range of imaginative ownership." In addition, Taylor unpacks the ideological import of the narrational strategies in the video version of *Many Adventures,* showing how, in "manufactur[ing] authenticity," "Milne's text is literally incorporated into the film" and Shepard's map, minus his figures, is made into the background for Disney's figures.

Yet Disney's semiotic strategies in the commodification of Pooh seem relatively simple compared with the intricate differentiation and combination of multiple registers of simulated authenticity, realism, historical accuracy, irony, truth, sincerity, fantasy, fiction and verisimilitude in Animal Kingdom. In chapter 8, "Truer Than Life: Disney's Animal Kingdom," Scott Hermanson approaches this recently constructed theme park in ways that complement Susan Willis's more historical analysis, and also focuses on different attractions. For Willis, "Animal Kingdom offers the most meticulously themed environments on the planet," and Hermanson demystifies the theming and branding of nature itself, a process facilitated by contemporary consumer culture's relegation of "nature to that which has no contact with humans. . . . nature [as] already a theme park, a fantasyland where we escape the rigors and frustrations of modern life. Animal Kingdom merely conventionalizes and commodifies this relationship in the easily understood genre of theme park."

One of the best-known formulations of Disney's formidable ideological power comes from postmodern theorist Jean Baudrillard: "Disneyland is presented as imaginary in order to make us believe that the rest is real, when in fact all of Los Angeles and the America surrounding it are no longer real, but of the order of the hyperreal and of simulation."[48] Pushing the concept of the social construction of reality to the point of relativism, Baudrillard here gnomically suggests a kind of vast semiotic jujitsu, in which Disney's fantasy lands act as illusory guarantors of the reality of what lies outside them, of a difference that only seems to make a difference. The popularity of this quotation speaks to the recognition of many that their everyday world of malls and suburbs and freeways is beginning to look less real and more like a theme park. Developing Baudrillard's insight, Scott Hermanson explores the individual "lands" in Animal Kingdom for their administration of modes of conventionalized authenticity and naturalized nature. It is likely not a coincidence that the two insightful essays on Animal Kingdom included here are written by literature professors working with the tools of critical cultural studies, since in its most recent park Disney has articulated and elaborated the codes of realism beyond anything it has done previously, and those sensitized to such conventions and codes are most skilled at deconstructing its intricacies. Animal Kingdom is a large, loosely interrelated system in which the parts (Camp Minnie-Mickey, the Kali River Rapids, Harambé, the Kilimanjaro Safari, DinoLand USA, the Tree of Life, and Conservation Station) are not only *pitched to* carefully differentiated demographic niches and combinations of niches but, as semiotically rich environments coded as finely varied mixtures of verisimilitude and fantasy, are *designed to manage the tastes of* those demographic categories with uncanny industrial precision. "Something is provided for everyone so that no one can escape," as Horkheimer and Adorno suggest.[49] Not only do the "lands" work internally, but Conservation Station and other elements act as guarantors of the whole: there Disney takes its most environmentally aware visitors behind the scenes, showing that it can respond to the skepticism of critical consumers. "Conservation Station definitively draws the line between real and artifice, putting the animals and their habitats clearly on the side of the real. Its magic is to change Animal Kingdom from just a theme park about animals into an ecologically informed utopia."

But the system is hardly seamless: Kali River Rapids, for example, "ecotourism [as] neocolonialist kitsch," tries to separate bad capitalism (illegal logging practices in developing countries) from its own good capitalism, but the contradictions and hypocrisies emerge in an analysis that goes beyond the "easy environmentalism" of Animal Kingdom to the realities of the global political economy, including the sweatshop labor around the world from which both Disney and the many investors among its affluent customers regularly profit.

In part V, "Urban Planning and Themed Environments," the final three essays examine some of Disney's most important recent initiatives within larger contexts of related developments. These initiatives bring up to the present and into the future a trajectory that is evident in the company's projects from the 1930s on. Walt Disney's own interests in theme parks and urban planning during this period are well documented, and he led the development of a corporate culture that continued the trajectory after his death in 1966. The distinctive characteristics of the Disney company and its products—fantasy storytelling, branding, theming, synergy, control—were expanded from animated films and merchandise into television and other realms but especially into theme parks, which extended the two-dimensional animated fantasies into three dimensions, so you could walk around inside that fantasy world.

But since Disney's post–World War II trajectory also generally matched the needs and directions of U.S. and global elites and the tastes of middle-class consumers, the company's theme parks increasingly became the models for other built environments. It was not so much Disney's direct influence on architects, urban planners, and policy makers. Instead, acceleration of the middle-class exodus from cities to suburbs, malls, and commuting; the increase in mass long-distance vacations enabling the success of theme parks; from the seventies, deindustrialization and downsizing, with tourism as a new and desperate economic hope for U.S. cities—all these postwar trends meant that urban planners, mall designers, and even sports stadium architects looked to attract tourists to themed environments. As the fantasy space of Disney cartoons extended into theme parks and then into public spaces, more and more built environments came to resemble theme parks.

It is within this context that we can understand the rise of the Walt Disney Company's development activities, inseparable from the Imagineering of the theme parks and other Disney products both in design and in corporate structure. These activities were brought together in 1984 as the Disney Development Company (and later part of Walt Disney Imagineering and Disney Regional Entertainment) as the company increased its involvement in design consultancy and real estate development in U.S. cities both on and off Disney property. This led in the late eighties and nineties to increasingly high-profile projects, including several very interesting failures. In chapter 9, "Saying No to Disney: Disney's Demise in Four American Cities," Stacy Warren brings a social geographer's perspective to several of Disney's failures in urban planning, providing a detailed history of these projects and what can be learned from them.

In its relations with various state and local governmental bodies and regulatory agencies around development issues over several decades, Disney developed a corporate modus operandi, what Warren calls the "Disney Planning Storyboard (DPS)." When they interact with the outside world, especially with planners and public officials over a large prospective Disney development, Disney representatives follow a rigid script that resembles the storyboard or blueprint for a Disney film. It is as if Disney expects that it can extend into the real, messy, public, and political world of urban planning the same totalizing private control it exercises in the construction and management of the fantasy worlds of its animated films and theme parks. The spectacle of large corporations extracting ever-escalating amounts of public resources from desperate, misguided, overwhelmed, and/or venal city and state governments in exchange for locating supposedly valuable revenue-producing facilities in that area has by now become depressingly familiar. The DPS, Disney's variation on this pattern, adds the corporation's distinctive public aura of quality family entertainment, its preference for secrecy, speed, and absolute control, and its often arrogant and sometimes self-defeating assumption that it is not subject to standard regulatory planning procedures or public oversight.

In four increasingly high-profile projects, Warren shows that the nimble, highly capitalized corporation did not always triumph over its bumbling public partners. In Seattle in 1985, Disney was asked to design a new city center as one of its first large-scale projects outside a theme park context. However, accustomed to dominating public-private partnerships, the Imagineers gave no attention to community and public issues in their proposals, one of which would have forced the city to charge admission to a public facility! Citizens and city council members eventually won out over the mayor and a progrowth business coalition, and Disney was in effect fired in 1989.

In 1989 Disney created a competition between the cities of Long Beach and Anaheim for a new theme park: in Long Beach it was a waterfront location, while in Anaheim an extension of Disneyland. The two cities came up with large "support packages" worth around $1 billion each, but in both cases strong local, regional, and state resistance from environmentalists and home owners emerged, and both projects were dead or on the way to radical revision by 1995.

In 1993 Michael Eisner announced plans for Disney's America, whose fate I have described above. The demise of this proposed historical theme park demonstrated the company at its most inflexible in dealing with regulatory agencies and citizens' groups, and became Disney's biggest public relations disaster.

Disney's problems in these four instances derived from its general unwillingness either to follow conventional urban planning structures or to include public participation in any of its projects. In contrast, the redevelopment of Times Square in the nineties followed a different scenario: whereas the public story of Disney's America became one of Disney spoiling a beautiful historical site and landscape, the story in New York was always primarily of Disney leading the cleanup of a degraded Times Square.

Warren's historical analysis joins essays here by Lee Artz, Sean Griffin, and others describing and/or calling for opposition and resistance to Disney's activities, part of a larger trend in studies of Disney (and other entertainment multinationals) that emphasize the real-world rather than fantasy dimensions of the company. Disney has become so large and multifarious that more and more of us are living with or even in Disney's lands, and two recent books place the company's development activities within strong analytical frameworks. *The Celebration Chronicles: Life, Liberty, and the Pursuit of Property Value in Disney's New Town,* by Andrew Ross, describes everyday life in Disney's town of Celebration during its early growing pains, with special emphasis on the town's New Urbanist roots, its inhabitants' desire for community, and the conflicts around the educational philosophy and practices of its high school. *Married to the Mouse: Walt Disney World and Orlando,* by Richard Foglesong, examines the complex relations between a global corporation and local governments from the sixties through the nineties, as Disney corporate behavior exhibits intensifying patterns of deception and abuse while its "marriage" partners in city and county government struggle to find ways to articulate public interests.

Stacy Warren's historical account of Disney's failures in urban planning is followed by Frank Roost's analysis of two more recent and more successful Disney urban projects. In chapter 10, "Synergy City: How Times Square and Celebration Are Integrated into Disney's Marketing Cycle," Roost, like Warren, brings the lenses of urban studies to a study of corporate activity. He sees these highly publicized city planning projects absorbing urban life and space into the priorities associated with Disney's distinctive operating approach: inhouse cross-promotion, or synergy. Others have told the story of Disney and Times Square, but here the project's popularity is explained, not just by the apparently near-universal desire to "clean up" this landmark, but through the integration of this desire into the marketing cycle by which Disney sells movies, merchandise, television, and itself.

Examples abound. After enormous favorable publicity casting Disney as the hero of Times Square redevelopment, the merchandising process began with the musical theater productions of *Beauty and the Beast,* then *The Lion King* at Disney's newly renovated New Amsterdam Theatre, both shows already presold through the successful animated films that preceded them, plus millions of toys and videos. (As Maurya Wickstrom shows, one of the main exits from the theater during the performance of *The Lion King* led into the Disney Store next door, filled with Lion King merchandise for every taste and budget.)[50] In June 1997 Disney promoted the opening of its animated feature *Hercules* with a whole weekend of activities around the city, centering on "The Hercules Electrical Parade," which traveled up Fifth Avenue from Forty-second Street to Sixty-sixth. This and other events brought the Disney theme parks into the heart of New York City, since the parade was "similar to Disneyland's 'Main Street Electrical Parade' and featured floats that had previously been used only for parades inside Disneyland and Disney World." An example of Disney products and activities advertising one another in "reciprocal synergy" is the

> $75 million *Good Morning America* studio on Forty-fourth Street, where ABC has produced its popular live TV show since 1999. . . . Because of this dominance of synergy, a much more important aspect for Disney's planners than the cost was

to build the studio with a large window so that ABC's stars would sit in front of a background showing Times Square. . . . Disney is able to advertise the destination Times Square to viewers all over the country every morning. And if they actually come, they are subjected to another Disney promotion. The studio's facade has large electric signs forming colorful bands that get the passerby's attention even in the neon-lit Times Square. On those bands are shown flashy computer-animated advertisements for Disney's several TV channels—alternating between commercials for ABC, ESPN, Lifetime, or the Disney Channel. In addition, a 585-square-foot video screen displays ABC's program as well as short ads for other Disney products like books or movies—exposing thousands of tourists to the company's products every day in intensive synergy at the "Crossroads of the World."

Of course there is a distinctive and public price to pay for this intensive privatization: the exclusion of the homeless and other marginalized groups, and the transformation of a place of social mixing and heterogeneity into a sanitized urban space for suburban tourists. Typifying the "public-private partnership" of the city and the local Business Improvement District (BID) is the Midtown Community Court, created specifically to deal with minor offenses in the Times Square area, and financially supported by area merchants. "In most cases the penalties imposed on the offenders . . . are so-called community services. . . . In practice, this means the delinquent must join the BID's cleaning crew and has to sweep sidewalks for several days." It would seem that even the legal system is drawn into the orbit of Disney's synergy.

In chapter 11, "Disneyfication, the Stadium, and the Politics of Ambiance," Greg Siegel brings the picture of Disney in the city into the present and the future. Noting that Disneyfication is by now much larger than the operations of the Walt Disney Company itself, he describes it as a dominant contemporary "mode of urban development, in which a circumscribed space is strategically sanitized and spectacularized for maximal and manifold consumption" to create "'urbanoid environments'—[architecture critic] Paul Goldberger's term for 'places that purport to offer some degree of urban experience in an entertaining, sealed-off, private environment.'"[51] Sectors of cities are privatized and militarized in ways that resemble the divided cities in many developing countries: "Rather than being woven into the existing urban fabric, hotel and convention facilities, sports stadiums, restaurant districts, and downtown shopping malls are cordoned off and designed to cosset the affluent visitor while simultaneously warding off the threatening native."[52]

Within these synthetic enclaves, sports stadiums seek to become tourist destinations with multiple attractions, including malls, restaurants, sports history museums, exercise facilities, playgrounds, movie theaters, and team-related activities. As with theme parks, the object is for tourists to spend more time there, and the family can go in different directions during the visit. The game and the home team become a theme that, "as deployed in Disneyland and Disney World, is more than a principle of semiotic coherence: it is an instrument of social control and a catalyst for consumer desire."

One of the distinctive features of the Disneyfied stadium is the large-screen video display, which provides another point of affinity with theme parks:

> Through the use of zooming close-ups, multiple angles, instant replays, and slow-motion effects, the large-screen video display confers on the sports spectator a visually/virtually mediated mobility. [Geographer Yi-Fu] Tuan argues that, for visitors who use them, Disneyland's rides, in addition to producing kinesthetic sensations, transform the visual landscape into an impressionistic panorama. . . . Disneyland's rides generate spectacle through machinic mobilization; the Disneyfied stadium's large-screen video display generates (virtual) mobilization—a flash of color and form, a feeling of rushing along—through machinic spectacle.

Cultural and political economies rearticulate in the historical formation of theme parks, sports stadia, and related "complete entertainment environments."

Making connections between political economy and cultural studies, between textual analysis and institutional analysis, and especially among different parts of the Disney empire and the larger historical forces it represents and opposes, these essays help bring critical studies of Disney into the twenty-first century, and point to the dynamic of public and private that defines so many of the struggles around this company.

Notes

1. Steven Watts, The Magic Kingdom: Walt Disney and the American Way of Life (New York: Houghton Mifflin, 1997), 284.
2. Janet Wasko, Mark Phillips, and Eileen R. Meehan, eds., Dazzled by Disney? The Global Disney Audiences Project (London: Leicester University Press, 2001), 342, n.1.
3. "Rethinking Disney: Private Control and Public Dimensions," an international conference held in Fort Lauderdale, Florida, in November 2000 and sponsored by the Ph. D. Program in Comparative Studies: The Public Intellectuals Program in the Dorothy F. Schmidt College of Arts and Letters at Florida Atlantic University. The conference was the source of the present volume.
4. Wasko et al., Dazzled by Disney, 331.

5. Janet Wasko, *Understanding Disney* (Cambridge, England: Polity Press, 2001), 208.

6. Ibid., 42.

7. John A. Byrne and Ronald Grover, "The Best and Worst Boards," *Business Week,* December 8, 1997, 90, quoted in Wasko, *Understanding Disney,* 40.

8. Wasko, *Understanding Disney,* 42.

9. "Paywatch Fact Sheet," NABET-CWA website, http://pw2.netcom.com/-nabet16/page24.html, using 1997 AFL-CIO data; cited in Wasko, *Understanding Disney,* 96.

10. Andrew Ross, *The Celebration Chronicles: Life, Liberty, and the Pursuit of Property Value in Disney's New Town* (New York: Ballantine, 1999), 296–298 and 337 n.3; Andrew Ross, ed., *No Sweat: Fashion, Free Trade, and the Rights of Garment Workers* (New York: Verso, 1997); Norman Solomon, "Kathie Lee, Disney, and the Sweatshop Uproar," www.monitor.net/monitor/sweatshop/ss-solomon.html, 2/17/05; "Sweatshop News Update: Disney Pulls Toys off Shelves," *Co-op America Quarterly* 55 (Fall 2001): 26. For further information on Disney and sweatshops contact the National Labor Committee at www.nlcnet.org or nlc@nlcnet.org, Global Exchange at www.globalexchange.org, or the Campaign for Labor Rights at www.summersault.com/~agj/clr or CLR@igc.org.

11. James F. Tracy, "Whistle While You Work: The Disney Company and the Global Division of Labor," *Journal of Communication Inquiry* 23, no. 4 (1999): 374–390.

12. John Gregory Dunne, *Monster* (New York: Random House, 1997); Wasko, *Understanding Disney,* 83–107.

13. Wasko, *Understanding Disney,* 84–85.

14. Jim Mullen, "The Disney Experience," *Public Management* 77 (October 1995): 4.

15. Mike Wallace, "Disney's America," in *Mickey Mouse History and Other Essays on American Memory* (Philadelphia: Temple University Press, 1996), 166.

16. Wallace, "Disney's America,"159–174; Carl Hiaasen, *Team Rodent: How Disney Devours the World* (New York: Ballantine, 1998), 21–24; Jon Wiener, "Tall Tales and True," *Nation,* January 31, 1994, 133–135; Patti Wolter, "Mouse Trap," *Neighborhood Works* 17, no. 6 (December 1994/January 1995): 17–20.

17. Norman M. Klein, *Seven Minutes: The Life and Death of the American Animated Cartoon* (London: Verso, 1993); Richard Schickel, *The Disney Version: The Life, Times, Art and Commerce of Walt Disney* (New York: Touchstone, 1985).

18. Schickel, *Disney Version,* 225.

19. Alan Bryman, *The Disneyization of Society* (London: Sage, 2004); George Ritzer, *The McDonaldization of Society* (Thousand Oaks, Calif.: Pine Forge, 1993).

20. Schickel, *Disney Version,* 12–13.

21. Walter Benjamin, "The Work of Art in the Age of Mechanical Reproduction." in *Illuminations,* edited and with an introduction by Hannah Arendt (New York: Schocken, 1969), 217–251.

22. Fredric Jameson, "Reification and Utopia in Mass Culture," *Social Text* 1 (1979): 130–148; Fredric Jameson, *Postmodernism: or, The Cultural Logic of Late Capitalism* (Durham, N.C.: Duke University Press, 1991).

23. Susan Sontag, *Against Interpretation and Other Essays* (New York: Farrar, Straus, and Giroux, 1966).

24. Peter Hansen, "Cultural Criticism," in Richard Wightman Fox and James T. Kloppenberg, eds., *A Companion to American Thought* (Malden, Mass.: Blackwell, 1995), 159–162.

25. As Dick Hebdige notes in the first chapter of this volume, "The decline since [the seventies] of Old Testament-style attacks on capitalist idolatry and yippie-style lampoons of Disney family values can be attributed in part to posture cramp/discourse burnout (polemical forms are as subject to fashion as anything else)."

26. Michael Warner, *Publics and Counterpublics* (New York: Zone, 2002), 149, 56.

27. See, for example, Walter Benjamin, *The Arcades Project,* trans. Howard Eiland and Kevin McLaughlin (Cambridge, Mass.: Harvard University Press, 1999); Max Horkheimer and Theodor W. Adorno, *Dialectic of Enlightenment: Philosophical Fragments,* ed. Gunzel Schmid Noerr, trans. Edmund Jephcott (Stanford, Calif.: Stanford University Press, 2002); Susan Buck-Morss, *The Dialectics of Seeing: Walter Benjamin and the Arcades Project* (Cambridge, Mass.: MIT Press, 1989); Miriam Hansen, "Of Mice and Ducks: Benjamin and Adorno on Disney," South Atlantic Quarterly 92, no. 1 (Winter 1993): 27–61.

28. Raymond Williams, *Marxism and Literature* (New York: Oxford University Press, 1977); Stuart Hall, *Critical Dialogues in Cultural Studies,* ed. David Morley and Kuan-Hsing Chen (London: Routledge, 1996).

29. Elizabeth Bell, Lynda Haas, and Laura Sells, *From Mouse to Mermaid: The Politics of Film, Gender, and Culture* (Bloomington: Indiana University Press, 1995).

30. Guy Debord, *Society of the Spectacle,* ed. Donald Nicholson-Smith (New York: Zone, 1995); Henri Lefebvre, *Everyday Life in the Modern World,* trans. Sacha Rabinovitch, introduction by Philip Wander (New Brunswick, N.J.: Transaction Books, 1984); Michel de Certeau, *The Practice of Everyday Life* (Berkeley: University of California Press, 2002).

31. Ariel Dorfman and Armand Mattelart, *How to Read Donald Duck: Imperialist Ideology in the Disney Comic* (New York: International General, 1975); Louis Marin, "Disneyland: A Degenerate Utopia," Glyph 1 (1977), 50–66; Umberto Eco, *Travels in Hyperreality* (New York: Harvest/HBJ, 1983); Sharon Zukin, *Landscapes of Power: From Detroit to Disney World* (Berkeley: University of California Press, 1991); Alexander Wilson, *The Culture of Nature: North American Landscape from Disney to the Exxon Valdez* (Cambridge, England: Blackwell, 1992).

32. The Project on Disney, *Inside the Mouse: Work and Play at Disney World* (Durham, N.C., and London: Duke University Press, 1995). See also Susan Willis, ed., *South Atlantic Quarterly, Special Issue: The World According to Disney* 92, no. 1 (Winter 1993); Willis, "Fantasia: Walt Disney's Los Angeles Suite," *Diacritics* 17 (1987): 83–96; and "Learning from the Banana," in Willis, *A Primer for Daily Life* (London: Routledge, 1991), 41–61.

33. Rick Lyman, "Box-Office Letdown for Disney Raises Worry about Animation," New York Times, December 5, 2002, 1. www.nytimes.com.

34. Willis, *A Primer for Daily Life,* 57; John Hannigan, *Fantasy City: Pleasure and Profit in the Postmodern Metropolis* (London: Routledge, 1998).

35. Steve Fjellman, *Vinyl Leaves: Walt Disney World and America* (Boulder, Colo.: Westview, 1992), 16.

36. Ibid., 14–15.

37. Eric Smoodin, ed., *Disney Discourse: Producing the Magic Kingdom* (New York and London: Routledge, 1994).

38. Alan Bryman, *Disney and His Worlds* (London: Routledge, 1995).

39. Raymond Williams, *Television: Technology and Cultural Form* (London: Routledge, 2003) (first published 1974).

40. Wasko, *Understanding Disney;* Klein, *Seven Minutes;* Esther Leslie, *Hollywood Flatlands: Animation, Critical Theory, and the Avant-Garde* (London: Verso, 2002); Watts, *The Magic Kingdom;* Richard E. Foglesong, *Married to the Mouse: Walt Disney World and Orlando* (New Haven, Conn.: Yale University Press, 2001).

41. Wasko et al., *Dazzled by Disney.*

42. Benjamin, *Arcades Project;* Michael Taussig, *Mimesis and Alterity: A Particular History of the Senses* (New York and London: Routledge, 1993). See also Maurya Wickstrom, "Commodities, Mimesis, and *The Lion King:* Retail Theatre for the 1990s," *Theatre Journal* 51 (1999): 285–298.

43. Saskia Sassen, *The Global City: New York, London, Tokyo* (Princeton: Princeton University Press, 1991).

44. Patricia Leigh Brown, "Disney Deco," *New York Times Magazine,* April 8, 1990, 18–22; Paul Goldberger, "And Now, an Architectural Kingdom," *New York Times Magazine,* April 8, 1990, 23–24. See also Herbert Muschamp, "Disney: Genuinely Artificial, Really Surreal," *New York Times,* October 4, 1998, AR41.

45. Sean Griffin, *Tinker Belles and Evil Queens: The Walt Disney Company from the Inside Out* (New York: New York University Press, 2000).

46. Foglesong, *Married to the Mouse;* Ross, *Celebration Chronicles.*

47. Craig Calhoun, ed., *Habermas and the Public Sphere* (Cambridge, Mass.: MIT Press, 1992).

48. Jean Baudrillard, *Simulations* (Brooklyn: Autonomedia, 1997), 25.

49. Max Horkheimer and Theodor Adorno, "The Culture Industry: Enlightenment as Mass Deception," in *Dialectic of Enlightenment: Philosophical Fragments,* ed. Gunzelin Schmid Noerr, trans. Edmund Jephcott (Stanford, Calif.: Stanford University Press, 2002), 97.

50. Wickstrom, "*Lion King*"; Wickstrom, "Commodities."

51. Paul Goldberger, "The Rise of the Private City," in J. Vitullo-Martin, ed., *Breaking Away: The Future of Cities* (New York: Twentieth Century Fund Press, 1996), 135–147.

52. Susan S. Fainstein and David Gladstone, "Evaluating Urban Tourism," in D. R. Judd and Susan S. Fainstein, eds., *The Tourist City* (New Haven, Conn.: Yale University Press, 1999), 21–34.

Part I

Alternative Histories

1

Dis-gnosis: Disney and the Re-tooling of Knowledge, Art, Culture, Life, Etcetera

Dick Hebdige

Introduction

This essay was written in 2000, hence before 9/11, the Dot.Bomb, the stock market crash, and the War on Terror, each of which may well have modified and/or intensified elements in the configuration proposed below. In an earlier draft, the essay accompanied an exhibition of Disney-influenced art entitled Never Never Land, curated by Omar Lopez-Chahoud. The exhibition was installed in 2000–2001 in art museums at Florida Atlantic University, the University of South Florida, and Rutgers University. The show featured work by Jim Anderson, James Angus, Markus Baenziger, Bonnie Collura, Rico Gatson, Arturo Herrera, Colin Keefe, Tommy Kenny, Mary Magsamen, Melissa Marks, Jason Middlebrook, Michael Minelli, Daniel Mirer, Takashi Murikami, Stephen Pascher, Daniela Steinfield, Gabriele Stellbaum, Brian Tolle, and Type A. Drawing alternately on the critical literature and fairy tales, the essay examines the integrated and integrative logics of, on the one hand, the Disney business plan and, on the other, the trademark Disney modes of narration. A broad range of "disneyfied" effects are proposed on everything from work, retail and consumer culture, to contemporary art and architecture. I argue that these effects are underpinned by a figuration and positioning of both childhood and "innocence" that is consistent across the entire spectrum of Disney products/texts and which is global in its scope and implications. "Disgnosis," a neologism coined for this essay, is related, though not reducible to, sibling terms like ideology, *mauvaise foi,* amnesia, and false consciousness. Dis-gnosis refers to the putative "knowledge" effect produced by the strategies, logics, and inferred purposes that form the objects of study.

1

Dis-ney Cor-por-ate Cul-ture (*diz'ne kor'pr'it kul'cher*) **n.1.** Of or pertaining to the Disney organization, as a: philosophy underlying all business decisions; b: the commitment of top leadership and management to that philosophy; c: the actions taken by individual cast members that reinforce that image.[1]

Once upon a time in 1928 there was a line that got up off a drawing board in Burbank and went for a walk around the world a few million times in a pair of outsize shoes stuck to one end of a skinny manic rodent. The "walk" was really a line of flight, syncopated and krazy like the Charleston: insolent and purposeless, unhampered at the outset by social conventions, moral rules, or by the laws of physics. But as the miles peeled away at mounting speed behind the clumpy shoes like celluloid spilling to the floor in an unattended projection booth, the line began to twist and morph until it formed itself, like irradiated DNA, into a menagerie of squawking ducks, singing mermaids, hunchback warblers, mute green flubber. As the dizzy Disney line accelerated into the millennium like the burgeoning necromantic flood destined to confound the bucket-wielding good intentions of the sorcerer's newly house-trained helper it began miraculously to shape itself in three not two dimensions, producing in the process a worldwide Magic Kingdom that at the time of writing (2000) consists of:

5 motion-picture studios,

2 major publishing houses,

7 theme parks (with 4 more imminent),

466 franchised retail outlets,

a major TV network (ABC),

21 radio and 20 TV stations,

a global chain of hotels and family restaurants,

several multimedia companies, sports franchises, and insurance companies, 2 "edutainment" universities (one affiliated with Disneyland, the other with Disney World),

a proposed $2 billion "creative campus" in Anaheim, and an entire planned community in Osceola County, Florida, called Celebration.[2]

A lot got turned around between points A and Z however. Most notably, somewhere (not too far) down the line the spirit animating the original enterprise—the insolence of pure kinesis, those whacky first cartoons!—congealed into its opposite : a mania for nothing less than absolute control.

Narrative, which is what the Disney name is famous for—theming, after all, is just narrative in three dimensions—is a means of imbuing time with the semblance of significance in order to control projected outcomes. The desired outcomes in the case of the generic Disney narrative include brand loyalty; return to point of origin (ideal/american/ized childhood); return to point of sale; serial selling (the integration syntactically of thematically linked products—films, soundtracks, merchandizing, vacations, etc.). At a more abstract level those outcomes extend to the suburbanization of the global imaginary; the Taylorization of leisure; compliance with the overall mission (e.g., internalization of the performance goals and obsequious behavioral norms of a hyper-conformist service economy); and something close to "disenstrangement": the domestication of all otherness, the subtraction of risk from pleasure.

To take just one goal: *integration,* the leading strategy of the corporate business plan, has been a Disney byword since at least the 1950s. As early as 1937, long before it became standard business practice, Walt was linking merchandizing to movie promotions, launching a line of toys and clothing to coincide with the release of *Snow White.*[3] In the years since Disney's death, merchandizing has become so thoroughly integrated into the packaging of Disney narratives that it can even function as a theme in the filmic diegesis. For example, when Hercules achieves hero-hood in Disney's 1997 eponymously named animated feature (an apotheosis rendered in the language of the chorus as his translation "from a Zero to a Hero"), his celebrity status attracts hordes of fainting fans and mega-wealth as, thanks to a series of lucrative endorsements of everything from Hercozade sports beverages to Air-Herc sports sandals, he becomes a bona fide brandname: Hercules dot com.

This marks a new departure:[4] the incorporation by Disney animators of postmodern irony into a classic story adaptation pitched at media- and consumer-savvy early teens and children including jokes directed at the visual design of American Express credit cards and mass-produced Greek urns turned out for the tourist market as well as a very old pun directed at the less-than-stellar earnings of their makers. Of course, the punning line ("He can tell you how much a Greek earns") contains a metaphorical reference to the animation labor process itself (studio animation tends to be regarded by people in the industry as not very well paid grunt work). Throughout the movie, the narrative designs on ancient Greek ceramics are presented as proto-cartoons so that the sequence detailing Hercules's apotheosis could even be said to contain a Brechtian laying-bare of the device as the animation cel containing a single gaunt figure bent with a paintbrush over a vase is suddenly replaced by an entire grid of identical figures as the frame (and here the homonymy between animation cel and prison cell is fortuitous) replicates into an entire sheet of cells, an entire prison-house of production. The animation process is figured here as an infernal cross between viral replication and Henry Ford–style conveyor-belt industrial production.

Such blatant references to the signifying-selling chain and the manipulative logic that—literally in this case—animates it are still rare in Disney vehicles, though as the threshold for training and targeting consumers drops daily closer to the cradle and as the dictatorship of the marketplace becomes the sole model of cultural as well as of economic value, it remains to be seen how long tomorrow's children (as opposed to tomorrow's happily regressed adults) will respond to story lines that insist on positioning them as innocent bystanders at the carnival of signs rather than as knowledgeable customers.

2

Disneyfication (*diz'ne fik'a'shun*) n.1. Neologism combining **Disney** (surname of Walt, founder of Disney Studios, etc. etc.) + **-fi-ca'tion** (from Fr *-fication;* L—*ficatio* from unstressed form of *facere,* to make, to do) a suffix meaning a making, creating as in, e.g., calcification, mortification, mystification. See also **imagineering; theming** (esp. of built environments); **hyper-realism** (also **hyper-retailism; hyper-conformism**); **privatization** (of public spaces, services); **californication** (formerly **"americanization"**); **repression** (esp. libidinal); **mono-logism** (also **mono-theism; mono-gamism; mono-railism**); **infantilization; bowdlerization** (of history, myth, existence, etc.); **homogenization** (of cultures, differences); **casualization** (of labor).

The Disneyfication fable seeks to upend the archetypal Disney narrative of Innocence Rewarded in order to emancipate arrested criticality (the surcharge extracted at the turnstile along with the ticket price). Like Snow White's poisoned apple, the knowledge that ensues spells exile from the Kingdom.

Disney bashers can be as aggressive and as totalizing in the scope of their (deflationary) ambitions as any Disney PR *apparatchik* out to meld the corporate mission with the future of democracy and the New World (Entertainment) Order (though the opposition, of course, tends to be somewhat less well funded). Virulently anti-Disney discourse flared throughout the Cold War period, at least on the Left, in the wake of the 1941 strike at Disney Studios and later in response to Walt's documented affiliations with the FBI and HUAC. It became a dominant motif in the '60s and '70s counterculture, where Disney—both the man himself and the emerging corporation—featured as the mean square opposition in the counterhegemonic culture war opened up by the new underground media as a secondary domestic front in the war against the war in Vietnam.

The decline since then of Old Testament–style attacks on capitalist idolatry and yippie-style lampoons of Disney family values can be attributed in part to posture cramp/discourse burnout (polemical forms are as subject to fashion as anything else). Old School Left–accented Disney bashing, an intrinsic component of the alternative late '60s student scene, is just one more casualty of fading twentieth-century Big Picture radicalism: another ailing critical formation buried in the rubble of the Berlin Wall.[5] (It remains to be seen where Disney will figure on the hit list of the new anarcho-left formed around Seattle-style resistance to global capitalism. Early indications are that post-baby-boomer brands with hipper target markets like Nike with its high-priced street-cred sports attire produced, as surely as any *Lion King* T-shirt, in Third World sweatshops and Starbucks with its multiple-choice cappuccino options and seize-every-other-street-corner business plan provoke more immediate hostility.)

Also Disney's notorious dual penchant for flattening all in-house opposition (and the "house," remember, these days is an entertainment nation-state) and aggressive litigation on copyright grounds against parodists out to diss the brand constitutes another double whammy to the overactive jaw of any smart-ass dumb enough to promulgate an insubordinate approach to corporate power.

In the more accommodated (some would say more canny) critical climate that prevails on most university campuses in the year 2000, knee-jerk anti-Disneyism tends to be regarded as passé: too crude and a priori an instrument to serve social science and cultural studies majors whose assignments are as likely to include appreciations of the complex nuances of consumer culture as essays on political economy or labor history. Similarly, while recent intimate, if ultimately no less hostile engagements, with the Mouse (e.g., by Susan Willis, Jane Kuenz, and Henry A. Giroux)[6] offer better-researched and more practical understandings of how the Disney machine actually operates than were available thirty years ago, raw antipathy to Disney is now less likely to be garlanded with the "progressive" label in fashion-conscious educated circles than written off as sour grapes elitism—the swan song of aging East Coast fuddy-duddies panicked by their loss of cultural influence into denigrating popular leisure preferences under cover of "good taste." Here, for instance, in the style of Gore Vidal is a huffy read of what Disney did to the Mediterranean Hercules myth with special reference (see *Disneyfication* above) to *mono-theism, monogamism,* and *bowdlerization* (or sanitization). Hercules, product in the ancient Greek original of a one-night stand between Zeus and Alcmene, Queen of Thebes, is portrayed in the Disney version as the legitimate heir of faithful marrieds, Zeus and Hera, happily nesting in an exclusive resort community sited on Mount Olympus. Hercules's tortured destiny, motivated in the myth by Hera's unrelenting spite, becomes in Disney's hands an uplifting tale of kidnap, Evil overcome, and, in the final reunion with Megara, monogamy eternally triumphant. (Needless to say, Hercules's subsequent abandonment of Megara following his incineration of the couple's children in a fit of Hera-induced [hence heaven-sent] madness is tactfully omitted.)

In the Disney version, Hercules and Megara, in fact, get stuck at the end of the film at the Platonic prenuptial stage preferred in Disney's cartoon world, where characters tend to arrive fully drawn, as Neville Wakefield points out, "without the messy inconvenience of personal history or sexual reproduction."[7] As Armand Mattelart and Ariel Dorfman argued in the 1970s in their banned-in-the-U.S. critique of Disney, *How to Read Donald Duck,*[8] the Disney tooniverse is organized as an avunculate oddly free of parentage. Furthermore, the prevalence of twins and triplets—Donald's nephews, Daisy's nieces, the three little piglets, etc.—indicates, as Wakefield, again, has perceptively indicated, a "preoccupation with cloning as the form of non-sexual genesis. . . . With no sexual reproduction liable to shuffle the genetic cards, diversity among the ducks is guarded against."[9] The ban on history, death, sex, reality, and difference brings us to Jean Baudrillard, who in the early 1980s identified Disneyland as the elephants' graveyard of the real: the place where all the big old mythologies of the West—history, politics, transcendence, etc.—come lumbering in to die.[10]

3

Dis-gnosis (*diz-'nosis*) **n.1.** Neologism combining *-dis* prefix meaning opposite of, lack of when placed before a noun and *-gnosis,* of or pertaining to knowledge, as in, e.g., dis-honest = not honest, cf., e.g., dia-*gnosis.*

Hence *dis-gnosis* means the opposite of knowledge or positively lacking in knowledge. *Disgnosis* refers in this essay to those culturally valorized mentalities and institutional modes of sanction which bestow a positive value on and reserve practical and professional benefits for a disposition towards awkward knowledge that resists its acquisition, that suppresses its articulation, that does not just idealize childlike states and the myriad associated simulacra that support *ad infinitum* the intricate machinery of not-and-never-knowing but actively rewards states of arrested development, denial, disavowal, and unacknowledgment.

A few miles north of CalArts at the Valencia town center, designed in the mid-'60s by Victor Bruen, who coincidentally invented the world's first shopping mall, there are a number of statues cast in bronze of human-scale idealized Valencians: a petrified host, frozen, like the denizens of Pompeii, as if by some catastrophe, arrested mid-stride, apparently while shopping. According to the letters page of the Santa Clarita *Signal,* a rumor circulates among local elementary schoolkids that the statues come to life at night and stomp about the neighborhood drinking children's blood. In the mall, a network of streets that appear to be constructed, like Main Street in Disneyland, to three-quarters normal scale, naughtiness is cast in bronze: a metal juvenile delinquent eternally tosses an empty bucket of water at a statue of an older girl (his sister?) by the fountain in front of the IMAX multiplex. Such behavior is, of course, not permitted in the animate zone. Valencia operates a zero-tolerance policy with regard to nonrational, nonpurposive conduct. Along with, inter alia, a prohibition on "bringing onto Center property any animals, living or dead," the Valencia Town Mall Code of Conduct (999–2) stipulates that it is forbidden to "engage in non-commercial expressive activity without the prior written permission of the management of the Center."[11] Commercial, nonexpressive activity, on the other hand is to be encouraged at all costs. A statue of a thirty-something male sits in all weathers in his (white) shirtsleeves on the steps outside a Starbucks clone reading a newspaper on which nothing is printed apart from the single word "RESIDENT."

It is important to note that *disgnosis* is not the same as "ignorance" (which can be imagined as the *raw,* as it were, to knowledge's *cooked*). *Disgnosis* is already cooked like vacuum-packed convenience food. And it has to be distinguished from "innocence," which is actually the opposite not of knowledge but of guilt. The word "innocent," stemming from the Latin *innocentem,* meaning "not guilty," meant originally in English "harmless," "blameless": two adjectival verdicts that are simply inapplicable to *disgnostic* states and subjects. In the late fourteenth century "innocence" acquired by association the further connotations of "simplicity" and lack of cunning."

Subsequently burdened with the legacy of two hundred years or so of European and American romanticism, "innocence" is now bound up with the linked notions of noble savagery, primitive simplicity, pre-lapsarian bliss and oneness with the world, impeccable awe and spiritual wonderment, openness to encounter, childlike purity. *Disgnosis* connotes, by way of contrast, simulated innocence. It thus contains a paradox as banal and yet as sinister as the one conveyed by "disingenuousness," a word that refers to "*simulated* candor," "*calculated* frankness."

Is it a coincidence that Radiohead's latest album is called *Amnesiac*, that the movie *Memento* uses memory loss as the organizing trope, that an anthology edited by Jonathon Lethen under the title *The Vintage Book of Amnesia* has just appeared in the bookstores? As Andrew Niederman, who has just published a novel called (of course) *Amnesia* said in a recent interview with the *Los Angeles Times*: "Anybody who suffers from amnesia is in a very vulnerable state. They have to accept on faith what they're being told about themselves and their past and their history."[12]

Disgnosis is a cause for genuine concern for all of us. As George W. Bush put it on the campaign trail just before the November 2000 presidential election: "Rarely is the question asked: is our children learning?" Please excuse any insubordination on my part because . . .

4

dis- Art- iculate: v. (. . . . .)

. . . insubordination has a limited and, in the end, annoying range, a fact of life regularly tested in the Art World where, to take a recent instance, the fatuous Britart "Sensation"(s) show, bankrolled by an advertising magnate, of large bisected animals suspended in formaldehyde or an unmade bed exhibited in white-box space represent punk rock provocations to the "classic" provocations of 1970s Conceptualism: the Disneyfication (accessible and cinematic) of Marcel Duchamp's legacy. Another less transparent, hence in the longer run more serviceable, response vocabulary to the post-1945 corporate landscape has, in fact, been available in the art world since the very early '60s when Lichtenstein and Warhol began replicating deadpan rather than subverting or interrogating corporate iconography.

Pop's accommodation with the irreversible facticity of corporate cultural dominance, its refusal of Marcuse's Great Refusal, marked a break with modernist angst and with the rhetorics of authenticity, commitment, and expression, which, for an older generation, had guaranteed Art's purity—its difference from commercial image-making. Much of what follows in the Smash Hits version of late-twentieth-century American art from ultra-clean flat-plane neo-Geo and digitally manipulated simulation through Richard Prince's minimally adapted Marlboro ads to the abjection-fest of a Mike Kelley installation or the regressive romper-room hysteria of a Karen Finley or a Paul McCarthy performance stems more or less directly from that accommodation. This is true even when, as in the latter cases, the intention seems to revolve, at least in part, round a willed rejection of the demand for personal coherence, boundary maintenance. and bodily discipline that so marks the regulated, ultra-sanitized spaces the Dilberts of this world are forced to occupy.

To blunder wild-eyed round a gallery in SoHo covered in mayonnaise and ketchup (McCarthy) or to stand naked, daubed with "excremental" melted chocolate (Finley) may seem a somewhat infantile response to an aggressively normative and expansionist corporate culture, but, at the risk of sounding overly reductive, that may be the point (if anything as finite as a point could find a purchase in such goo). Infantilization—the rendering mute, dependent, powerless—of large sections of the adult population is one result of a process whereby employees ("cast members" in the Disney argot), bludgeoned into submission by downsizing, deskilling, and temporary contracts, are made to audition for their jobs on a daily basis, are expected, on pain of summary dismissal, to defer automatically to all "superiors," to stay "in role," "on script," and "in view"—subject to surveillance by company-appointed supervisors for however long the shift lasts at the workplace (or, in Disney-speak, for however long the worker is "on Property").[13] Increasingly the expectation and demand is that they stay "in character" 24/7 whether physically "at" work or not.

The generalization of the surveillance model (reality TV, security video, e-mail-tracking software, consumer profiling by banks, etc.), together with the decay of public/private distinctions and of the fragile discretionary etiquettes that made those distinctions viable, threaten to project the recalcitrant opacity of human existence into its inimical opposite—what Henry Giroux describes as "a world of clean, well-lighted places, a world in which adult preoccupations with complexity and moral responsibility appear . . . out of place, or, perhaps, simply irrelevant."[14]

Like good disciples of the Stanislavsky Method, we all feel more and more compelled these days for the sake of an "easy" life (if not a good one) to take our work (*personae*) home with us. In the meantime middle-aged empty-nesters standing next to families with excited tots and teens line up patiently in Anaheim determined to stretch the envelope one more time on Roger Rabbit's Car Toon Spin or happily aver to Celebration's writer-in-residence that living in a Disney-designed township helps to reanimate "the Mickey within us."15

The art world's fascination in the '90s with adolescent postures of abjection and sullen noncompliance, its embrace of work devoted to the elaboration of perverse liminalities and hyper-diaper-narcissism, has endorsed one set of tactics for young and young-at-heart practitioners confronted by a socioscape in which no one is allowed to grow up gracefully or to secede without a note from mom or dad. Hence the procession of celebrity Sick Boys and Bad Girls trooping back and forth between Manhattan and LA (and the pages of *Art Forum*): models of dysfunction-chic as arresting and as individually forgettable as those spectral Calvin Klein folk plastered to the advertising hoardings on Forty-second Street.

More recent exhibits like the contemporary art component of Made in California at the Los Angeles County Museum of Art (LACMA), which opened in the fall of 2000, proclaim a movement even further back as the museum space gets converted into a playpen designed explicitly for kids complete with hands-on interactive art work. Wooden noisemakers (Martin Kersels) are laid out like antique toys beneath the Christmas tree alongside installations with a climbing-frame component (Allan Kaprow, Elinor Antin). Here established artists engage Disney on its own turf as a contest is joined for the very soul of childhood. At LACMA, "innocence"—Disney's raw material *and* its finished product—is alternately narrativized or freed from narrative altogether via unstructured polymorphous play induced through unframed encounters with loosely signifying constellations of objects: an antique antic counterproposition to the programmed theme-park ride.

Regression as reward and as revenge for the corporate way of life and labor has served as an object of perpetual fascination throughout his career for Jeff Koons, who from the early '80s on "takes the Mickey" out of Art's (in his view doomed) attempts to separate itself from the banalization process. Grafting a high camp tone onto the floppy sculptural aesthetic pioneered four decades back by Oldenburg, Koons has sought to amplify the invasive power of kitsch by exhibiting handcrafted knock-offs of commercial figurines in toney galleries or by erecting giant floral replicas of begging cartoon dogs in public squares in Europe and New York. For younger artists growing up in a digital environment where all forms (including DNA) are reducible to code and hence intrinsically transmutable/transposable, the eternal tooning of matter into energy and back again is hardly news. In fact it comes as second nature to many of the artists on show in the Never Never Land exhibition, so much so that Koons's public "provocations" to the *kunst-und-kultur* mavens threaten to appear as archaic and contrived as countercultural grand-standing no doubt once appeared to Koons when he was starting out.

Just as Pop once mirrored back within the Art World the monumental icons of the analog phase in marketing, so artists like Melissa Marks, Takashi Morakami, and Fabia Closson explore the sculptural and existential implications of digital mimesis in a world where nothing exists outside the manipulated image. A world where the *conduit* that connects the screened model to its three-dimensional "realization" or its "audience effect" is open and the traffic runs both ways. Walt presides over this imagineery universe as First Fabricating Principle. A throwback to a cruder and more vital phase in the history of manipulation, he is positioned in the current exhibition like *Itchy and Scratchy* and *Terence and Philip,* the TV cartoon shows aired within the cartooned real respectively of Springfield (*The Simpsons*) and *South Park* at a point beyond, yet at the (couch-potato) center, of the animated world. At this zero point everything is animate yet subject to control. Everything has been simultaneously anthropomorphized and rendered alien, brought to life and put to bed.

The paternal annexation of the Art World by the Magic Kingdom has been presaged many times, most famously in Michael Eisner's Medici-matching patronage of celebrity architects, hired to design the flagship Disney structures of the '90s. Philip Johnson, Michael Graves, Charles Moore, Helmut Jahn, Aldo Rossi, Arata Isozaki, Cesar Pelli, Frank Gehry, Robert Venturi, and Denise Scott Brown have all been enlisted to place their trademark signatures on the Disney built aesthetic.[16] Many of those same signatures have been used to underwrite the New Urbanist experiment of Celebration. So secure is the link between the company name and high-end decorative postmodernism that "The Art of Disney" was chosen as the theme for the American entry to the 1996 Venice Architectural Biennale. As Norman Klein has argued,[17] the ambition to contain and shape the cultures of the world now far outstrips the literal simulation logics of the theme park. What Klein calls the "scripting" of spaces extends beyond the construction and ideological enframement of the physical environment and the mediascape to potentially envelop, beneath its branded forms, the entire human habitat, to englobe the human project as neatly as Mary Magsamen's pallid diorama patrolled by miniature security guards is englobed in her snow cone piece entitled *Gotchyer.*

One of the final projects overseen and sponsored by Walt Disney just before his death in 1966 was the building in Valencia, a planned community in northern LA County, of CalArts, an institute devoted at the outset to experimental practice, experimental pedagogy, and the "cross-pollination" (now "synergy") of all the arts. A monument to the Disney genius for compression,

CalArts houses in one building programs dedicated to the pursuit of excellence in art, dance, film/video, music, theater, and critical studies (the school, coincidentally, where Norman Klein and I were both teaching at the time of writing). Tempered in the embers of the '60s avant-garde and the student counterculture, the Institute's foundation stones remain indelibly scored with the runes of early '70s radicalism: revolutionary polemics, performance art and agit-prop, conceptualism, the Women's House, dissonant proto-electronica. Thirty years on, the echoes still resound, so that the institute at times turns into Arts Land, a veritable Bermuda Triangle of echoes, where animatronic avant-gardists endlessly recapitulate the doctrinal spats and schisms of yesteryears long gone. Nonetheless, contrary to vulgar expectations deriving from the donor links to Disney, thirty years down the road CalArts, nestled in a suburb (pop. 146,979) a few miles south of Six Flags Magic Mountain Theme Park on Interstate 5, continues to function as a microcosm of the possibilities for experimental art-making available in www.americaworld.com.

5

Meanwhile in Democracyland trouble is brewing. Deep in downtown LA, the recently opened Staples Center is surrounded for one week in August 2000 by a fourteen-foot wire fence erected to protect the proceedings of the Democratic National Convention from the anticipated protests of the sundry groups of dissidents assembled at its edges. Organized marches snake their way between the office buildings at preset times along routes agreed weeks in advance between rows of armed police. An area facing the conference entrance, bounded on three sides by metal fences, has been earmarked for a conference on the opening night by Rage Against The Machine, a magnet for the "trouble-making element" that, for months now, has preoccupied LA law enforcement. At the center of this protest playpen, a giant plastic Liberty Bell inflatable bobs and wobbles in the breeze. The concert goes off without incident. As the crowd begins to disperse, a few individuals jump onto the fence. Some plastic water bottles get thrown about. Police in full riot-gear advance in military formation to clear the area in five minutes with CS gas and rubber bullets.

> More than 200 million people a year watch a Disney film or home video; 395 million watch a Disney TV show every week; 212 million listen or dance to Disney music, records, tapes or compact discs. . . . More than 50 million people a year from all lands pass through the turnstiles of Disney theme parks.[18]

The line still spinning out of Burbank . . . that dizzy Disney line . . . goes on forever morphing like the fauna in Ovid's famous poem. The metamorphosis to watch out for, of course, is the one where the People—that ancient fairy-tale protagonist, bumptious, contrary, politically driven, and politically di-verse—gets turned into livestock, "cattle" as George Carlin puts it,[19] reared not for the slaughter but to graze the verdant malls and media-ways, to graze forever on the Astroturf, to graze and blink and wear the brand.

Notes

1. John Van Maanen, "The Smile Factory: Work at Disneyland," quoted in Henry A. Gi-roux, *The Mouse That Roared: Disney and the End of Innocence* (Lanham, Md., and Ox-ford: Rowman and Littlefield, 1999). According to Giroux, this definition is given to new employees at Disneyland to memorize "to give them an emotional lift as they begin their workday" (50).
2. Statistics gleaned from Henry A. Giroux and from "Eisner's Big Fiscal Adventure" (*Los Angeles Times,* September 19, 2000). Since the publication of Giroux's book, Disney merchandising has slumped, so the number of retail stores is probably reduced today. For an excellent account of the development of Disney animation from 1928–1947 see Norman Klein, *7 Minutes: The Life and Death of the American Animated Cartoon* (Lon-don: Verso, 1993).
3. The apogee of first-phase integration (i.e., integration prior to the Internet) occurred with the advent of TV. Shows like *The Mickey Mouse Club* functioned not just to ad-vertise Disney theme parks, film products, and character-related paraphernalia (Mickey Mouse ears, Zorro masks, Davy Crockett hats, Old Yeller dog food, etc.) but the logos and products of program sponsors like GM, the American Dairy Association, Hills Bros Coffee, and Portland Cement. Both here and in the parks, Disney pioneered the art of product placement, domesticating in the process the now familiar constella-tion of blue-chip US brands by turning logos into household names and placing them on TV screens inside the nation's homes. The launch in 1961 of *Walt Disney's Wonder-ful World of Color* gave the corporation an opportunity to sell the very technology through which the program was delivered: the show was sponsored by NBC's parent company, RCA Victor, the leading manufacturer in the early 1960s of color TV sets.
4. But see also the merchandising strategy adopted for Steven Spielberg's *Jurassic Park* (1993), in which T-shirts with the *Jurassic Park* logo and plastic dinosaur toys based on the genetically engineered "originals," both of which figured in the fictional scenario, were manufactured in bulk and sold to the movie's fans.
5. By coincidence, Michael Eisner points to Disney's role in the destruction of the edifice in question: "The Berlin Wall was destroyed not by force of Western arms, but by the force of Western ideas. And what was the delivery system for those ideas? It has to be

admitted that to an important degree it was by American entertainment." Quoted in Giroux, *Mouse That Roared*, 28.

6. See The Project on Disney (Karen Klugman, Jane Kuenz, Shelton Waldrep, Susan Willis), *Inside the Mouse: Work and Play at Disney World* (Durham, N.C.: Duke University Press, 1995), and Giroux, *Mouse That Roared*.

7. See Neville Wakefield, *Postmodernism: The Twilight of the Real* (London: Pluto Press, 1990), 102. Wakefield's analysis of Disney in chapter 7 of his book is concise and inspired.

8. Ariel Dorfman and Armand Mattelart, *How to Read Donald Duck: Imperialist Ideology in the Disney Comic* (New York: I.G. Editions, 1975). The authors' analysis of the disgnostic erasure of origins in Disney cartoon characters is especially compelling:

> [They] only function by virtue of a suppression of real and concrete factors; that is their personal history, their birth and death, and their whole development, as they grow and change. Since they are not engendered by any biological act, Disney characters may aspire to immortality: whatever apparent, momentary sufferings are inflicted on them in the course of their adventures, they have been liberated, at least, from the curse of the body. (35)

9. Wakefield, *Postmodernism*, 102.

10. Jean Baudrillard, *Simulations* (New York: Semiotext(e), 1983).

11. Code of Conduct (999-2) issued at Valencia Town Center when the shopping mall that formed the hub of the commercial development was opened in 1992. Here is the code in its entirety:

> Welcome to Valencia Town Center. In order to make your visit, and that of your fellow shoppers a pleasant one, we kindly ask that you refrain from the following activity while shopping at Valencia Town Center:
>
> 1. Using physical force, obscene language, obscene gestures, or racial, religious or ethnic slurs which are likely to create a disturbance or impinge on the hearing or peace of other patrons of the Center.
> 2. Physically or verbally threatening any person, fighting, spitting, annoying others through noisy or boisterous activities or by unnecessarily staring, by following another person through the Center or by using sexually explicit language or conduct, or in any other way creating a disturbance which is disruptive or dangerous to the Center's patrons or its commercial functions.
> 3. Running, skating, skateboarding, bicycling, obstructing or interfering with the free flow of pedestrian traffic or with patrons' view of windows and other tenant displays, or assembling for the purpose of disturbing the public peace or committing any unlawful act. Skateboards must be checked at the Concierge upon entering the Center.
> 4. Creating litter, or throwing, discarding or depositing any paper, glass or other matter of any kind in this Center, except in designated trash receptacles.

5. Defacing, damaging or throwing any real or personal property constituting part of, or located in or on, the Center and belonging to the Center, its patrons, or its tenants, including writing, spraying, scratching or otherwise affixing graffiti on such property.

6. Bringing onto Center property any animals, living or dead, with the exception of animals in the company of and trained to assist physically-challenged patrons.

7. Yelling, screaming, singing, playing of musical instruments, radios or tape players or otherwise communicating in a manner which creates noise of sufficient volume to impinge on the hearing or peace of the general public.

8. Engaging in non-commercial expressive activity without the prior written permission of the management of the Center.

9. Soliciting money or other contributions or donations, or distributing commercial advertising or promotional material of any kind, or offering samples of items which are sold, available for sale, or available in exchange for a donation or contribution, except with the prior written permission of the Center.

10. Failing to be fully clothed, or wearing apparel which is likely to provoke a disturbance or embroil other groups or the general public in open conflict.

11. Sitting on planters, handrails, stairs, escalators or trash receptacles.

12. Possessing any open can, bottle or other receptacle containing any alcoholic beverage, except in those areas specifically designated for the consumption of alcohol.

13. Smoking while in any store, Common area or within the Center in any location.

14. Engaging in any unlawful activity or behavior.

12. *Los Angeles Times,* August, 24, 2001.

13. For a fine ethnographic study of the Disney workplace see Jane Kuenz, "Working for the Rat," in Karen Klugman et al., *Inside the Mouse,* 110–162. Also John Van Maanen, "The Smile Factory: Work at Disneyland," in Peter Frost et al. (eds.), *Reframing Organizational Culture* (Thousand Oaks, Calif.: Sage, 1991).

14. Giroux, *Mouse that Roared,* 34.

15. Andrew Ross, *The Celebration Chronicles: Life, Liberty, and the Pursuit of Property Value in Disney's New Town* (New York: Ballantine, 1999). "Several Disneyphilic (seniors) spoke wistfully of reactivating the emotional link with their childhood—'the Mickey within us'—through their newly intimate association with the company name" (216). Ross's highly readable close-up study of Celebration as an experiment in corporate New Urbanism looks set to become a sociological classic.

16. See Shelton Waldrep, "Monuments to Walt," in Klugman et al., *Inside the Mouse,* 199–229. Many of those same signatures have been used to underwrite the architectural credentials of Celebration as a model of Andres Duany–style New Urbanism (see Ross, *Celebration Chronicles*).

17. Norman M. Klein, *The History of Forgetting: Los Angeles and the Erasure of Memory* (London: Verso, 1997). Also *The Vatican to Vegas: A History of Special Effects* (New York: New Press, 2004).

18. Quoted in Giroux, *Mouse That Roared,* 19. Originally from Michael Eisner, "Planetized Entertainment," *New Perspectives Quarterly* 12, no. 4 (1995): 8. Andrew Ross adds more statistics: Disney-owned radio stations reach 123 million people each week; Disney earnings revenues are in the region of $22 billion annually; Disney World is the largest single-site employer in the United States (51,500 workers, almost 15.,000 of them part-time). Although a 36 million hike in attendance seems a little much even by Disney standards, Ross also revises the estimate of annual Disney theme park visits upward from Eisner's 50 to 86 million (See Ross, *Celebration Chronicles*).

19. George Carlin, interviewed on NPR (broadcast September 22, 2000). Carlin foresees a time when Pepsi-Cola will pay parents $100,000 to have the company logo tattooed on a newborn's forehead (the tattoo to be removed at company cost on the bearer's twenty-first birthday).

Disney's Bestiary

Susan Willis

"That's not real."

"Yes it is. Its nose is wiggling."

Mother and child looking at a muntjac

"Africa is to your right. Asia is to your left." This is how the uniformed guide greets visitors to Disney's Animal Kingdom theme park. As with Disney's other lands, it's best to start with a map, if only to rid ourselves of the geographies we learned in school. For here, constructed out of Florida scrub, are the imagined realities not only of Africa and Asia, but the dinosaur badlands of South Dakota, a Minnie and Mickey Mouse wilderness camp, a geographically nonspecific rain forest, and something of a Polynesian fantasyland.

Because Disney's topographies are themed environments, they can be read like narratives. Coincidentally, each geographic region is defined by a particular dominant narrative genre. Africa smacks of adventure, while India is imbued with history. Other genres include fable and the tale of species extinction. The only prerequisite to reading Disney is to bear in mind that nothing is real but the meanings.

Hippos and Gorillas: The Narrative Adventure

A visit to Disney's Africa begins with a stroll through the marketplace of Harambé, gateway to the wilderness and wild animals. For its sienna hues, brightly costumed cast members, imported South African musicians, east African craftsmen, and saucy aromas wafting from the Tusker Restaurant, Harambé offers an enticing and altogether pleasing environment. Indeed, Disney's imagineers assembled an impressive array of decorative detail to create the aura of a present-day east African coastal town curiously caught in a time warp that has filtered out all the objectionable features of globalization and consumerism, such as cell phones and boom boxes, and left behind quaint Victorian signage, a mother's voiceover heard from an upstairs hotel window, and a genuine baobab.

Harambé serves as staging ground for Africa's version of a thrill ride: a safari quest for wild animals. Visitors familiar with Walt Disney World's Magic Kingdom may find themselves tempted to compare the safari to the Jungle Cruise, long a favorite of Adventureland. The Jungle Cruise has become something of a cult classic for its punsters who man the boats and banter with the tourists while avoiding the hazards posed by fake hippos and headhunters. It's possible that the original 1950s audience saw this as a thrill ride. Today the Jungle Cruise is generally perceived as an over-the-top excursion into a pastiche of a 1950s Tarzan-like adventure film.

Whether Animal Kingdom's safari sounds hauntingly like the Jungle Cruise depends largely on one's safari guide. Some drivers offer innuendo and ironic puns, while others treat the ride as a serious excursion into the African savannah. The drivers' uncertainty over how to present the safari has a lot to do with the competing narratives that define it. For the safari is freighted with all the ideological baggage that derives from the real-life history of big-game hunting (all the big-money philanthropists who shot the animals now stuffed and on view in New York's Natural History Museum), as well as all the fantasy baggage cranked out by Hollywood from *King Kong* to *Indiana Jones.* These adventure narratives collide with today's passion for environmental protection and species preservation, making the Disney safari a mixed message. It offers all the accoutrements of adventure: a battered safari vehicle, a khaki-clad driver, a jouncy ride across potholes, flooded roadbeds and rickety bridges, and sightings of dangerous animals: hippos, rhinos, lions, elephants—all in close proximity. But like true eco-tourists, we're here to see the animals, appreciate their diversity and uniqueness, and shoot them with cameras—not weapons. The safari's adventure tale morphs into a story about conservation when our guide picks up a radio communication from an aerial patrol. Apparently, poachers are in the area, and they are attempting to make off with an elephant. At this point our driver "leaves" the prescribed safari route and heads off in hot pursuit. In true Disney fashion, we (the audience) arrive just as a rifle-toting game warden enacts the apprehension of the suspects. We are center stage in a drama that coalesces contradictory strands of narrative into one fun-filled eco-friendly package.

Our driver's uncertainty whether to play to the adventure or the conservation narrative may have something to do with the effect of the built environment on the perception of reality. On the one hand, the safari includes a lot of real animals, perhaps more species than one would actually see on a real safari. On the other hand, the entire landscape is so artfully contrived as to render the animals props in an elaborate stage set. Indeed, our driver knows what the animals probably sense, as well, that both are cast members expected to provide a good show for us, the avid spectators.

As the audience, we see and journey through a savannah and upland forest. There are trees and bushes, rock outcroppings, termite mounds, rivers and ponds. We do not see ha-has, fences, moats, turnbacks, bollards, and walls — but they are there. We see open vistas and animals ranging freely. We do not see that "onstage habitats are often long and narrow, strung along the winding vehicle ride track."[1] A description of the hippo enclosure reveals the unseen technologies that define animals as cast members:

> The safari vehicle seems to plunge through Hippo River with the two-ton critters threatening to swamp the jeep from both sides. Actually, concrete fins with a 45-degree angle — called hippo bumpers — turn the beasts back from their pools' walls on both sides of the road. The angle is so steep that the animals can't get their feet up on them; the length of the fins also keeps the hippos in the center of the rivers so that the guests can see them. Water pumped over the ride path creates the illusion that the two pools are connected and that the vehicle is fording the river.[2]

The staging of conservation reaches its apex in the Harambé Research Station, which visitors are encouraged to visit either before or after their safari ride. The research station is reached by way of a footpath, the Gorilla Falls Exploration Trail, whose signage is bilingual, given in Swahili and English. The trail winds past the site of an animal kill (staged with tracks in the concrete and a corpse in a tree), through an aviary annex of the station, and finally into the actual facility, which gives onto Disney's gorilla habitat. The research station conveys the tone of a rustic field station headed by a fatherly local scientist, Dr. K. Kulunda, and staffed by an assortment of international students.

Traces of the apocryphal Dr. Kulunda are so strong one expects a holographic image to appear at any moment. However, Disney imagineers eschewed advanced technology and instead produced the impression of Dr. Kulunda out of the assembled clutter of written documents and artifacts that decorate the field station. The visitor with an eye for detail who pauses to read the posted journal entries and letters will construct a notion of the facility's personnel and imagine that Dr. Kulunda and his associates have just stepped out, providing an excellent opportunity to explore the station and its research. The latter focuses on totally dissimilar mammals: naked mole rats and gorillas. One side of the research station is a cutaway exhibit that allows us to peer into the subterranean world of the naked mole rats; the other side is a viewing porch that gives onto Gorilla Falls. The exhibit puts us in the position of researchers like Ray Mendez, who brought the naked mole rats to public attention, and Dian Fossey, who dramatized the life of gorillas. It asks us to imagine the days, months, years spent observing and documenting the minutiae of a species' physical and social attributes. It's a setting not suited to the Disney temporality, which generally urges visitors on with scheduled attractions and a fastpass for the most popular rides. If visitors linger here, it's because the animals are themselves compelling: the mole rats for their obscenely vulnerable bodies and beehive sociality; the gorillas for their hauntingly human looks and behaviors. What we see here are antithetical poles of mammalian life. It's a stupendous show whose spectacular qualities redefine the humble research facility as something of a theater in the round built for an ambulatory audience.

At Disney, conservation is more than a narrative; it's a spectacle whose main show is housed at another site far more modern than Dr. Kulunda's humble field station. This is Conservation Station, a multimedia theater equipped with sound booths, video and computer monitors, and performance areas that demonstrate veterinary care, nutrition, and animal tracking. Here guests are bombarded with images of some of the conservation projects that Disney funds. These, according to one researcher, must meet the dual criteria of "good science and good show."[3] Am I wrong to think these two attributes might be antithetical?

At Disney nothing can be perceived as antithetical, because narratives slide seamlessly into one another under the umbrella of "show." While the safari casts conservation as the adventure of catching poachers, Dr. Kuluda's station recasts it as the meticulous, possibly tedious, work of doing science. Significantly, the facility's rustic décor and the Victorian gentility of its head anchor the theme of science in a temporal frame that includes the era of the big-game hunts that gave rise to the adventure narrative. From this perspective the narratives of conservation and scientific investigation are shown not to be in competition with adventure, but imbued with its spirit. The conflation of narratives sends a message about gorillas and mole rats as well. That is, animals once defined as objects of the hunt and accessible only by harrowing overland treks now live as extensions of research stations, where they serve as objects of scientific investigation.

Tigers: The Narrative of History

Disney's exhibit of Asian animals is presented in a built jungle and savannah environment dubbed the Anandapur Royal Forest. This is one enclave of the larger themed continent of Asia that also includes a colorful and richly aromatized market and a thrill ride that courses visitors through river rapids and forest fire. Tame by comparison, Anandapur offers the visitor the Maharajah Jungle Trek, something of a self-guided trail that winds past a Komodo dragon grotto, through bat and bird enclosures, past the sanctuary of a pacing tapir, and finally into a clearing where tigers loll in the ruined shell of what we're told was once a royal hunting lodge. The architecture is beguiling. The unroofed palace consists only of colonnade walls whose arching doors and windows give onto vistas of open savannah where blackbuck and deer graze. The courtyard includes a fountain, clean and flowing, even though the palace appears to have been abandoned for centuries. The interior of the palace, home to the tigers, is carpeted with grass, lending an atmosphere of architectural decomposition to the surroundings.

Serendipitously, the trail does not skirt the Maharajah's lodge but enters into its heart. We traverse the ruins and come nose to nose with the tigers, all safely separated from us by glass partitions, whose transparency demarcates the absolute separation of humans and tigers, tigers and deer. We are all in our proper niches in a staged environment that gives the illusion that we humans might enter the tigers' court while the tigers might stalk off into the bush to tackle a herbivore.

The tigers are captivating. Huge and sleek, they lie about or leisurely stroll, unperturbed by the droves of tourists who pass by the glass partition, some calling out mock growls, others rapping on the glass or pressing their faces against it. Maybe the partition blocks our scent so that we appear to the tigers like images on a screen: a human video parade. Similarly, the tigers pay little attention to the deer. Perhaps they've learned that they are forever tantalizingly unattainable. Tourists on one side, deer on the other, the tigers are surrounded by images, animal spectators inside a 360-degree IMAX projection.

The Maharajah's palace is a three-dimensional tableau, a complicated diorama that the viewer traverses. It is a meticulously staged environment wholly devoted to rendering fascinating images of splendid tigers amidst the decayed elegance of a bygone aristocracy. The exhibit catapults the entertainment features of a penny arcade into the twenty-first century. Indeed, the tiger tableau is not unlike the kinetoscope that we peer into and crank to watch its animated images dance. Peering through the glass partition, we watch the tigers, animated not by a crank but by carefully contrived "enrichment" devices that ensure the animal actors will always be onstage. Scents, sometimes of food, often of urine, are the lures (called spikes). These are planted at strategic sites chosen to keep the tigers in view and active.[4] Moreover, the offstage tunnel that connects the two areas of the tiger exhibit is perversely "cooled in winter and warmed in summer so the cats will not linger there but will use it only for traveling back and forth."[5]

As actors in an architectural kinetoscope, the tigers depict a story, one framed by the overarching narrative of the larger Anandapur Royal Forest, which is given on a sign at the entrance to the Maharajah Jungle Trek:

Since very ancient times, the Rajahs of Anandapur have hunted tigers in this forest.

In AD 1544, King Bhima Disampati decreed the forest a Royal Preserve, closed to all save his guests, and built a royal hunting lodge whose ruins lie nearby.

After 1948, the Royal Forest was given to the people of Anandapur. Today the forest protects not only the remaining tigers and other wildlife, but is a valuable watershed of the Chakranadi River and some of the last remaining virgin forest in this region.

Royal Wildlife and Forestry Authority[6]

The exhibit's defining moment is the near past, 1948, when the royal lands passed into the public domain. (Although the Royal Wildlife and Forestry Authority, which issues the statement, suggests the Maharajah is still alive and unwilling to cede control to either nation-state or community.) The year 1948 is the temporal platform from which the distant past, the Maharajah, and his hunting lodge can be cast in a halo of nostalgia. All that remains of the aristocracy is the decrepitude of their architecture and the legacy of their custodial oversight of the tigers, which ensured the animals' preservation—if only as objects of the royal hunts. The year 1948 is also the platform from which the present is ambiguously sketched in the environmentalist lingo of watersheds

and virgin forests. The precise choice of 1948 significantly avoids all possible negative connotations—those associated with the more distant past, when Maharajahs and the British held sway, and those associated with India's present, fraught with the politics of nuclear proliferation and border conflicts. Moreover, 1948 neatly sidesteps the tumultuous events of 1947, marred by partition and Ghandi's death. Finally, 1948 represents the spirit of a newly independent nation—one capable of looking to the future by creating wildlife preserves while remaining curiously devoid of politics.

Indeed, Disney's representation of Asia as a whole, as well as Animal Kingdom's other themed worlds—Africa, America's dinosaur country, even Camp Minnie-Mickey—are all themed to represent the near past. The telling historical marker is usually an automobile, suggesting that Americans locate themselves historically with reference to the cars we own and drive. For Dino-Land it's a late 1950s Rambler and a pea-shaped camper trailer. For Anandapur, it's a 1950s bus, bedecked with flowers and mirrors. Indeed the only contemporary vehicle in the park is a safari-style jeep, used to designate the information station for tourists interested in buying a Disney Vacation Club time-share. The only other reference to present-day realities is Conservation Station, the state-of-the-art animal care facility and conservation classroom. Otherwise, a visitor to Animal Kingdom is enveloped in a Third World Never-Never Land amenable to American sensibilities. It's exotic, but comfortable;

different, but recognizable. It's a Third World reaping the benefits of modern industry, but not yet ruined by rampant and exploitative development. Hence Disney's India harks to a time of nascent electrification well before the era of petrochemical development that christened India with the horror of Bhopal.

From the sagging single-strand electric wires to the Bodhi tree where villagers leave garland offerings, Animal Kingdom offers the most meticulously themed environments on the planet. As such it outdoes all other previous Disney elaborations of theming, specifically EPCOT's World Showcase, whose renderings of Germany, France, Mexico, and a host of other nations once took the prize for the detailed allegiance to authenticity. In thematic hyperdrive, Disney's Animal Kingdom all but overwhelms the visitor with sensory cues: aromas, music, speech, dress, architecture, landscape, décor, horticulture, images, theatrics—all registers are activated to produce an unmistakably identifiable place or milieu. In this overabundant and thoroughly contrived and controlled setting, real animals cannot but be seen as elements of décor. The Maharajah's tigers are living, breathing, flesh-and-blood ingredients of a theme. As such, they are components in a narration. But they do not tell of tigers. Even the native informant, appropriately brown skinned and dressed in khaki or a version of native dress, who comes from Japan, Indonesia, Thailand, or Tibet and stands beside the tiger exhibit, speaking in Asian-inflected English, cannot tell the tiger's story even though he/she describes the tiger's physical attributes and habits. This is because the native informant is a scripted actor in the Disney narrative. And in this narrative, history stopped in 1948. Nature encroached on its course, just as it did in the Harambé savannah, and civilization never progressed beyond nascent low-impact development.

But maybe *this* is the tiger's story, and the world the way the tigers would want it. Maybe the world of 1948 contained the last remnants of possibility for tigers. After all, it's doubtful that anyone, even Disney's imagineers, can cast a future for tigers on the basis of our world today. So maybe the tigers spoke through the imagineers to frame themselves in a 3-D animated postcard sent from their no longer retrievable past and delivered into their already foreclosed future.

Teals and Tamarins: The Narrative of Fable

Around the base of the massive baobab, the still-life sculpture that defines the artificial core of Animal Kingdom, are a number of traditional zoo exhibits. These feature a particular animal species in an open-landscaped grotto-like enclosure. There are a roseate spoonbill, capybara, marbled teal, Galapagos tortoise, and cotton-top tamarins. Each is identified with a plaque in the shape of an open storybook where a trite rhyming refrain tells us something about the animal's physical or social attributes. The spoonbill gets short shrift with a poem that does little more than point to the shape of the bird's bill. One line from the poem unintentionally points to the spoonbill's survival dilemma: "Would a beak less unique find the food that I seek?"[7] The spoonbill in Disney's enclosure, not unlike spoonbills in the wild, is besieged by local native birds—herons and egrets—who aggressively use their less unique beaks to steal the spoonbill's food.

The storybook presentation of these animals harks to other areas in Walt Disney World—most notably the Magic Kingdom—that are grounded in Disney's sense of the child's experience and perception. The infantilization of imagination is a Disney hallmark that has important consequences when carried into the world of animal pedagogy and preservation. The refrain that introduces the cotton-top tamarin, an endangered primate from the rain forests of Colombia, anthropomorphizes the tamarin and endows it with "family values."

> When we are born
> (We're usually twins)
> It's truly a family event
> Our Mom keeps us fed
> And Dad gives us treats
> Sweet fruit just to
> Keep us content
>
> I'm carried by parents and siblings
> Right from the very first day
> It's part of our family values
> The cotton-top tamarin way[8]

The refrain that introduces the marbled teal makes no attempt to assimilate the bird to human lifestyles. Rather it casts the teal as expendable in a contest with humans for hegemony over the land.

> I only live near shallow lakes
> Since the foods that I like best,
> Are grasses and reeds that grow nearby
> And they also make quite a nest

But this land that I love is fertile
And the lakes are easy to drain
When humans turn them to farmland
My loss becomes their gain[9]

These messages are telling in their content and no less ideological in their form. As animal fables they compare with the medieval bestiaries. And like the bestiaries, they tell us more about ourselves—our culture and values—than they do about the animals.

Medieval bestiaries turned rudimentary—sometimes erroneous—information about animals into affirmations of divine omniscience and the totalizing oneness of the Christian worldview. Many tales are told of the lion, king of beasts, including this one that equates the lion with the resurrection of Christ:

> When the lioness gives birth to her cub, she brings him into the world dead and by her mouth: he is nothing but a piece of flesh in the shape of a cub. For three days she watches over him, dead as a stone. On the third day the lion arrives to breathe and roar over him: such growling, roaring, and snuffling, that he resuscitates and brings the little cub to life with his breath and his voice. The cub leaps to his feet when he hears his father's growling and follows him. Thus, the all-powerful Heavenly Father brought to life his blessed Son, our Lord, Jesus Christ, on the third day, of whom Jacob said: "He slept like the lion, like the lion's cub." (My translation)[10]

In a tightly construed allegory such as this, the lion's tale is anagrammatic of Christ; the two figures overlap like mirror images, each giving off the other's reflection.

It is no stretch of the imagination to read the divine presence in animal figures typically associated with the good, such as the lion, eagle, dove—even the elephant and peacock. But what about all the beasts associated with evil? The genius of the medieval bestiary is to demonstrate how even maligned beasts such as the serpent can be refashioned in order to illustrate divine purpose:

> When the serpent grows old and his sense of sight weakens, if he wants to rejuvenate himself, he only has to restrict his food intake and fast for days and days, until he floats in his skin; then he looks for a narrow crack in the rock, and there he brushes and rubs himself, until he leaves behind his old skin. Let us charge ourselves also to put aside our former self and its clothing by way of the bodily restrictions and abstinence that Christ embraced. Let us search for the Rock that is Christ, and the crack which is the "narrow door." (My translation)[11]

In the medieval bestiary, animals are never animals in their own right, but instruments of allegory. As such, they are the embodiments of biblical truths and teaching. They are also much more subtle and complex than Disney's teal and tamarin. Because medieval Christianity posited a world wholly defined by the conflict between good and evil, but one just as wholly dominated by divine will, the symbolic meanings of animals are never one-dimensional. Indeed, double and triple meanings can better elucidate the power of divine knowledge. Thus, the serpent can simultaneously bode death and redemption:

> "As Moses exalted the serpent in the desert, so the Son of man must be exalted, for whomsoever believes in him shall not perish, but will possess life eternal." In this case, the serpent represents the death of Christ. This death saves humankind, whose God-given salvation was sidetracked by the wicked counsel of that serpent of antiquity. (My translation)[12]

Using logic as convoluted as the serpent's coiled body, the bestiary imagines the serpent as symbol of Christ's death, which is necessary for human salvation. This in turn redeems the serpent of Eden by translating damnation into salvation.

Just as the medieval bestiaries were elaborated in a variety of media (script, sculpture, tapestry, stained glass), so too does Disney's bestiary assume numerous forms. In fact, it is possible to read the entire Animal Kingdom as a multigenre bestiary whose summation is embodied in the giant Tree of Life sculpture that serves as the park's main focal point and orientational hub for the visitor's exploration of the park. Standing 140 feet high, capable of withstanding hurricane-force winds, supporting "45 secondary branches, 756 tertiary branches, 7,891 end branches, and 102,583 green plastic leaves,"[13] the Tree of Life resembles a colossal baobab. In Africa, the baobab might well be associated with life for its appearance of stoic endurance and for the myriad life-giving uses its wood, fruit, seeds, and leaves provide. Disney's baobab is designated the Tree of Life for the four hundred animals sculpted into its trunk, lower branches, and upheaved roots. The artists, primarily Native Americans, were hired because of "their feeling for animals."[14] Indeed, the tree seems to have exuded the animals out of its interior resin. Most curiously, Disney's baobab seems to include the possibility for all species of tree as well as animal, as the various animal attributes (stripes, scales, fur, hide), are rendered in a variety of bark textures: oak, cedar, banyan. Then too, scale is not an issue. Many insects are the size of the tree's mammals. Rather, overall conformation to design and the requisite filling of space dictate the size and placement of the animals.

© KAREN KLUGMAN

In this, the Tree of Life is very like the bestiaries sculpted into the architectural features of medieval churches. What's most interesting about medieval animal sculpture is the elision and interlacing of forms, often across species lines. Mammals elide into reptiles while others sprout from vines or spit foliage out of their mouths. A beast with the head of a lion might curl about itself and end with a dragon's tail. Humans, too, might assume the shape of animals as sirens and centaurs. Other sculptures are complicated for the interweaving of figures. Mouths bite necks, necks wrap around torsos, and tails loop back around the heads. Where the untrained eye is apt to see cacophony, the medieval scholar recognizes the perfect mesh between aesthetic freedom, formal constraint, and divine plan.

Much like the animals on Disney's Tree of Life, the choice and placement of animal sculpture in medieval churches was first of all determined by architectural features—*chapiteau*, tympan, medallion, portal, pillar—and by the aesthetic dictate to fill that space in a balanced and symmetrical fashion. The structural constraints posed by architecture had the counterintuitive effect of freeing the aesthetic imagination. Animals could be bent, juxtaposed, and interlaced to fit the available space. And because form was such a strong determinant, animals from various allegorical registers could occupy the same space—even the same body. In this, form gives expression to the larger religious meaning of the sculptures. Because everything exists to glorify God, everything is possible. As medieval scholar V. H. Debidour puts it, "Dieu est géomètre":15

God gave Adam all the animals of his creation, the useful and the hostile alike, but He also gave him all the unreal monsters because He gave them to him to imagine: more than useful these are malleable as he sees fit, more than hostile, these are diabolic. The Romanesque artist renders them to God, not in a desperate and feverish display; but instead, translated in a double and unique language wherein the body is a geometry, and the soul is prayer: a double bridge from man to God. With his harpies, his dragons, his eagles and his lions, the twelfth-century sculptor says, perhaps without explicitly knowing it, these are the highest and most joyous truths with which he is imbued by intuition, by faith, by love: that Satan also is part of God's creation, that every creature, real or not, is of and for God; and that "God is the geometer." (My translation)[16]

If in medieval sculpture the artist conjoins with the Christian faithful to recognize and celebrate the all-encompassing multiplicity of God's design, how does Disney's Tree of Life function with respect to its coreligionists? The initial response of most visitors is to stare in awe of its monumental proportions and wonderment of its interconnecting sculpture. The moment of awe and wonder is, however, fleeting and quickly replaced by the desire to find the best photo opportunity place. Predictably, there are a number of optimal sites, most of which afford the possibility of framing the entire family in the tree's embrace. Closer inspection of the tree comes next. This invariably elicits a version of the Where's Waldo game. In this case, visitors challenge each other to find a particular animal. Some test their long-range vision in a contest to determine who can see and count the most animals. Somehow these trivial pursuits don't reduce the tree's grandeur, but they do underscore the fact that most tourists don't know what to do with the tree or what to make of it. It is simply there, and this is a bit odd because everything else in the park is so clearly supplied with a readily available meaning or use.

Dinosaurs: The Narrative of Extinction

The meaning of life is death. To understand the Tree of Life requires an excursion into death, which Disney provides in the dinosaur badlands of South Dakota. A celebration of the tacky and the scientific, DinoLand combines a diner and roadside tourist trap with a fossil laboratory where real scientists and technicians open plaster casings and clean dinosaur bones. The dinolab reiterates the small-scale, nuts-and-bolts simplicity found in Dr. Kulunda's field station — both, then, operate as illusionary disclaimers of the massive large-scale technological reality of the Disney operation as a whole. Cotton candy and curios frame DinoLand in the aura of roadside attraction. This enhances our already commonly held sense of dinosaur research as popular, rather than real, science. The only thing lacking in DinoLand's décor is Burma-Shave highway signs — but then, an extinct company is not a viable Disney sponsor.

For amusement, DinoLand offers a boneyard playground where kids scamper on and amongst huge fossil replicas, and the Countdown to Extinction,[17] a thrill ride that puts visitors on a collision course with the meteorite that ended the real world of the dinosaurs. Countdown to Extinction features an impressive assemblage of state-of-the-art audio-animatronic "Saltasaurus," "Parasauolophus," "Styracosaurus," and "Alioramus," all possibly apocryphal but so dramatic that Michael Eisner was wont to comment, "It's the first time I've been sorry they are extinct."[18] Rather than God the geometer, Countdown to Extinction dramatizes the unseen technological wizardry of Disney's imagineers, who found a way to bring subtle lifelike movement to ponderous eighteen-foot-high robots whose false skin alone weighs upward of five hundred pounds.

DinoLand is a perverse celebration of life in death. For a culture that has banished the presence of death with assisted-living enclaves for the aged, antiseptic funeral practices, and cemeteries that qualify as proving grounds for corporate landscape architects, DinoLand offers a brush with death — haunting but safe, because the fact of dying is displaced onto the dinosaurs. Entering DinoLand, we cross a bridge through the articulated skeleton of an immense brontosaurus. We are, thus, birthed into the world of the extinct. Here, kids

whose parents would never dream of letting them play in a graveyard cavort on the unearthed remains of the dinosaurs. Like zombies in a shopping mall, we stare at the displays of dinosaur eggs, teeth, and footprints, wondering how to distinguish the real fossils from Disney knock-offs. Not all of us will be brave enough to hurtle with Countdown to Extinction into the moment of the dinosaurs' demise, but we will all come away with the message that extinction is as much a part of Disney's Animal Kingdom as conversation. This marks a bold departure from the message offered by every other zoo, whose mantra is to preserve and protect wildlife and wild lands so that our children's children will be able to marvel, as we do, at the lions and tigers and bears. If in a zoo, extinction comes up at all, it's never more than a warning footnote—a poster of a dodo, once the world's largest flightless bird, alongside the current record holder, the ostrich.

By devoting an entire subpark to the theme of extinction, Disney situates its wildlife and wild lands in a countdown to the inevitable. This is no warning footnote in a larger message devoted to celebrating and preserving life; rather it reveals the fossilized climax of Disney's other narrativized species. From this point of view, the enshrined tigers inhabit a picturesque mausoleum; the mole rats, a theatrical tomb; the gorillas, a sepulchral garden; and the teals and tamarins, a parable of death. All are rescripted under the aegis of the narrative of extinction as flesh-and-blood embodiments of the life force that once quickened the dinosaurs.

But have no fear, Disney is here! And Disney can build life better than the Stepford Wives ever dreamed possible. If the Disney imagineers can engineer a dinosaur, they can certainly build a tiger. Would we know an audio-animatronic tiger from a real one? Those tigers in the Maharajah's palace who respond to enrichment "spikes,"—are they appreciably different from Deckard's electric sheep in Philip K. Dick's disturbingly bleak novel that inspired the movie *Blade Runner?*

> It [the sheep] lay ruminating, its alert eyes fixed on him in case he had brought any rolled oats with him. The alleged sheep contained an oat-tropic circuit; at the sight of such cereals it would scramble up convincingly and amble over.[19]

Is Disney, the corporate zookeeper, appreciably different from the novel's Rosen Corporation, producer of androids (humanoid robots) virtually indistinguishable from humans? Deckard's visit to the Rosen Corporation reads like a sci-fi version of the reaction many tourists to Animal Kingdom have when they wonder if an animal is "real":

> "A major manufacturer of androids," he said thoughtfully, "invests its surplus capital on living animals."
>
> "Look at the owl," Rachael Rosen said. "Here, I'll wake it up for you." She started toward a small, distant cage, in the center of which jutted up a branching dead tree.

There are no owls, he started to say. Or so we've been told. Sidney's, he thought; they list it in their catalogue as extinct: the tiny type, the E, again and again throughout the catalogue. As the girl walked ahead of him he checked to see, and he was right. Sidney's never makes a mistake, he said to himself. We know that, too. What else can we depend on?

"It's artificial," he said, with sudden realization; his disappointment welled up keen and intense.[20]

To paraphrase: Disney, a major manufacturer of illusions, invests its surplus capital on living animals, so as to stage them in artfully contrived settings (some with a "branching dead tree") and thereby reap a profit off our desire not to feel the "keen and intense" disappointment that the discovery of artificiality might render.

Juxtaposing the Disney and Dick versions of the corporate zoo casts the Tree of Life at the heart of Animal Kingdom in a new, laser-clear light. The tree's celebration of life is no deeper than its bark-like skin. What the tree monumentalizes is technology itself: the union of computer and rebar and the omnipresent but unseen corpus of the corporation whose mole-rat managerial staff pulled it all together. As paean to the artificial, the Tree of Life welds the narrative of extinction to conservation by giving us a pleasingly packaged clone. Tourists who quickly exhaust the tree's possibilities with their photos and Where's Waldo games unknowingly confront the bleak hollowness of a tree built on technology. Bemused, they wander off—no one wants to experience the keen and intense disappointment that comes with seeing the artificial for what it is.

So as not to recognize the heart of extinction at the core of Disney's zoo, we beguile ourselves with Disney's myriad fantasy replacements for the world's endangered species. There are whimsical beasts—perhaps more numerous than the real animals, who greet us, parade about, and interrupt our trajectories with their shows. Homespun bugs wearing afghans, imaginary birds on stilts, even a leaf-clad ivy person who drapes herself around lampposts. These are some of Disney's strolling players who celebrate nature as artificial. Rather than the tragedy of extinction and the grim "We Can Build You" corporate solution to an imperiled planet, the costumed characters suggest that we can play at what's becoming extinct. In fact, Disney's actors can be more colorful, more fun, more imaginative than anything created by God or evolution. What's most telling about the strolling players is that none pretends to be a "real" animal. Indeed, all reveal human faces as proof that human artifice can supersede both animal and plant forms. The play of artiface and face is reiterated in the face-painting booths, where children can have their faces transformed into humanoid versions of lions and gorillas. Or we might pose for an "animalture," an artist's rendering of our body in the shape of an animal.

With so many imaginative variations on the theme of animals, do we really need real ones? Besides, the human monkeys in Disney's Tarzan show, roller-blading acrobats in brilliant orange suits, do things that real monkeys wouldn't dream of doing.

Disney's bestiary carved in the Tree of Life is not a totemic celebration of life, but icon to the powers of corporate industry. It stands as leaf-covered pinnacle to the 4,400,000 cubic feet of earth moved to create Disney's Animal Kingdom; the 60 miles of pipe, 1,000,000 square feet of rockwork, 600 miles of electrical conduit, and the 15,000,000 gallons of water moved in the park per day to create an ambient setting for stories about animals.[21] These tell us about ourselves and our world. They tell of our nostalgia for the past, for, unlike androids, we dream of real tigers. They show us how our nostalgia is reworked into a celebratory veneer—all the props, packaging, and playacting that constitute leisure but mask a world not driven by nature, or God, or do-gooders like Dr. Kulunda, but by incalculable investment capital, massive development, and technologies that make life improbable. This is a bestiary whose electric sheep is named Dolly.

Notes

1. Melody Malmberg, *The Making of Disney's Animal Kingdom Theme Park* (New York: Hyperion, 1998), 108. This is the official guide to the theme park and includes all the facts and photos approved by the Disney corporation.
2. Ibid., 109.
3. Ibid., 171. Malmberg quotes Dr. Anne Savage, who evaluates the projects showcased at Conservation Station.
4. Most zoos now use enrichment devices such as puzzle box feeders to keep animals mentally alert and active. Many also use scented spikes to keep animals inquisitive. These are often placed so as to bring the animals into view. At Disney's theme park, enrichment dovetails with the emphasis on theatricality and promotes animal activity as part of their performance.
5. Malmberg, *Animal Kingdom*, 181.
6. Verbatim message on sign at entrance of Maharajah Jungle Trek.
7. Quoted from plaque in front of roseate spoonbill exhibit at Disney's Animal Kingdom theme park.
8. Quoted verbatim from plaque in front of cotton top tamarin exhibit at Disney's Animal Kingdom theme park.
9. Quoted verbatim from plaque in front of marbled teal exhibit at Disney's Animal Kingdom theme park.

10. *Bestiaire Roman,* tr. E de Solms, intro. Dom Claude Jean-Nesmy (Paris: Zodiaque, 1977).
à l'heure où la lionne enfante son lionceau, elle le met au monde par la bouche, et tout mort: ce n'est que pièce de chair en forme de lionceau. Trois jours le garde ainsi, tout mort. Au troisième jour vient le lion, qui souffle sur lui et mène grand bruit: tant gronde tout autour, rugit, et souffle, qu'il lui donne vie et le ressuscite, et par souffle et par voix. Le petit saute sur ses pieds, par le grondement que mène le pere, et il le suit. Ainsi le Pere tout-puissant ressuscita de mort au troisième jour son saint Fils, notre Seigneur Jésus-Christ, dont Jacob dit "Il a dormi comme le lion, comme le petit du lion."

11. Ibid., 153.
Quand le serpent devient vieux et sa vu baisse, s'il veut se rajeunir il n'a qu'à se priver de nourriture et jeûner des jours et des jours, jusqu'à ce qu'il flotte dans sa peau; il cherche alors une étroite fissure de rocher, y pénètre, s'y frotte, s'y rape, et finit par y laisser sa vieille peau. Efforçons-nous donc, nous aussi, de déposer notre vieil homme et son vêtement, à force de restrictions corporelles et d'abstinence embrassées pour le Christ: Cherchons le Rocher qui est le Christ, et la fissure qui est "la porte étroite."

12. Ibid., 155.
"Comme au desert Moïse a exalté le serpent d'airain, il faut aussi que soit exalté le Fils de l'homme, afin que quiconque croit en lui ne périsse pas, mais possède la vie éternelle." En ce cas le serpent représente la mort du Christ. Cette mort sauva le genre humain, que la ruse de l'antique serpent avait, par un malin conseil, frusté du salut que donnait le Créateur.

13. Malmberg, *Animal Kingdom,* 38.

14. Ibid., 120.

15. V.-H. Debidour, *Le Bestiaire Sculpté du Moyen Age en France* (Paris: Arthaud, 1961), 171.

16. Ibid., 170–171.
Dieu a donné à Adam tous les animaux de sa création, serviables ou hostiles, mais aussi tous les monstres irréels, puisqu'Il lui a donné de les imaginer: plus que serviables, ceux-ci, malléables à sa guise, et plus qu'hostiles, puisque diaboliques. L'artiste roman les Lui rend tous, non pas dans un déballage fiévreux et desespéré, mais traduits dans un double et unique langage dont le corps est géométrie, et l'âme prière: double pont de l'homme à Dieu. Avec ses harpies, ses dragons, ses aigles et ses lions, ce que dit le sculpteur du XIIe siecle, sans le savoir explicitement peut-être, ce sont les hautes vérités joyeuses don't il est impregné par intuition, par foi, par amour: que Satan aussi est de Dieu, que toute créature, crée ou non, est de Dieu, et pour Dieu; et que "Dieu est géomètre."

17. Countdown to Extinction has been renamed DinoLand to function as a tie-in with Disney's movie by the same name.

18. Malmberg, *Animal Kingdom,* 91.

19. Philip K. Dick, *Do Androids Dream of Electric Sheep?* (New York: Ballantine, 1987), 6.

20. Ibid., 36–37.

21. Malmberg, *Animal Kingdom,* 192.

Part II

Capitalism, Commodification, Globalization

3

Monarchs, Monsters, and Multiculturalism: Disney's Menu for Global Hierarchy

Lee Artz

Disney leads the world in the production and distribution of popular culture. Although AOL–Time Warner may be the media giant in assets, none challenge Disney as the primary purveyor of entertainment nor approach its perennial popularity and box-office success in animated feature films. Indeed, animation is central to Disney's economic vitality and cultural influence. In the last decade, Disney has sold over $3 billion in toys based on characters from its animated features. Disney theme parks, featuring popular film characters and settings, now have more visitors each year than all of the fifty-four national parks in the United States.

Although Disney produces nonanimated films through its Miramax and Touchstone movie studios, its economic and cultural strength remains in animation. Using profits from its global sales of animated films, Disney has acquired the ABC television network, mass-market radio stations, and cable channels such as ESPN and A&E. Disney's cartoon channels successfully air spin-off programs such as *Timon and Pumbaa* (from *The Lion King*), *Lilo & Stitch,* and *Jungle Cubs* (from *Tarzan* and *The Jungle Book*). Remarkably, eight of the top-ten-selling videos in the world are Disney animations, including *Lion King* (1994), *Pocahontas* (1995), *Tarzan* (1999), and *Lilo and Stitch* (2002).

The Lion King has grossed over $1 billion in video sales and merchandising. Now, allied with Pixar—the digital animation company headed by Steven Jobs—Disney has seamlessly expanded to lead in digital animation as well: *Toy Story* (1995), *Bug's Life* (1998), *Toy Story II* (1999), *Monsters, Inc.* (2001), *Finding Nemo* (2003), and *The Incredibles* (2004) have been major box-office successes. Indeed, *Finding Nemo* has become the highest-grossing animated film of all time. Moreover, each success at the box office has carried a parallel triumph in marketing Disney toys, games, videos, and clothing, among other commodities.

The centrality of animation to Disney's corporate success and the corresponding centrality of Disney animation to global popular culture forms and themes require some exploration. This inquiry should entail both a political-economic and a cultural studies approach given the apparent parallels between Disney's corporate practices (from investment and workplace practices to technological production and mass distribution) and the ideological themes of Disney's animated narratives (including race and gender equality). Investigating the construction, content, and persuasive appeal of Disney animations suggests that Disney consistently and programmatically produces "commodities-as-animated-feature films" that promote an ideology preferred by Disney and global capitalism—an ideology at odds with democracy and creative, participatory social life. Of course, post-structuralists and theorists of polysemy will contend that audiences construct their own meanings, whatever the meaning preferred by the media author. As interesting and significant as that conversation might be, one must still decide if an authorially preferred meaning can first be recognized. In the case of Disney, there is no doubt about the intent, the themes, and the dominant meanings preferred. Moreover, whatever readings individuals or particular social groups might perform, there is also a discernible media effect on the popular consciousness and vocabulary because we all use predominant "words and images to create and sustain social relations,"[1] even if we use them in negotiated or oppositional ways. In a society and culture ostensibly democratic, it is unsettling to find the major distributor of global entertainment promulgating narratives that simultaneously soften and defend messages of social-class hierarchy and antisocial hyper-individualism.

Animation in a Digital World

Animation—including its digital manifestation—provides the material, technical, and aesthetic basis for popularizing Disney content. Animation exhibits and employs features of all visual communication, blurring the "margin between fiction and reality."[2] The frame, the shot, the scene, the sequence—

these articulate cinematic images by virtue of their composition: characters and actions are highlighted and thus valued by their on-screen prominence. Animation has considerably more representational purchase than nonanimated film: image, size, movement, color, lighting, and continuity are easily altered with the stroke of a pen or a keystroke. All "films claim to show the truth, and constantly deceive,"[3] but animation excels at both owing to its artistic and technical flexibility, especially including computer-generated images that can more "accurately" visually approximate the material world. No documentary could reconstruct the anthropomorphized characters and stories of Disney's *Lion King* (1994), the *Bug's Life* (1998), or *Finding Nemo* (2003)—because the natural world disallows the fictional representations necessary for the narrative content. Animated characters and settings can be graphically adjusted to empower desired meanings: Sully, the "scarer" of *Monsters, Inc.* (2001), and Stitch, the cuddly, aggressive alien of *Lilo and Stitch* (2002), obtain human characteristics and movement through the "real"-ization of animation and digitization. Sully's more than 2,300,000 digital hairs bounce, flow, and move as "naturally" as the hair on a brown bear. Additionally, idealized character traits may easily be exhibited through visual representations that trigger audience recognition and either sympathy or antipathy: Good characters (e.g., Simba, the Sultan, Flick, Lilo, Sully, and Crush) are drawn in curves (smooth, round, soft, bright) and feature appealing juvenile traits such as big eyes, round cheeks; villains (e.g., Scar, Jafar, Hopper, Randall, and the Sharks) have sharp angles, jagged, rough edges, and are usually dark and oversized.

Animation has the same artistic capacity as illustration, where color, shape, and size evoke certain psychological responses and attitudes. Mickey Mouse's head, for instance, is composed of three symmetrically attached circles. As former Disney artist John Hench explains, "Circles never cause anybody any trouble. We have had bad experiences with sharp points, with angles, but circles are things we have fun with . . . circles are very reassuring."[4] To know Disney's attitude toward a character, one must simply describe its graphic depiction. Although screenwriters and cinematographers regularly and effectively express ideas through visual metaphor, animation has more technical opportunities and fewer creative obstacles, because animation is "freed from the limitations of physical laws and formulae"[5] and more easily disarms resistance to fiction and fantasy with its symbolic personification of values and ideals.

Children are particularly attuned to animation because it visually stimulates their emotions.[6] Bjoerkqvist and Lagerspetz found that children respond both cognitively and physiologically to the meaning of animation.[7] For children, animation pierces the consciousness and physical existence with experiential meaning, accessing a realm of understanding unavailable via literature or noncinematic physical activity. And in the world of animation, Disney, more than any other filmmaker, has shown itself "capable of understanding the way children think and feel."[8] Observe any preschooler or grade-schooler watching Disney—their eyes are wide and their bodies quake; laughter is spontaneous and fright discernible.[9] Adults likely interact with cinema in a similar though less transparent way, given their socialization to self-control and public self-consciousness, while recognizing animation as fictive, not real. Yet, the narrative and the animated motion attract attention, mitigating graphic fictions. Digital representation of animation further enlivens visual metaphor in character and setting, because it more closely and consistently approximates animal and human physiology and movement. Moreover, in Disney, fantasy and reality do not compete but "unite in a droll way."[10] For children and adults, Disney stories are exempted from the cinematic norm of fidelity to natural or historical conditions, largely because the presentations please us visually, viscerally, and psychologically.

Disney fantasies and their narratives are shielded from external critiques, in part, because they are based on widely accepted cultural myths and mores. Whether based on European folktales and Western myths (from *Cinderella* and *Snow White* to *Tarzan, Toy Story,* and *Pocahontas*) or adaptations of other cultures' stories (e.g., *Lion King, Mulan,* and *Bug's Life*), Disney animation always reaffirms "basic, commonly experienced social psychological needs which are connected with the socialization process and through it with the larger social structure,"[11] but leaves "nothing to make a child think or feel or imagine," and borrows without regard for the anthropological, spiritual, or psychological truths of the folk stories.[12] In short, Disney versions replace prior accounts and meanings, erasing much of the potential empowerment once offered by fairy tales and fantasy.[13] In recent animated features, Disney has even moved from nonhuman heroes in *Lion King* (1994), *Toy Story* (1995, 1999), and *Bug's Life* (1998) to nonnatural heroes and monsters in *Monsters, Inc.* (2001) and aliens in *Lilo and Stitch* (2002). In each instance, driven largely by preconceived marketing goals (e.g., toys, games, clothing, other media spin-offs), Disney crafts highly stylized, naturalistic graphics with realistic narratives that are entertaining and persuasive precisely because they have become so familiar and comforting.

Familiar visual metaphors, naturalistic scenes and settings, anthropomorphism of animal and fantastic creatures, and the appropriation of comforting cultural codes, overlaid with pop music sound tracks, are but some of the defining characteristics of Disney animation—characteristics established by Walt Disney but perfected by corporate Disney in the 1990s. Not only have Disney animators received little credit for their talent and creativity over the years; they have had little control over how their talents will be used. As one animator explained, "you drew Disney-style or else. No real experimenting, no breaking the mold."[14] Looking for creative variation in Disney is like looking for menu choices in McDonald's or some other industrialized fast-food chain. The one instance of Disney using an outside artist for a feature animation (*Hercules* 1997) was a box-office failure because it violated established visual codes, animation techniques, and narratives perfected as "Disney." Animation at Disney is preordained: the institutional structure and practices subsume creativity within established production technique and artistic form—from the hiring of artists, job divisions, and work rules to the decision-making chain of command from storyboard artists to corporation board members. Disney's five-feature long-term agreement with Pixar further privileges executive over artist—technology and technical workers have replaced cel painters, storyboard illustrators, and other individual art workers. Pixar's amazing Renderman (the high-powered digital production software used in animation) cannot begin without an original creative rendering by a human artist who likely commands considerable remuneration for the initial idea; a large workforce of artists is no longer needed. Not surprisingly this institutional structure of hierarchical mass production finds an echo in the narrative structure of Disney feature animations.

Disney uses its trademark techniques (color, movement, background) and forms (fictional creatures, animal buddies, youthful hero narratives) to tell stories with popular yet enduring themes vital to the contemporary capitalist culture of the United States (e.g., coming-of-age, personal responsibility, search for individual happiness, stratified social order). Indeed, Disney narratives are unsurpassed in their narrative fidelity to dominant ideology and cultural values, consistently asking audiences to enter believable fantasy worlds. In *The Lion King*, Disney captures our continuing cultural attraction to royalty and noble beasts to construct a fictional world where animals of prey bow to—rather than flee from—the predator. In *Monsters, Inc.*, Disney caricatures industrial piecework and idealizes the production line of "scarers" in terms of a rationalized, cartoonized free market enterprise. In these and other films, Disney can dismiss social inequality and the brutality of feudalism and capitalism by creating representational characters with familiar and believable connotations controlled not "by the properties the [subject] actually has but by those it is widely believed to have":[15] a cuddly sultan (*Aladdin*), a benign emperor (*Mulan*), a just queen (*Bug's Life*), magnanimous supervisors (*Lilo and Stitch, Monsters, Inc.*). Meanwhile, Disney easily denigrates democracy by casting secondary characters as bumbling or threatening to the collective good (as in *Pocahontas, Mulan, Monsters, Inc., Finding Nemo*, among others). In short, Disney can render history and nature in very antihistorical and unnatural ways (e.g., a sultan who ignores social class, a baboon that cooperates with lions, workers intent on saving the company, sharks and birds that don't eat fish), because animation allows realistic reconstructions of narratives, fables, and even extant material conditions. Indeed, because Disney excels at wrapping the fantastic in the natural, its animated narratives assume much of the verisimilitude of "real" movies.

With the communicative power of animation and digitization in narrative realism and the dominance of Disney as the most popular purveyor of the art form, there is a consensus that Disney supplies a stable diegesis for socialization.[16] In his appraisal of mass-mediated culture, for instance, Michael Real determined Disney has replaced schools, churches, and families in teaching society right and wrong.[17] Kathy Jackson argues that Disney and its vision "permeates our culture."[18] Annalee Ward further believes that for children the social values of Disney stories "form the standards for testing the truth of other stories later in life,"[19] while film critic Michael Medved even predicts a historic cultural shift to family values led by Disney.[20] Unfortunately, the pro-social values that Ward and Medved perceive in *The Lion King* and the feminist virtues that Henke, Umble, and Smith find in *Little Mermaid* and *Pocahontas* are surface readings of Disney's adjustment to its market needs.[21] Close attention to the narratives and character traits suggests that although Disney animations remain "naive, childlike, even childish,"[22] they are not the fairy tales of imagination that children need,[23] nor are they socially progressive. Rather, Disney animations are self-contained confections mass-produced by adults writing, selling, and promoting themes for product licensing and private profits, with consumerist values and ideologies supportive of capitalist globalization.[24]

Significantly, Disney's animated visions not only thrive in the United States but predominate in international entertainment, partly because, more easily than any other global communication form, animation crosses borders. Unlike nonanimated television and film, animation does not need to be dubbed or fitted with subtitles: cartoon characters are multilingual. Consequently, the costs for international distribution of animation are low, while the possibilities for cross-cultural reception are high. Raised by the apes, Tarzan speaks German. The Powhatan Pocahontas may not know her own language, but she speaks fluent French and Italian. Stitch and Flik converse in Malay and Spanish but not Arabic, as that film market is too small. In its commitment to market diversity, Disney also willingly edits any culturally unfavorable textual content as in *Pocahontas* and *Aladdin* because it is "determined to release non-controversial" animated films to maximize profits.[25] The apparent preference for animals, aliens, and monsters in recent Disney/Pixar releases is likely due to a recognition that such protagonists communicate no obvious offense to any culture while being universally marketable.

Disney animations are not only linguistically adaptable; they also have long lives. In addition to the toys, clothes, and other products that outlive the theater runs, Disney animations are re-released on video, and characters reappear in various video and television spin-offs. Actors age and die; cartoon characters are eternal. Based on fairy tales and historic myths rather than current events, Disney features do not become dated as quickly as other genres. Snow White, Bambi, Pinocchio, Peter Pan, and now Simba, Mulan, and Tarzan will likely thrill future audiences as their contemporaries.

Disney animation has already become popular with international audiences, which eagerly anticipate and are willing to pay for each new release. Disney develops its films according to a strict artistic and corporate protocol,[26] displaying an identifiably consistent naturalistic style with richness of color and shading, depth of detail in background, full musical scores, and of course consistent themes, narrative, and ideologies. When Disney used an outside artist for *Hercules* (1997) (violating its own established techniques, codes, and forms), audiences rejected the departure from the expected Disneyfied fare and the film stumbled at the box office. Meanwhile, Steven Spielberg's DreamWorks studio has had some success in challenging Disney with *Shrek* (2001), as has Fox with *Ice Age* (2001)—both of which, incidentally, depart ideologically from Disney formulae by encouraging group solidarity. Yet, Disney's latest offerings, *Monsters, Inc.* (2001), *Lilo and Stitch* (2002), and *Finding Nemo* (2003) (at $850 million gross), reaffirm Disney's overwhelming box-office superiority.[27] Like all televised entertainment, animation carries no sanctions, only gratifications to deliver meaning.[28] The popularity of Disney suggests that audiences receive considerable pleasure, while the pervasive redundancy of Disney animations assures that Disney's vision will be seen, understood, and remembered—three requirements of effective propaganda. Given evidence that children causally equate narrative outcomes with behavior (bad actions are punished, good are rewarded),[29] it is also likely that Disney's morals and hierarchies will be acted on as valid and preferred. The magic of Disney—its ability to communicate ideas to millions—comes from offering children and adults alike a visual sweet, desired and satisfying. Of course, for all its pleasure, a high-sugar diet is not the most nutritious. Likewise, the messages in Disney's vision do not encourage healthy communities or democratic societies.

A textual analysis of themes in recent Disney animated features reveals that Disney's dreamworld of individual heroes and royalty rests on cultural privilege, social inequality, and human alienation—the same ingredients obtained and produced by the socioeconomic practices of Disney and other capitalist enterprises—validating the observations of Dorfman and Mattelart nearly three decades ago that Disney's representations promote capitalist hegemony and political quiescence.[30] In short, Disney's symbolic production parallels the social production of global capitalism as recognized in part by Ricker and Wasko.[31]

Artz's textual analysis based on the audio dialogue, the published scripts, and the visual graphic representations of *Aladdin* (1992), *The Lion King* (1994), *Pocahontas* (1995), *Mulan* (1998), and *Tarzan* (1999) was an attempt to examine the common features of the most popular and financially successful Disney animations of the 1990s.[32] The study unearthed some larger themes that clarify how "dominant culture constructs its subordinates."[33] A second study of Pixar/Disney projects— *Toy Story* (1995), *Bug's Life* (1998), *Toy Story II* (1999), *Monsters, Inc.* (2001), and *Finding Nemo* (2003)—further validated the earlier findings. As discussed above, Disney creates its ideal world through an animated narrative realism. Each narrative tells a story of the way things are, or are supposed to be. Each story (and every Disney product) represents the myth of "how things are done, not then or now, but always in the life of the living being, group, or culture."[34]

Each Disney narrative features some characters, events, and perspectives, instead of others, in order to entertain and to communicate a particular meaning. Presenting some characters and events as more entertaining, dramatic, humorous, or enlightening, and "real"-izing them through animation, the Disney narrative "suppresses" other characters or events as less important, less entertaining, indeed, uninteresting, even boring.[35] Importantly, in all narratives, the story develops through the action and discourse of the lead characters. Characters can be evaluated by when, how, and how often they speak and act, by what they say and do, how they interact among themselves, how they are rewarded in the story, and, important in any audiovisual medium, how they look and sound. Thus, Hoerner defines a story's hero, or heroine, as the central character determined by time on screen, lines of script, and the focus of the story, while the villain is defined as anyone who acts in opposition to the hero.[36] In Disney characters, the distinction between good and evil, proper and improper behavior, is always clear in the character's actions.[37] Characters narrate the values and myths dear to the producer, representing the producer's preferred values and themes to the audience.

From this perspective, the analysis offered here considers Disney narratives in terms of character action (including dialogue) and character visual depiction (including shape, size, color, and other descriptive graphic features). The markers of character trait, social position, and dramatic value discovered within the narratives appeared in bundled themes that seem to crystallize Disney's ideological project. The distinguishing themes in Disney animated features include (1) the naturalization of hierarchy; (2) the defense of elite coercion and power; (3) the promotion of hyper-individualism; (4) the denigration of democratic solidarity. Analytically distinct, the four themes are necessarily intertwined, serving as complementary supports for each and all, and are dramatically apparent in each film. Digital Disney advances the same ideological content, with an occasional creative wrinkle. The following discussion summarizes instances from over a dozen Disney features that illustrate consistent hierarchical narratives that contain complementary positive representations of elite coercion, and that obviously omit or reject democratic cooperation and social concerns.

Naturalizing Hierarchy

Hierarchy in a social order indicates a ranking according to worth, ability, authority, or some other attribute. In Disney, these values are combined with goodness and physical appearance such that, in each animated narrative, heroes and heroines are invariably good, attractive, capable, worthy, and ultimately powerful while in service to the narrative's social order.

From the opening "circle of life" scene in *The Lion King* we cannot mistake the social order and its validity. All species bow before the rightful king. The heavens open and a (divine?) light shines on the new lion cub. This future king is held before a multitude of reverent and bowing beasts whose happiness and very existence depends on the maintenance of the established and rightful hierarchy. The visual metaphors of good and evil are simple and transparent: a regal king and his heir; an evil uncle who covets the kingdom; and lesser, passive animal-citizens overrun by social undesirables in need of leadership. The meanings are animationally inescapable—the King and his son, Simba, are brightly drawn, muscular, and smoothly curved; the villainous uncle, "Scar," is dark, angular, thin, and disfigured; the hyenas, likewise, are angular and unmistakably black and Latino (in the voice, diction, and verbal styles of Whoopi Goldberg and Cheech Marin); the socially irresponsible meerkat and boar, more cartoonish, less naturalistically drawn, live beyond the pride lands. The dialogue and action indicate importance, as well. Mustafa speaks in the King's English, usually from on high. Scar, the villain, lurks in shape and movement, languid, lazy, and foppish, narratively manipulating other characters through deceit. The hyenas have secondary roles with fewer lines, delivered comically, with slapstick interactions that are nonetheless understood as threatening to the smaller, younger, and naive lion cubs. In short, from theme song and graphic representations to story line, Disney establishes a series of relationships of power that are maintained throughout.

Similarly, *Aladdin* has a favorably drawn picture of hierarchy. The hero, Aladdin, lives above Agrabah and its smarmy merchants, murderous palace guards, and suffering street urchins, at eye level to the sultan's palace—a clear visual metaphor of Aladdin's social equality with the princess Jasmine. Significantly, Aladdin has little interaction with any human character other than Jasmine. He has a monkey companion and, of course, his friendly genie. Jasmine, one of Disney's recent "feminist" heroines, is spunky, adventurous, and independent—although ultimately she needs male guidance, rescue, and approval. This fantasy of youthful rebellion and romance occurs completely within the Disney world of hierarchy. The hero never questions or challenges the feudal order: Aladdin does not use the magic lamp to feed the children, aid the poor, or disarm the sultan's army. No, this "diamond in the rough" only strives to win the princess and defeat Jafar, the archvillain. Jafar, described narratively as "a dark man . . . with a dark purpose" is drawn darkly, highly angular, threateningly tall, with a long mustache and large nose. The Sultan of Agrabah, in contrast, is round, with a white, fuzzy beard, jovial features, a bumbling gait, and short—the representational personification of benevolence, Santa Claus without the red suit. Jafar speaks with a thick Arab accent, plotting overthrow and subterfuge throughout the story. The sultan has a cheerful British accent and plays with toys, largely oblivious to the political intrigue. Light-skinned Aladdin, the only male without facial hair in the movie, saves the sultan and Jasmine, and Agrabah returns to the normal elite order required by Disney.

The narratives of *Pocahontas, Mulan, Tarzan,* and other Disney animations are formed from the same redundant template of elite hierarchy, albeit with hegemonic variation. In *Pocahontas,* the standard Disney coming-of-age romance has been updated with a feisty, independent heroine in a narrative advocating cultural tolerance but following the trail of all Western captivity narratives with its "noble" Powhatan, "savage" warrior Kocoum, and "Indian princess" Pocahontas.[38] John Smith, blond, smoothly muscular, and athletically animated, fulfills the heroic ideal in vision and plot, while Chief Powhatan appears more sedate in bold, symmetrical strokes, with slower, more dignified screen movements and dialogue. These two elites survive the actions of the reactionary Kocoum and villainous Ratcliffe. The stoic, irrational Kocoum has few lines and dies at the hands of a naive colonialist. The Ratcliffe character reveals in dialogue that he is indulgent, pompous, greedy, incompetent, and not respected by the British nobility. He appears as the largest figure in the film, obese, with a huge nose, big lips, and pencil-thin triangular mustache.

The narrative's social relations are hierarchical: lower-class Anglos work for Ratcliffe or Smith; native soldiers and villagers follow Powhatan's directives. In the end, the "good" colonialist John Smith intervenes to save Powhatan and order the arrest of Ratcliffe; Pocahontas presumably finds her true path as a peacemaker and daughter; and the rest of the natives and English adventurers assume their prescribed subordinate positions, awaiting further orders from their superiors. In *Pocahontas,* two hierarchical orders are defended and left intact, although the extended visual metaphor of John Smith saving Powhatan and wanting to civilize Pocahontas indicates that the colonial is dominant over the indigenous.

The heroes in Pixar features have similar characteristics, rendered more dramatically by digitization. *Bug's Life,* the Disney rewrite of Aesop's "Ant and the Grasshopper," portrays an entrepreneurial, patriotic inventor as savior of the monarchy. The hero, Flik, is slender, athletic in form and action, and albeit amusing, a thinking ant. The caring queen ant—complete with crown—has large round eyes, long eyelashes, and a robust torso. The evil leader of the grasshoppers, Hopper, has a tough exterior, multiple jagged appendages, sharp facial features, large, angular eyes, and sports a military-style high-collar jacket. The story's moral of hard work, subservience to hierarchy, and defense of the status quo is barely disguised in the construction of marauding grasshoppers laying waste to an industrious ant colony. In *Monsters, Inc.,* the heroes are not only good-natured scarers, cuddly, furry, oval, pastel-colored, with big round eyes; they understand, defend, and work to maintain the corporate order, to keep corporate secrets, to increase piecework production, and to thwart attempts at industrial sabotage or disruption. The evil Randall is snakelike with wide, narrow lips and a mouthful of sharp-pointed teeth. As superchameleon, Randall deceives through manipulation of appearance. All heroic pals are round, furry, somewhat sheepish no matter their size, and equally committed to corporate success—the perfect quality circle.

Given the prevalence of elite narratives in Disney animations, it appears that hierarchy is a structural prerequisite. Graphic representations verify such a conclusion. In *Mulan,* the treacherous, invading Hun towers over all other characters, hulking, hooded, and with sharp, foreboding facial features: angled eyes, triangular eyebrows, long angular mustache, and tight lips. His giant steed snorts, his falcon pierces the air with hooked beak and sharp wings, and his dark minions hack, maim, and kill with vigor. In contrast, the Emperor of China is slight and thin, almost wispy, and moves gracefully across the screen. Barely defined graphically, a mass of bowing, passive, and helpless citizens provides background filler for the antagonism between the Huns and the heroine. Mulan has fewer Barbie-esque features than other Disney females and generally is less on display, although she is drawn with the requisite oval face, large eyes, and graceful body lines.

In the story, Mulan disguises herself as a man to replace her father in the military draft—temporarily violating the law against female fighting. She performs courageously, and through wit, physical skill, and the assistance of some barely competent assistants, Mulan overcomes the invading Huns and saves China. Of course, she returns to her "proper place" at her father's side in the family garden to be courted by a handsome nobleman she met during her adventure. Ultimately, traditional romance and Chinese feudalism survive.

Edgar Rice Burroughs's myth of Tarzan is well known and in little need of Disney's creative license. Raised by apes, Tarzan, king of the jungle, rescues Jane and retires to an idyllic life of swinging vines and fresh fruit. Disney lushly animates the narrative with visual metaphors of good and evil within a clear social hierarchy. Once again sharp, angular depicters carry the villain on screen. Clayton has a big head, protruding nose, cavernous mouth with huge teeth, jutting chin, and the sinister little mustache of melodramatic villainy. Clayton has a fondness for weapons, easy wealth, and large ascots. When he speaks, his face contorts and his mouth twists ungraciously. Like other Disney villains, Clayton is the largest human character in the film—graphically representing dangerous power. Tarzan is angular, muscular, Aryan. His demeanor on screen is athletic and coordinated, yet in dialogue he is innocent and naive, evidence of the backwardness of his jungle family. Jane teaches him, as the Western world civilizes Africa; but his prowess saves Jane, as men protect women. Jane's colonizing father is a graphic tracing of the sultan: short, round, furry, and nonthreatening. Apes, baboons, an elephant, and Clayton's men furnish the requisite comic filler or stereotypical representation of the mass: alternately witless, awestruck, and obedient to elite leaders or witless, hungry, and easily roused to treachery by the villain.

Disney provides multiple variations on the hierarchy theme, yet each narrative establishes a clearly differentiated power. As Wilson observed about theme parks, "the organising principle of the Disney universe is control."[39] In animation, race, gender, and particularly class act as recurring indicators of hierarchy. A charting of authority suggests that elite authority communicates social legitimation within the narrative.[40] Mustafa instructs Simba in his duty. Porter approves Jane's decision to stay with Tarzan. The queen ant rules in *Bug's Life;* happiness depends on maintaining the proper social order, with her approval. Once Woody and Buzz Lightyear share authority—metaphorically validating the combination of Old West libertarianism with technological individualism—any threat to the toy world can be defeated; toys are saved and may return to their patronage responsibility for pleasing humans. Despite their considerable intellectual and technological power, even intergalactic beings pale when faced with the creative superiority of preadolescents in *Lilo and Stitch*. In short, in each animated narrative, a princely elite (animal or human) conveys and protects the ideals, values, and traditions of the social order.

While the hero and heroine are always noble and attractive by birth, villains are privileged and titled only because of the misplaced magnanimity or whim of a legitimate superior. Villains are unattractive, semielite social misfits. Jafar is grand vizier, adviser to Sultan; Scar is King Mustafa's disgruntled brother, ineligible for legitimate succession; and Ratcliffe's governorship is a reluctant sop from more worthy elites. Randall remains on the monsters' payroll only through his deceit, which ultimately is discovered by the hero, Sully. In each of these narratives and many others (e.g., *Little Mermaid, Beauty and the Beast, Fox and Hound*), the dominant social class has no villainy, producing only good souls who never abuse their authority. We understand this viscerally by the soft, cuddly caricatures that Disney creates. Abuse comes solely from those elevated beyond their goodness, villains who would reach beyond their status and disrupt the social order. The structure of overworked employees is never questioned: only crustacean Henry J. Waterhouse III must be removed for violating the social responsibility that generations of monster CEOs had felt for the business. But villainy is always undone, because as Disney's *Comic Book Art Specifications* dictate, only elites can triumph; there is "no upward mobility" in Disney lands.[41] In the fairy-tale world of the dominant, class rules apply: a frog becomes a prince only if he was a prince before. Rulers may change among the elite (from Mustafa to Simba, from Sultan to Aladdin, Flik gets royal privilege), but the rules and ruled remain. And, in Disney's world, the only just rule is class hierarchy.

In addition to providing heroes and villains with clearly drawn markings of social status, Disney illustrates social position and worth of secondary characters with variations appropriate to their relationship to hero or villain. Thus, aides to the hero/heroine are invariably animals, friendly and "cute," as Uncle Walt dictated decades ago: Meeko the raccoon; Mu-Shu the scrawny dragon; Timon and Pumbaa, the Laurel and Hardy of the pride lands; Terk, the ape sibling, and Tantor the jovial elephant; lively crabs; comic birds; lead scarer Sully has a one-eyed monster sidekick; rescue-ant Flik has a circus troupe of bumbling aides; to find Nemo, Marlin reluctantly teams with an ADHD, memory-challenged female fish, while Nemo has an entertaining "tank gang." Only Jasmine's companion tiger-bodyguard and Aladdin's genie possess any visual strength, but narratively they both live to serve their owners. Villains occasionally have animal assistants, some of which are cast as unenthusiastic participants who find pleasure in other characters' misfortunes—that is, not so cute.

Each villain's animal companion has some graphically or narratively suggestive objectionable feature: grating voice (Jafar's bird), mean-spiritedness (hyenas and Ratcliffe's pampered dog), or violent nature (the Hun's falcon); Hopper's brother Molt is lazy and dim-witted. Humans loyal to the heroic characters and awaiting more powerful leaders have less character development (like the colonial workers in *Pocahontas,* passive ant-citizens in *Bug's Life*), while the collective population frequently appears as largely motionless, two-dimensional spectators (as in *Aladdin, Mulan,* and *Nemo*), illustrating their passive role in both the narrative and Disney's social vision. *Monsters, Inc.* deviates slightly from this formula by elevating the narrative value of labor, choosing a heroic and moral worker as protagonist—a monster who scares small children into screaming, which generates energy in the monster world. Yet, despite labor's violation of accepted practices, in the end, proper corporate order is established.

Evil henchmen, such as Clayton's sailors or the Huns, are consistently shabbily dressed or disheveled, dark, often bearded, usually armed, speak harshly in short sentences, and mete out their brutality only as long as the villain commands. In Disney, lower-class characters do not act on their own. Large groups are often cast as mob-like in action and graphic: jeering primates terrorize Jane; wildebeest stampede without regard for others in *The Lion King;* native warriors huddle around the fire waiting for orders to attack; the Huns shout and howl above the thunder of their horses' hooves; grasshoppers and sharks indiscriminately attack. Whether African, Arabian, North American, Chinese, or nonhuman, few from the good citizenry or evil troops are individualized; even fewer have articulate voices, appearing but as replicates from two or three stencils, graphically reflective of their necessarily subordinate position in Disney's hierarchy. In sum, Disney films all play a similar refrain: a stylized, naturalized, and Westernized elite hero combats a privileged antisocial oversized villain, while cute animal sidekicks and thuggish rebels knock about in front of a shapeless, faceless humanity. Animating hierarchy centers Disney's vision, whatever the era, geography, or species.

Ordering Coercion and Power

To underscore this essential Disney law, narrative resolution in each film defends and reinforces the status quo. Nothing is resolved until the preferred social order is in place. No one lives happily ever after until the chosen one rules. All is chaos and disorder in the pride lands until Simba returns as monarch. Even nature withholds its bounty, pending the proper social hierarchy. Nemo's mistake is curiosity about another world: when he leaves the security, safety, and proper place of the coral reef, disaster strikes. Saving China is only a youthful adventure: Mulan's "place in life" is in the family garden. Even the wisest of apes knows Tarzan is superior. The fictional multispecies cooperation in *Bug's Life* occurs to defend monarchy and the colony, not to build a democratic order. Sully and company rescue the corporation from its treacherous owner, not to establish a cooperative, but to reorganize an improved hierarchical order. And so it goes, in Disney animation. Hierarchy is essential and sacred, from animal and human to monster and alien.

We all need true rulers who are wise, benevolent, and powerful. Any other arrangement is unworkable. Villains may attain power, but as nonelite, false leaders, they are ill equipped to rule. Their reign is disastrous and temporary. Soon the hero will save the day and the hierarchy. "As evil is expelled, the world is left nice and clean," and well ordered.[42] Thus, zebras bow, faceless Chinese cheer, and, in general, the working masses rejoice (and happily resume their subservience) upon the triumphant defense of the hierarchy. The pleasant narrative outcome verifies the virtue of hierarchy and models Disney's actual institutional hierarchy in everything from animation production to cruise ships, theme parks, and town life in Celebration, Florida.[43] In its digital production, Disney replaces piecework animation artists with piecework technicians in a hierarchical structure dedicated to marketing entertainment commodities for shareholder profit—no cooperative here, no creative exchange between artists, technicians, and citizen-parents. The story scripts in narrative and in production and distribution conform to market dictates and capitalist production norms, including corporate elite control.

Preference and justification for elite control can be observed in the attributes of each narrative's leading authority: this character is morally good and invariably benevolent. The sultan may be disoriented, but he is a gentle soul, impervious to evil. A compassionate John Smith—"the perfect masculine companion"—is willing to sacrifice his own life to avoid further bloodshed.[44] In contrast to the malevolent Huns, Mulan's emperor exudes warmth for his docile subjects. Tarzan demonstrates his human compassion and species superiority in saving his ape family (and Jane). For Disney, all elite authority figures are good, caring, and protective of their wards. In a telling statistical analysis of eleven Disney animations, Hoerner found that heroic protagonists exhibit 98 percent of all pro-social behavior in the films.[45] Disney's subsequent animated films maintain the same class-based morality, as do Disney's digitized features *Toy Story* and *Toy Story II*, although, as noted above, *Monsters, Inc.* exhibits some variation.

Rulers are also responsive to the individual needs of their duly anointed successors, frequently revising rules that do not overturn the status quo. The sultan changes the laws of royal matrimony. John Smith orders the arrest of a governor. Mulan's father, emperor, and royal suitor all forgive her individual indiscretion, but the discriminatory laws against women are not revoked or even questioned. After witnessing Tarzan's rescue of his ape family, Kerchak puts aside his species bias and declares Tarzan king of the jungle. The queen ant rewards Flik after he saves her colony. James P. Sullivan, Sully, can violate rules for protection of corporate secrets and success. Significantly, once their individual needs are met, all heroes and heroines come to accept the wisdom of established authority and norms.

A consistent haloing of hierarchal power as preferable for all organizes the films' moral conflicts and elite responses to challenge. In all cases, elite heroes and heroines use coercion with impunity, continuing a Disney tradition that dates back to Snow White. Elite coercion varies from the Beast's abuse of Belle to the colonialist's murder of Kocoum. Mulan slaughters dozens of Huns; Tarzan wrestles with Clayton, who accidentally falls to his own death. Villains Randall, Waterhouse, Hopper, and various aliens are similarly dispatched by elite violence. In addition to coercion, elites frequently employ deceit. Everywhere and always Disney's heroic elites are stronger, smarter, and victorious in the final conflict (even when performing antisocial acts). In each case, the protagonist earns riches, power, and happiness.

In contrast, villains—who almost exclusively exhibit antisocial behavior and violence—suffer calamity or death: Jafar is imprisoned for thousands of years; Scar dies; Kocoum dies; Ratcliffe is arrested; the Hun dies; Clayton dies; Randall and Hopper are ultimately dispatched. One need not consult a literary critic to understand the moral of these stories. In all fairy tales, good triumphs over evil, but for Disney good is the exclusive genetic and social right of the elite. Elites are attractive, benevolent, good, and successful; villains are misshapen, treacherous, and evil and cannot win. The rest of the Disney world is undifferentiated, passive, dependent on elite gratuity, and largely irrelevant except as narrative fodder.

Community and Democracy

At least since Snow White, the path to happiness and self-fulfilment has not existed for most characters in Disney animation. Although one might expect some contemporary modifications with the passing of Walt and Roy, or with the development of digital technology, corporate Disney has only further institutionalized the classic formula for feature-length filmed fairy tales. There is nothing new in theme, character, or representation. Despite narrative openings that might lead to some collective action for change, ultimately the protagonist reasserts the film's fidelity to hierarchy and individual gratification.

Disney's naturalization of hierarchy, its defense of elite coercion, and its promotion of unrestricted elite individualism coalesce in stories that undermine and denigrate societal responsibility, democracy, and human solidarity. Thematically, Disney's opposition to democracy and solidarity is apparent in its graphic illustrations of nonelite characters, the lack of dialogue for nonelite characters, its consistent slights of group interests, and the narrative and visual naturalization of unfavorable social conditions.

In focusing exclusively on individual elites, Disney dismisses group solidarity and the public interest as unimportant to the story. Although each narrative includes dozens of nonelite characters, they appear primarily as background or as proxies for the protagonists—as exhibited by Nemo's "tank guy" buddies. In fact, "every Disney character stands on either one side or the other of the power demarcation line. All below are bound to obedience, submission, discipline, humility. Those above are free to employ constant coercion, threats, moral and physical repression and economic domination."[46] Before Pixar's *Bug's Life* and *Monsters, Inc.,* producers were mostly absent in Disney animations. In ridding the animated environment of work and its necessary social relations, "all the everyday functions of the city have been hidden or banished."[47] Thus, the contributions and value of the majority of society disappear as well. Necessities of life in Disney's world appear magically; so feudal exploitation and other undemocratic conditions can be ignored, as can the individual and collective participation of farmers, workers, artisans, and other producing human beings, leaving Disney free to focus on the lives of the rich and fantastic. In *Monsters, Inc.,* a story about the lives of "scream workers," the diegesis centers on the star monster, presents the social and hierarchical conditions of production as a given, and avoids any possible collective action, cooperative communication, or conscious choice by monster workers. As in many recent United States television sitcoms (e.g., *Grace Under Fire, Home Improvement, Drew Carey,* and *Roseanne),* the work site is simply the backdrop for self-centred, ego-driven protagonists modeling appropriate middle-class, entrepreneurial values and practices.

Individualism and competition—buzzwords for capitalism—are reserved for Disney's fantasy elites, who have no moral or social peer. Elite ideas and actions are right, good, and ultimately successful. Villains may have ideas and take action, but they are wrong, bad, and doomed to fail. In such a fantasy world, no other ideas or actions are needed; hence Disney's animated public seldom speaks, exhibits limited thought, and undertakes little independent action—and never, ever, does a nonelite character freely broach the question of equality, democracy, or social justice.

Nonelites have little self-interest. They have no personal ambition. Indeed, life below affords no individual distinction, at all. All nonelites are traced from similarly static outlines. Yet Disney cannot imagine they have any similarity of interest. At most, Disney's animated populations appear as "average" characters, either acting irresponsibly as inferiors, squabbling over trifles or passively waiting for mobilization orders from a superior. Most secondary castings are not particularly bright in dialogue or graphic portrayal except for aides, who are often mischievous but harmless, comic animals. Less enlightened nonelites tend toward antisocial behavior as thieving hyenas, tormenting monkeys, or devious monsters. Having baser instincts, "bad" nonelites (unshaven, partially dressed, usually large) are also prone to violence and easily misled by nefarious Disney antagonists: Arab bandits work for Jafar; sailors join Clayton in kidnapping; hordes follow the Hun; Randall directs his monster minions; and grasshoppers pillage for Hopper.

Predictably, according to Disney, most nonelites tacitly or enthusiastically understand that hierarchy is good and support the social order no matter who rules. The citizens of Agrabah bow to the sultan, Jafar, then Aladdin on each successive command; no animals rise up against Scar; the colonists obey Ratcliffe, then Smith; and all apes obey Kerchak, then Tarzan; the Queen rules over all bugs: long live the monarchy!

According to Disney, workers, sailors, farmers, and other producers are wretched, irrational, chaotic, and passive, unable to act in their own interests—at best they may be motivated to protect the hierarchical social order. Some may be roused to mob action under the wrong leader, but all will be happier if the proper order is fulfilled—the hierarchical natural order of the animal kingdom or the hierarchical social order of an Arab sultanate, Chinese empire, British or ant colony, toy room, scare factory, or ocean. Group action, in other words, occurs only at the whim of the powerful.

Worthless individuals would likewise collectively amount to nothing, so Disney omits any independent, cooperative action by nonelite citizens or community members. Nonelite characters seldom, if ever, recognize their own democratic interest. Moreover, in Disney animations, actions by leading characters thoroughly shred any semblance of collective interest. Aladdin deserts the orphans and his neighborhood; Pocahontas betrays her nation; Tarzan betrays his family; Mulan deceives her family and compatriots; Simba returns to the pride lands only out of royal duty; Flik imperils the colony; Marlin has no concern beyond Nemo. Disney never animates democracy or social responsibility. Disney heroes in all their wit and wisdom never seek happiness or fulfillment through commitment to improving the human condition. Instead, all Disney animated stars indicate that acting against the public interest in one's search for individual gratification is natural, legitimate, and preferred. Community or family interests or democratic concerns do not appear in Disney, while the box-office success of Fox's *Ice Age* indicates that narratives that include group efforts are creatively and financially possible.

It seems that Disney's message to the world is: Take what you can by force, deceit, or luck. The future of the world depends on the self-interested actions of naturally-superior elites. Thirty years after Dorfman and Mattelart described the world of Disney as "a nineteenth century orphanage,"[48] Disney is animating twenty-first-century gated communities for a global consumerist culture where the only actions relevant are by those living inside the circle of capitalist life, or "going with the flow" of the global order. Solidarity among the majority populations on the outside is unthinkable for Disney's "imagineers."

The Realities of Fantasy

Disney is a world leader in mass entertainment implicated in the globalization of capitalism and a concerted effort to deregulate and privatize world culture. A highly proficient producer and international distributor of capitalist cultural products, Disney advances an ideological content that parallels the social and political requirements of capitalist economic activity: hierarchy, elite coercion, hyper-individualism, and social atomism.[49] In particular, Disney's animated features communicate a clear message to the world: The individual elite quest for self-gratification, adventure, and acquisition is good and just. This cultural edict suggests that the momentary pleasures of entertainment will free us from the throbbing anxiety of daily life. So, just as Disney's animated masses await their rescue by some benevolent noble, millions of spectators anticipate successive Disney films for pleasure and distraction.

Disney's fabrication of culture as individual consumption is built on the backs of masses of farmers, garment workers, technicians, illustrators, retail clerks, and other working people, but from the pinnacle of power and in front of the movie screen, such details of production are irrelevant. Wealth appears and riches flow to all deserving elites. To be rich is to be good—and a little lucky. To be poor is to be bad and unfortunate. A world designed by Disney directors and other cartoon representatives would "naturally" have social problems and economic inequities, individual capitalists would deny responsibility, and the poor would have to accept their plight or be removed.

However, Disney does not conspire to build such a new world order. No, its pro-capitalist ideological premise is patently obvious, redundant, and pervasive. Disney themes, characters, and animation style have been thoroughly institutionalized in practice and procedure—from the scriptwriters, animators, and technical producers who create the actual films to the market researchers and integrated marketing directors who conduct product research and focus groups to spot trends and advise editors on socially sensitive issues—all are geared to maximizing corporate profits. Pixar's innovations digitally improve Disney content and productively improve Disney's market dominance. Furthermore, dominance in the production of commodified animation and its spin-offs indicates that Disney's narratives resonate with appreciative mass audiences, suggesting that Disney's hierarchical themes are also culturally acceptable, at least tacitly. Individual pleasures or meanings derived from Disney commodities reinforce, but should not be confused with, the overarching, consistent themes of self-fulfilment through consumption. Disney's ability to market popular films and the public's delight in consuming their little pleasures can best be understood as a negotiated hegemonic activity.[50] Like modern advertising, Disney worlds are fanciful, optimistic, and tidy.[51] And like advertising, Disney has become part of everyday life, commercially and culturally institutionalized by design.[52] But in Disney's case, the medium is also the advertisement. Disney products are themselves advertisements for Disney and for its ideological and cultural themes.

While one might hope for a more open system that allows for some nuanced messages, the evidence indicates that Disney's dominance is secured through its conscious and selective application of technology, technique, and culturally palatable content. First with Walt, then Roy, and now Michael Eisner, Disney has organized a bureaucratic, hierarchical system of production that severely limits the creative contribution of individual animators. The resulting symbolic product mirrors the organization of material production. Moreover, the naturalized animation of cultural truisms combined with a hierarchical narrative realism stimulates mass audiences to collective anticipation, surprise, and wonder. In appreciation, we consent to our own satisfaction and distraction. As audiences, we are busy enjoying the stylized graphics and familiar narratives, while Disney successfully reflects, clarifies, and popularizes existing dominant cultural values and meanings. Indeed, the communication of specific dominant themes such as individual happiness, family values, and the triumph of good over evil is remarkably consistent across cultures: in a preliminary look at audience reception, The Global Disney Project found that more than 85 percent of respondents in eighteen countries who had seen a Disney film shared similar interpretations of meaning.[53] Even critics committed to the power of the reader admit to the difficulty of finding "resistant readings" in Disney animation.[54] In the process of being entertained, we are held hostage to a highly individualistic, consumerist perspective that leads us to understand these films in terms of social privilege and individual escapism.[55]

The interpretation of Disney animation presented here is intended only as an entry to discussing Disney's vision of globalization. Understanding Disney clarifies the global intent of corporate capitalism. Without deviation Disney animates and narrates myths favorable to a corporate culture, including its own. The emerging world capitalist culture revels in the ideology distributed by Disney, an ideology that aligns the morals of every animated film to class hierarchy, thereby denigrating and dismissing solidarity, democracy, and concern for community needs and interests.

Those interested in improving world social conditions and human solidarity should take note of the cultural power of animation, narration, and entertainment. Disney's application is one variant extremely useful to global capitalism. The practice of individual consumption of entertainment commodities (which further promote individual consumption) subverts collective reflections and discussions that could lead to solidarity. Rather than searching for the occasional instance of tweaking by resistive animators or hoping that individual subversive readings may prompt a social movement, those who oppose Disney's autocratic production model and generic content should replace them with cooperative creations and narratives.

Artists, illustrators, historians, animators, technicians, storytellers, and individual citizens must collectively take hold of technology and technique for democratic purposes. For American audiences, animated films featuring historic figures such as Simón Bolívar, Touissaint L'Overture, Joe Hill, Mother Jones, Sojourner Truth, and Green Water Woman could foreground movements for liberation and equality. Historic struggles for freedom elsewhere supply an abundance of other possibilities—in folk tales (not appropriated by Disney or some other corporate producer) and in accounts of popular heroes and heroines, such as the Colombian fight for water rights or the Zapatista struggle for land and community. Rather than viewing heroes who only want more stuff, children and adults could become acquainted with protagonists and behaviors that validate social interaction, social responsibility, and social justice. Such heroines and heroes would be worthy of emulation. Of course, the struggle over culture will not be decided by cartoon figures, but surely working classes around the world need a vibrant, animated democratic culture as a necessary forum for communicating and organizing a political power against real hierarchies. Creating our own entertainment would be one way to practice democratic communication and international solidarity for human liberation.

Notes

1. Ann Ricker, "The 'Lion King' Animated Storybook: A Case Study of Aesthetic and Economic Power," *Critical Studies: A Journal of North-South Dialogue* 10, no.1 (1996): 41–59. (Quoted on p. 42.)
2. James Chesebro and Dale A. Bertlesen, *Analyzing Media: Communication Technologies as Symbolic and Cognitive Systems* (New York: Guilford Press, 1996), 143.
3. Trevor Whittock, *Metaphor and Film* (New York: Cambridge University Press, 1990), 35.
4. Robert W. Brockway, "The Masks of Mickey Mouse: Symbol of a Generation," *Journal of Popular Culture* 22, no. 4 (1989): 25–34.
5. Fritz Moellenhoff, "Remarks on the Popularity of Mickey Mouse," *American Imago* 46 (1989): 105–119. (Quoted on p. 116.)
6. Ibid., 105.
7. Kaj Bjoerkqvist and Kirsti Lagerspetz, "Children's Experience of Three Types of Cartoon at Two Age Levels," *International Journal of Psychology* 20 (1985): 77–93.
8. Joel Rosenbaum, "Dream Masters II: Walt Disney," *Film Comment,* January–February 1979, 68–71. (Quoted on p. 69.)
9. Noboru Takahashi, "Developmental Changes of Interests to Animated Stories in Toddlers Measured by Eye Movement While Watching Them," *Psychologia* 34 (1991): 63–68.
10. Moellenhoff, "Remarks," 114.
11. Winfried Fluck, "Popular Culture as a Mode of Socialization: A Theory about the Social Functions of Popular Culture Forms," *Journal of Popular Culture* 20, no. 4 (1987): 31–46. (Quoted on p. 39.)
12. Frances Clarke Sayers quoted in Janet Wasko, *Understanding Disney: The Manufacture of Fantasy* (Williston, Vt.: Blackwell, 2001), 126.
13. Wasko, *Disney,* 15.
14. Quoted in Stefan Kanfer, *Serious Business: The Art and Commerce of Animation in America from Betty Boop to Toy Story* (New York: Scribner, 1997), 224.
15. Michael Beardsley, "The Metaphorical Twist," in *Philosophical Perspectives on Metaphor,* ed. Michael Johnson (Minneapolis: University of Minnesota Press, 1981), 105–122. (Quoted on p. 107.)
16. Miriam Hansen, "Of Mice and Ducks: Benjamin and Adorno on Disney," *South Atlantic Quarterly* 92 (1993): 28–62.
17. Michael Real, *Mass-Mediated Culture* (Englewood Cliffs, N.J.: Prentice-Hall, 1977).
18. Kathy Jackson, *Walt Disney: A Bio-bibliography* (Westport, Conn.: Greenwood, 1993), 109, argues that Disney and its vision "permeates our culture."
19. Annalee Ward, "The 'Lion King's' Mythic Narrative," *Journal of Popular Film and Television* 23 (1996): 171–178, believes that for children the social values of Disney stories "form the standards for testing the truth of other stories later in life," 177.
20. Michael Medved, "The Box Office Word: Give Culture Back to Families, *New Perspectives Quarterly* 15, no. 3 (1998): 86–87.

21. Jill B. Henke, Diane Zimmerman Umble, and Nancy J. Smith, "Construction of the Female Self: Feminist Readings of the Disney Heroine," *Women's Studies in Communication* 19 (1996): 229–249.

22. Moellenhoff, "Remarks," 114.

23. Bruno Bettleheim, *The Uses of Enchantment: The Meaning and Importance of Fairy Tales* (New York: Random House, 1977).

24. Edward S. Herman and Robert W. McChesney, *The Global Media: The New Missionaries of Corporate Capitalism* (New York: Cassell & Continuum, 1997): 54.

25. Gary Edgerton and Kathy M. Jackson, "Redesigning Pocahontas: Disney, the 'White Man's Indian,' and the Marketing of Dreams," *Journal of Popular Film and Television* 24, no. 2 (1996): 90–98. John A. Lent, ed., *Themes and Issues in Asian Cartooning: Cute, Cheap, Mad and Sexy* (Bowling Green, Ohio: Bowling Green University Press, 1996). Robert Ostman, "Disney and Its Conservative Critics: Images versus Realities," *Journal of Popular Film and Television* 24, no. 2 (1996): 83–89. (Quoted on pps. 86–87.)

26. David Kunzle, "Introduction," in *How to Read Donald Duck: Imperialist Ideology in the Disney Comic,* ed. Ariel Dorfman and Armand Mattelart (New York: International General, 1975), 11–24.

27. http://www.pixar.com.

28. Robert Hodge and David Tripp, *Children and Television: A Semiotic Approach* (Stanford, Calif.: Stanford University Press. 1986).

29. Paul Jose and William F. Brewer, "Development of Story Liking: Character Identification, Suspense and Outcome Resolution," *Developmental Psychology* 20 (1984): 911–934. Paul Jose, "Just-World Reasoning in Children's Immanent Justice Judgments," *Child Development* 61 (1990): 1024–1033.

30. Ariel Dorfman and Armand Mattelart, *How to Read Donald Duck: Imperialist Ideology in the Disney Comic* (New York: International General, 1975).

31. Ricker, "Case Study," and Wasko, *Disney.*

32. Lee Artz, "Animating Hierarchy: Disney and the Globalization of Capital," *Global Media Journal* 2 (2003): http://www.globalmediajournal.com.

33. Eric Smoodin, *Disney Discourse: Producing the Magic Kingdom* (New York: Routledge, 1994): 36.

34. Will McWhinney and José Batista, "How Remythologizing Can Revitalize Organizations," *Organizational Dynamics* 17 (1998): 46–58. (Quoted on p. 47.)

35. Edgerton and Jackson, "Redesigning," 94.

36. Keisha L. Hoerner, "Gender Roles in Disney Films: Analyzing Behaviors from Snow White to Simba," *Women's Studies in Communication* 19 (1996): 213–228. (Quoted on p. 227.)

37. David Berland, "Disney and Freud: Walt Meets the Id," *Journal of Popular Culture* 15 (1982): 93–104. (Quoted on p. 101.)

38. Michael T. Marsden and Jack Nachbar, *The Indians in the Movies: Handbook of North American Indians* (Washington, D.C.: Smithsonian Institution, 1988).

39. Alexander Wilson, "Technological Utopias," *South Atlantic Quarterly* 92 (1993): 157–173. (Quoted on p. 166.)

40. Artz, "Animating."
41. Kunzle, "Introduction," 16.
42. Dorfman and Mattelart, *How to Read,* 89.
43. Celebration, Florida, is Disney's model perfect community located five miles from Disney World with state-of-the-art schools, pedestrian malls, and public spaces—all closely governed by the Disney corporation.
44. Derek T. Buescher and Kent Ono, "Civilized Colonialism: Pocahontas as Neocolonial Rhetoric," *Women's Studies in Communication* 19 (1996): 127–153. (Quoted on p. 140.)
45. Hoerner, "Gender Roles," 222.
46. Dorfman and Mattelart, *How to Read,* 35.
47. Wilson, "Technological," 164.
48. Dorfman and Mattelart, *How to Read,* 35.
49. Göran Therborn, "Why Some Classes are More Successful Than Others," *New Left Review* 138 (1983): 37–55.
50. Antonio Gramsci, *Selected Writings, 1918–1935,* ed. David Forgacs (New York: Schocken, 1988). Lee Artz and Bren Murphy, *Cultural Hegemony in the United States* (Thousand Oaks, Calif.: Sage, 1990).
51. Paul J. Croce, "A Clean and Separate Space: Walt Disney in Person and Production," *Journal of Popular Culture* 23, no. 3 (1991): 91–103. (Quoted on p. 91.)
52. Pamela C. O'Brien, "The Happiest Films on Earth: A Textual and Contextual Analysis of Walt Disney's *Cinderella* and *The Little Mermaid,*" *Women's Studies in Communication* 19 (1996): 155–181. (Quoted on pps. 173–75.)
53. Wasko, *Disney,* 191–193.
54. See special issue of *Women's Studies in Communication* 19 (1996).
55. Miriam Hansen, "Of Mice and Ducks: Benjamin and Adorno on Disney," *South Atlantic Quarterly* 92 (1993): 28–62. (Quoted on p. 40.)

4

The Lion King, Mimesis, and
Disney's Magical Capitalism

Maurya Wickstrom

An ad in the program for the *The Lion King*, Julie Taymor's stage version of the original Disney film, which opened in November 1997 at the New Amsterdam Theatre in New York, reads, "Enjoy your audience with the King. And remember, even in the jungle, American Express helps you do more."[1] What is so striking about this ad is not only its blatant construction of the mutually beneficial relationship between theater and the market but also that it places audience members bodily inside the fiction of the musical. They are not merely an audience watching the lion king Mufasa on a stage; they are in the play, enjoying his audience. The market, in the form of American Express, has a clear commercial interest in encouraging consumers to slide from their actual role as spectators of a show to a fictional role as participants in the stage drama, which, in this case, is a multimillion-dollar commodity.

The Lion King and its relationship to the Disney store that was originally adjacent to it an excellent study of the ways in which capital has further developed its centuries-long relationship to performance, mimesis, and the body. In the postmodern period, it has not been enough to encourage consumers to possess a commodity; we must be compelled to merge into the commodity as its life force. The market depends on the commodity's kinesthetic claim on the mimetic imagination of consumers; we desire to be bodily like the commodity. It waits for us to bring it to life.

Since *The Lion King* opened, however, Disney's fortunes have changed. This essay is a study of what I call Disney's magical capitalism as it emerged in the heyday of the Disney stores and in the huge success of *The Lion King*. I also mark the struggle of the faction led by Roy Disney to maintain the Disney company narrative about its own innocence and "magic" in the face of the raw corporatism Roy Disney attributes to Michael Eisner.

Magical Capitalism

I have invented the phrase *magical capitalism* as a way to differentiate one set of corporate practices from another as I try to articulate the crisis that has unfolded within the Disney corporation. I chose the word "magical" because the word "magic" has been at the center of Disney's presentation of its products, forming the core of Disney's stranglehold on American culture. But it also carries with it the connotations of the mimetic. The mimetic is a strange and wonderful proclivity. Disney has long understood this, and drawn mimesis into its corporate imagination.

I'll begin by clarifying the particular meanings of mimesis that I am using and, in the process, looking at some of the ways that Disney has used mimesis as a key strategy for the success of magical capitalism. I'll then move on to a description of Julie Taymor's production of *The Lion King*, and, finally, to a brief look at the distress of Disney fans in the face of Eisner's leadership. Eisner has disrupted Disney's long-entrenched success with mimetic techniques. Led by Roy Disney, these loyalists clearly believe, although they would not articulate it in these terms, that the success of contemporary capital remains dependent on awakening the mimetic desire of consumers and wedding that desire to its products.

In his book *Mimesis and Alterity*, Michael Taussig builds a theory of mimesis based on foundations laid out by Benjamin, Marx, and Adorno. In its classical formulation mimesis has tended to be largely ignored in recent years, especially by poststructuralists who regard it as a discredited representational modality. But the mimesis they are rejecting, that of a copy which creates a transparent window onto an underlying truth, is only one of the possible ways to go about thinking of mimesis.

For Taussig, as for Benjamin, mimesis depends on tactility, on the senses, and on the materiality of perception and knowing. It involves not only copying but also deep contact. Taussig argues that human beings have a propensity to become other through this copy/contact. Our mimetic tendency, he says, draws us into an "ineffable plasticity in the face of the world and the world's forms of life."[2] In this relation to the other, this "sympathetic magic," mimesis is a bodily relation to otherness in which a being becomes like, but also touches, or absorbs, the other, so that the boundaries between self and other are blurred. Importantly for our purposes, the copy takes into itself the power of the original.

This way of thinking about mimesis undoes the binary notion of original and copy, and as such helps us to understand the profound pleasure humans are able to take in the play of the real and the made-up.[3] Further, in Taussig's vision, the indeterminacy of mimesis, both between the real and the made-up and between forms, confounds practices of domination. Mimesis can be a rejuvenative alternative in a "disenchanted" world (made in the Enlightenment image of master), where we are cut off from any mimetic relation to otherness. We are positioned to implement a mastery over nature, others, and our own selves, where all that we "know," including that which comes to us through our senses, is banked, put away as an investment for some future opportunity. We accumulate the sensations of our body as private property.[4] A mimetic relation to the world, by contrast, is a "spiritualized" world, with animals, plants, and humans miming, becoming one another, giving the self away, into an exchange with otherness that then comes full circle in a cycle analogous to that noncapitalist economy of the gift society.

Postmodern capitalism, though, has drawn upon mimesis with a great deal of sophistication. The pleasurable intersubjectivity that gets played between the real and the made-up has thus been diverted from the radical potential that Taussig says it has into the service of corporations like Disney. A few years ago, a report by Robert Spiegel of National Public Radio on the "boy band" 2-gether provided a delicious example of how the sophistication of the postmodern consumer includes pleasure taken in the simultaneity of the real and the made-up. The band 2gether was originally formed with the intention to parody boy bands like 'N Sync and Backstreet Boys. The five members of the band, including thirty-five-year-old Kevin Farley, who describes himself as overweight and bald, approached MTV with their "mockumentary," in which they sang satirical songs. In a completely unexpected turn of events, they became overnight sensations. Teenage girls have gone as crazy for 2gether as they did for 'N Sync, even though they are completely aware that 2gether is not a "real" boy band.

Robert Spiegel comments in his report that "some of the press coverage of 2gether has portrayed the band's teen-age fans as hapless, hopeless victims, adolescents too unsophisticated to distinguish what's real from what's fake."

However, he continues, "Mark and Brian Gunn prefer to see it another way. They view the fans' embrace of 2gether, not as evidence of the teenagers' lack of sophistication, but rather as a signal that they are in fact more highly evolved consumers."5 He quotes Kevin Farley's own insight on this. Farley says,

> What's interesting to me is that people watch so many shows right now that plug themselves as reality shows and yet, also people know that they're engineered in countless ways. And people are able to hold within themselves something being an artifice and something being real at the same time. And in many ways 2gether is a lot like pro wrestling. All the fans completely know that it's fake and yet they give themselves over to it wholeheartedly. And what's interesting to me is that in some ways now, you have to admit of the form. You have to show both the artifice and what motivates that artifice. And I think, actually, I give credit to people not for mistaking the construct, but for admitting of the construct and being able to indulge in it at the same time.6

Farley's perceptive comments point to a postmodern capitalism where it just isn't the case, as is often imagined, that consumers are merely duped with a sleight-of-hand trick whereby they take as real what is only simulation. They are, rather, playing, allowing forms to shift into each other, "indulging" a mimetic pleasure in allowing things, which are simultaneously made-up and true, this indeterminacy. Disney, early in the twentieth century, led the way in embedding this indeterminacy, this mimesis, at the heart of its marketing strategies and corporate identity.

In particular, Disney seized on the mimetic proclivities of children. Walter Benjamin, who, like Taussig, looked for the ways that commodity culture is punctured by mimesis, derived much of his mimetic theory from watching the play of children. He observed that children easily occupy imaginary worlds, physically seizing hold of them, becoming them, with a creativity inseparable from action. But in dystopian inversion of this theory, Disney learned quickly to position its movie characters to take advantage of children's almost automatic desire to enact what they find compelling. A significant and early strategy for this operation, this suturing of child to character, was the Mickey Mouse clubs.

By the end of 1930, 150 movie theaters across the country had Mickey Mouse clubs. Designed to facilitate the merchandising of toys that were spin-offs of the animated films, the clubs had strategic alliances with department stores like Bloomingdales, where Mickey and Minnie were appearing "in the flesh." At Kresges, Mickey and Minnie introduced Santa Claus to children and handed out toys. Children seeking membership in the clubs had to go to the department stores to procure and fill out the necessary application. Once accepted, members met at a participating movie theater for the Saturday matinee. The lobby of the theater would typically be displaying Mickey merchandise for sale and giveaways. Each meeting consisted of "the recitation of the Mickey Mouse Club Creed, the singing of 'America,' a stage/show or contest, the Mickey Mouse Club Yell, the Mickey Mouse Club Song,"[7] and then the feature film for the day. But not only did these clubs spur the children's desire to have Disney products, they were also formulated around the children becoming the product, or enacting the product with their bodies. According to deCordova, photos from the club show child members dressed in the very popular Mickey and Minnie playsuits. Club members were also instructed to greet each other by saying, "Hi Minnie!" or Hi, Mickey!"[8] and to use a Mickey Mouse handshake.[9]

This mimetic absorption in Minnie or Mickey, or other Disney characters, became a signature feature of the corporation, part of its "magic." When I first began studying the Disney stores, I visited the first to open in New York City, which was in the Staten Island Mall. I was struck, during my first visit there, by the installation above our heads just inside the entrance. There was Donald Duck with a cartoon character film crew; he sat among a three-dimensional cartoon rendition of all the apparatus for making movies: a crane, a tracking system, movie lights. The clapperboard identified the movie being made as "Movie Magic—Backstage Antics, Director: Mickey." Donald, the cinematographer, was aiming an old-timey cartoon film camera at shoppers as they came into the store. Minnie Mouse cranked the film through the camera from behind him, and out the images rolled, on the film negative curling out into the air at the top of the store. Donald's holding on to his hat, oh boy! His legs swing up, whooping, he's delighted with the results; we're no longer ourselves. In our passage through the Disney camera, we were, as Peter Quince in *A Midsummer Night's Dream* says of Bottom, "translated." On the negative were the silhouetted forms of the Disney characters we became: Minnie, Mickey, Pluto, Dumbo. Film spilled out from the reel, curling in and through the airspace above the store. Each image on the film was an image of a different cartoon character. It was as if the "magical" machinery of Disney's production apparatus transformed each shopper into Disney characters. It was as if we had been absorbed into the very heart of the Disney brand and welcomed to a life inside it.

By the 1990s, Disney was dipping the packaging of its products in baths of copy so that the products were dripping with promises of "magical" transformation into "being" something different from what you were. Everywhere in Disney environments there has been an invitation to an interchangeability of forms. The toys that crowded the stores in their heyday invited enactment.

The child, the packaging promised, could "become a real Indian chief," "live as," and "experience just like" Pocahontas, or John Smith. Similarly, the costumes hanging everywhere in the stores invited children to perform as Disney cartoon characters, both animal and human. The Disney stores of the mid-1990s were filled with endless racks and shelves of clothes that were invitations to this dress-up play. If they were not Pocahontas, Cinderella, and Snow White costumes, they were infant playsuits, school clothes, denim shirts, ties, all emblazoned with Disney characters. At the Staten Island Disney store, Mickey stood on a shelf over our heads, costumed in his role as the Sorcerer's Apprentice from *Fantasia*. He looked directly down at us, wand raised, book of spells opened. His gaze was direct, casting his spell. Watched over by this Mickey, I asked a little girl who was trying on a Snow White costume, why she wanted to wear the costume and she said, "To try and try and try to be a princess."

Commodity Fetishism: The Store, the Theme Parks

The mimetic propensity to become another thing, to take on the life of another thing, becomes shaded, in the practice of Disney, by an unavoidable association for any clear thinking person between commodity fetishism and this phenomenon where little boys and girls (and the rest of us) are bringing a thing, a Mickey, a Pocahontas, a princess, to life in their own bodies.

Jack Amariglio and Tony Callari say that Marx, when devising his theory of commodity fetishism, used the religious vocabulary of the fetish to suggest the absence of a fixed human subject and to propose in its place a subject continually forged within commodity exchange: "In our view, Marx's choice of the figure of fetishism to convey the mystery of commodity exchange suggests his own commitment to depicting the creative, innovative, and even fantastic process that creates the reality/myth of the 'individual,' the form of subjectivity that is continually shaped by and, in turn, shapes market relations."[10] In magical capitalism, mimesis, diverted from its radical potential, is precisely this "creative, innovative, and even fantastic process," that positions humans as creative agents of "market relations."

One particular advertisement has become emblematic for me of corporate strategies for the bodily enactment of the commodity, mimesis lived as commodity fetishism. One of the billboards dominating "the new Times Square" in 1998 advertised Disney's across-the-street competitor, Warner Bros. In the ad, the head of Tweetybird filled the billboard on one side and, on the other side, a young girl was wearing a shirt emblazoned with the head of Tweetybird. Above the shirt her face mimicked the expression that Tweetybird characteristically wears. It was as if by costuming herself as (or becoming like) Tweetybird, she was infused with the life of Tweetybird, who is, after all, a commodity. Her expression was the expressiveness of the commodity. The words "show your character" were written on a blank blue area between the two images. The ad played on the meanings of character as both the unique properties belonging to the individual and a persona that is adopted through mimetic play. Inside the store (which, like the Disney store), is now closed, the advertisement and its message was repeated everywhere with slightly different images. For instance, a girl "showed her character" by wearing a baseball cap decorated by Tweetybird's eyes. The cap was pulled down so that instead of seeing her eyes, we saw Tweetybird's eyes taking their place.

It's a chain of copy and contact, sympathetic magic à la Taussig. The girl touches and copies the commodity and absorbs its power. But the commodity is also copying her, the human, and acquiring her power. The girl/human and commodity lose the boundaries that differentiate one from the other. In an interrelated chain of reification and fetishization, girl and commodity are co-created. The thing derives life from the human. The human derives life from the thing. Human is woven into thing, and ultimately, thing appears the most lifelike, pulling its aura out of its contact with the human, seeming to be magical, and one of a kind.

At the Staten Island Mall Disney store there was a store within the store, a kind of inner sanctum selling limited-edition versions of the animation characters being sold in the rest of the store as the playsuits, and those endlessly replicated toys promising children that they could "become" John Smith, or Pocahontas. On the wall directly across from the door into the room there was an ornately carved, gilt frame encasing a video screen. It resembled nothing so much as an altar. The interactive touch screen on the video allowed me to choose to call up any of a selection of topics. Almost without exception Walt introduced the short film clips. In each, he said he was about to let me in on the secrets of Disney's "magic." On one of the clips the voice-over crooned, "There's a lot of knowledge we have about how to entertain people by bringing *things* to life."

I chose a clip called "Audio-Animatronics." An extremely proud Walt appeared as soon as I pressed the image. He wanted to show me how his lifelike creations, the audio-animatronic robots, were made. First I saw the gelatinous, clear heads filled with tubing and mechanisms, still in the workshop. The workings of these internal mechanisms were demonstrated, and then the skin was put on. Then the video cut to a now fully fashioned robotic "person" sitting comfortably with his newspaper, on stage in a cozy, Americana living room set, conversing with Walt! Cut to backstage, where there was a human being strapped into a device that looked eerily like an electric chair. His head was in a metal cap; his back and limbs were attached to metal rods. He was the source of the robot's "life," animating it through this full-body remote control. Walt, chatting agreeably with the automaton, never addressed the human who labored to make this "thing come to life." Walt ostensibly defetishized his automaton: he did show us the human labor that animates it. But he showed us only to show us how much less "magical" is the human. It's the human who looked thing-like. The worker looked much more dead than the automaton. Against the background of his effacement, the "magic" of Disney appears in very sharp relief. The "thing" is defetishized and then refetishized, into the life we wish we had because it is so "magical."

The context for showing the workings of the robot was a glimpse into the "science" of Disney's "magic." It's an instance of Disney's manipulation of our perception of the power the brand has to subordinate the human to its own goals, versus our subsequent denial that the brand has any goals at all, or even exists as an entity differentiated from our own "selves." The productive power of the corporation must seem inevitable and the subordination of the human desirable as the commodity takes on the auratic magic of the human it copies, and whose energy it draws upon. We are meant, I think, to be awed by the power of the corporation to give life, to feel our own diminishment in the face of that creativity, but not with regret or rancor. Rather we are meant to wish ourselves to be as lifelike as that thing.

This is a realization of Benjamin's idea of "empathy" with the commodity. He uses the word empathy to describe a mimetic relationship of both being like and being, by which commodity and human being become undifferentiated. He uses the prostitute, for instance, as a figure for the human as commodity, not only in the sense that the seller and the object for sale are the same, but also in the sense that, in the streets of Paris, prostitution was so common that the women appeared almost as reproductions, identical, like the chorus line dancers he also wrote about.[11] He writes, "Love for the prostitute is the apotheosis of empathy for the commodity."[12]

In one fragment from Benjamin, humans empathize with the commodity because their labor corresponds to the absolute invariance of the units by which exchange value is measured. Both the underlying terms by which the value of a commodity is assessed and the labor time that produces the value are invariable and invariably the same. Benjamin writes,

> It is only as the commodity that the thing has the effect of alienating human beings from one another. It produces this effect through its price. What is decisive is the empathy with the exchange value of the commodity, with its equalizing

substrate. (The absolute qualitative invariance of the time in which labor that generates exchange value runs its course—such absolute equality is the grayish background against which the gaudy colors of sensation stand out.)[13]

There's a kinship between human and commodity that comes gradually to be greater than the kinship between humans. The kinship is grounded in mass reproduction. We can feel closer to the mass-produced object, because of this substratum of gray, exchangeable time, than we can to a unique, unreproducible object. Alienated from other human beings by the commodity, which differentiates consumers by virtue of its price, as Benjamin points out, we turn to our kinship with the commodity. The commodity, as mass reproduction, feels more like us. This isn't a kinship that's apprehended intellectually. It is a physical, tactile identification, which comes about because our very senses have been changing along with the changes in production.[14]

The costumed workers in the Disney theme parks provide another remarkable example of this empathy with the commodity, although in the theme parks, in contrast to Walt's demonstration of the robot, the human animating the commodity is specifically kept hidden. Jane Kuenz has done an alarming study that reveals the extent to which labor conditions in the theme parks enforce the total translation of the human into the copy that has appropriated its powers. The mimetic exchange is ongoing. The human and the commodity are touching (here in a most literal and grueling way), each absorbing the other, but the totalizing power of the commodity as a life force is what must be staged.

I encountered on a Disney Web site a fan's description of her almost feverish anticipation of a trip to Disney World:

Gwen and I leave for Disney World tomorrow morning. I can't explain it, but I get butterflies in my stomach at the thought of the trip, and I keep seeing shapes of Mickey Mouse in the most ordinary objects in my office, at home, even while sitting in traffic. Why, there's one stoplight that has cable in a circle on both sides of the light. The red light is Mickey's head; the circular cable, his ears. . . . I am on a growth path. Disney is part of that path. I follow the Mouse, because he represents quality, innocence and hope. . . . I am part of his family. In Walt Disney World, I am more accepted than I ever was by my parents, my siblings, and some of my friends."[15]

A visitor like this is coming to meet her Mickey, the Mickey who is already part of her. Here the thing must be alive, auratic, "magical." The literalization of the "magic," a glimpse of the human surrendering its energies to make the thing come alive, would undo the mimetic absorption into this world that the park visitor seeks. For this woman seeing Mickey in everything, Mickey is her real life, more meaningful, and more loyal, more hopeful, than the world of human relationships. For the making of a subjectivity so cathected to Mickey, so identified as him, the commodity must be fully a fetish, without question completely alive, independent of the social relations or human labor that produced it. The mimetic exchange in the parks is set up to be between the living commodity and the human who hopes to be absorbed into its magical life and, as a result, be enlivened by it.

And so, the rules about workers' performance while wearing the huge cartoon heads are extremely strict. Because the "heads" are heavy and the Florida heat is extreme (although workers are allowed out only twenty minutes at a time), many vomit or pass out inside their character heads while "onstage," as the public areas are called. This happens because no matter how sick a performer becomes, she will lose her job if she removes her head for any reason before reaching a "backstage" area. Corporate policy states that if a child were to witness a "head-less" character, her faith in "magic" would be ruined for life. One man Kuenz interviews describes his job, which is to drive around in a little cart and retrieve the unconscious bodies of passed-out performers. He says, "One day I picked up three at one stop, Donald, Mickey, and Goofy. It's frightening because you can die on your own regurgitation when you can't keep out of it. I'll never forget Dumbo—it was coming out of the mouth during the parade. You have a little screen over the mouth. It was horrible."[16]

The employees of the theme park must be fashioned as humans willing to undergo these conditions. Miraculously, Disney pulls this off, hiring people who specifically want to be part of the "magic," who come to get jobs hoping specifically to be allowed to become Mickey, or Minnie, or Snow White. To this end, Disney uses the language of the theater to encourage the mimetic features of this character labor, just as the Warner Bros. sign exhorting consumers to "show your character" does. In the parks there is an "onstage" and an "offstage," and workers are "cast members." According to Kuenz, workers are unfazed by their conditions of employment because their personal investment in the transformative powers of Disney is extreme. Disney workers often describe themselves as unable to stop being their character after work. In their interviews with Kuenz, they go in and out of speaking as a character, seemingly without noticing. Kuenz writes,

> Disney's metaphoric translation of workplace, worker, and labor into theatre, cast and performance is crucial to understanding how Disney workers make sense of themselves on the job. This is a place where an entire work force shows up each day, not in uniform, but in costume. Most have internalized this distinction; they

never say uniform just as they always say cast, on stage, and backstage. Apparently this transformation to Disney product is what many of them want when they apply to the park in the first place. [They came here] to be part of the magic, familiar and reproducible.[17]

The commodity bodies enlivened by the disappeared human bodies that populate the theme park are echoed, albeit in a "high art" key, in Julie Taymor's production of *The Lion King*, which opened in New York in November 1997. In this production, the "magic" of commodity fetishism has earned rave reviews and leads to a "transporting" experience.

The "Magic" of *The Lion King*

The production translates the flat, broad surfaces of the animated film into a marvel of mimetic fluidity, human into animal, into landscape, into plant, into animal. Like the film, it tells the story of a young lion, Simba, the son of the king, Mufasa. Simba is a mischievous cub who continually gets into trouble. His uncle, the villain Scar, takes advantage of the cub's disobedient curiosity to lead him astray. He offers to show him the elephant graveyard and, once there, sets his minions, the hyenas, in pursuit of Simba. Simba is lost and gets caught in a wildebeest stampede. His father finds out, goes to rescue him, and Scar kills Mufasa just as Mufasa is about to save Simba. In the second half, Simba, in the company of his two comic cohorts, Timon and Pumbaa, a meerkat and warthog, grows to young manhood. He is only occasionally haunted by the memory of the events of his childhood as he plays with his companions and sings, "Hakuna Mutata," or "no worries." Eventually the young lioness Nala, his childhood playmate, who has been victimized by Scar, comes in search of him to bring him home to the starving Pridelands, desperate under Scar's rule. Simba comes back with her, defeats Scar, takes his rightful place as ruler of the Pridelands, and produces, with Nala, a new little lion heir, thus completing the reproductive circle, known in the production as "the circle of life."

Taymor has crafted each animal as a marvel of puppetry. Humans, whose own bodies are molded into service, animate full-body carapaces to bring these characters "to life." For instance, the giraffes are people walking on all fours on stilts, with their faces just visible below the giraffe's neck and head, which is worn like an enormously elongated hat. The gazelles are mounted, in units of three, on the head and both arms of actors who are camouflaged in their shades and patterns.

Taymor, of course, doesn't see the actor/dancers in their animal carapaces as humans bringing "things" to life, a mimetic absorption of self into commodity. For her, showing the labor of the humans animating their puppet carapaces means that she's able to achieve something "human" that special effects in films are unable to do. The puppeteers give us a chance to connect to the human spirit because we can see it at work, see that the human spirit can make a thing, a puppet, come to life. She says, "Audiences relish the artifice behind the theater. When we see a person actually manipulating an inanimate object like a puppet and making it come alive, the duality moves us. Hidden special effects can lack humanity, but when the human spirit visibly animates an object, we experience a special, almost life-giving connection."[18]

Interestingly, fetishism has been linked to mimesis in ways that precede the postmodern capitalist translation of mimesis into commodity fetishism and are potentially transformative. It seems to me that Taymor may be reaching for this kind of fetishism, as opposed to commodity fetishism, but misses the boat. Marx himself, early in his life, used the "primitive" practice of fetishism to help develop a materialist theory of sensuous, mimetic relationship to objects, whereby a certain animateness of all things suggests their mutual interrelationship, relation rather than domination. William Pietz reads Marx as using the "savage subject of religious fetishism"[19] as a sort of judge or measure of capitalist fetishism. The primitive fetishist (along with the proletariat) is able to identify capitalist fetishism because, for the primitive fetishist, objects and other forms of life are animate but, unlike the apparently animate commodity, are available for relationships, interchange, a kind of radical intersubjectivity. This "primitive" fetishism, or true materialism, is very different from the possessing relationship to other beings and to objects that characterizes capitalism.

Taussig furthers this argument in working to formulate the difference between capitalist commodity fetishism and a postcapitalist fetishism. He writes,

> Under capitalism the animate quality of objects is a result of the radical estrangement of the economy from the person. Post-capitalist animism means that although the socioeconomic exploitative function of fetishism will supposedly disappear with the overcoming of capitalism, fetishism as an active social force inherent in objects will remain. Indeed it must not disappear, for it is the animate quality of things in post-capitalist society that ensures what the young Marx envisaged as the humanization of the world.[20]

Taymor's production comes enticingly close to representing the postcapitalist animism that Taussig describes. Her marvelous scenic devices, which in a single sweep transform a group of humans into a savannah of waving grasses, certainly describe a relation to nature that is "yielding" rather than dominating.[21] Her human bodies placed in an almost inextricable interplay with the animal bodies they inhabit are certainly protean selves, knowing the other by losing oneself in it.

But the catch is that this utopia is performed within a system of economic and cultural circulation in which the "primitive" fetish, animated through a radical mimesis, can only be an alibi for the capitalist fetish. Each character onstage is, after all, already a Disney character. The onstage Mufasa, that marvelous interplay between human and animal body, is a representation of the lifelike-ness of its commodity form, the children's playsuit, endlessly replicated on the shelves of the adjacent Disney store. The child (or adult) who is drawn to the evocation of "primitive" mimesis onstage is drawn to "become" that thing that seems so "magical": the character she's watched in probably endless repetitions of the video of *The Lion King* in her home come to "life."

The first glimpse of the puppets/performers is when they process from the back of the house and onto the stage. Because there is a Disney store directly adjacent to the theater lobby, just steps away from the doors into the theater itself, and because before the show the doors to the store were open onto the lobby, the animal/actors appear to be coming from the store, which is filled with various reproductions of Mufasa and the animals in his kingdom, from playsuits to stuffed animals to toys that can help children "become like" the characters. The puppet/human characters seem to be their commodity parents translated, come to life and flowing down the aisle in what Ben Brantley described in his *New York Times* review as "the transporting magic wrought by the opening ten minutes of *The Lion King*."[22]

An ad from the program places the bodies of the audience inside the fiction of the musical and simultaneously directs them to the consumption that will enable even "more" absorption: "Enjoy your audience with the King [Mufasa]. And remember, even in the jungle, American Express helps you do more." And, indeed, after intermission, the theater is full of shopping bags.

Art, or the Alibi

A certain rhetoric of complexity and artistry surrounded the show's opening, from both critics and Taymor herself, in seeking to differentiate what she had made from the film version. In this rhetoric, the special attributes of the theater become a kind of alibi for the commodified Disney context in which the production takes place, all the while facilitating the circulation of objects and images from the play as commodities. Reimagined by Taymor to become art objects, the Simba playsuits in the store are transmuted onstage into puppet objects of the highest artistic caliber. The theater, as opposed to film, is the medium for this effect. In the course of their apparent procession out of the store and into the theater, the Disney characters change from mass-produced objects into priceless works of art.

Critic Linda Winer notes the advent of Disney's foray into Broadway theatrical production and then marks the peculiar feat of Taymor's production: that it transposes the commodity from what might otherwise have been a display of raw corporatism into the enchanting essence of a thing of quality (and, in so doing, proves the instrumentality of theater to Disney's corporate strategy). The production convinces Winer, at least, that Disney has deeper and more meaningful motives than corporate greed. Magical capitalism weaves its spell around her.

> When Disney made its first assault on Broadway with *Beauty and the Beast* we were dispirited by the laziness of sprawling corporate-culture. Instead of some state-of-the-art Hollywood wizardry or even ordinary modern Broadway know-how, the best we got from the legendary entertainment giant was a tracing paper blow-up of a cartoon hit—just creaky old children's theatre at Broadway prices. That show is in its fourth year now, with cash-happy clones around the planet, and Disney would seem to have no possible reason to change the formula. But hold on to your Mickey souvenirs. Disney opened *The Lion King* and both the show and the playhouse are enchanting. If this is the dreaded Disneyfication, well, come on down. Disney has taken a huge risk and dug far into the theatre's parallel universe to hire the unlikely Julie Taymor, visionary director-designer of rarefied folk-tale extravaganzas. If this is Disney's idea of a theme park, however, we are delighted to report that the theme is quality.[23]

The use of art as an alibi for the reproduction of the commodity, while fully developed and expressed through Taymor's production, is a theme that Disney also explores in its stores. The Disney store at the New Amsterdam Theatre, like the one in the Staten Island Mall, had its own room at the back that worked as a kind of inner sanctum devoted to the art object, in this case, *The Lion King*. Here is where memorabilia from the production were sold. When I first saw the production, in previews in November of 1997, the memorabilia were limited to T-shirts, mugs, and programs emblazoned with the image of Mufasa as a kind of golden cutout, which has become the signature image of the production. After the show opened, however, the room became more elaborate. It began to function partially as an art gallery, featuring some of

Taymor's "priceless" original models for the characters in *The Lion King*, which were not for sale. Next to the cases where the models were displayed were stacked hundreds of four types of Beanie Babies, which loosely reproduced the models in the cases, sporting the same kind of brilliantly colored and extravagantly designed mask and body costume, and labels saying "an original Taymor design." They were ten dollars apiece, whimsical versions of made-up African trickster characters named Tricksters 1, 2, 3, and 4.

This room was intended to be saturated with the aura of the original, the art object, the one-of-a-kind. At the same time, it eased visitors through the transition from singular art object to reproduced commodity and back again, with the Beanie Baby copy presumably picking up the power of the original in the exchange. It was the purchasable fetish, enlivened with the auratic energy of the original. The stacks of souvenir commodities in the store as a whole, in turn, received some of their power from their mimetic proximity to both the art objects and the copies of the art objects in the inner sanctum. The room neither confirms nor denies the ascendancy of the art object, but preserves the commodity alongside the original. The commodity that, after all, must retain enough allure to be purchased, receives that allure from the original. And in this mimetic circuitry between original and copy, the theater is the ultimate inner sanctum, the place where the commodity is transcended by magic. Circulating between the store and the theater, consumers are absorbed into the *Lion King* backstory, enjoying their audience with King Mufasa, American Express card at the ready, buying their way into an experience by which they will be transformed into the magical essence of the commodity. Supposedly free of the corruptions of capitalism (if we believe Winer), this essence is made by what Benjamin called the "rotten spell" of commodification. It is magical capitalism, where the crass commodity is translated into a commodity fetish living through the bodily enactment of formerly one-of-a-kind human beings.

The Lion King: An Excursion into Primitivism and Mimesis

Finally, it is important to look at *The Lion King*'s use of the black body and its conjuring, thereby, of the primitive.[24] The production is saturated with primitivism. It is almost a textbook case for modernity's need to call the primitive into being, in order, through difference it thereby makes visible, to determine the western subject as the knower, the looker, and the master. The mimetic, conjured in modernity's construction of primitivism, becomes a property of the primitive from which the Westerner is differentiated by his quantifying, rational, scientific mode of inquiry into that primitive being. The Westerner assumes that he doesn't share the mimetic tendencies of the primitive, although it is precisely those tendencies that he is drawn to in the primitive, causing him to conjure and reconjure the primitive for a glimpse, a touch, of the mimetic.

In *The Lion King* Taymor's most extraordinary scenic devices are mimetic. The production conjures and stages an achingly beautiful mimetic saturation of one form of life into another, animal into human and back again, human into jungle flower, losing the boundaries of self in the form of what one is not. That is, in a single sweep, a group of humans (the chorus) become and turn the stage into, for example, a savannah of waving grasses. There is at every turn, in the scenic magic implemented through the bodies of the chorus, that "yielding relation to nature" that Taussig uses to characterize mimesis.

In modernity's relation to its primitive, the rational Westerner is colored white, whereas the primitive mimetic body is dark, African, Indian, the colonial subject. So, it's not surprising that Taymor conjures the mimetic through black bodies. For all the members of the chorus are black, and many of them are African. The Taymor production team deliberately hired many African singers, apparently, to render the African-derived theme and the African-derived music both authentic and politically correct. But this way, it is not just any bodies but black bodies who morph into extravagant foliage, undulating grasslands, the animals of the savannah. The production repeats modernity's operation in conjuring a primitive to whom is ascribed properties that, it is assumed, we do not share but that we find alluring and compelling and want to know, own, bank on.

Hal Foster's analysis of the modernist appropriation of African art in a Picasso exhibition at MOMA can illuminate the relationship between mimetic allure and commodification. He says,

> Meanwhile, the tribal object with its ritual/symbolic exchange value was put on display, reinscribed in terms of exhibition/sign exchange value. In this way, the potential disruption posed by the tribal work—that art might reclaim a ritual function, that it might retain an ambivalence of the sacred object or gift and not be reduced to the equivalence of the commodity—was blocked. And the African fetish, which represents a different social exchange, became another kind of fetish: the "magical" commodity.[25]

So the primitive is concocted onstage, so that through a chain of copy and contact the Beanie Babies in the store can be saturated with the power of otherness, and thereby pull the self of the consumer into a desire to experience that otherness—specifically, and only, though, in the form of the Simba playsuits tucked into the shopping bags that fill the theater. The primitive is conjured to create a certain kind of commodity form. Westerners are not, in modernity's myth, mimetic creatures. Westerners are rational creatures. But they acquire the properties of the primitive as commodities, as values that can circulate in our economies of exchange, imbued with the aura or the allure or that otherness. Western commodities can copy the primitive and receive thereby its value, its aura, sympathetic magic creating the "magical commodity."

At the same time, the use of the black bodies stages the domination of the primitive body itself. For all the mimetic allure of these bodies appearing with the swaying grasslands of Africa on their heads, they are also the stage machinery. They are black bodies through whose labor the stage picture appears. Here, mimesis is conjured while at the same time subjected to control and domination. The yielding of these bodies into the grasslands of Africa re-creates a trope wherein black bodies labor to produce the commodity that brings wealth to the masters even as they are themselves commodities.

Eisner (the Ogre) and the Battle for the Magic of the Magic Kingdom

I originally wrote about Disney starting around 1996, and on into 1997, with the opening of *The Lion King*. This period marked a certain height of Disney hubris; Michael Eisner was in business with Mayor Giuliani and the Times Square Development Corporation, *The Lion King* opened to extravagant reviews in the beautifully restored New Amsterdam Theatre, formerly a Ziegfeld house, and the flagship Disney store, which opened right into the theater, was a centerpiece of a newly "revitalized" and sanitized Times Square, a very magnet for tourists wishing to experience the centerpiece of global capitalism.

But in the last few years, Disney has turned away from the "magical" illuviation of the commodity into the body, and the body into the commodity, preferring instead the colder outlines of the hard sell. This shift has created a crisis within the corporation, a face-off with Eisner-bred raw corporatism that reveals just how important to the market is "magical" embodiment, the weaving through of commodity and human. Because of the shift in Disney's corporate tactics, the company may lose revenues as it loses some of its power to enlist people in a process of shaping their subjectivity in a corporate image.

During the winter of 2004, the company was brought into severe crisis by a takeover bid by the communications giant Comcast. The takeover was averted, but the tensions surrounding the bid have foregrounded the seething discontents at the heart of the corporation. Roy Disney, Walt's nephew, though only a very minor shareholder and largely inactive in the company, has recently resurged as the voice of the traditional company in opposition to CEO Michael Eisner, who, in the first week of March 2004, was voted out as chairman of the board and replaced by former senator George Mitchell. (Eisner will remain CEO until 2005.)

Roy Disney has positioned himself as a purist and an antibureaucrat who rejects, at least for Disney, the concept of "branding," which he associates with bureaucracy. He wants to establish distance between Disney and this cornerstone of contemporary capitalism. For him, "Branding is something you do to cows,"26 and making Disney a brand "degrades Disney into a 'thing' to be bureaucratically managed, rather than a 'name' to be creatively championed." Eisner, Roy says, has corrupted everything Disney stands for with his ruthless capitalism, making the company "rapacious, soulless, and always looking for a buck."27 Behind Roy are many Disney fans, expressing themselves on Roy's own Web site, SaveDisney.com, or on other Disney-related sites like Mouse-Planet. One such fan says, about Eisner and Comcast, "It feels like they just killed the dream, magic and Walt."28

In this clash of corporate wills, Roy has no qualms about championing the company, heretofore untainted by the sordidness of branded capitalism, as a deep well of "magic," a well at risk of being capped by a greedy CEO who doesn't recognize "magic" as the inherent source of its value.

It is fascinating that at this moment—when one corporate scandal after another adds up in the minds of Americans to a general picture of the greed inherent in capitalism—two supposedly different Disneys are being opposed to one another. The company Roy would lead is a "magic" kingdom, which, as Walt once said, serves an "audience" that "is made up of parts of people; of that deathless, precious, ageless, absolutely primitive remnant of something in every world-wracked being which makes us play with children's toys—and laugh without self-consciousness at silly things, and sing in bathtubs, and dream . . . you know, the Mickey in us."29 The company Eisner would lead would be guided by ruthless, corporate rapaciousness.

A pro-Roy document published on the Web dramatizes the conflict in fairy-tale format. In "The Emperor's New Greed," by Dave Pruiksma, Eisner, the "evil ogre," is contrasted to Walt Disney. In the story there once was a King Walt, who ruled over a "beloved and peaceful Eden, a humble kingdom." But after King Walt's death, an ogre took over and began at once with his evil plotting: "'Just look at those fools down there,' the evil ogre muttered to himself smacking his hideous lips over his great, weasel-like teeth, 'Can't they see the gold mine they are sitting on? I can practically *smell* the hidden riches that King Walt has left behind as their heritage!'"30

The plot revolves around a miraculous golden goose that lays the beautiful golden eggs that somehow (there is no buying or selling in Walt's kingdom) create the "magical kingdom's" revenue. Under King Walt, these eggs, treated as objects of art, are cared for with reverence. They are what "sustains the [magical] kingdom." But the ogre doesn't recognize the value of the goose, choosing at first to discard her and focus instead on other sources of revenue in the magic kingdom. King Walt's loyal faithful somehow manage to keep the belittled goose alive and nurtured, and still laying its golden eggs, eggs suffused with the aura of the one-of-a-kind, and therefore unassociated with market relations.

The discourse of the fairy tale is unremitting in the way it opposes the ogre/Eisner's selfishness, avarice, bureaucracy ("which confuses and ultimately paralyzes the people of the kingdom"), looting, pillaging, outsourcing, and the constructing of "great, gaudy, dreadful structures with tacky, garish facades and little substance beyond that" to the goodness and generosity and magic formerly inherent in the kingdom grown from the bounty of the golden eggs. Eventually, the eye of the ogre turns back to the goose, whose value he begins to see. He demands a frenzy of production from the goose, but the desires of the ogre and his "ministers" are "insatiable." They want more and more of the eggs produced, and with the eggs they attempt to make themselves "omnipotent." Our poor fabulist cries out, "It was no longer enough just to be the leaders of King Walt's once magical kingdom."

This insatiable drive causes the ogre to seize the goose for himself and take it away from its loving caretakers, the surviving retinue of dead King Walt. Predictably, under his "noxious" care, the eggs decline in size and soon become rotten. Subjected to conditions of production probably not unlike those that workers laboring for Disney contractors suffer around the globe, in other words, ordinary conditions of production, the eggs wither in value. Produced in an uncaring and alienated circumstance, they are just, well, rotten eggs. The tale has a happy ending, though, when King Walt's loyal nephew surfaces and restores the near-dead goose to health. The ogre's "tower of terror" crumbles, and all begin to "rebuild and recreate the once happy and magical little hamlet."

It is difficult for this author, in his account of Eisner's rise to power, to sustain the egg metaphor. While he makes the eggs the source of Disney's value, he struggles hard with trying to avoid any suggestion that they are related to capitalist modes of production (only the ogre/Eisner engages in these), even though they are produced over and over again, each the same as the last. Without the author's being able to say so (for fear of disenchanting us; such a mention might reek of Haitian sweatshops), the goose is the machinery for mass production upon which Disney's profit depends. He wants us to know the power of Disney's productive machinery, the unstoppable force of the iterated egg, but to simultaneously idealize the goose and her eggs as quite an opposite thing—one of a kind, "magical," unquantifiable.

The awkwardness of the story reveals the uneasy positioning of the loyalist faction. What Roy and the other loyalists want is for the company to go on accumulating wealth for its shareholders through ever broadening world markets. Simultaneously though, since they believe that it is in the experience of Disney's "magic" that the guarantee of that profit lies, they have to use "magic" as an alibi for their own corporate greed, and the alibi doesn't seem to stretch quite far enough. It's almost as if, with the crisis, Disney's cover has been blown.

The seizure of the mimetic faculty, particularly in children, has long served the company as the means by which to create and reproduce this experience and ideology of "magic." Eisner has exposed the profit-driven underbelly of Disney's "magic," thereby puncturing the processes of fetishization that uphold it. Children taken to Disney stores recently find themselves wearing cheap, low-quality outfits made in sweatshops with the picture of a Disney character or two stuck to them, rather than becoming a princess.

Roy Disney, protesting his faith in the "magic kingdom" but all the while heavily invested in the company's profits, fears that magical capitalism, built on the mimetic desire diverted to commodity fetishism, is the only way those profits can be sustained. Eisner sees other means, perhaps, by which the Disney corporation can be a figurehead for corporate attempts to make a final, decisive takeover of human life. But the strength of the resistance to Eisner is a measure of the investment by corporate culture—not only Disney, but many other companies as well—in mimetic techniques for the absorption of consumers into a corporate imaginary.

The crisis in the Disney corporation is ongoing, and it is not certain whether Roy will be able to enthrone himself and/or his magical capitalism at its center. Perhaps Disney's particularly ruthless experiment in the forging of subjectivity through and as the face of the commodity has had its day. *The Lion King* is still running, still successful. But the store adjacent to it is closed. The store I first visited in the Staten Island Mall is just a shadow of its former self. The doorway into the inner sanctum still has *Fantasia* Mickey poised over it, but the opening itself, the theater for the production of the original, the aura, that proscenium arch of a video screen which let loose the spirit of the dead Walt, my fingers on the interactive screen touching the object to conjure the magic from inside it—that opening is blocked off with an ugly temporary shelf unit covered in the same stuffed animals that populate a store that no longer sells dress-up character clothes, only "real" clothes, like any other clothing store, even if they do have Disney characters on them. If there's any of Disney's "magic" here, it's not evident.

Nevertheless, the company's legacy as the innovator in mimetic techniques will linger. So it is still important to ask, why *does* this mimetic tendency, this great pleasure, this terrifically sensuous reach into others, or otherness, this play whose remnants outside of commodification linger in the act of making theater, or in isolated instances of the play of children, why *does* it get expressed through the commodity, why *do* we set ourselves into a mirroring relation of "copy and contact" with commodities instead of with other human beings, or animals, or any other forms of life or being? Why do we not, rather, find a way to an animist, antibanking, bodily reach, an inter-becoming empathy with other humans?

I think, quite simply (or perhaps not so), that this is because we have made ourselves as social beings in and through the commodity. The commodity comes into being and attains its "power" as a mimetic thing. It copies our energies and our desires, and we, in turn, copy the commodity, touching as we go. With ever greater force the commodity has become more human than ourselves. It has taken on the life force, the vibrancy, of the human we want to be, which we then copy, often in the utterly material life of our own bodies. Commodities are the other selves, the alterities we want to touch, copy, become. The mimetic chain of our relationship to commodities creates the fetish commodity, the mysteriously alive thing that is recognizably the shape in which a significant portion of our own open-ended process of formation as individuals occurs.

Joseph Roach writes in *Cities of the Dead*, "The restored behavior [his own version of copy/contact] of the marketplace created by its synergy a behavioral vortex in which human relationships could be drained of sympathetic imagination and shaped to the purposes of consumption and exchange."[31] Without sympathetic imagination, our relation to other humans is as competitors, as hostile units. Humans are reminders of alienated social conditions. We take our anger out on other humans. One has only to drive on the New Jersey Turnpike, or any American road, with the man or woman wearing the carapace, the body, of her Lexus SUV bearing down on you, honking, swerving, driving a foot from your bumper. Other people are in her way, reminders that she cannot get all that she wants as fast as she wants. But as she enacts "the character" of the Lexus, the luxury vehicle, she takes on the living social force of the commodity, in the path of which the human, already evacuated, turns away, like a shade, a memory of a different human history.

This is the power of the golden egg: Being the commodity seems necessary because, after a chain of mimetic copying, and countercopying, it seems the source of life. In this way the commodity in particular, and corporate power in general, can come to seem the ineradicable source of ongoing life, whereas the human is only something in our way, dying, being blown up, suffering, needing, hungry, decisively unmagical.

Notes

1. Playbill, *The Lion King,* New Amsterdam Theatre, New York, November 1997, 28.
2. Michael Taussig, *Mimesis and Alterity: A Particular History of the Senses* (New York: Routledge, 1993), 34
3. Ibid., 86.
4. Ibid., 99.
5. Robert Siegel, *All Things Considered* (National Public Radio: Transcript, November 2, 2000), 4 of 4.
6. Ibid., 4.
7. Richard deCordova, "The Mickey in Macy's Window," in *Disney Discourse: Producing the Magic Kingdom,* ed. Eric Smoodin (New York: Routledge, 1994), 207.
8. Ibid., 211.
9. Richard Schickel, *The Disney Version: The Life, Times, Art and Commerce of Walt Disney* (Chicago: Elephant Paperbacks, 1997), 167.
10. Jack Amariglio and Antonio Callari, "Marxian Value Theory and the Problem of the Subject: The Role of Commodity Fetishism," in *Fetishism as Cultural Discourse,* ed. Emily Apter and William Piez (Ithaca, N.Y.: Cornell University Press, 1993), 203.
11. Walter Benjamin, *The Arcades Project* (Cambridge: Belknap Press of Harvard University, 1999), 346. "In the form taken by prostitution in the big cities, the woman appears not only as commodity but, in a precise sense, as mass-produced article. This is indicated by the masking of individual expression in favor of a professional appearance, such as makeup provides. The point is made still more emphatically later on, by the uniformed girls of the music-hall review."
12. Ibid., 375.
13. Ibid., 386.
14. Philip Auslander argues in his book *Liveness* that all arguments that advocate for the uniqueness of performance on the basis of the unique, unmediated aura of the performer's presence are specious. He says that the proliferation of technologically reproduced performance has so substantially shaped our sensual apparatus that we can feel close to a live performance only through a mediated form.
15. http://www.dannhazel.com/Gay%20disney%20Guide%20Sample%20. Chapter.htm.
16. Quoted in Project on Disney, *Inside the Mouse: Work and Play at Disney World* (Durham, N.C.: Duke University Press, 1995), 135.
17. Ibid., 112, 137.

18. Playbill, *The Lion King*, 31.

19. William Pietz, "Fetishism and Materialism: The Limits of Theory in Marx," in *Fetishism as Cultural Discourse*, 143.

20. Taussig, *Mimesis and Alterity*, 99.

21. Ibid., 46.

22. Ben Brantley, "Cub Comes of Age: A Twice-Told Cosmic Tale," *New York Times*, November 14, 1997, B1.

23. Linda Winer, "Lion King Leads a Magical, Rich Jungle Parade," *New York Newsday*, November 17, 1997, B3.

24. I want, in my use of the word primitive, to preserve an ambiguity. The word must be used in a way that acknowledges the fact that the word is a product of imperialist ideology. But it's also possible to use the category of the primitive for the purposes of teasing out difference. In *Art, Spectacle, Cultural Politics* (Seattle: Bay Press, 1985: 199), Hall Foster distinguishes the category of the primitive, which he attempts to refunction as an index of critical difference, from the discourse of primitivism. This he characterizes as follows: "Primitivism not only absorbs the potential disruption of the tribal objects into western forms, ideas and commodities; it also symptomatically manages the ideological nightmare of a great art inspired by spoils."

25. Ibid., 193.

26. http://savedisney.com/news/essays/rd020904.1.asp, p. 1.

27. Alex Berenson, "The Wonderful World of (Roy) Disney," *New York Times*, February 15, 2004, sec. 3, p. 6.

28. http://www.forbes.com/business/newswire/2004/02/11/rtr1257547.html.

29. Schickel, *The Disney Version*, 158.

30. http://www.pruiksma.com/A%20NOT%20So%20Silly%20Symphony.html, p. 2.

31. Joseph Roach, *Cities of the Dead: Circum-Atlantic Performance* (New York: Columbia University Press, 1996), 213.

Part III

Hierarchies: Race, Class, Gender, Sexuality

5

Curiouser and Curiouser:
Gay Days at the Disney Theme Parks

Sean Griffin

Beginning in 1978, various events at both the Disneyland theme park in Anaheim, California, and Walt Disney World in Orlando, Florida, have catered to
homosexual consumers. The emergence of these "Gay Days," as they are generally known, presents an ongoing discourse between the Walt Disney Company
on the one hand and the "gay community" on the other. Over the years, how
these events have been organized, experienced, and even defined by both sides
has changed. What had been viewed originally (by participants, the Walt Disney
Company, and those reporting on the events) as an overt cultural confrontation
has been reframed as a charity event, as a vacation free of political agendas, and
as a lavish "circuit" extravaganza. This evolution reflects shifting patterns in the
power dynamic between Disney and the gay community, responding to each
other as well as to other groups (such as the Christian Right). The various conceptions of Gay Days have resulted from the various parties employing different assumptions and strategies to gain control over how these events are framed
and discussed. The political economy of Gay Days has strongly affected the discourse, for consumer capitalism (and its effect on identity) strongly conditions
these annual occasions and the discussion about them by Disney, by the gay
community, by the news media, and by the Christian Right.

The discourse around Gay Days has often become part of negotiations about public and private behavior, such as the public use of a privately owned space and the public expression of conventionally private desires. The emphasis on the public/private dichotomy reflects its importance to both Disney and sexual desire. The Walt Disney Company is a private business, but a publicly traded one that promotes itself as pro-family and pro-community. On the other side, gay rights activists often argue that sexual orientation is a privacy issue (as exemplified by the arguments that helped end laws against sodomy) yet also often present "coming out" publicly as fundamental to attaining those rights. As will be discussed, modern capitalism affects the shifts in the public/private dichotomy, as well as shifts in the meaning of Gay Days, and even in the meanings of "Disney" and "the gay community."

1978: Gay Day as Guerrilla Raid

For many years, management at Disneyland has allowed private parties to rent the park after normal working hours during the off-season (roughly October through January). In 1978, an organization naming itself the Los Angeles Bar and Restaurant Association reserved the park for such a party. Just before the night of the party, Disneyland realized that the association consisted of gay male restaurants and bars, and had been selling tickets to the event to all its customers. Unable to stop the event completely at such short notice, Disneyland made preparations "for the worst." All live music was canceled to keep from encouraging same-sex couples to dance. Security was beefed up, and park supervisors "said that, for a night, courtesy was optional."[1] According to different accounts, about fifteen thousand mainly gay male guests aggressively took over Disneyland that night. Some of the guests were heterosexual families who had no idea that they had bought tickets for a gay event and were shocked to find very open displays of affection between men. Yet the majority were homosexuals running rampant through the park, occasionally having it out with homophobic employees, and joyfully engaging in what has been described by many of the people who worked at the park that night as a free-form orgy. Various stages of sexual coupling occurred in bathrooms, on park benches, and even on the Submarine Voyage.[2]

Such is the beginning of the history of Gay Days at the Disney theme parks. This narrative of the event posits quite clearly the discursive positions of Disney and the gay community as antagonistic. Disney at this point was positioned (both by the gay men who attended the event and by park authorities) as a representative of the traditional old-fashioned heterosexual patriarchy that demonized and discriminated against homosexuality. Disney management seems pretty obviously to have regarded the event as a form of warfare, with gay men invading the sacred hallowed grounds to loot and pillage, while park officials literally called in reinforcements and laid out emergency defense plans. Telling workers that courtesy was not mandatory implies that Disney regarded these customers not as guests but as the enemy.

Those who attended the event seemed eager for Disney management to view the night as a guerrilla raid. This was not a case of Disney security coming in with nightsticks and beating up innocent gay victims, and it must be stressed that I have found no evidence of physical harassment by Disney workers toward anyone at this event. Accounts of this night present the homosexual customers as very consciously conceiving of their presence as a radical political intervention, aggressively challenging both workers and straight customers through open displays of sexual behavior. Even a homosexual employee at the park who worked that night describes the customers as practically spoiling for a fight: "Oh my goodness! There were men cruising men all over, . . . and they were obnoxious. . . . Even the gay people like myself were a little appalled. Because we thought, 'Well, this is a little—pushing things too far.' I mean, it's one thing to come and have fun, but they were really in your face."[3]

Such raids were a common strategy during the first decade of modern gay activism. In the wake of the protests that occurred in Greenwich Village in June 1969 outside the Stonewall Inn,[4] gay rights activists began taking their cues from the radical protests of groups such as the Black Panthers and the National Organization of Women. Instead of marching peaceably in a circle while wearing "respectable" clothes, these groups organized confrontational demonstrations aimed at jolting the complacency of those who would deny them their rights. The Black Panthers began training their members how to handle weapons; women burned bras in Atlantic City just before the 1968 Miss America pageant. Foremost, the new group of gay rights activists saw "coming out" as the most basic and important political action an individual could make. If enough individuals overtly announced their self-identification as a homosexual, the rest of society would eventually see (1) how many homosexuals actually exist; and (2) that homosexuality encompasses a diverse realm of individuals instead of only the stereotypical versions of feminine men and masculine women. Among the methods of gaining attention were anniversary celebrations of the Stonewall riots. By the end of the 1970s, the end of June had become Gay Pride week, and most large cities witnessed annual Pride parades attended by thousands of lesbians and gay men.

Gay activists also organized highly visible confrontations to make their presence known to the larger society. Kiss-ins were held at restaurants that refused to serve gay customers; lesbian and gay couples made sure the media were present when they attempted to apply for marriage licenses; a protester broke onto the set of CBS News during one of Walter Cronkite's live broadcasts. "Zapping," as it was labeled by gay activists, became quite prevalent during the early and mid-1970s, as lesbians crashed the National Organization of Women (who were attempting to distance themselves from lesbianism) and gay men and women shouted down supposed experts on homosexuality at conventions of the American Psychiatric Association (which labeled homosexuality as a mental disorder until the protests helped overturn that decision in 1973).[4] The goal of these actions was to invade the publicly visible "space" of perceived upholders of the dominant heterosexual paradigm, taking over the space to celebrate the wealth of sexual possibilities.

Since the 1930s, the Walt Disney Company had cultivated an image of conservative American cultural values—values that uphold the heterosexual patriarchal family unit as a nostalgic ideal. The use of narratives of courtship and romance (whether with Mickey and Minnie Mouse, or with various princesses and their Prince Charmings) reinforced both approved gender behavior and heterosexual normativity. This discourse extended to the theme parks, where it was almost impossible to miss the repeated construction of the typical visitor unit as a heterosexual family of four. This was plain to see, for example, in the original House of Tomorrow (which assured visitors that the future would be designed with the two-child patriarchal heterosexual family in mind); the seating diagrams for the Matterhorn roller coaster (showing the international symbols for girl-boy-woman-man getting into cars in that order); the photos of happy heterosexual families in the Disneyland brochures given to everyone who entered; the decades-old jokes about mothers-in-law recited by the operators of the Jungle Cruise boat ride; the Pirates of the Caribbean chasing lustily after female prey. The assumption and reinforcement of heterosexuality could be found wherever one turned.[6] With this image in place for decades, Disneyland became an obvious target for the gay activist zapping that occurred in 1978.

Yet, certain aspects of the event suggest that, while each side expressed animosity toward the other, seeds of complexity lay hidden within the monolithic conceptions that each side held of the other. While activists seemed to view Disney as homophobic and discriminatory, a number of lesbians and gay men worked as employees at the parks at this time. Establishing the number of such employees is practically impossible, due in large part to various levels of closetedness. Yet, the existence of these employees complicates the assumption of automatic antagonism by everyone at Disneyland toward its gay customers on that night in 1978. Further, the concentration of gay men among the customers at the park exemplified shifts within the gay rights movement. The term "gay" had encompassed both men and women in the immediate post-Stonewall period, but the overemphasis on men's issues in much of the movement resulted in many lesbians disassociating themselves from "gay." By the end of the 1970s, "gay" meant predominantly "homosexual male." In fact, lesbian separatism became widespread—detaching lesbian activists from gay male society and, as much as possible, the patriarchal system itself.[7] So, while zapping Disneyland, the gay male customers were also displaying their dominance in the homosexual community.

Also, while overtly positioning themselves as insurrectionists, by all accounts the gay men at Disneyland on that night were *enjoying* themselves. Although perhaps not in the manner the management would have preferred, these customers were still using the theme park space for an evening of fun and recreation—and some may have entered the park hoping to feel that, as homosexuals, they could still become (for a night) part of "the Happiest Place on Earth." While some in the zap may have wanted to take Disney down, others may have instead wanted to revel in Disney, to be included in what had traditionally been viewed as a "straights-only" space. Such complications would shift the understanding of how a Gay Day at the theme parks could be put together.

1980s: Gay Day as Discreet Charity Event

In the wake of the 1978 event, Disney management succeeded in preventing any further zaps at either Disneyland or Walt Disney World. The closest anything came to a similar event happened in the summer of 1980, when two gay male teenagers attended a Date Night at Disneyland and purposefully danced together at the Tomorrowland Terrace in order to challenge the park's policy against same-sex dancing. As in 1978, both sides viewed each other as antagonists, with Disney security forcibly escorting the two men off the floor and out of the park, and the two men responding by filing a lawsuit. (In 1984 a jury found in favor of the couple.)[8]

During the 1980s, though, the positions of both Disney and the gay community altered, creating the opportunity to frame the concept of a Gay Day differently. The emergence of the AIDS crisis in the early part of the decade signaled a new era in gay rights activism. With death rates among gay males soaring, and the Reagan administration refusing even to acknowledge AIDS (much less pave the way to fund research and treatment), individuals began to come together in a shared cause. Lesbians joined with gay men in the fight against AIDS. Safe-sex organizations attempted to reach out beyond the largely middle-class white populations of gay men in the "gay ghettos" to the African, Latino, and Asian American communities. Radical activist groups such as ACT UP gathered members from a number of diverse communities in order to demand attention. As with the zaps of the 1970s, these groups broke into press conferences, government offices, and medical labs to stage demonstrations and gain publicity for their cause.

In gaining the attention of the media, these groups attempted to wrest control away from medical, corporate, and governmental authorities and advance a different perspective for understanding the crisis. One of the main strategies for framing the discussion was in getting people to stop thinking of AIDS as a homosexual disease. Rather, these groups stressed that anyone was a potential victim, regardless of sexual orientation. In this way, homosexuals with AIDS were perceived not as sinners being punished but as unlucky individuals who deserved compassion and help. Such tactics favored an inclusionary attitude within these groups, welcoming all who shared the same cause regardless of perceived identity differences (in race, gender, and even sexual orientation). A result of this development was a reinvestment in the term "queer," which had been previously used as an epithet to demean anyone who did not conform to gender or sexual normativity. Groups like Queer Nation and an entire trend in academic thought now began using the term to acknowledge the diversity of sexual desire and the oppression nonpatriarchal heterosexuals shared. "Queer" encompassed gay men, lesbians, bisexuals, transgendered people, and even "straight queers" who were either sympathetic to nonheterosexuals or felt their heterosexual desire in nonprescribed ways.

In aiming at institutions that were blocking or thwarting the search for a cure, the availability of medical treatment, or the acceptance of nonheterosexuality, radical AIDS activists might have logically targeted the "heterosexual family values" image of Disney much as gay zappers did in 1978. On occasion, some groups still did target the parks to disrupt things. The activist group Boys with Arms Akimbo, for example, visited Disneyland in 1989, strutting their wild retro-1970s outfits in a comparison of their queer look to the excessive style of the park itself.[9] Yet the playful nature that the group brought to its visit differed from the more aggressive behavior of the 1978 zap. In the 1980s, Disneyland and Walt Disney World took on special meaning and importance for a number of people with AIDS (PWAs). Many PWAs visited Disneyland and Walt Disney World, some repeatedly, specifically seeing their trips as a way of dealing with their status. The fascination with the theme parks (and Disney in general, as judged by the number of Disney images found on the AIDS quilt) may have tied into a need by many PWAs for momentary escape and fantasy. For many, the parks provided an actual location where "dreams come true," a vacation from the hardships and hatred in the outside world. Many who attended the parks also seemed to enjoy how the space brings out the child in people, possibly allowing nonstraights and PWAs to return in fantasy to a time before the disease or before the onset of sexual awakenings (and the oppression that resulted). In other words, the theme parks increasingly became regarded by some PWAs (and those around them) not as a bastion of heterosexual presumption but as a haven from homophobia and rampant AIDS panic.

Disney had also undergone some major changes during the 1980s that may have militated against zapping. The 1970s had been generally stagnant years for Walt Disney Productions, as executives attempted to keep company policies and strategies frozen in time after Walt's death in 1966. Such decisions proved increasingly misjudged. The studio's income steadily decreased, from a $34.6 million profit in 1981 to $19.6 million in 1982, then to a $33.3 million loss in 1983.[10] In 1983, the studio would release only three films. The theme parks did only marginally better than the film division. While they consistently made money for the company, profits remained stable rather than increasing. Between 1983 and 1985, the Imagineering workforce (as the Walt Disney Company designates those who help create the attractions for the parks) was reduced from 2,000 to 450.[11] The economic precariousness of the firm resulted in repeated worries during the mid-1980s about corporate raiders stealing the company and selling off all its assets.

Deciding that a major executive shake-up was needed, the board of directors brought in Frank Wells and Michael Eisner in 1984 to helm the company. Their reign over the studio almost completely and immediately revamped the philosophy and the day-to-day experience of life in the company. They did whatever they felt they could to build the strength of the company, even if it seemingly flew in the face of the Disney image and reputation, such as releasing R-rated films (through Touchstone Pictures). The new Disney also made a concerted attempt to be taken seriously by those working in the entertainment industry and to attract talent that had never previously considered making a film for the company. In this new atmosphere, no one seemed to care what you did in your private life, as long as you helped bring in revenue. By 1991, the Walt Disney Company formally instituted a nondiscrimination policy based on sexual orientation, and anecdotes indicate that Michael Eisner personally figured that about 40 percent of the Disney workforce was gay or lesbian.[12]

The year 1986, two years after Eisner and Wells took over the company, saw another Gay Day at the Disneyland theme park. Like the 1978 event, it was organized as a private party held after the regular working hours for the parks. Unlike 1978, though, Disney and the event's participants were not on opposite sides of a battle line. Instead, everyone seemed to be working together. In conjunction with AIDS organizations in Orange County, Disneyland held a benefit at the park to raise funds for AIDS Project Los Angeles. Not only was this 1986 event sponsored directly by the company, but also Disney pledged to match the money raised by ticket sales with an equal donation from corporate coffers. The success of the event led to subsequent benefits at both Disneyland and Walt Disney World through the rest of the decade.

Both the gay community and Disney found advantages to this rapprochement. To the gay community, such events not only materially helped AIDS patient care but also seemed to demonstrate the extension of acceptance from a major corporation. The events provided a momentary space for lesbians, gay men, and other queers to experience being part of the majority instead of a minority. The smiles on people's faces as they felt safe and free to hold their partner's hand in public, or give each other a hug, expressed that sense of "dreams coming true." For the newly reconfigured Disney, such events worked to boost the company's public image ("we care") and, management hoped, provided a side benefit of customer brand loyalty from an undermarketed population group just when Disney needed to bolster its coffers. (The increased number of openly homosexual employees would also alter general attitudes within the company toward such events.) Hence disparate needs brought the previously antagonistic groups together.

Such connections, though, were predicated on a carefully planned discourse defining these mutual benefits. Just as different factors brought Disney management and the gay community together to organize these occasions, various motivations also brought them together in agreement about their meaning. Although I have used the general term "Gay Day," the charity events of the 1980s never once actually used the words "gay," "lesbian," or "homosexual" in their announcements, posters, tickets, or press releases. Instead, these events were described as "AIDS benefits" or "special parties" with proceeds going to various AIDS charities. Both Disney and the AIDS groups involved in organizing these events stood to gain from the official elision of homosexuality, even as the majority of the people who attended through the years were lesbians and gay men who read between the lines. (Many lesbians and gay men in the Los Angeles area commonly referred to these events as "Gay Night" rather than using titles like "A Private Holiday Party at Disneyland," as the 1994 event, for example, officially called itself.)

Refusing to label these benefits as "Gay Days" worked to further the activist discourse that was trying to frame AIDS not as a gay disease but as one that could afflict anyone. Disney was also invested in keeping the word "gay" out of the official discourse for these events (as were major corporate sponsors of other

AIDS events). In its effort to boost revenue, Disney executives wanted to tap new markets, but not at the expense of losing their established customer base. In other words, Disney sought a method of appealing to homosexual customers without potentially disturbing the heterosexual families on which the company still depended. Framing these events as AIDS benefits kept the company from specifically championing gay pride. Lesbians and gay men could read this as much-needed support for the number of homosexuals with AIDS, but Disney could promote the event more broadly. This was never more apparent than in the benefit held at Disneyland in January 1990, attended by former president Ronald Reagan, which raised $50,000 for the Pediatrics AIDS Foundation.[13]

The AIDS benefits of the 1980s were major events, with Disneyland attracting headline celebrities (such as Reagan and Elizabeth Taylor) and charging higher ticket prices. As the decade ended, the benefits grew smaller in scope. The Odyssey Adventures travel agency began in 1992 to rent the park one night a year (usually during the early winter, traditionally a slow period for the park) to hold less extravagant private charity events. Following in the tradition already established, the parties never used the words "gay" or "homosexual," and only the knowledge that the locations where you could buy tickets were lesbian/gay community centers or that "a portion of the net proceeds [would go] to benefit Aid for AIDS" would tip off a potential customer. Another change began with the advent of the Odyssey benefits: other than signing the contract to rent the park, Disney was no longer involved in the organization of these events. This new development allowed Disney even further absolution from culpability in endorsing homosexuality.

The use of the "AIDS benefit" discourse had its drawbacks for Odyssey Adventures. In 1995, word spread throughout the area that Odyssey was making only token donations of the proceeds to the Aid for AIDS charity—even though the event's publicity prominently described it as a charity event. Attendance dropped precipitously as potential customers began perceiving the event as a con job. The following year, Odyssey Tours decided not to donate proceeds to any charity and dropped mention of any such charity in its ads for the event. In 1998, Odyssey announced that it would no longer be organizing its annual private party. The official reason was that Disneyland had announced that it would remain open late for a longer portion of the year, necessitating cuts in the number of dates open for private groups to rent the park. Yet Odyssey had definitely been burned by its involvement with the events, and its move to begin organizing private parties at the Magic Mountain theme park may have signaled a desire to start over somewhere else.

Both Odyssey and Disneyland would remain involved in Gay Days, but for both the terms of how such events were managed had changed. While

Odyssey would still refer to its events at Magic Mountain as "private parties," the travel group began using a pink triangle as its logo, and its website would contain links to explicitly gay organizations (with the word "gay" in the Web addresses). On the other side, Disney's Gay Days began being referred to specifically by that name (though, as will be shown, not directly by Disney itself). These events were directly influenced by a new model that had taken root at Walt Disney World while Odyssey was still announcing AIDS benefits. The exponential growth of these events at the Orlando park indicates how new needs by both Disney and the gay community resulted in another definition of what Gay Days are.

1990s: Gay Days as Apolitical Vacation

About the same time that Odyssey began organizing its evening events at Disneyland, another yearly event was beginning at Walt Disney World—but organized by a loose coalition of queer individuals rather than by a business. In 1991, subscribers to CompuWho? (an Orlando computer bulletin-board service that linked gays and lesbians in the area), picked the first Saturday in June for a group outing to the Magic Kingdom. Through e-mail and fliers handed out at local bars, attendees were encouraged to show up in red shirts so that people could identify each other among the rest of the guests at the park that day.[14] Unlike the carefully coded advertising done by Odyssey, ads for the Disney World gathering simply announced it as "Gay & Lesbian Day At the Magical Kingdom That Walt Built." That first year only a few hundred responded, but the event was considered enough of a success to make it an annual occurrence, scheduled for the first weekend in June. Attendance grew steadily and markedly each year. By 1994, the fourth event was being advertised and cosponsored by *Out* magazine. Estimated attendance went from 32,000 in 1995 to 125,000 in 2002,[15] and by the year 2000 "common knowledge within the park [was] that . . . [Gay Day] is one of the busiest days of the year."[16] Since 2000, almost an entire week of activities has been scheduled and advertised each year. In 1998, less than a year after Odyssey announced the cancellation of its annual private party at Disneyland, groups had organized what they labeled a (one-day) "Gay Day" at the Anaheim park modeled after the growing success of the more extensive Gay Days at the Orlando resort. Although Gay Day at Disneyland is much smaller in scale than what has evolved at Disney World, lesbians, gay men, bisexuals, and their straight friends and relatives enter the park during regular park hours on an October Saturday in their requisite red T-shirts for a day of revelry in the Magic Kingdom.

As Gay Days at Disney World grew, Disney at first responded with guarded alarm. In contrast to the AIDS benefits of the 1980s, Disney management had not been involved in the organization of these events. Since this event was not a private party but took place during regular working hours, worries about a melee such as had occurred at Disneyland in 1978 seemed to proliferate. Security was beefed up secretly on the first Saturday in June for the first few years. Placards were placed at the entrance informing visitors that homosexuals were arriving en masse. Disney gave surprised and angry heterosexual customers shuttles to other theme parks, passes to return on another day, and (for those who accidentally showed up in red) complimentary white T-shirts.

While Disney readied for confrontation, though, the people who congregated for Gay Days were not nearly as anxious to create an incident as the zappers of the 1970s. Doug Swallow, the CompuWho? member credited with founding the event, remembers, "Back in 1991 when we started it, it was truly . . . 'Why not tell everybody else about it at the bars and see who would show up?' I'm sure there was a little bit of, you know, 'It'll be fun to see how Disney reacts to this.' But it wasn't meant to be in-your-face—'Hey look at us, we're going to make a mess in your park.' It was meant to be, 'We're going to go out and have fun like everybody else.' That was how it began."17 This description, while acknowledging that a transgressive thrill may be part of the enjoyment of a Gay Day at Disney, foregrounds the way organizers have repeatedly framed the event: as apolitical and nonconfrontational. Jeff Truesdell, reporting for the *Orlando Weekly*, stated plainly that "Orlando's Gay Day had no activist or fund raising agenda." The programs distributed each year also proclaim this loudly. The 2000 *Gay Day 2K Pride Guide* announced, "It's not about politics. It's not about issues like equal rights, marriage, or adoption laws. . . . And it's not about making a statement. . . . It's about having fun."18 The *Gay Days 2002 Program* similarly declared, "What is our stated purpose? To have fun. What is our hidden agenda? There is none."19 Founder Doug Swallow positions Disney World's Gay Day in distinction to other events normally held during the Gay Pride month of June: "All month long you're bombarded with 'give me money for this, give me money for that, donate here, donate there, fight for our rights.' It gets to be a bit much . . . I was just wanting to see something done for fun."20

Various people within the queer Orlando community have even actively worked to keep Disney World's Gay Days from becoming confrontational. In 1993, the third year of the event, a dozen gay and lesbian Disney World employees (or, as they are called, "cast members") decided to welcome red-shirted customers near the entrance and spell out the rules, such as keeping the shirts on and making no overt sexual conduct. Later, in the park, they made certain that parade lines were kept unobstructed and broke up any spontaneous obscene group chants. Not only did these people defuse any activist sentiment—but they did so on their own initiative during their off hours. Consequently, Disney World authorities got thousands of well-behaved customers who were guided and watched over by unpaid volunteers.[21] Such policing has also been done subtly by those organizing the events. The annual programs not only attempt to define these events as merely "fun" but also make certain to give advice on what is meant by "fun." Trying to prevent the eruption of public sex or other scandalous forms of pleasure, the *Gay Day 2K Pride Guide* pointed out that "it's easy to 'Get a room!,'' when there are thousands on the property."[22] In the 2002 program, the advice was even more overt: "Don't be shy about holding hands if you have a mind to. Don't feel constrained to hide your affection from one another, but by the same token, remember that grand displays of physical interaction are never considered in good taste under any circumstances."[23]

The work by the promoters to present Gay Day as apolitical and nonorgiastic probably helped assuage the fears of executives at the Walt Disney Company. Further, the growing acceptance of homosexuality within the Walt Disney Company at large meant that corporate reaction to such an event would be more tempered than in 1978. By the end of the 1990s, Disney had gone beyond the inclusion of sexual orientation in its equal employment opportunity policy to the granting of domestic partner benefits to homosexual employees. Various company-sanctioned lesbian and gay employee groups had formed within Disney (LEAGUE at the studio, LEAGUE/Disneyland and ALLIANCE at Disney World). These changes in Disney, and in how the gay community of Orlando was positing what a Gay Day meant, helped ease worries about the events among Disney executives—and the enormous growth of visitors during what had previously been a period of low attendance was certainly appreciated. Consequently, Disney went along with the apolitical frame—that anyone was welcome to attend the park.[24] By 1996, the warning placards had disappeared. In coordination with Gay Days, Disney even began allowing gay party promoters to plan events throughout the resort, such as the "Beach Ball" nighttime extravaganzas at Typhoon Lagoon water park and the "One Mighty Party" events held at the Disney/MGM Studios theme park.

While Disney would obviously prefer to frame Gay Days as just a vacation and not a political statement, why the gay community would promote this viewpoint is not initially as obvious. A simplistic argument would be to accuse those in the gay community surrounding Orlando of being influenced by the conservative environment in which they live and work. Situated in the midst of the "Bible Belt," parts of the Orlando area harbor strong sentiments against homosexuality. Hence the desire to present Gay Days as apolitical might be an attempt to diminish its importance. Although some of this may apply, such reasoning makes sweeping and generalized assumptions about homosexuals in the area. Further, "Gay Days" now attracts people from across the country (and even outside the United States) and has been a source of major media attention—so the "apolitical" framework has certainly not kept the event hidden. A stronger argument can be made that the concept of "just fun" actually has a subtle political goal in mind. In claiming to be apolitical, the planners seem to hope to bring down homophobic defenses. If successful, "Gay Days" may advance general public acceptance of homosexuals. While repeating constantly that there is no agenda, the *2002 Program* also ends its welcome with a somewhat overt announcement of what "Gay Days" hopes to accomplish. "By the end of the day most will come to realize that we are 'just people.' . . . Remember, it's not us versus them. It is quite simply 'we the people.' Collectively, we are all part of the human family."[25] Referencing the U.S. Constitution reveals the potential political benefits for the gay community that lie within such a supposedly apolitical discourse.

Of course, this essay is not the first to recognize the ideological implications of fun, and the fun of Gay Days is quite ideologically overdetermined. Since Gay Days at Disney World are held during regular park hours, and not as a private event, homosexuals and heterosexuals are copresent—but with queers tending to outnumber straights. The sense of liberation is thus not only in the freedom to show same-sex affection but in being able to consider heterosexuals as the minority group. Such a reversal of balance also allows traditionally marginal viewpoints to be more strongly expressed throughout the parks. A participant in the 1998 Gay Days described some of the alternate reading strategies employed:

> When you put 100,000 gay people within [the park], . . . even familiar rides take on whole new connotations. The dark solitude of the "cars" at the Haunted Mansion, for example weren't so much an attraction as an opportunity. Gives the term "thrill ride" a whole new meaning. . . . At what other time of year could I have gotten applause in The Hall of Presidents for booing a certain jelly bean loving individual? And the fabulous EPCOT attraction, Ellen's Energy Adventure . . . became like a gathering of disciples come to worship. As an additional bonus, waiting on lines . . . becomes a lot more fun when you can spend the time cruising.[26]

One of the most popular events each year occurs on Thursday night at the Mannequins nightclub at Disney World's Pleasure Island complex. As the gay zine *4Front* noted, "Unofficially, Mannequins is gay every Thursday,"[27] attracting the gay employees at the resort as well as the rest of the queer community in the Orlando area. During "Gay Days," the club becomes literally packed to the rafters, having to open out onto a patio area to contain the crowds that willfully disregard the signs demanding that people not take off their shirts. The fact that Pleasure Island's name was originally used in Disney's *Pinocchio* for a land of excess, ribaldry, and overt lawlessness seems ironically to apply to the general atmosphere, as partyers at Mannequins often gleefully fail to follow the self-policing advice written up in every year's program.

Such ideas of fun have enraged groups antagonistic to gay rights, groups refusing to accept the apolitical discourse about Gay Days promoted by the organizers and implicitly endorsed by Disney. The growing crowds wearing red T-shirts (or no shirts) soon attracted the notice of religious conservatives, who launched a media campaign against the event in 1994. Although protesters did not appear in front of the park's gates, David Caton, director of the American Family Association, told reporters that the AFA had sent "non-confrontational observers" (possibly in an attempt to intimidate some patrons as well as to take notes on how Disney itself dealt with the "homosexual element").[28] Protests against Gay Days grew over the next few years and were a strong factor in leading the Southern Baptist Convention to announce a boycott of the Walt Disney Company in 1997. In 1998, Operation Rescue, ostensibly an antiabortion group, planned to protest outside Walt Disney World during that summer's Gay Days weekend, and attempted to charter a private airplane to circle the park with the banner "Jesus Saves." (Similarly, a Christian conversion-therapy group tried to get legal clearance to fly a banner over the park during the 2003 Gay Days.) In 1999 and again in 2001, members of the Christian Action Network surreptitiously videotaped the parties at Mannequins, attempting to embarrass Disney and enrage conservative stockholders.[29] Intriguingly, though, an Associated Press report in 2001 referred to the videotapers as "Christian guerillas," indicating that the Christian fundamentalists, rather than the homosexuals, were now being perceived as interlopers.

Both Disney and the organizers of "Gay Days" have attempted to downplay the demonstrations against the event through a variety of strategies. One method has been to reassert the idea of apolitical "fun." Doug Swallow responded to the videotaping by the Christian Action Network by wondering "why they're so intent on doing this, that they would go to extremes to ruin someone's vacation."[30] Disney has also reiterated that this is no company-organized event, that people are just "on vacation" and everyone is welcome. By refusing to let the demonstrators alter the structure of the discourse, the political benefits of being "apolitical" also continue. In advising attendees to "treat all others in the park with kindness, most especially those who are not kindly toward you. Take the higher ground!"[31] the strategy of defining the situation as apolitical works to make the demonstrators look petty and hateful, and the queer visitors as sweet and well behaved. As the *2002 Program* proudly states, "The espionage efforts have proven expensive and ineffectual. The Southern Baptist boycott has been pretty much a failure, and Pat Robertson's dire warnings of hell and brimstone have failed to set the city on fire. Now, . . . the Mayor of Orlando and the Chairman of the Board of County Commissioners have offered Gay Days visitors a hearty welcome."[32] Such a description implies that, repeated pronouncements of "just having fun" notwithstanding, some sort of political battle was being waged, and that "in the end, persistence, tolerance and economics won out."[33] It is this last plank, "economics," that still needs to be addressed, for nowhere are the political ramifications of the latest round of Gay Days more pronounced than in the event's ties to consumer culture and late capitalism.

Gay Days as Circuit Event

One of the major methods Christian fundamentalists began using to protest against Disney's growing acceptance of homosexual employees and customers was through the pocketbook. The American Family Association in 1998 planned to picket Disney stores, and the year before the Southern Baptists passed a resolution to boycott all of Disney. With fundamentalists boycotting on one side and thousands of queer customers spending money on Disney on the other, the economic dimension of Gay Days becomes vital to discuss. "Just having fun" means opening up the pocketbook, and in the political economy of Orlando, tourist dollars pull a lot of weight. (The entire state of Florida is highly structured around tourism: the lack of a state income tax is partly made up for in the state budget by a high sales tax paid by both state residents and tourists.) The events of 2002 reportedly infused the local economy with over $90 million. Representatives for Gay Days were being interviewed by the media to talk about "economic impact and entertainment value rather than conflict and comets from hell."[34] Such a statement points out how economic power could be wielded against the fundamentalists. Hotels and motels began signing a "Gay Days Friendly Pledge" to get in on the potential cash windfall, and 2002 saw the first corporate sponsors of Gay Days: Bud Light and Showtime.

Orlando had been a relatively small town in the 1960s, with its economy mainly focused on livestock. The debut of Walt Disney World in 1971 changed the community practically overnight, and now the surrounding area is littered with motels, hotels, theme restaurants, and a variety of theme parks and water parks competing with Disney World (including Universal Studios/Orlando and Sea World). With so many people working in the tourist/service industry, it is not surprising that the members of CompuWho? (the Orlando lesbian/gay Internet group) would conceive of a group meeting as a theme park excursion in 1991. Gay Days at Disney World also began when the homosexual community at large entered a new economic phase in its history, what many at the time joyously proclaimed as the "Queer Moment" of the early 1990s. With the presidential election of Bill Clinton in 1992, hopes soared that a new era of acceptance was on the horizon. The critical attention being given to New Queer Cinema and the inclusion of more and more homosexual characters on network TV (climaxing in the "coming out" of the main character on *Ellen* in 1997 and the debut of *Will and Grace* in 1998) seemed to reinforce that outlook. Yet, one of the most recognizable features of this Queer Moment was the attention that homosexuals began receiving not from politicians but from businesses. The 1990s saw the explosion of target marketing toward gay consumers, treating them as a niche group for selling music, movies, fashion, and alcohol. Items such as Pride Beer, "lesbian chic" fashion, and the variety of pink-triangle and rainbow-colored knickknacks indicated that homosexuals would increasingly be defined not as political activists but as a consumer base.

Stuart Ewen speaks of modern industrial capitalism (and the advertising that supports it) endowing the mass audience with an "industrial democracy"—in which the individual is made to believe that freedom and equality are defined as the ability to consume and acquire, effectively supplanting the desire for actual social reform.[35] A dissatisfied individual is encouraged to create change not through collective protest and revolt but through individual consumption, which only reinforces the established system that made the individual dissatisfied initially. With regard to the call for gay rights, the influx of corporate interest in the gay community encourages lesbians and gay men to show their pride and political commitment by buying a solid gold AIDS ribbon, a rainbow bumper sticker, or a vacation package for Gay Days at Disney World rather than protesting for domestic partner benefits or national health care. The *Gay Day 2K Pride Guide* points out that it named itself a "pride guide" because of the lack of any other Gay Pride events in the Orlando area that year—that Orlando did not hold a Pride parade in 1999 or 2000.

One of the major growth areas in attracting homosexual consumers is the travel/tourist industry. The number of lesbian and gay cruises escalated through the 1990s, and lesbian/gay travel guides became so numerous that many gay bookstores gave them their own section—and in 2003 that section would include *Queens in the Kingdom: The Ultimate Gay and Lesbian Guide to the Disney Theme Parks*.[36] Gay Days at Disney World has profited handsomely from the growth of gay tourism. Possibly the best example of this rise in gay tourism is the development of what is commonly referred to as "the circuit." Beginning in the late 1980s as parties to raise funds for AIDS research and care, events like the White Party in Miami soon proliferated around the globe and morphed into extravagant blowouts for thousands of revelers, most of them no longer organized as AIDS benefits. The term "circuit" developed as the parties began being planned so as not to compete with each other, and partygoers could "do the circuit," traveling every weekend to the next town for the next wild weekend. Miami Beach quickly became one of the main circuit destinations, with a thriving gay community and a highly developed tourist industry. By 1996, Miami's party promoters extended the circuit to Orlando and Gay Days. The success of Jeffrey Sanker's "One Mighty Party" private events at the Disney/MGM Studios soon made Gay Days a major circuit stop. Currently, circuit party events happen almost every night of the six-day event. By 2001, "The Circuit Dog," a website devoted to the circuit, had awarded events at Gay Days four different awards, including Best Circuit Party, Best Runner-Up, and Best Weekend.[37]

The circuit has evolved into a subculture with its own slang, zines, and spaces. It has also become the subject of major discussion in the gay community over the past decade as it has come to dominate conceptions of gay male social life. A number of articles in the gay press, as well as books and films like *Circuit* (2002) and *When Boys Fly* (2002), have attempted to address "circuit culture." The general attitude toward the circuit within the gay community can be described as ambivalent. A number of people (including myself) often disparage circuit culture; at the same time, many gay men (including myself) are simultaneously attracted to it. Criticisms often focus on two aspects. First, circuit parties are notorious for heavy drug use (the alphabet soup of E or X, K, and G or B, as well as crystal meth), and many of the first major analyses in the gay press about the circuit resulted from overdoses, comas, and deaths on the dance floors at some of the events. The second criticism revolves around the sense that, in order to be accepted at a circuit party, one has to conform to a certain body image: beautiful, highly muscled with incredibly low body fat. Defenders of the circuit attempt to minimize these aspects in favor of the "tribal" sense of family they feel at the circuit. Certainly one can experience that sense of bonding, and people *do* attend events completely sober and/or not conforming to the muscle-boy look. Yet the attraction to the circuit is often based precisely in the wild abandon of music, lights, and a highly sexualized environment that drugs and perfect bodies help reinforce.

These factors have forced Gay Days to negotiate its growing association with the circuit. The *Gay Day 2K Pride Guide* tried to describe the circuit parties held during the week as inclusive: "A misconception about the circuit party scene is that one has to be a certain type or classification to enjoy the night's festivities. . . . Gay Day weekend has distinguished itself purely as a 'gay' event—not just a muscle-boy event. . . . This is a celebration of all lifestyles." Further, in describing the Beach Ball event at the Typhoon Lagoon water park, the *Guide* announces, "This isn't an evening about high profile DJs spinning. And it doesn't revolve around the fear of a pill not kicking in at the appropriate time."[38] Evidence at the event itself in 2000 proved mightily to the contrary. Admittedly, one could find an example of almost every subgroup within the queer community wandering around Typhoon Lagoon that night. Predominantly, though, muscle boys in skimpy shorts populated the scene, and the usual party enhancements were being discreetly consumed in the locker areas of the park. The aforementioned article also forgets, by the fifth paragraph, its opening argument that Gay Days is not about circuit-star DJs and muscled bodies, announcing "circuit sensation DJ Manny Lehman" spinning at the House of Blues for an evening entitled "Muscle and Sweat," describing how the Magic Journeys party at Arabian Nights in Kissimmee "flexes its circuit muscle," and listing every major DJ spinning at all the other parties that weekend.[39] The *Guide* actually includes a separate article listing, quoting, and describing each and every DJ.[40]

Disney has remained mum about the links between Gay Days and the circuit, although the video taken in 1999 by the Christian Action Network at Mannequins of two male stage dancers performing simulated sex may have led to making certain the dancers reined in their behavior in subsequent years. This silence not only keeps Disney from being forced to answer uncomfortable questions but also allows Disney to keep raking in the profits from such circuit events. The Beach Ball and One Mighty Party events (not to mention Thursday nights at Mannequins) bring an avalanche of cash to Disney every year. Further, while the drugs and sex that accompany the circuit may not be condoned by Disney (or, at least officially, the promoters), the concept of the circuit is fully in line with the discourse of fun that has defined these latest Gay Days. Circuit events are moments for enjoyment and not politics.

Yet just as the supposedly apolitical framework of Gay Days obscures the political work of assimilation and acceptance, so too does this discourse work to obscure how capitalist interests may affect issues of sexuality. Using major vacation sites as spaces to expose and celebrate sexual diversity amid the general population may create a sense of liberation for those in attendance; having to pay to do so complicates how liberating these events are. Frederic Jameson contends that this latest stage of capitalism now isolates and commodifies time, space, and even psychic spaces or definitions of identity.[40] As Bill Short writes: "Many of us who wish to maintain a gay identity, actually *buy* that identity. . . . We are forced to prove we exist by projecting a gay image or lifestyle."[42] Consequently, when engaged in marketing to homosexuals, corporate interests attempt to define the identity of the gay community, defining it to suit their own needs. Events such as Gay Days exemplify how the relationship between homosexuality and capitalism is a constant tension between autonomy and exploitation. The gay community tries to use capitalism to advance its causes, but the community is simultaneously used by corporations interested mainly (if not solely) in profit. While the apolitical discourse may work covertly to help win acceptance by corporations and citizens, it also ensures that the community will police itself and not detract from Disney's goal of attracting tourists' dollars.

Corporate interests also work to define who gets to be regarded as part of the homosexual community. Karen Stabiner's research into the beginnings of gay marketing in the early 1980s revealed that the boundaries of the gay market as defined by corporate interests were very narrow. "Seventy percent of [the 1980 *Advocate* readership survey] . . . were between the ages of 20 and 40, and their annual median income in 1980 was $30,000 . . . 28 percent . . . earned over $40,000 in 1980, while nationally, the number of men earning over $35,000 was only 6.9 percent."[43] Furthermore, she pointed out that "most people who talk about the 'gay market' make the implicit assumption that it is a male market."[44] Such concepts of a "gay market" held into the 1990s and the "Queer Moment." In a 1995 promotional video, the gay-owned marketing firm Ron/Owen and Associates asserted to its potential clients that the average homosexual made over $50,000 a year, while showing images of almost exclusively white men—and nobody over thirty-five years old. While a more recent study done at the University of Maryland by economist Lee Badgett revised those figures downward ($34,000 for gay men, $20,000 for lesbians),[45] businesses still tend to consider "the gay consumer" to be a young, white middle- or upper-middle-class man. All those who define themselves as homosexual but do not fit these additional parameters are not considered or addressed (and there is no conception of such "queer" individuals as bisexuals or transgendered persons). The cycle of "lesbian chic" in the 1990s widened the circle only slightly to include young, white, moneyed lesbians. The few women appearing in the Ron/Owen presentation, for example, fit this narrow conception of the lesbian consumer.

The gay circuit supports rather than resists this conception of "the gay market." Staying on the circuit requires a lot of money—flying all over the globe, making hotel reservations, paying close to $100 (sometimes more) per event, as well as spending money on the right outfits and the right drugs (which could include steroids) for every party. Circuit events often create an atmosphere of "more"—more bodies, more music, more lights, more everything. Although people from across the globe attend circuit parties, thus ensuring a variety of racial, ethnic, and national identities, global capitalist economics tend to privilege the "white" people, who still usually make up the largest percentage of circuit goers. Also, while not absolute, the circuit is primarily a gay male environment.

As part of the circuit, the first weekend in June at Walt Disney World is susceptible to falling into this exclusionary pattern. The title itself serves as a perfect example: "Gay Days." Although both women and men were part of the Orlando Internet group that met that first time in 1991, by the end of the decade gay men seemed to have taken over. The subheading for the 2000 *Guide* article titled "Gay Day for Grrls" pointed out, "This first weekend in June is for 'family' in Orlando, but somehow there always seems to be more brothers than sisters. Where are all the women?"[46] The article reported that "women's events put on by outside production companies haven't caught on due to their lack of local promotion," and actually suggested venturing away from Disney World in order to find lesbian life![47] Such feelings of exclusion have not been limited to lesbians. At a Gay Day in 1998, one male customer entered the park in drag—and was "politely but firmly steered into a store on Main Street USA to pick out other apparel" (although Disney did agree to pay for it.)[48] Four years later, in 2002, the *Orlando Sentinel* interviewed an African American man "attending [his] first Gay Days in search of events that didn't target only single white men."[49] Gay Days planners did attempt to address the lack of attention to women's events in 2001, by hiring female party promoters Alison Burgos and Pandora to organize the "Girls in Wonderland" event, with headliner DJs, a light show, live performances, and go-go dancers.[50] In 2002, more parties were lined up for women (even though male events still outnumber female ones). Hence, the terms of the circuit were revised, but not replaced.

By marketing only to a select group of people within the homosexual community, advertising prizes this subgroup and holds its members as representative—an ideal that the lesbian or gay subject is taught to measure him or herself by. Writers such as Mary Ann Doane have discussed how traditionally the female has been constructed in economic terms as both consumer of commodities (subject) and as commodity herself (object), that "all consumerism involves the ideal of self-image."[51] In order to "be" a "true" woman, the female consumer is urged to consume—to buy cosmetics, clothes, perfume, etc., which will transform the body—usually with the fetishized female body presented directly in the ad. Marketing thus works not only to describe and promote the product but also to describe and promote a specific type of identity, an identity that will conform to the needs of modern industrial society—a "commodity self," as Ewen terms it.[52] One can easily expand this concept beyond the female body to images of masculinity, of sexuality, of race, and of class. Part of the criticism within the gay community (and beyond) of circuit culture is in how the young, white, muscle-boy image makes many who do not fit that look dislike themselves and their bodies. Ads aimed at white, middle- or upper-middle-class gay male consumers thus affect not just those within the targeted group. By teaching them to admire this image, these ads also send messages to nonwhite, working-class queer individuals that they are somehow "less valuable." As a consequence, when the slogan for the 2002 Gay Days was "It's All About You!" the issue of who got to be included in that pronoun was up for debate. The program may have touted the event as celebrating "quite simply 'we the people,'" but some people have been getting more attention than others.

Conclusion: Which Gay Days Did You Attend?

Although the political economy of this latest incarnation of Gay Days (at both parks) seems to circumscribe how the event is supposed to be understood (and, to a degree, who is encouraged to attend), the actual events reveal a diversity of experience. In fact, Gay Days has expanded so much that currently different guests can have totally different vacations. While one person can spend a different day at each of the multiple parks in the Disney resort (as well as Sea World and Universal), another person can spend the entire time doing nothing but going from circuit party to circuit party without ever once getting on a ride. Lesbians now have an entire separate schedule of women-centered events.

The proliferation of opportunities mirrors the multiplicity of identities as well. While the official *2002 Program* focused almost exclusively on circuit events and the men (and now separately, women) that attend them, one could easily find noncircuit types roaming around. Bears (hirsute, heavier and/or older men) were conspicuously in attendance at the Magic Kingdom, particularly in front of the Country Bear Jamboree for an unofficial gathering early Saturday afternoon.[53] While circuit boys crowded the official host hotels for Gay Days, a number of lesbian and gay parents with children stayed at various Disney hotels. The Family Pride Coalition announced through its website its own schedule for queer families to meet each other at various points during the weekend. The gay Catholic organization Dignity also arranged for a gay-accepting mass to be said on Saturday evening at the Grosvenor Resort just outside the Disney World grounds.

The involvement of Dignity and the Family Pride Coalition has also underlined that, regardless of the promoters' attempts, not every one of the 125,000 or more who attend agree to abide by the conception of Gay Days as apolitical. The year 2002 saw a rising scandal in the American Catholic Church over priests sexually abusing children, and some looking for scapegoats (including a few church authorities) associated these revelations with homosexuality in the priesthood. A Dignity mass at Gay Days in the midst of these revelations could not help but remind people of these issues. Similarly, the presence of lesbian and gay parents at Gay Days in 2002 provided an easy reminder that Florida prohibits homosexual adoption of children. Rosie O'Donnell made national news only months before when she came out of the closet in order to support gay and lesbian parents trying to challenge this statute. One local Orlando television news program framed its coverage of Gay Days around this issue, interviewing a gay couple wanting to adopt with Cinderella's Castle poised right behind the duo.

The *Orlando Sentinel* also framed its 2002 coverage around a current issue in gay rights: the fight to legalize gay marriage.[54] On Thursday, May 30, 2002, Steven Hoff and Jeffrey Carlson commemorated their third anniversary of meeting (at the 1999 Gay Days) by holding a wedding ceremony at one of the host hotels. The wedding was even hosted by the organizers of Gay Days, inviting everyone to attend and providing a DJ for the reception. The ceremony exemplifies how Disney World's Gay Days can use its apolitical discourse toward political ends: while the ceremony consciously entered the debate over gay marriage, it also functioned as just another celebration. As the *Sentinel* reported, "Carlson and Hoff did not intend for their ceremony to be a political statement."[55]

Therefore, while Gay Days has expanded in scope and meaning, it has remained within the apparently apolitical framework that the tourist economies of Disney and the Orlando area prefer. If anything, the diversity of Gay Days refers more to the increased methods of spending—going beyond even Disney itself. By 2002, it was literally impossible to attend all the events scheduled, because various parties were often in competition, particularly the number of events being held at Universal in an attempt to woo some of the tourist money away from Disney. The range of events, while sometimes acknowledging the diversity of people that fell within the definition of "the gay community," also functioned to further break this group down into marketable niches. Whether gay male or lesbian, single or with kids, somebody had something to sell to you.

The increasingly rampant attempts to squeeze every possible cent out of gay customers became so heated that a potential crisis point happened during the Gay Days of 2003. A circuit party held at the Hard Rock Coliseum at Universal Studios almost turned into a riot. The party promoters reportedly oversold tickets for the event. By 11:00 PM, usually when such parties are just beginning, security felt the venue was at capacity and refused to let anyone else enter. Huge crowds were outraged, and some minor confrontations occurred as people who had already paid their money angrily tried to storm the entrance. On a less volatile scale, customers who went to the annual Beach Ball event at Disney World's Typhoon Lagoon were met with no music for the first few hours because someone had reportedly not brought phonograph needles for the DJ. On various websites and chat rooms throughout the week of activities, people wrote in steaming about how they felt cheated out of their money.[56] Some have even suggested that 2003's Gay Days were an indication that "the Golden Age of the Circuit" has come to a close.[57] Only a few months later though, on October 4, 2003, Dutch gay magazine *Gay Krant* sponsored the first Gay Day at the Paris Disneyland.[58]

As the events of 2003 show, the balancing act between using and being used by corporate capitalism continues unabated. A final image from 2002 seems to encapsulate how the political economy of Gay Days functions for both the queer community and Disney. Among that year's red-shirted attendees at the Magic Kingdom were a male and female pushing a carriage with child. Such individuals exemplify the notion of "queer." Were they a gay male and the straight mother of his child? A lesbian and the straight father of her child? A gay man and lesbian who were this child's parents? Or were they a heterosexual family who were showing support and acceptance of their fellow homosexual guests? Or something else? It did not seem to matter. In a way, that is empowering and a step forward politically. But, what did matter—at least to Disney—was that the couple and child paid to enter the park.

Notes

1. David Koenig, *Mouse Tales: A Behind-the-Ears Look at Disneyland* (Irvine, Calif.: Bonaventure Press, 1994), 134.
2. Personal interview with the author, name withheld by request (March 13, 1994).
3. Personal interview with Sue Schiebler, Los Angeles, Calif. (May 31, 1994).
4. Most lesbian and gay historians regard the events around Stonewall as landmark. Instead of allowing themselves to be arrested in yet another bar raid by the New York

police, patrons of this Mafia-controlled gay bar fought back, instituting demonstrations that lasted for three nights. Allen Ginsberg would say, when viewing the area during the riots, "They've lost that wounded look that fags all had ten years ago." Word of this local incident rapidly spread to homosexual communities throughout the country, even though mainstream newspapers barely reported on the incident. Soon, a number of groups coalesced (mainly on college campuses such as UC Berkeley and Harvard) to organize political demonstrations for gay rights—groups like the Gay Liberation Front and the Gay Activists Alliance. For a wider history of this event, see Martin Duberman, *Stonewall* (New York: Dutton, 1993).

5. For more on this era, see John D'Emilio and Estelle B. Friedman, *Intimate Matters: A History of Sexuality in America* (New York: Harper & Row, 1988), 318–325.

6. Disneyland decided to tone down the jocular portrayal of rape presented in the Pirates of the Caribbean ride in 1996 by altering the scenes to intimate that the pirates were after the *food* the women were carrying. Certain customers complained about the change, claiming that chasing women was what pirates did historically. None of these complainers seemed to want the historical accuracy to include pirates chasing after young boys as well. Currently, at both parks, the scene has been changed yet again so that now the women are chasing the pirates with brooms. Similarly, the Jungle Cruise hosts have toned down the sexism of the patter. Intriguingly, the parks tried to introduce female ride operators in the 1990s but returned to male operators when it was perceived that having women tell the typical type of jokes didn't work.

7. For more on lesbian culture in the 1970s, see Lillian Faderman, *Odd Girls and Twilight Lovers: A History of Lesbian Life in Twentieth-Century America* (New York: Penguin, 1992), 215–245.

8. Koenig, *Mouse Tales,* 209.

9. Frank Browning, *The Culture of Desire: Paradox and Perversity in Gay Lives Today* (New York: Vintage Books, 1993), 72–73, discusses the group and its visit to the park in more detail.

10. Joe Flower, *Prince of the Magic Kingdom: Michael Eisner and the Re-making of Disney* (New York: John Wiley and Sons, 1991), 96.

11. Ibid., 188.

12. Steven Gaines, "Will the Mouse Come Out," *Buzz* 6, no. 4 (May 1995): 68.

13. Rick Vanderknyff, "Ronnie, Mickey Mark Disneyland Milestone Theme Park," *Los Angeles Times,* January 12, 1990, A6.

14. Jeff Truesdell, "How Gay Day Pushed Disney Out of the Closet," *Orlando Weekly,* June 1–7, 2000, 16.

15. "Survivor—Gay Days," *Gay DayS 2002 Program,* 14.

16. Scott Smith and Kirk Hartlage, "Why Gay Day 2K," *GD2K Pride Guide,* June 1–5, 2000, 11.

17. Truesdell, "How Gay Day," 17.

18. Smith and Hartlage, "Gay Day 2K," 11.

19. "12th Annual Gay Day in The Magic Kingdom," *Gay DayS 2002 Program,* 28.

20. Truesdell, "How Gay Day," 17–18.

21. Ibid., 18.

22. Smith and Hartlage, "Gay Day 2K," 12.

23. "12th Annual Gay Day," 28.

24. An example of Disney's official response comes from Disney spokesperson Rena Callahan, who told a reporter that "Gay Days" is "not a Disney-sponsored event and our parks are open to everyone everyday." Mike Schneider, "'Christian Guerillas' Infiltrate Gay Days," Associated Press (June 1, 2001), reprinted at www.gayday.com/news/2001/ap_000601a.asp.

25. "12th Annual Gay Day," 28.

26. Eddie Shapiro, "Gayety in the Magic Kingdom: Even the Wrath of Pat Couldn't Stop the Fun," *4Front Magazine* 3, no. 24 (August 19, 1998): 12–13.

27. Shapiro, "Gayety in the Magic Kingdom," 13.

28. "Gay Day at Disney World Goes Off Without Incident, Park Aide Reports," *Los Angeles Times,* June 5, 1994, A21.

29. Schneider, "Christian Guerillas."

30. Ibid.

31. "12th Annual Gay Day," 28.

32. "Survivor—Gay Days," 15.

33. Ibid.

34. Ibid., 14.

35. Stuart Ewen, *Captains of Consciousness: Advertising and the Social Roots of Consumer Culture* (New York: McGraw-Hill, 1976).

36. Jeffrey Epstein and Eddie Shapiro, *Queens in the Kingdom: The Ultimate Gay and Lesbian Guide to the Disney Theme Parks* (Los Angeles: Alyson Books, 2003). The book is a general "year-round" guide rather than a guide to Gay Days events at either park.

37. As reported on the Gay Days website, www.gayday.com/default.as.

38. Tony Hayden, "Plugging into the Gay Day Circuit," *GD2K Pride Guide,* June 1–5, 2000, 26.

39. Ibid., 26–27.

40. Kirk Hartlage, "You Spin Me Right Round, Baby," *GD2K Pride Guide,* June 1–5, 2000, 29–31.

41. Frederic Jameson, "Postmodernism, or the Cultural Logic of Late Capitalism," *New Left Review* 146 (July/August 1984): 78.

42. Bill Short, "Queers, Beers and Shopping," *Gay Times* 170 (November 1992): 20.

43. Karen Stabiner, "Tapping the Homosexual Market," *New York Times Magazine,* May 2, 1982, 36.

44. Ibid., 74.

45. Jeremy Quittner, "Where to Put Your Money," *Advocate* (April 30, 2002): 33.

46. Jenn Gargiulo, "Gay Day for Grrls," *GD2K Pride Guide,* June 1–5, 2000, 34.

47. Ibid., 38.

48. Truesdell, "How Gay Day," 17.

49. Kelly Brewington, " 'Holy Union' Accents Gay Days," *Orlando Sentinel,* May 31, 2002, B1.

50. "What's a Girl to Do?" *Gay DayS 2002 Program,* 26.

51. Mary Ann Doane, "The Economy of Desire: The Commodity Form in/of the Cinema," *QRFV* 11, no. 1 (1989): 30.

52. Ewen, *Captains of Consciousness,* 36.

53. With the elimination of the Country Bear Jamboree attraction, the gathering place for gay male bears has become the Winnie-the-Pooh attraction in Fantasyland.

54. Brewington, "Holy Union."

55. Ibid.

56. Among the websites consulted during the week was http://www.gayday.com/forum/topic.asp?t=1205, which included posts such as "The point is Mark Baker & Gay Days.com [the party promoters] are in it only for the money. ONLY THE MONEY," from "Kevin Marks" (June 14, 2003) and "I feel lucky now that I stopped the gym and my circuit boy career now that I see the problems created by these blood suckers that prey on the well to do gay boys," from "ftlvorlons" (June 14, 2003). Note that GayDayS.com and gayday.com are not the same organization.

57. While not laying the blame solely on the 2003 Gay Days debacle, Tony Hayden from thecircuitdog.com writes in "The Golden Age of the Circuit" (April 29, 2004), "Gay Day Disney is everything that is wrong with today's party scene. . . . Before the anti-Christ could walk and talk I'm sure he was a cute baby as Gay Day Disney once was. But it grew into something ugly, Wal-mart'ish and threatening to its own scene. . . . Gay Day Disney's radiant glow was SO BRIGHT that it practically burned several HIV/AIDS charitable parties right off of the circuit calendar" (http://www.thecircuitdog.com).

58. "Disneyland 'Gay Day' Idea Crosses the Atlantic," *Reuters Newsline,* October 5, 2003, found at http://in.news.yahoo.com/031005/137/287an.html.

6

Anglophilia and the Discreet Charm of the English Voice in Disney's *Pocahontas* Films

Radha Jhappan and Daiva Stasiulis

Introduction

Recent Disney animated feature films such as *Pocahontas* (1995) and *Mulan* (1997) and Dreamworks's *Prince of Egypt* (1998) have attempted to move beyond the white solipsism and Eurocentrism of previous productions (such as the widely criticized *Aladdin* [1992]) and to offer more "sympathetic" portrayals of racialized "Others." In fact, most of the critical commentary about these films has focused on the constructions, be they friendly or hostile, of the racialized "other." In the case of *Pocahontas,* for example, analyses have largely centered on the colonial imaginary of "civilized" white settlers and American "Indian" "savages" disrupted by a Native American heroine (also a corrective to the customary androcentrism). Various reviewers and scholars have examined the distortions of the historical record (such as it is) of Pocahontas's life, Smith's possibly fictitious account of his "rescue" by her,[1] continued stereotyping of Native Americans, and the cultural politics of the babelicious Buckskin Barbie body the Disney Imagineers conjured from the Noble Savage branch of white mythology about indigenous Americans.[2] Some have even commented

151

on how "an episode historians have characterized as a genocide against the Powhatan Indians is reworked into a thrilling, bitter-sweet adventure/love story between a busty native *Babewatch*-style gal and her commanding white lover, who looks like a dancer from Chippendale's."[3]

The construction of whiteness, indeed Britishness, in Pocahontas, and particularly in the 1998 made-for-home-video sequel, *Pocahontas II: Journey to a New World*, has, by way of contrast, received very little critical analysis. The relative inattention to the construction of the British in *Pocahontas I* is perhaps understandable, given that this was Disney's first conscious attempt to present a sensitive and more culturally accurate image of an indigenous nation. Moreover, scholars have generally concentrated on high-profile theatrically released feature films rather than their straight-to-video sequels, even though children probably see the latter nearly as much as they see the originals with higher production values. While the important breakthrough in the *Pocahontas* films is Disney's attempt to present a sympathetic and respectful portrait of Native Americans, it is arguably almost as significant that, for the first time in a mainstream American animated feature film, the whites are not necessarily the good guys. In fact, the two *Pocahontas* films engage the issue of racial/cultural superiority by questioning the white/English claim to civilization versus savagery.[4]

Scholars working in the field of whiteness studies remind us that whiteness is invisible and ubiquitous in dominant/white discourse. Whiteness is usually represented as prototypical, normative, the default human norm. Other people are raced, whereas white people are just people. As Dyer notes, "there is no more powerful position than that of being 'just' human. The claim to power is the claim to speak for the commonality of humanity. . . . Raced people can't do that—they can only speak for their race."[5] "The equation of being white with being human," Dyer argues, "secures a position of power."[6] Disney's *Pocahontas* films appear to be decentering and/or racializing whites in general, and the British in particular, through four principal textual strategies: (a) showing how, from the cultural viewpoint of American "Indians," it is the white British who are savages and barbarians; (b) offering dual viewpoints, or alternating the action and point of view between Pocahontas/the Powhatans and Smith or Rolfe/the English; (c) decentering the myth of whiteness as the pinnacle of physical beauty and courage in offering up Pocahontas as the beautiful and fearless "other"; and (d) depicting an interracial heterosexual romance and thus challenging taboos against miscegenation. The question raised by these two postmodern texts is: are they dislodging whites from the position of power by undercutting the authority with which they speak and act in and on the world? Our response to this question is that, in spite of studied efforts at cultural relativism in *Pocahontas I* and *II*, the answer is no. The films ultimately absolve the

English and thus whites of the history of colonial genocide. This end is accomplished by adopting key assumptions of Anglophilia, namely, that despite the odd quirk or anomalous behavior by isolated individuals, English culture represents the pinnacle of civilization.

Our examination of one recurring aspect of Disney animated features, namely, the implicit equation of Britishness with civilization, high culture, knowledge, intelligence, erudition, and authority, suggests that Disney, like other corporate cultural producers, plays into and thus reinforces residual North American Anglophilia (the elevation of things British, from the royal family to English culture, literature, language, actors, films, television, and other cultural products). Anglophilia is seemingly an international phenomenon, but it is particularly virulent in (formerly British) white settler colonies such as the United States, Canada, and Australia. As Aristides points out, in America it appears in many guises: in movies wherein "the English came off as the most suave, most intelligent, most heroic of fighters"; in the modeling of elitist American schools on English prep schools and Oxbridge; in the preference for the teaching of English over American literature and for English theater and writing of all sorts; in imported conceptions of "honor, courage, romance, and decency"; and in the adoration of English speech, accents, pronunciation, locutions, and use of language, such that "a good English accent can still be worth an additional ten to thirty thousand dollars in an annual academic salary."7 Anglophilia presents an image of the English as brilliant, sensible, fair-minded, decent folk, positively brimming with goodwill, good humor, common sense, administrative genius, courage, and the stiff upper lips needed to fulfill their "duty" to "civilize" the world.

Anglophilia is neither unique to the *Pocahontas* films nor merely a result of their subject matter (the "encounter" between the Powhatans and the British). On the contrary, it is a common feature of Disney and other American cultural products. Of note, for example, are the British voices in other Disney animated films where the cultural context does not call for them. Indeed, it has become a virtual Disney convention to have male lead characters in positions of power/authority voiced by British actors (for example, the vaguely British accent of the Sultan in *Aladdin,* and Patrick Stewart as Pharaoh Seti I and Ralph Fiennes as Ramses in Dreamworks's *Prince of Egypt*). Even where such accents attach to evil (but powerful) characters—Jeremy Irons as Scar in *The Lion King* (1994) (a characterization no doubt inspired by George Sanders as Shere Khan in *The Jungle Book* [1967]), Tony Jay as Frollo in *The Hunchback of Notre Dame* (1997), and the Anglo-Arab voice of Jafar in *Aladdin* (1992)—they still function to mark the character off as possessing superior intelligence. In casts where the heroes and heroines almost invariably have American accents, what are the meanings coded within the casting of British voices in Disney animated films?

Shohat and Stam have drawn attention to the ideological import of sound and language in cinema, suggesting that "formulating the issue as one of voices and discourses helps us get past the 'lure' of the visual, to look beyond the epidermic surface of the text."[8] As a methodological alternative to the study of stereotyping of racial/ethnic oppressed communities within Hollywood films, they suggest that film scholars pay more attention to the aural aspects of film, including voices, intonation, and accents. As they further aver, "a voice is never merely a voice; it also relays a discourse, since even an individual voice is itself a discursive sum, a polyphony of voices."[9]

Scholars and cultural critics have virtually ignored the uses, functions, and meanings of spoken accents in animated films, though *Aladdin* elicited some commentary as its anti-Arab, anti-Muslim text relied on portrayals of Aladdin and Jasmine as essentially American-sounding teenagers, while the evil Arabs pointedly did *not* sport American accents.[10] But there has been no real analysis of such matters as the presumptive authority of specifically *English* speech (accents, pronunciation, locutions, and use of language); the assumption that the English voice signals intelligence, erudition, and sophistication; and the complex meanings inherent in that voice's association in animated features with malignant male power. Although the latter is beyond the scope of the present analysis, we would venture to explain it in terms of two factors: first, America's fundamental ambivalence toward its former rulers; second, America's anti-intellectualist popular culture that, in a Kantian sense, distrusts high intelligence and exalts medium or even lower intelligence combined with goodwill/nature/motivation. In Disney animated features, the American-sounding protagonists, regardless of their epidermal cast (whether wooden as in *Pinocchio,* furry as in *Lion King,* or brown-skinned as in *Aladdin*), are good-hearted, adventurous, and fun loving, rather than highly intelligent or wise.

Disney's Pocahontas Fable, Parts I and II

Disney's *Pocahontas,* the studio's first animated feature based on real historical figures and events, engages one of America's key foundational myths. Set in 1607, it opens with the voyage from London to the "New World" of a ship-full of gold-seeking "adventurers" led by the greedy governor of the Virginia Company, John Ratcliffe, and including an intrepid and handsome soldier named John Smith. Meanwhile, in Virginia, Pocahontas, the beautiful daughter of Chief Powhatan, ponders her path in life and dreams about what lies "just around the river bend." The British arrive on the shores of the Powhatan territory and immediately start digging up the countryside in a frenzied search for nonexistent gold. John Smith, in charge of security, scouts the area and meets Pocahontas. They soon overcome communication/language barriers (Pocahontas instantly becomes fluent in both the King's English and Broadway Musical Theater once she listens with her heart, as Grandmother Willow advises) and find that they are attracted to one another. She introduces him to a world he never knew he never knew, the natural world of rocks, trees, and creatures endowed with living spirits. However, relations between the British and the Powhatans are not so cordial. Governor Ratcliffe is convinced that the "Indians" are trying to prevent him from finding gold and prepares to eliminate them, once and for all. When the "Indians" capture Smith and prepare to execute him, Pocahontas throws herself in front of him, telling her father she loves Smith and asking him not to choose "the path of hatred." Smith is released, and combatants on both sides lower their weapons, save Ratcliffe, who shoots Smith, claiming that it was Smith's own fault for stepping into the line of fire.[11] The wounded Smith's only hope of survival is to return to England for treatment, and he and Pocahontas kiss and part with heavy hearts as he and his comrades return to London.

Disney's straight-to-video sequel of 1998, *Pocahontas II: Journey to a New World,* picks up several years later, and centers on Pocahontas's trip to the "old world." Again, the film opens in London, where, set up by Ratcliffe, Smith escapes arrest for treason by the King's guards. The King has dispatched John Rolfe to the New World to bring back the "Indian chief." As the ship arrives at Jamestown, Pocahontas is once again wondering, "where do I go from here?" and once again, she prevents war when an incident on the dock prompts the Indians to attack the English. As Powhatan refuses to cross the salt water to visit the King, he sends Pocahontas on the diplomatic mission to find out what the English want. Pocahontas is overwhelmed by everything about London, from the buildings to the people, fashions, streets, commerce, art, and even the cuisine! Though the King is angry that Rolfe has brought back a mere woman instead of the chief, Ratcliffe, anticipating that she will offend English etiquette, suggests that Pocahontas attend the Hunt Ball. The King decrees that if she can prove she is civilized, he will call off the armada that is about to go off to destroy her people. In a Pygmalion-like transformation, the powdered, corseted, and gowned Pocahontas charms the court, until a cruel entertainment with a tortured bear (set up by Ratcliffe) prompts her to accuse the English of barbarity, whereupon the King has her locked up in the Tower of London. Rolfe and Smith (who emerges from hiding) return the famous rescue favor by springing her from the Tower. She later climbs over the palace wall and warns the King that her people will fight to the last warrior, while Smith chimes in that there is no gold and that Ratcliffe has lied about everything. On the King's order that Ratcliffe must be stopped, Smith and Rolfe halt the armada in a swashbuckling finale. The film ends with Pocahontas and Rolfe kissing as they sail off into the sunset back to the New World, or "home" as he now calls it.

Textual Strategies Decentering "Whiteness"

Mutual Attributions of "Savagery"

As many have noted, in the *Pocahontas* films, Disney made an attempt to offer a sympathetic and respectful portrayal of the "Indians," even employing Native advisers[12] and Native actors, including one of the cofounders of the American Indian Movement, Russell Means.[13] More significantly, at least in terms of the focus of this discussion, Disney's portrayal of the English was surprisingly (though not wholly) *un*sympathetic. In an unprecedented display of cultural relativism, Disney's *Pocahontas* features fairly lengthy sequences and songs in which each side, English and Powhatan, attribute savagery in customs and manners to the other. Secondly, *Pocahontas* subtly undermines one of the key justifications for the Europeans' dispossession of the indigenous nations— that they were nomads who did not cultivate the land—by showing the Powhatans' well-tended corn and other crops (nontipi) permanent housing, etcetera. Thirdly, and critically, it problematizes, from the Native point of view, the behavior and attitudes of the English, particularly their alienation from nature, their greed, and their unquestioned assumptions of their right to ownership of other people's territories. From the beginning, the shaman's visions of the English reveal these qualities: "These men are not like us . . . they prowl the earth like ravenous wolves, consuming everything in their paths." Kekatough's prescience plays out when no sooner do they land than the English get to work digging ugly great holes in the ground and blowing up the trees as the odious Ratcliffe sings "It's gold and it's mine, mine, mine." Later, during their illicit liaison in the forest, after Smith tells Pocahontas that the English are going to build roads and "decent houses," that they have "improved the lives of savages all over the world," she sings an angry response that challenges his racist assumptions: first, of the Europeans' presumption of their inalienable right to the land of others ("You think you own whatever land you land in"); second, the presumption of European superiority/Native inferiority ("You think the only people who are people, are the people who look and think like you"); and third, his/their alienation from nature ("the earth is just a dead thing you can tame"). The English attitude is, of course, authorized in the Christian tradition where, in the opening book of the bible (Genesis 1:26), God says, "Let us make man in our image, after our likeness: and let them have dominion over the fish of the sea, and over the fowl of the air, and over the cattle, and over all the earth, and over every living thing that creepeth upon the earth." In contrast with the Christian/European "human dominion over nature" approach, Pocahontas's Native American spirituality sees humans as only one among many elements of creation, all of which are animated by spirit ("but I know every rock and tree and creature has a life, has a spirit, has a name").

The climax of the first *Pocahontas* comes as the two sides prepare for war, Ratcliffe's vocal stylings leading the English chorus, while Powhatan and Kekataugh direct the warriors. Each side tars the other with the "savagery" brush: Ratcliffe asks what can be expected of "filthy little heathens," "vermin" whose whole disgusting race is a curse." Echoing the infamous proverbial invective that "the only good Indian is a dead Indian" ("their skin's a hellish red, they're only good when dead"), the English chorus chants that these "dirty shrieking devils" are "savages, savages, barely even human, savages, savages, drive them from our shores." Interestingly, although the British have only just arrived, the lands of the Powhatan nation have already become British lands, "our shores." In almost a mirror image, the Powhatans characterize the British as "demons" who are only capable of feeling greed, since "beneath that milky hide, there's emptiness inside" and, because "they're different from us," they cannot be trusted. The scene terminates with each side insisting they must "sound the drums of war."

As the *Pocahontas* lyricist, Stephen Schwartz, put it, "'Savages' is a very powerful song that attempts to expose the ugliness and stupidity that results when people give in to racism and intolerance. This song deals with one of the most adult themes ever in a Disney film. . . ."14 By venturing to suggest that the savagery might be on the English side, Disney is indeed breaking with its Eurocentric convention. It may even be that, on balance, the Indians' view wins out, as children today are much more concerned with ecological issues, one of the issues that condemns the English. Similarly, in *Pocahontas II* the charge of savagery is aimed at the English court when Ratcliffe's plot to flush Pocahontas out by staging a cruel bearbaiting is successful: she protests that the bear is a helpless animal and that "*Your* behavior is savage. You and *your* people are the barbarians!" The English cruelty to animals certainly casts a pall over their claims to be the font of civilization, especially when read in the context of the anthropomorphized Disney animal kingdom.

It is perhaps not surprising (given their self-image as the civilizers of the world) that the portrayal of the English in *Pocahontas* triggered outrage in the British press. The *London Times,* for example, published a scathing review that liberally deploys racist terminology ("squaw," "Redskins") even while attempting to distance the English from the American "bad conscience" and "xenophobia," as if the English had nothing to do with colonization and genocide in the Americas:

> [Pocahontas is] history's most famous squaw. . . . The English are thugs, all greed, gold and guns, and they treat natives like savages. The Indians, by contrast, are civilized, peace loving and eco-conscious. The animators have significantly made the Redskins look pretty much like modern paleface Americans, and speak like them too. . . . Disney's fable of an arcadian American history wrecked by incursions from the Old World is obviously a means of allaying a bad conscience, while voicing xenophobic resentments about corrupt Europeans.[15]

A subsequent *Sunday Times* review went on the attack against Pocahontas in particular, and her people in general:

> The film's heroine is based on the 12-year-old Indian girl—who was bald as the baldest bald eagle—who treated [John Smith] to what, from all accounts, sounds like a series of fireside orgies. Disney has certainly come a long way of late in the portrayal of its heroines, but one would hazard a guess that bald nymphomaniacs are still something of a no-go area. So it is that when we first see Pocahontas in Disney's film, she's standing atop a rock, her hair flowing in the wind: national pride incarnate, her lustrous black locks doubling up as the flag that native Americans never had. That they spent most of their time not airing their scalps but depriving the English of theirs is a fact swept under the carpet with the efficiency of a barbershop broom.[16]

As noted above, although the "Indians" might come out looking better on the issues of cruelty to animals and the environment, the mutual attribution of savagery is not as evenhanded as it might first appear, since it is offered in a cultural context of dominant discourses in which, for centuries, Natives have been labeled "savages" (noble or ignoble) by whites. As noted by Nash, the English had been primed by the Spanish and Portuguese to regard the nations of the Americas as savages. It was an image that enabled the Europeans to justify their invasion in legal and moral terms, either by claiming that they were exchanging the use of abundant lands for the "benefits" of an advanced civilization, or by simply denying the humanity of indigenous peoples and thus their right to possess the land.[17] As Pauline Turner Strong points out, "for many Native Americans 'savage' is the 'S' word, as potent and degrading as the word 'nigger.'"[18] In the framework of ongoing constructions of Native Americans as "primitive" if exotic peoples, the continuous repetition of the word "savages" plays into an already existing racism that patently does *not* attach to the English at anything more than a superficial level. In fact, despite the attributions of savagery by the "Indians," the films, particularly the sequel, nevertheless present the British in general as good and honorable (with the exception of the villainous Ratcliffe), and Britain as the hub of civilization to which the "Other" wishes to assimilate.

Apart from the environmental and cruelty to nonhuman animals issues, the films conceal the real savagery of the British, Smith in particular (whose good looks carry his virtue), in the murders of Powhatans. In fact, the savagery of the British is individualized to one scapegoat, Ratcliffe, the bad apple. It should be noted that the real Ratcliffe was not the governor but a captain, whose execution (with thirty of his men) by the Powhatans in 1609 (seven years before Pocahontas's visit to England) was one of the reasons the English captured Pocahontas.[19] Nevertheless, Disney's barrel-chested bombast who wears poncey tights and high-heeled buckle shoes is an avaricious, vain liar, who exploits his working-class crew (whom he calls "witless peasants") and makes them dig up the countryside in the vain search for gold. It is Ratcliffe who looks for any opportunity to attack the Indians, lies to the King to get Smith arrested, manipulates the King into sending the armada to kill the Powhatans, and sets up the bearbaiting (or rather the Indian princess baiting) to fluster Pocahontas into insulting the King, leading to her arrest. In the words of Duncan Marjoribanks, supervising animator for the character:

> Ratcliffe carries the racism and greed of the movie. He represents the aristocracy and his greatest fault is that he ignores everything about this new land that he's come to. He is more of a colonialist than a settler. Instead of adapting himself, he becomes more European than ever.[20]

Thus, by individualizing the qualities of greed, vanity, deceit, and aggression, the thesis of the two films is that the bad things that happened to the indigenous Americans were caused by the actions and the misunderstandings that resulted from the malignant acts of one dishonorable individual.

Ratcliffe aside, however, British culture (at least upper-class British culture) is painted as fundamentally honest and honorable, exemplified in various ways. One important instance occurs in Pocahontas II, when Rolfe intervenes in an altercation between Pocahontas and the ship's captain who is objecting to her "stowaway" pets, the raccoon and the bluebird. "Like it or not, you are the envoy, and I am honor-bound to protect you," Rolfe tells her, "and honor is the backbone of our civilization."

In the minds of the Imagineers, the racism Pocahontas encounters in London is not an intrinsic requirement of the imperialist project but is a figment of the warped pathologies of a random few (such as Ratcliffe). For example, the King, who is otherwise a buffoon manipulated by Ratcliffe, regains his sense of honor when he discovers he has been lied to by the one bad apple (there is no gold, and the Indians are not savages). Indeed, the whole premise of *Pocahontas II* is that if only Pocahontas can "prove" she is "civilized," King James will refrain from sending his armada to "destroy the heathens" and claim the gold of the "New World." The fiction that the English invasion was simply called off when Pocahontas proved herself *au fait* with English fashion, manners, and ballroom protocol is, of course, nonsensical. In fact, the opposite seems to have been the case, as "her presence at the English court had the effect of attracting increased financing for the Virginia colony,"[21] thereby speeding up the colonization process and the destruction of the Powhatans (and ultimately other Native American tribes), who were to be confined to a reservation by 1658. The impression left at the end of each film, that British imperialism was called off, is indeed one of the most fanciful yet serious departures from reality committed by Disney's narratives.

Along with the individualization of racism, greed, and bad faith, and the portrayal of the English in general as good eggs, Disney's Anglophilia appears in yet another guise. Disney's "old world," represented by a sparkling clean London, a city painted in cheerful colors, full of charming Tudor cottages, bright awnings, trees and gardens, is the very epicenter of civilization. This pristine and inviting image of England's capital is exemplified in the song that greets Pocahontas's arrival, "What a Day in London," which features clean, loving, cheery citizens going about their quaint trades. Interestingly, there are two references in this scene to England's ugly underbelly: the pastiche shows an undertaker hauling a coffin through the streets, as well as a disabled beggar who sings happily "We thank the lord / And kiss the ground / For bed and board in London town." This is no doubt a reference to the Elizabethan Poor Laws, which made some meager provisions for the "deserving poor," though begging was prohibited and savage punishment was visited upon vagrants or those displaced from the land by the Enclosure Acts and the industrial revolution.[22]

Indeed, far from Disney's quaint, pastel city thronging with cheery, pink citizens, early seventeenth-century London (like the London of the centuries before and immediately after it) would more accurately have been represented as a wretched, miserable place, seething with poverty, disease, crime, horror, and cruelty. Ravaged by virulent infectious diseases such as syphilis, the sweating sickness, and "the maladies tedious, loathsome or abhorrible to be looked upon" associated with but not limited to the poor,[23] seventeenth-century London was a toxic purgatory. As Stannard notes, "epidemic outbreaks of plague and smallpox, along with routine attacks of measles, influenza, diphtheria, typhus, typhoid fever, and more, frequently swept European cities and towns clean of 10 to 20 percent of their populations at a single stroke."[24] As Europeans knew little of hygiene, "roadside ditches, filled with stagnant water, served as public latrines," while "the practice of leaving the decomposing offal of butchered animals to fester in the streets" cannot have done much to improve public health. London, in particular, kept "poor holes," into which the corpses of the poor were stacked in rows, to be covered with a layer of soil only when each hole was full. Moreover, "a modern visitor to a European city in this era would be repelled by the appearance and the vile aromas given off by the living as well [since] most people never bathed, not once in an entire lifetime," and it was the norm for men and women to have "bad breath from the rotting teeth and constant stomach disorders which can be documented from many sources, while suppurating ulcers, eczema, scabs, running sores and other nauseating skin diseases were extremely common, and often lasted for years."[25] In the epicenter of this "civilization," Lawrence Stone noted, the typical English town "was a place filled with malice and hatred, its only unifying bond being the occasional episode of mass hysteria, which temporarily bound together the majority in order to harry and persecute the local witch."[26]

In his account of her trip to London, Barbour notes that Pocahontas became ill within a short time after her arrival, as "the air of London was far from clean and a girl accustomed to the unsullied breeze of the virginal forest could not have found the air breathable."[27] Pocahontas was so ill from the bad air, in fact, that she had to stay in Brentford, outside London. But finally, while waiting to return by ship to Jamestown, like three of the Powhatan delegation who had already died in the "unfriendly climate" of London,[28] Pocahontas succumbed to either consumption or smallpox and died at the aptly named Gravesend. Like many important events in her life, Pocahontas's death is not recounted in the cartoon as "Disney chooses to suspend the narrative at the moment of tragic sentiment and unconsummated miscegenation."[29] The truth is, London, the hub of civilization that mesmerized the Disney Pocahontas, actually killed her.

Dual Points of View

One of the significant departures from convention in Disney's *Pocahontas* films is the attempt to capture each culture's point of view about the other.

Disney indeed presents a more complex picture than the usual Europeans/ goodies versus Indians/baddies story through a number of devices. For example, rather than turning on the gaze of one character or group, the narrative shifts viewpoints, alternating the action so that the audience can see things from each "side" (through Pocahontas's/Powhatan eyes, and through Smith's/ Rolfe's/English eyes). This is a salutary innovation in a cultural industry that has contributed so much to the racist constructions of Native Americans. But does this device dislodge the hegemony of the British/white gaze, and/or the audience's identification with it? Does it de-other the Other?

We would argue that to some extent it does. We, as audience, are certainly permitted to see events from the Native point of view, as a number of scenes in each film are set among the Powhatans and are white-free, and English behaviors and attitudes are explicitly critiqued in each of the films. However, the effect is subdued by the fact that each narrative *begins* in London. *Pocahontas* opens with an upbeat scene of the good-looking ship's crew preparing to set sail, kissing their loving wives and children good-bye, and singing a jaunty chantey ("In 1607, we sailed the open sea, for glory, God, gold and lumber and the Virginia Company"). The fact that the British point of view comes first positions the audience to identify with the English as "us," so that when they finally reach the "New World," and when the action shifts to the Powhatans, we have already been primed to consider them "them." The English crewmen are humanized throughout the film, and are painted as under the class and military authority of the evil Ratcliffe, who exploits their labor and orders them to fight the "savages" against their better judgment. In *Pocahontas II,* it is true that the King, in accordance with Disney iconography of ridiculous kings,[30] is portrayed as vain, rather idiotic, and under Ratcliffe's control, but he does the right thing in the end once he knows the truth. Yet neither he nor Ratcliffe carry the English point of view. Smith represents this in the first film and Rolfe in the second, and *they* are decent, honest, charming, well meaning, and heroic.

It is also true that the other eye of the dual gaze/point of view is that of Pocahontas. But Pocahontas's eye is hardly that of the resisting, anticolonialist Native American. For one thing, in Disney's accounts, Pocahontas loves two Englishmen, and is willing to risk her life to save theirs. Partly as a consequence of this individualized heterosexual love, she is sympathetic to the English in general, speaking up for them to her people, saving them from certain annihilation on several occasions, and thus helping them to get a foothold in the territory of her nation. Whenever other Powhatans are suspicious of the motives of the English ("Your kind are barbarians. They only want our land. They mean to destroy us!"), Pocahontas questions their mistrust as if it is caused by nothing but ignorance, as if the Englishmen's motives would turn out to be benign, if only they were asked (*"Is* that what they want? *You* don't know."). "You speak with the tongue of a pale one," says one of the warriors in *Pocahontas II,* "you belong with them. You should go." She does, and she does, and she does. As Bird notes:

> The American Indian princess became an important, non-threatening symbol of white Americans' right to be here because she was always willing to sacrifice her happiness, cultural identity, and even her life for the good of the new nation. . . . The prevailing view of the princess was that she was gentle, noble, non-threateningly erotic, virtually a white Christian, and yet different, being tied to the native soils of America. As Tilton explained, the Princess Pocahontas story enabled the white U. S., but especially the South, to justify its dominance, providing a kind of origin myth that explained how and why American Indians had welcomed the destiny brought to them by whites.[31]

Of course, Pocahontas was a Christian by the time she went to England, having "converted" during her almost two years of captivity by the English (of which more will be said later), when she was "educated" in English manners, customs, language, and dress.[32] Indeed, according to Woodward, Pocahontas told her brothers that "she had been so well treated by the English she intended to remain with them, now preferring them to her own people."[33] In view of this, many Native Americans regard Pocahontas with skepticism, to say the least. For example, Lester Brown, acting director of American Indian Studies at Cal State Long Beach, made the point that "[t]o many [Native Americans] she seemed too eager to embrace European ways." He explains her popularity in terms of her acceptability to white society in view of her acceptance of *it.* She is

> a good Indian, a tame Indian. Of course [American] culture would embrace her, of course they'd make a movie about her, because she served the Europeans' needs. . . . The problem is that Euro-Americans have never viewed Indians as people equal to them. . . . So the only time they embrace an Indian is when that Indian embraces European culture.[34]

According to Leland Conner, national director of the American Indian Lore Association, unlike the nature lover portrayed in the film, Pocahontas seems to have been "a child smitten by the goodies English culture had to offer." Thus, the beloved American icon who, schoolchildren learn, saved the life of an innocent white man and believed in peace among all people is seen by many Natives at best as "a naïve pawn of those who would eventually wreak havoc upon them, and at worst, a villain and a traitor."[35] Thus, the choice made by Disney to make an animated feature on *this* colonizer-friendly Native American female protagonist, as opposed to the many women who resisted European colonialism and Euro-American subjugation, seriously compromises Pocahontas's role as conduit of the Native viewpoint.

Finally, the dual viewpoint is undermined by the two *Pocahontas* films' "regime of linguistic non-reciprocity," or "colonial bilingualism," whereby the dialogue in English diminishes the self-representation of the Powhatans.[36] In *Pocahontas,* Powhatan greets an elder in *Renape,*[37] but then the dialogue among the Powhatans reverts to English. Pocahontas, remarkably and instinctively, is not only able almost immediately to communicate with John Smith but, by "listening to her heart," is able to do so in standard English. In both films, the Powhatans are heard to speak *Renape,* but only as background babble. At one point in *Pocahontas II,* Powhatan men speak audibly in their native tongue, but no effort is made to translate, the implication being that what they are saying is not important. While it could be argued that subtitles of *Renape* dialogue would not have worked for a film whose target audience was young children, the linguistic structure of the *Pocahontas* films nonetheless reinforces Hollywood's colonizing history, which assumed that "to be human was to speak the colonizing language."[38]

Decentering the White Beauty Myth?

There has been much commentary, even celebration, of the fact that in *Pocahontas,* Disney broke the mold of its standard heroines to the extent that, in the words of producer James Pentecost, Pocahontas is "the strongest heroine ever to appear in a Disney film. She is open, athletic, dynamic, intelligent, and quite beautiful."[39] In her portrayal as a strong character, Pocahontas also breaks the mold of Disney's pale, pathetic, passive heroines in the sense that some critics argued Beauty did in *Beauty and the Beast.*[40] She is also Native. Indeed, as Leslie notes, Disney's Pocahontas "appears as the spirit of America. She is a virgin terrain, a child-like innocent resonating with myth not history."[41] Along with this portrayal of the purity of the land that Pocahontas symbolizes, it could be argued that Disney's *Pocahontas* decenters the idea of whiteness as the pinnacle of human beauty. In white culture, white is beautiful because it is, coincidentally, the color of virtue, purity, transcendence, cleanliness.[42] In these animated films, however, Pocahontas, the Native American woman, represents these qualities.

On the other hand, the idea that whiteness is decentered in the construction of Pocahontas is countered by the fact that her body is changed to complete the effect of what Disney (and Euro-American society) deems beautiful. Although there are no reliable images of the real Pocahontas as a child, as anthropologist Helen Rountree points out, in Pocahontas's day, prepubescent girls of her nation generally had shaved heads and went about naked. Indeed, according to Rountree, one of the historically reliable accounts was of Pocahontas "turning stark-naked cartwheels around the settlers' stockade, provoking the men inside." It came as no surprise to her, however, that once Disney "did" Pocahontas, she would be transformed into "a buckskin-clad Barbie—doe-eyed, docile and utterly romantic."[43]

In fact, quite apart from the baffling facts that they changed her from a ten-to-twelve-year-old child to a twentysomething woman and sexualized her in the process (presumably they advanced her age so as to avoid making child pornography re her fictional romance with Smith), Disney's Pocahontas is not Native American at all. Supervising animator Glen Keane describes Pocahontas as "an ethnic blend," whose convexly curved face is African; whose dark, slanted eyes are Asian; and whose body proportions are Caucasian. "Because we are Disney," he explains, "the ethnic qualities are softened a little bit."[44] It is possible that Disney created a hybrid, this Cafricasian, for her cross-cultural, multiethnic appeal. But surely the point of the Pocahontas story is precisely that she was a Native American, not an African, not an Asian, not a Caucasian. As bell hooks points out:

> The very choice of Pocahontas has to do with the cultural fascination with an ideal of beauty that is ethnically indeterminate. In traditional racist terms, that particular beauty was mixing white Victorian purity with the more soulful, sexualized quality of the darker races.[45]

While there is no one "look" that is "authentically" Native, in the case of Disney's Pocahontas any of the "darker races," *except* the one to which she actually belonged, would do. Although she *was* Native, and that is pivotal to the story, Disney's Euro-aesthetic deliberately undermines the representation of her *looks* as Native. In the genealogy of discourses on Native Americans, there are several that undermine the ability of American popular culture to see as beautiful those shoved to the bottom of the racial/ethnic hierarchy.

And whereas Pocahontas is the beautiful, sexualized "Other" (actually, some other "Other"), Disney also beautifies the bodies of the Johns (Smith and Rolfe), their beauty functioning to cloak some unpalatable realities of their characters and roles in the Powhatan genocide. Smith, the key adventurer character in the white American imaginary, had in reality been a beggar, a pirate in the tradition of Sir Francis Drake, who robbed the Spanish of the gold and silver they stole from the nations of the Americas.[46] He had also been a mercenary for Hungary, which had pensioned him off and awarded him a shield depicting three Turks he had beheaded.[47] Disney made the thirtysomething, short, red-haired, bearded mercenary, "who more resembled a brick than a blonde Adonis,"[48] into a tall, handsome, blond, square-jawed, smooth-shaven twentysomething romantic hero.

It is notable that the voice of John Smith does *not* bear an English accent but is voiced by Mel Gibson, one of the most idolized of Hollywood actors, best known for his starring roles in action films. Although John Smith, the English mercenary and Indian fighter, undoubtedly had an English accent, he has been mythologized in numerous accounts for American schoolchildren as "the best-known early *American* explorer and settler,"[49] thus establishing a heroic link between British colonialism and American internal colonization of indigenous peoples. Moreover, the choice of Gibson's voice is appropriate for reasons other than box-office draw, the continuation of the Disney (and Hollywood) tradition of transforming the heroic protagonists of all nations into Americans, and the sought-after identification of American audiences with an American-sounding hero. Born in New York, migrating at age twelve to Australia, starring in Australian films, then becoming a Hollywood star, Gibson himself embodies the links of British settler colonialism and thus is well suited to voice the crossover colonialist.[50]

According to published histories, Smith first met Pocahontas at his first audience with Powhatan, and the supposed rescue episode "was almost certainly a combination of mock execution and salvation, in token of adoption into Powhatan's tribe."[51] In spite of this, however, from 1607 to 1646, but for a few short cease-fires, English colonists were in an almost constant state of warfare with the Powhatans. Contrary to their manufactured image as humanitarian colonizers, the English committed numerous acts of barbarism:

> When one [raiding party] returned after a particularly successful massacre, they were admonished for having brought back alive the chief's wife and two children. To remedy the situation, the children were thrown into the river and their brains shot out; as for the mother, the president insisted they should burn her, for strangling on the gallows was too good.'. . . Some time later, the English lured 200 Pamunkey Indians to peace talks and murdered them with poison wine, then killed and scalped another fifty.[52]

The historical record shows that Smith, who became virtually a military dicta-tor in Jamestown, took to his work with a relish that appeared unseemly, even to the Virginia Company, which sent him letters complaining of his "need-lessly cruel attitude towards the savages":[53]

> he had behaved throughout his governorship as a pure opportunist. . . . Above all, he had held resolutely to the theory that the Indians were inferiors, to be bullied, threatened and tortured at pleasure, and his downfall came, not through the Indian resistance, but through the fact that he could not obtain fresh supplies (thanks to a bad harvest) . . . [and he was sent back to London] to answer for his misdemeanors.[54]

None of this historical reality is allowed to sully Disney's romantic hero, whose square-jawed handsomeness and familiar Mel Gibson voice is designed to in-still a sense of trustworthiness, a disbelief that he could be anything other than honorable, honest, and a friend to the Indians, as he is indeed portrayed in the two films. Smith is kind to animals, jumps into the swelling ocean to rescue a man overboard, and, in *Pocahontas,* he (in exact opposition to the historical Smith's actions) tries to stop Ratcliffe from "eliminating the savages once and for all" by telling him that they are not really savages and that "they can help us, they know the land." He subsequently warns Pocahontas of the imminent En-glish attack (an inversion of the historical record that it was she who warned him of the Powhatans' plans) and, ultimately, takes a bullet for Powhatan (an-other fabrication). In *Pocahontas II,* Smith rescues Pocahontas from the Tower of London and, with Rolfe, halts the armada with some tricky swordplay.

Similarly, John Rolfe is beautified by the Imagineers in *Pocahontas II,* and voiced and gestured as the disarmingly charming Hugh Grant of the Seven-teenth Century by the American actor Billy Zane. There is little to distinguish Disney's characterization of the two Johns, save John Rolfe's upper-class Brit-ish (versus John Smith's American Hollywood) accent, and Rolfe's preoccupa-tion with English manners and ballroom etiquette. With his crisp British ac-cent, Rolfe provides American audiences with the "familiar Other," or not so much an "Other" as an antecedent.

Apart from the fact that the real Rolfe was (already) married to Pocahontas, his other claim to fame was his experimentation with tobacco growing (dis-covered by the "Indians"), which led to the reorganization of Jamestown, then Virginia, and later much of the South along West Indian–style plantation cul-tivation by black slave labor.[55] Naturally, none of this appears in the film. Phys-ical beauty in Disney is code for unimpeachability, the automatic presumption attaching to the English heroes.

Finally, along with the issue of beauty, there is the matter of individuality. Whereas there is little variation in the Powhatans' appearance (in either their physical features or their style of dress), the English are marked by their endless variability in phenotypes and fashions. The diversity of the English is also manifested in their accents, which reveal different classes and indeed nations in the British Isles (one ship crew member speaks with a Scottish brogue). When Pocahontas arrives in London in the second film she is incredulous at the fact that Londoners/the English come in all shapes and sizes. The stereotyping re homogeneity and interchangeability of subordinated social groups "is one of the means by which they are categorized and kept in place, [while] white people in white culture are given the illusion of their infinite variety."56 So, although the "Indians" are "more human-looking, if nippleless, and are indeed more human or humane than the nasty, brutish colonists who stem yet from cartoon's native domain—caricature,"57 the physical and linguistic diversity of the English serves as a device to distinguish them as individuals and, ultimately, as more "human."

Interracial Heterosexual Romance

The Imagineers at Disney went to considerable trouble in *Pocahontas* to arrange an interracial romance between Pocahontas and Smith, changing their ages, physiques, and the historical facts.58 Such a romance was a bit easier in the sequel as the filmmakers were able to use the man Pocohantas actually married, although they altered the true sequence of events and omitted some important ones. It should be noted that interracial marriage was a huge taboo and illegal in most parts of the United States until well into the twentieth century. In 1924, for example, the Virginia legislature revised the state's antimiscegenation laws (dating from the 1600s) to exempt white descendants of Pocahontas so that people with less than one-sixteenth of American Indian and no other non-Caucasian blood would be considered white.59

The taboo on filmic representations of interracial romance/marriage/miscegenation is barely a bygone, so Disney's creation of one such romance in the first film might be seen as a breakthrough, especially for a mainstream animated feature film. The Smith/Pocahontas relationship is, of course, a metaphoric romance that stands in for the colonial encounter in the white imagination. However, Dyer makes the point that interracial heterosexuality "threatens the power of whiteness because it breaks the legitimation of whiteness with reference to the white body . . . if white bodies are no longer indubitably white bodies, if they can no longer guarantee their own reproduction as white, then the "natural" basis of their domination is no longer credible."[60] Is it possible to understand the interracial romances in each of these films as threatening the power of whiteness? We argue that it is not.

In the first place, the manufactured romance between Pocahontas and Smith carries multiple meanings beyond the attraction of opposites and the mutual desire of the colonizer and the colonized. For example, in *Pocahontas,* our heroine sings a song in which she wrestles with the question of whether to marry the serious Kocoum and thus end her dreams of what might be "Just around the Riverbend." In fact, similar sentiments have become the norm in other recent Disney animated features. From Ariel in *The Little Mermaid* to Belle in *Beauty and the Beast,* the central female character longs for something more, and will only be satisfied when a man, a *different* kind of a man (or beast) comes into her life. This theme is repeated post-Smith in *Pocahontas II* when, in "Where do I go from here?" (her "I don't fit into my culture" song), she sings that "in my heart, I don't feel part of so much I've known." Her relationship with Smith, then, has alienated her from her own culture. No white character sings or speaks of not belonging in his, especially not as a result of the encounter with Native Americans. Pocahontas's exposure to the English has left her bereft; she finds her own culture wanting; she no longer fits; she longs for the colonizer in the embodied form of a lover but also in the form of the "new world," their world, to which she has been exposed. This is not an instance of decentering of whiteness/the British then, but of the decentering of Pocahontas.

Moreover, the putative romance between Pocahontas and Smith in *Pocahontas* is not consummated—Smith goes home; she stays home. Why, then, did Disney go to so much trouble to fabricate it? This romance surely serves other purposes. In fact, virtually all of Disney's animated feature films center on a compulsory heterosexual love story, whether between humans (*Snow White,* 1937; *Sleeping Beauty,* 1959; *The Jungle Book,* 1967; *Aladdin,* 1996; *Hercules,* 1997), cats (*Aristocats,* 1970), dogs (*Lady and the Tramp,* 1955), lions (*Lion King,* 1994), or even interspecies (a mermaid and a man in *Little Mermaid,* 1989, a woman and a beast in *Beauty and the Beast,* 1992). Presumably, Disney felt that a romance between Pocahontas and one of her own people would have little dramatic appeal, whereas one between her and the Englishman she purportedly saved would work at various levels. Peter Schneider and his development team at Disney had been considering an animated Romeo and Juliet for the previous eight years, and this story had many of the same elements.[61] Mike Gabriel, *Pocahontas* creator and director, made it clear that the project was conceived principally as a love story:

We are doing a love story. So (at least in these Disney animated films) you do need a male to go along with the love story. You could almost call this one, *John Smith and Pocahontas*. . . . Because it is really, from the large scope, the story of the American Indian and the effect of the European invasion of the continent, it never really felt right to try to end this happily ever after. We didn't for a minute want to tell kids, "isn't it wonderful and love conquers all," because it really is a tragic story.[62]

Oddly enough, Pocahontas's love does seem to conquer all in the first film—war is averted and the English go home, a good result from the Powhatans' point of view. How would that be tragic, other than the fact that it was not true? In fact, the true history is tragic from the point of view of Native Americans, but Disney has made it look as if colonization did not proceed after Smith sailed back to London.

Most important, within a narrative of colonization, the interracial love story between Smith and Pocahontas serves to legitimize that colonization. The "Other" must love us, must want us, must desire us. Diane Krumrey, a literary critic who has done extensive research at Princeton University on the many ways the Pocahontas story has been told, makes the point that "Americans need to retell the story of the first contact between Euro-English settlers and Native Americans to make it a loving, interactive and mutually satisfying encounter, to knit themselves into the landscape with a love story that would produce a true American progeny."[63] Indeed, it is surprising that Disney did not invent Pocahontas having Smith's baby!

It is interesting, in fact, that the "true American progeny" that Pocahontas *did* produce was excised from the Disney stories. In order to fashion a new romance between Pocahontas and Rolfe, which would bloom during their trip to London, the Imagineers imagined that she was not already married to him, and that she had not already borne him a son about a year before the fateful journey to London (who was left there by his father until he returned to Jamestown as a young man). In order to do that, they also had to imagine that the English had not kidnapped Pocahontas. Pocahontas was known as a liaison between the Powhatan alliance of thirty-two tribes and the English settlers who arrived in 1607, and she warned the English about any troubles coming from her people. The English rewarded her for this by kidnapping her and ransoming her back to her father. In 1613, at the instigation of Captain Samuel Argall, Pocahontas was kidnapped for the English by a chief called Jopassus (or Japazeus) and used as a bargaining chip to secure the release of British soldiers being held prisoner by Powhatan. Although he released seven prisoners, she was not returned. About a year into her captivity, John Rolfe declared his love for her and his intention to marry her;[64] she was baptized in 1614 and given the name Lady Rebecca Rolfe.[65] According to Woodward, "the marriage symbolized for the colonists a lasting union between themselves and the New World," and Powhatan's consent to it suggests that it may have been a political marriage that was seen as beneficial by both sides.[66] It has even been suggested that Powhatan used Pocahontas, encouraging her to make friendships among the English to find out what they wanted.[67]

Why was Pocahontas's marriage to Rolfe, and more important, the child of that marriage, concealed in the Disney films? Was it simply to have an uncomplicated narrative in which they could develop the "romance" between them at a later stage than their actual relationship had happened in their lives? Or was it to avoid the issue of interracial sex and miscegenation? As Dyer argues, "the fact of reproduction does not necessarily, nor perhaps even usually, enter directly into the representation of interracial sexuality, yet it is what is at stake in it."[68] Unlike the situation in countries such as Mexico and Brazil, where *mestizaje* (the process of racial and cultural miscegenation) is part of these countries' founding myths, a miscegenation story might evoke unease in the United States, which lacks any such national mythology, and indeed where nation-building proceeded on the explicit separation of more from less "desirable" races.

Of course, we can only speculate as to the motives of the filmmakers. But concealment of the fact of miscegenation/interracial sex (as evidenced by the offspring) has the effect of keeping Pocahontas virginal, but desirous of her colonizer, as opposed to the wife and mother she actually was. This, of course, is consistent with Disney's convention of centering the action on young singles on their journeys to self-discovery and heterosexual bliss. It keeps alive the romantic notion, as expressed by the closing song of Pocahontas II, that the colonizing encounter was one of "Building a Bridge of Love between Two Worlds."

History and Authenticity

Disney's fabricated Pocahontas stories are, of course, cartoons whose purpose is entertainment and commercial profits. So what if they are not historically accurate? As the producer of *Pocahontas I,* James Pentecost, claimed:

> Nobody should go to an animated film hoping to get the accurate depiction of history. . . . More people are talking about Pocahontas than ever talked about her in the last 400 years, since she lived. Every time we talk about it, it's an opportunity to talk about what was, what was known about her and what we created out of our imagination.[69]

The question is, why should we have to spend time undoing *un*truths? The *Pocahontas* films use a mix of very fine-detailed accuracy with sweeping inaccuracies/downright lies, and yet nowhere does either one offer any kind of disclaimer such as "The characters and incidents portrayed and the names used herein are fictitious and any resemblance to the names, character or history of any person is coincidental and unintentional."[70] Of course, no one expects such a disclaimer from a children's cartoon, but Disney claims to be aiming at the teen, young adult, and mature adult audiences as well. Given that these films purport to tell the story of a real person who lived in real historical time, and whose story is the stuff of contemporary American founding mythology, the truth status of these narratives is surely a core issue. For unlike Disney's other animated features that are based on fairy tales and have no claims to truth, the *Pocahontas* films engage the Euro-American imagination in a tissue of deceits that end up redeeming the colonization project as a love story between two different worlds, rather than depicting it as the holocaust it was for the Native Americans. It is telling that while Disney employed American Indian advisers in the making of the two films, the offers by the Powhatan Renape Nation "to assist Disney with cultural and historical accuracy were rejected."[71] It is interesting that the corporation tried to fudge the historical-accuracy criticism leveled by modern-day descendants of the Powhatans when a Disney executive told the *Washington Post* that "nobody knows the truth of her legend," so the studio "simply set out to make a beautiful movie about the Native American experience."[72] In a conventional Disney response to charges of the historical inaccuracy of one of its products, *Pocahontas* art director Mike Giaimo stated, "Even though we wanted to be very historically accurate . . . at the same time our story is all about enchantment."[73] What, one wonders, was so beautiful or enchanting about the Native American experience of genocide?

Jacquelyn Kilpatrick makes the point that most of the adults who see Disney's *Pocahontas* do not have the background to judge whether it is accurate or not, particularly as much of the media hype has been focused on the "political correctness" of the film, a characterization that gives the impression of accuracy.[74] As for children, in her view, "[t]he visual is emotionally more compelling than the written word . . . and since few people will read about Pocahontas, this film will exist as 'fact' in the minds of generations of American children."[75] As "fact," the *Pocahontas* films, while not simple depictions of British superiority, nevertheless pander to white America's residual admiration for the rulers they eventually repulsed in favor of the republic, for they are "us." By appealing to the audience's identification and pleasure with pristine innocence, high adventure, and heterosexual love stories, *Pocahontas I* and *II* draw on American Anglophilia and the discreet charm of the English voice to construct a form of "nostalgic imperialism" and a "politics of forgetting," at the expense of the Powhatans and other American Indian nations.[76]

As Lowery points out, the corporation knew that Native Americans were wary of its retelling of their history, and Disney was also "well aware that non-Native Americans would not sit, or purchase metric tons of merchandise, for a film that labeled white settlers as invaders, plunderers and murderers."[77] So the filmmakers transformed it, in the words of Roy Disney, vice-chairman of the Walt Disney Company and head of the feature animation department, into "a story about people getting along together in this world,"[78] a story about "building a bridge of love between two worlds" in fact.

Notes

1. Sarah Kershaw, "Coming to Classrooms: The Real Pocahontas Story," *New York Times,* July 12, 1995.
2. Gary Edgerton and Kathy Merlock Jackson, "Redesigning Pocahontas," *Journal of Popular Film and Television* 24.2 (1996): 90–98. Michael Lind, "Dishonest Injun," *New Republic,* June 1995, 13.
3. Gary Morris, "The Incredible Shrinking and Expanding Ethnic Minority, or the Racist in the Cupboard," *Bright Lights* 15 (1995): 42–43.
4. Disney's *Pocahontas: Production Information* (1995, 35) quotes Thomas Schumacher, senior vice president of feature animation, as follows: "'Pocahontas's is much more than just a love story or entertainment. It is a story that is fundamentally about racism and intolerance and we hope that people will gain a greater understanding of themselves and the world around them. It's also about having respect for each other's cultures."
5. Richard Dyer, *White* (London: Routledge, 1997), 2.
6. Ibid., 9.
7. Aristides, "Anglophilia, American Style," *American Scholar* 66.3, Summer (1997): 327–336.
8. Ella Shohat and Robert Stam, *Unthinking Eurocentrism: Multiculturalism and the Media* (New York: Routledge, 1994), 214.
9. Ibid., 215.
10. Erin Addison, "Saving Other Women from Other Men: Disney's *Aladdin*," *Camera Obscura* 31 (1994): 5–26.
11. Smith was actually incapacitated by a severe burn caused by a gunpowder explosion that probably mutilated his genitals, while sailing down the James River 1 September 1609. He left for England within a month. J. A. Leo Lemay, *Did Pocahontas Save Captain John Smith?* (Athens: University of Georgia Press, 1995), xvi.
12. According to Disney's *Production Information,* advice and participation from Native American leaders, educators, and groups was sought. For example, Jim "Great Elk"

Waters, a tribal leader and artist/musician/poet, was brought in with an ensemble to provide authentic Algonquin music and speech; Native American choreographers and storytellers were consulted to ensure that the Powhatan lifestyle and customs were portrayed accurately. Unfortunately, Shirley Little Dove Custalow McGowan, a key consultant on the film who teaches Native American education at schools including the University of Virginia, was unhappy about the final content of the film: "Disney promised me historical accuracy, but there will be a lot to correct when I go into the classrooms." McGowan had raised objections in August 1994, but was told the project was too far along. Meanwhile, the response of the film's producer, James Pentecost, was that "people are still arguing about who killed Kennedy and Lincoln. The further back you go, the more complicated it gets. We never say that the two end up together . . . but as in all great romances, the implication is there." (Elaine Dutka, "Disney's History Lesson," *Los Angeles Times,* February 9, 1995, F2/F4.)

13. Russell Means is quoted in Disney's *Production Information* (34) for the film as saying: "I think 'Pocahontas's is the single finest work ever done on American Indians by Hollywood. When I first read the script, I was impressed with the beginning of the film. In fact, I was overwhelmed by it. It tells the truth about the motives for Europeans initially coming to the so-called New World. I find it astounding that Americans and the Disney studios are willing to tell the truth. It's never been done before . . . and I love it. The co-operation I got with every suggestion I made, even the smallest little things about our culture, have been incorporated into the script. I'm very proud to be associated with this film."

14. Disney, *Production Information,* 52.

15. Gilbert Adair, "Animating History," *Sunday Times* (London), July 30, 1995, 10.

16. "Disney's Not so Noble Savage," *Sunday Times* (London), October 8, 1995, 10. The *Sunday Times* obviously was not aware that it was the Europeans who started the practice of scalping to ensure that bounty hunters had really killed the number of Indians they claimed. Olive Dickason, *Canada's First Nations: A History of Founding Peoples from Earliest Times* (Toronto: McClelland and Stewart, 1992). (Ronald Wright, *Stolen Continents: The "New World" through Indian Eyes since 1492* (New York: Viking Penguin, 1992).

17. Gary B. Nash, *Red, White, and Black: The Peoples of Early America* (Englewood Cliffs, New Jersey: Prentice-Hall, 1974).

18. Edgerton and Jackson, "Redesigning Pocahontas," 40–41.

19. Philip L. Barbour, *Pocahontas and Her World* (Boston: Houghton Mifflin Co., 1970), 63–64, 103.

20. Disney, *Product Information,* 40.

21. Grace Steele Woodward, *Pocahontas* (Norman: University of Oklahoma Press, 1969), 182.

22. Geoffrey Taylor, *The Problem of Poverty, 1660–1834* (London: Longmans, Green and Co., 1969), 26, 46.

23. Paul Slack, *Poverty and Policy in Tudor and Stuart England* (London: Longman, 1988), 24.

24. David Stannard, *American Holocaust: Columbus and the Conquest of the New World* (New York: Oxford University Press, 1992), 57.

25. Ibid., 58–59.
26. Lawrence Stone, *The Family, Sex and Marriage in England, 1500–1800* (New York: Harper and Row, 1977), 77–78.
27. Barbour, *Pocahontas and Her World,* 163.
28. Ibid., 179.
29. Esther Leslie, "Pocahontas," *History Workshop Journal* 41 (1996): 239.
30. Elizabeth Bell, "Somatexts at the Disney Shop: Constructing the Pentimentos of Women's Animated Bodies," in E. Bell, L. Haas, and Laura Sells, eds., *From Mouse to Mermaid: The Politics of Film, Gender and Culture* (Bloomington: Indiana University Press, 1995), 107–124.
31. Elizabeth S. Bird, "Gendered Construction of the American Indian in Popular Media," *Journal of Communication* 49.3 (1999): 72.
32. Woodward, *Pocahontas,* 158.
33. Ibid., 164.
34. Steve Lowery, "Pocahontas: Peacemaker or Pawn?" (Long Beach) *Press-Telegram,* June 12, 1995, F2.
35. Ibid.
36. Shohat and Stam, *Unthinking Eurocentrism,* 193.
37. Chief Roy Crazy Horse of the Powhatan Renape Nation points out that while "Powhatan refers to our political identity, . . . *Renape* refers to our ethnic/language identity." Chief Roy Crazy Horse, "Powhatan History," http://www.powhatan.org/history/html.
38. Shohat and Stam, *Unthinking Eurocentrism,* 192.
39. Kershaw, "Coming to Classrooms."
40. Jack Zipes, "Breaking the Disney Spell," in Bell, Haas, and Sells, *From Mouse to Mermaid,* 37.
41. Leslie, "Pocahontas," 235.
42. Dyer, *White,* 72.
43. "Pocahontas Legend Hides Chromatic Realities," *Los Angeles Times,* June 24, 1995: B4-B5.
44. Ilene Rosenzweig, "And Disney Created Woman," *Allure* (1995): 87.
45. Ibid.
46. Jack Weatherford, *Indian Givers: How the Indians of the Americas Transformed the World* (New York: Fawcett Columbine, 1988), 21–38.
47. Lind, "Dishonest Injun," 13.
48. Jacqueline Kilpatrick, "Disney's 'Politically Correct' Pocahontas," *Cineaste* 21.4 (1995): 36–39. (Quoted on p. 36.)
49. Lemay, *Did Pocahontas Save Captain John Smith?* 1.
50. In the smaller-budget, straight-to-video *Pocahontas II,* Donal Gibson, Mel Gibson's brother, voices John Smith, who is featured in a smaller role than in the original.
51. Barbour, *Pocahontas and Her World,* 24. Robert S. Tilton, *Pocahontas: The Evolution of an American Narrative* (New York: Cambridge University Press, 1994), 5.
52. Lind, "Dishonest Injun," quoting Arthur Quinn, followed by his own words.
53. John Gould Fletcher, *John Smith, Also Pocahontas* (New York: Brentano's, 1928), 234.

54. Ibid., 247, 250.

55. Lind, "Dishonest Injun."

56. Dyer, *White*, 12.

57. Leslie, "Pocahontas," 237.

58. After the first film was released, Robert Eaglestaff, principal of the American Indian Heritage School in Seattle, sent an e-mail to teachers across the city saying: "Educators, please be aware of what Disney is promoting in their release of 'Pocahontas.' They are promoting racism, rape and child molestation." Eaglestaff referred to an account of the relationship between Smith and Pocahontas, said to be in Smith's diaries, in which Smith raped and impregnated Pocahontas: "It's like trying to teach about the Holocaust and putting in a nice story about Anne Frank falling in love with a German officer." Kershaw, "Coming to Classrooms."

59. Lind, "Dishonest Injun."

60. Dyer, *White*, 25.

61. Disney, *Production Information*, 36.

62. Cathy Thompson-Georges, "Gabriel's Bullhorn," *Entertainment Today*, June 29, 1995, 4.

63. Kirk Honeycutt, "Lion Roars on Disney Stage," *Hollywood Reporter*, March 18, 1994, 20.

64. "Love" might be a misleading term, for Rolfe's own words show him to have been rather conflicted about his feelings. He wrote a letter in which he said that the woman with whom he had fallen in love was "one whose education has bin rude, her manners barbarous, her generation accursed, and so discrepant in all nurtriture from myself that oftentimes with feare and trembling I have ended my private controversie with this: surely these are wicked instigations, hatched by him who seeketh and delighteth in man's destruction; and so with fervent praiers to be ever preserved from such diabolical assaults (as I tooke those to be) I have taken some rest." Quoted in Woodward, *Pocahontas*, 164–165.

65. Ibid., 154–157.

66. Ibid., 166.

67. Minnie-Ha-Ha Custalow, quoted in Lowery, "Pocahontas," F1-F2.

68. Dyer, *White*, 25.

69. Quoted in Kershaw, "Coming to Classrooms."

70. Natalie Zemon Davis, "'Any Resemblance to Persons Living or Dead': Film and the Challenge of Authenticity," *Historical Journal of Film, Radio and Television* 8.3 (1988): 268–283. (Quoted on p. 270.)

71. Chief Roy Crazy Horse, Powhatan Renape Nation, "Pocahontas Myth," http:www.powhatan.org/pocc.html.

72. David Andrew Price, "The Real Pocahontas," *Wall Street Journal*, June 13, 1995, 87, quoting *Washington Post* interview.

73. Quoted in Allen Malmquist, "Pocahontas: Team Disney Tackles Historical Fact, but Keeps the Magic in Animation," *Cinefantastique* 26.5 (August 1995): 14–15.

74. Jacqueline Kilpatrick, *Celluloid Indians: Native Americans and Film* (Lincoln: University of Nebraska, 1999), 154.

75. Kilpatrick, "Disney's 'Politically Correct' Pocahontas," 36.

76. The term "nostalgic imperialism" is Renato Rosaldo's (quoted in Giroux below). The "politics of forgetting" is Giroux's term for the process by which Disney produces a particular set of comfortable, sanitized mythologies that profoundly affect the public culture's view of history, racial identity, and nationalism. Henry A. Giroux, "Memory and Pedagogy in the 'Wonderful World of Disney' Beyond the Politics of Innocence," in Bell, Haas, and Sells, *From Mouse to Mermaid*, 43–61.

77. Steve Lowery, "Pocahontas Works Too Hard to Have Fun," (Long Beach) *Press-Telegram,* June 23, 1995, 5.

78. Disney, *Production Information,* 33.

Part IV

Representation, Simulation, Appropriation

7

Everybody Wants a Piece of Pooh: Winnie,
from Adaptation to Market Saturation

Aaron Taylor

On August 29, 1998, the Walt Disney Company acquired the British rights to
A. A. Milne's Winnie-the-Pooh from the Garrick Club until 2026 for the tidy
sum of sixty million dollars. Disney already owned the copyright until 2006,
but renewed its rights to produce both animated films and merchandise for at
least another twenty years. Earlier, in 1996, Disney had re-released *The Many
Adventures of Winnie the Pooh* on video (the film was originally produced as a
short cartoon in 1966 and then expanded into a feature in 1977). To corre-
spond with the release of the video—which went on to be one of the company's biggest moneymakers on the video market—Disney also launched a
worldwide marketing campaign for product tie-in.

Within months, international markets became saturated with a glut of Pooh
products—from plush toys to women's underwear. By 1999, the Disney Store
online catalogue alone featured 366 different Pooh products, while a search for
Pooh-related Web sites could generate almost fifty-eight million hits.[1] According to a study conducted by *Forbes* in 2003, Pooh is not only the company's
highest-grossing character but is in fact currently the most profitable fictional
character with a copyrighted image: licensing revenue for the character came to
a hefty $5.9 billion for that year.[2] The revenues generated from Pooh products

181

far exceed those of any other character. At the Disney Store, for example, the Winnie the Pooh Mini Bean Bag Plush line was the number one seller in 1998 and the most successful line in store history. More than eighty thousand units were sold in North America alone.[3] Only three years earlier, the company had acknowledged that Winnie the Pooh was second only to Mickey Mouse as its "most loved and trusted character."[4] But 1998 proved to be the Year of Pooh. "Forget the mouse," the *Los Angeles Times* trumpeted, "the bear owns this town."[5] The supremacy of Pooh's revenue-generating prowess remains indisputable, as the character's enterprise was estimated to contribute to as much as one-fifth of the company's $25 billion gross globally in 2001. The exact dollar value of the character is a matter of some controversy. Disney CEO Michael Eisner and President Robert Iger claimed publicly in February 2002 that the bear earns between $3.4 and $4 billion for the studio. In turn, their figure was contradicted by Disney attorney Daniel J. Petrocelli of O'Melveny and Myers, who places Pooh's profits at a much more modest $1 billion—"about three or four percent" of the company's corporate revenues.[6]

Interestingly, the merchandising of Pooh products followed an unconventional conceptual approach. Disney received its original and exclusive North American merchandising license from the Slesinger family in 1961 and soon afterward relicensed the characters to Sears, Roebuck & Company. As part of its efforts to centralize control over its product tie-ins, Disney did not renew its contract with Sears when it expired in 1996. In the distribution of Pooh licensing that followed, the company offered merchants a choice of selling either of two lines of products: the recognizable Disney character or "Classic Pooh," which closely replicated Ernest A. Shepard's original drawings. "Classic Pooh" had been developed as early as 1988, with Disney licensing the trademark to a few select "high-end" manufacturers. By 1996, the "Classic" design had spread out of the fine china shops and into malldom, in the form of Gund plush figures and nursery wallpaper.

At no other time in company history had an adapted character been promoted by reintegrating the original source material into the campaign. Disney's utter conceptual monopoly on Pooh is an atypical example of schizoid marketing. Pooh bear is now, in some sense, a split subject (insofar as fictional characters can possess a subjectivity), with his dualistic visual design as a battleground in the marketplace. He is not just another commodity to be circulated in the "endless round of self-referential co-advertisements" of the Disney empire.[7] The invention of a "Classic Pooh" has led to issues of a problematic authenticity with which other Disney characters have not had to contend. Which is the true Pooh?

On the one hand, his "Classic" persona has allowed independent businesses to acquire less expensive licenses to sell Disney-related products; on the other, Pooh as commodity is oversaturated within the market. Such a surfeit of product may even diminish Pooh as an icon of children's literature and a British cultural product. One need only recall New York mayor Rudolph Giuliani's "war to keep Pooh in New York" in 1998 as an example of Pooh's total Disneyfication. Chinese philosophy has also adopted the little yellow bear as a master of Taoism, as demonstrated by Benjamin Hoff's best-selling *Tao of Pooh* and its sequel, *The Te of Piglet*. Even Canada has tried to wrest a piece of the cultural and capital pie, as evidenced by the CBC's "Winnie Heritage Moment" and Canada Post's quick-cash Pooh stamp scheme.

If locating an authentic bear of little brain among such capitalistic furore is possible, one must be prepared to wade through a veritable mountain of products. Perhaps trying to certify the authentic is a misguided project. After all, the various cultural, corporate, and artistic voices laying claim to Winnie-the-Pooh are enough to give a silly old bear due course to adopt his pseudonym of Mr. Sanders for good and head for a much more reclusive Hundred Acre Wood. Instead, the focus should be directed to the ways in which Disney's dualistic circulation of Pooh products and the character's subsequent cultural dilution appropriate and commodify an already existing work of art. The case of Winnie the Pooh is in many ways different from other examples of Disney's literary acquisitions; the company has completely absorbed the character, right down to the original conceptual design, spitting out only the hyphens in its original name. No other source material for a Disney animated film has undergone the total corporate integration of Milne and Shepard's work.

What can be gained from such an example of artistic expropriation is the knowledge that an empire such as Disney cannot "remain faithful" to a work through adaptation; the company can only swallow it whole, leaving other cultural and corporate agencies to snap sycophantically at the few remaining traces. At best, then, the Disney machine merely *replaces* the source material — whatever the company touches becomes irrevocably stamped by "the Disney vision." As David Buckingham asserts, "it is hard to think of a fairy tale or a 'classic' children's book which children will not now encounter first (and in most cases *only*) in its 'Disneyfied' version. Symbolically—and in many cases legally—Disney now 'owns' nearly all the fictional characters who have populated children's imaginations over the past century."[8] It is unlikely, then, that one could return to the original Hans Christian Andersen or Brothers Grimm tales from which many of the studio's features were pilfered without inevitably associating them with the animated films.[9]

However, the way the company has done the most violence to its source material is the way it has imprisoned Pooh bear. By devising a "Classic Pooh," the company does not promote an artistic alternative by showcasing the original work of art but instead incorporates it within Disney's own hierarchical canon and *authenticates* its popular appeal. If "there is something sad in the manner in which Disney 'violated' [Winnie-the-Pooh] and packaged his versions in his name through the merchandising of books, toys, clothing, and records," these "violations" deserve exploration.[10] Investigating the Pooh explosion is therefore not simply an elitist wail to preserve a "purer" children's literature but a call to critique the corporate modes of production that may one day turn Milne and Shepard into just a couple of guys who worked for Disney.

Pooh Goes to the Movies

The proliferation of Pooh products can undoubtedly be attributed to the success of the animated films. Both of the first two features— *Winnie the Pooh and the Honey Tree* (Wolfgang Reitherman, 1966) and *Winnie the Pooh and the Blustery Day* (Wolfgang Reitherman, 1968)—were incredibly well received by audiences and critics alike. *Blustery Day* even picked up an Academy Award for Best Cartoon Short Subject in 1968. According to Disneyphile Leonard Maltin, "it took a fresh beguiling subject . . . to bring out the very best in Disney and his staff once more. 'Winnie the Pooh and the Honey Tree' and its sequel . . . were undoubtedly the most charming cartoons, both visually and otherwise, that the studio had created in years."[11]

Part of the films' success may be attributed to a perceived faithfulness to their source material. The studio's desire to remain as close as possible to the spirit of Milne's writing and Shepard's drawings is well publicized. Even the short documentary feature at the beginning of the video release of *The Many Adventures of Winnie the Pooh* emphasizes the connection to Milne's stories.[12] In an attempt to reinforce historical authenticity, Christopher Robin's original stuffed toys are hauled out of their hallowed display case at the Donnell Library Center in New York and filmed sitting on black velvet in loving soft lighting. Photographs of Milne and son abound, as well as the covers for Milne's *Now We Are Six* and *When We Were Very Young*. There are also several juxtapositions of the studio's concept art and publicity stills with the Shepard drawings to accentuate the similarities between the two. Ironically, these similarities are often superficial. Characters may share the same positions in two similar tableaux, or assume analogous poses in two different drawings, but there ends the congruency.

Moreover, there is no reference made to Shepard at all. His drawings are simply shown without connecting them to an author. They are rendered anonymous, their material and historical connection obscured, making the Disney project of appropriation all the easier. In a telling blunder, Maltin claims that the Disney animation "captur[es] the flavour of *A. A. Milne's* original drawings and tak[es] them a few steps further with delightful results."[13] Not only does Maltin mistakenly attribute the drawings to Milne rather than to Shepard, but he implicitly articulates a dissatisfaction with the original drawings. By claiming that Disney "takes [the sketches] a few steps further," Maltin voices a preference for the cartoon incarnations, implying by unspoken extension that the "Classic Pooh" is deficient in some way.

Disney, then, colonizes these "deficient" representations of Pooh and replaces them with a "corrected" version. Pooh's Disneyfication begins immediately in *Many Adventures*. The opening credits are superimposed over live-action shots of a boy's room that the narrator informs us belongs to Christopher Robin. Various stuffed animals populate the room, but not all of these are facsimiles of the toys introduced to the viewer in the opening documentary.[14] Significantly, the red-shirted, glaringly yellow Disney version replaces the more traditional teddy bear that the original Pooh resembles. There is even a Disney Pooh on the cover of a copy of Milne's book that rests next to the stuffed animal. The camera tracks in to a close-up of the cover (on which Milne's name, but not Shepard's, is clearly legible), and the book opens up to a re-creation of the map that Shepard drew for the original stories. Superimposed on the map are the Disney figures, which immediately come to life. Shepard's figures are nowhere to be seen. The illustrator is reduced to the status of a background artist, his "deficient" drawings "corrected" (or "taken one step further," if you prefer) by simply stuffing the principal character into an ill-fitting red halter-top. That Shepard's heirs denounced the film as "a complete travesty" therefore should come as no surprise.[15]

The studio is able to credit Milne unequivocally since his literary contribution (compared to Shepard's illustrative work) has little bearing (pun intended) on all subsequent merchandising. After all, there is no prose to be read and admired on a backpack, a bath toy, or a pair of women's underwear, and thus, no need for representatives of the Milne estate, or Dutton's Children's Books (who still owns the rights to reprint Milne's stories) to sniff around for royalties. Disney may stress the "literariness" of its films with impunity since the original author does not explicitly determine the way in which the visuals (the ultimate selling factor of product tie-ins) are articulated. Although quotes from the Milne texts are inscribed on many of the "Classic Pooh" products, these items would obviously not be marketable without corresponding imagery.

Many Adventures is an anomaly in that it represents one of the few *explicitly* intertextual examples of Disney's adaptations. Milne's text is literally incorporated into the film. Other animated adaptations (*Snow White and the Seven Dwarfs,* for example) begin with an ornate storybook opening to reveal its contents, thus providing both a narrative frame and an immediate association of the animated film with a "classic" literary masterpiece. Whereas the storybook frame disappears once the narrative begins in these films, the text returns repeatedly in *Many Adventures,* often becoming physically embodied within the narrative itself. Pages turn, characters continually hop over the bindings between the pages, and words become physical entities to be used as props (Tigger escapes from a high tree when the "book" is turned sideways — he simply hops onto the horizontal safety of the text itself). References are made to page numbers, characters comment on their own textuality ("I nearly bounced right out of the book!"), and an intradiegetic narrator "reads" the viewer the stories.

Voice-over narration allows for an even larger kernel of manufactured authenticity. Besides Christopher Robin, the narrator is the only other character in the film to speak with a British accent, and such a linguistic connection leads the viewer to assume that it is the voice of Milne, the storyteller himself. It is a voice of mastery and omniscience, and one that even the characters hear in a few select moments of self-reflexivity. "What will happen to me?" asks a curious Pooh bear at the end of an episode; "Wait and see," is the narrator's reply. His authority is never questioned but is simply accepted as apropos. Tigger *nearly* gets suspicious. While stuck at the top of a tree, he interrupts the snickering narrator to ask, "Hey! Who are *you*?" The reply is immediate: "Why, I'm the narrator." Hegemony is immediately restored in the Hundred Acre Wood as Tigger takes the evasive answer in typical stride: "Oh. Well then, narrate me down from here, would ya'?"

Tigger's unquestioning acquiescence is unfortunate in many ways since, to a certain extent, the narrator is a representative of the strategies of domination that seek mastery over the text. By continually calling attention to the presence of the text, Disney is able to extend its authority over Milne's work. Not only are the characters appropriated, but the film absorbs the book itself. The Disney version underwrites Pooh's textuality through processes of revision. Montage sequences streamline loquacious prose (for example, "Owl talked all the way from page forty-one until page sixty-two"), not just for the purposes of narrative economy, but to avoid undue "wordiness." Milne's charming circumlocutions are stripped to the bare essentials of plot development. Moreover, the narrator asserts his own autonomous dominance over the text. We begin to doubt that the narrator actually is Milne speaking from beyond the grave when his voice-overs diverge from the written text that appears on the screen. Characters within the diegesis also have a tendency to ignore Milne's dialogue, preferring their own virtual ad-libs (carefully scripted by Disney writers, of course). Such revisionist underwriting makes the process of appropriation and subsequent commodification all the easier. Milne's text is submerged and transmuted within Disney's authorial discourse, and the adaptation produces a corporate text, ready-made for profit and licensed by all the trappings of a "literary" heritage.

While the film ostensibly remains true to the "Milne spirit" by emphasizing its connection to its literary predecessor, the above examples are instances in which Disney discourse overwrites Pooh's authorial source. Pooh purists would certainly be outraged, especially those who espouse fidelity as a criterion for successful adaptation. Fidelity criticism, however, is a notoriously monologic system. It "depends on a notion of the text as having and rendering up to the (intelligent) reader a single, correct 'meaning' which the filmmaker has either adhered to or in some sense violated or tampered with."[16] Since the ultimately subjective readings of filmmaker and audience cannot completely coincide (some critic will inevitably invoke the term "hatchet job" in a review of an adaptation), "the fidelity approach seems like a doomed enterprise."[17] Nonetheless, there is a substantial difference between, on the one hand, unfairly criticizing the Disney studio for failing to live up to the impossible task of capturing a transcendent "authorial intent" and, on the other, voicing legitimate concern over possible strategies of cultural and economic colonization.

Disputed Origins and the Question of Ownership

The majority of complaints from British audiences are expressions of dissatisfaction with Pooh's "Americanization" and concern over a perceived supplanting of English heritage. Is "Classic Pooh" an evocation of Pooh's lost Britishness and an acknowledgement of his Disneyfication? More precisely, is the manufacturing of a schizophrenic Pooh a veiled apology to British nationalists and Milne/Shepard fundamentalists? After all, there seems to be a historical precedent for the studio's assuagement of outraged British sensibilities. Shortly before the first animated short's original release in 1966, the studio received a barrage of cables organized by the *Evening News* film critic Felix Barker demanding a redubbing of Christopher Robin's voice—replacing the original American inflection with "a standard southern English accent."[18] His campaign actually succeeded, and the film was redubbed at great expense. Whether or not such a concession represented a triumph for the British heritage industry, many critics in the United Kingdom were disgusted with the film and even more perturbed by the subsequent scramble among American manufacturers to acquire the merchandising rights. According to *Daily Mail* critics, "none of this wheeler-dealing with a part of the British heritage disturbs [the short's director] and his cohorts. To them, it appears Winnie the Pooh is not really all that different from Mickey Mouse."[19]

Disney's appropriation and commodification of a British cultural object may not be a venial sin, despite the protestations of angry English Pooh fans. According to an outmoded but formerly popular theory of filmic adaptation, the filmmaker "looks to the characters and incidents which have somehow detached themselves from language and . . . have achieved a mythic life of their own."[20] The company's ownership of and revisions to the characters could therefore be justified beyond the level of legalities. On a quasi-metaphysical level, if Pooh and company somehow achieve transcendence from their literary roots because of their "classic" status, then issues of authorship and cultural specificity are rendered moot. The text is just so much raw material that can be molded according to the wishes of the filmmaker. In this way, the studio could justify its postmodern (and neo-imperialist) "borrowings" that disregard the historical and national contexts of the textual source.

Could Winnie, then, conceivably become "just another bleedin' Yank?" So acute are British neocolonial anxieties that upon hearing that Disney would cover one-third of the cost of repairing the crumbling Pooh Sticks Bridge in East Sussex, "local people feared that Disney's involvement . . . might lead to the growth of a mini theme park."[21] Imagine how these poor residents would feel if they realized that although "Milne [did] not live to see what Walt Disney did to *Winnie the Pooh,* he might not have objected so much as some people assume."[22]

In fact, Milne relied heavily on American idiom—gleaned from "read[ing] any amount of Scott Fitzgerald and Mark Twain and back copies of *Movie Moments*"—in his original drafts of the stories.[23] Only after receiving numerous complaints from his publisher (for example: "As things are, you will confine the appeal to a handful of illiterates munching hamburgers in Kalamazoo") did Milne make an effort to "flatten the antics of the characters, reduce the pace, and downgrade the style to impeccable scholarly English."[24] To an extent, Pooh's appropriation and midwesternization by Disney (noticeable mainly in the accents of many of the characters in the animated shorts) may represent a homecoming of sorts. Much to the chagrin of the Empire, it appears the bear has Yankee roots.

And yet, national distinctions between the "Classic" and Disney animals are still vehemently asserted and constructed according to a misguided belief in the former's inherent authenticity. For example, Ann Thwaite asserts that "the Walt Disney film versions . . . loathed as they were by Shepard's admirers, and by many admirers of Milne too, increased awareness of the characters but apparently did nothing to diminish sales of the *real thing*."[25] Her elitism and nationalism extend to the critique of Pooh merchandise as well: "There is still a great deal of Disney-based merchandise about and some particularly unattractive Poohs, which bear no resemblance to the real thing."[26] However, she acknowledges a potential remedy by positing that "the situation has improved since Disney realized the value of the Shepard material itself. Disney now authorizes the marketing of a great many attractive bits and pieces with the authentic Shepard images."[27] Leave it to the cultural refinement of a British gentleman to add some class to the garishness of American imagination. If the invention of a "Classic Pooh" is a measure of apology and a revaluing of the original (read: "superior") material by Disney, the rift between the two animals could not be wider. For Pooh purists, the "Classic" line is both an accreditation of the source material and a means of discriminating the "tasteful" aficionado from the "vulgar" consumer. Such an upper-class animal thus becomes a cultural articulation of social and economic hierarchies. Yet, it is Disney who retains the last laugh (and the profits). The company has indeed "realised the value of the Shepard material," only insofar as it allows Disney to reach a wider market of consumers. Far from acknowledging Shepard's artistic "superiority," the value of his material is exclusively monetary.

Meanwhile, both the United Kingdom and United States continue to assert their respective natural rights to the characters. On February 5, 1998, MP Gwyneth Dunwoody initiated a campaign to repatriate the original stuffed animals that E. P. Dutton had donated to the Donnell Center, a branch of the New York Public Library. Her project sparked the wrath of Mayor Rudolph Giuliani, as mentioned earlier, who claimed that he would "risk a war with Britain" to keep the toys in New York.[28] Even President Clinton acknowledged that "the loss of Pooh [would] be utterly unbearable."[29] Dunwoody's efforts came to naught, and the toys remained in the States. Although the tongues of these public figures were undoubtedly clamped firmly in their cheeks, the debate over nationalistic ownership of the character is demonstrative of a skirmish between two imperialist powers, both jockeying for privileged positions within a global marketplace.

Various other nations and cultures vied for Pooh control as well, with Canadian arrogations being perhaps the most embarrassing examples of all. Not only had the culture machines laid dubious claim to Superman a few years earlier in a CBC "Heritage Moment," but a subsequent television short was commissioned to milk nationalistic capital from Winnie's seventieth anniversary.

The black bear who enthralled Milne's son at the London Zoo was originally from White River, Ontario, and her original owner, Lieutenant Harry Colbourne, hailed from Winnipeg (hence "Winnie").[30] Nationalists had a field day, and Canada Post even released commemorative stamps detailing the character's development from caged animal to Shepard to Disney.[31] Never mind that the other half of Winnie's name is derived from another (non-Canadian) animal at the zoo—a swan named "Pooh"—if the short documentary that begins *Many Adventures* is to be credited.[32] An article by Ross Kilpatrick even makes the astounding claim that "the plot of the very first chapter of Winnie-the-Pooh . . . is the creation of a New Brunswicker, Sir Charles G. D. Roberts," even though "there is no direct evidence that he knew A. A. Milne."[33] In another proud Canadian moment, the absence of historical factuality fails to inhibit nationalistic enterprise.

Far be it from me to favor other nationalist claims to Pooh (and certainly, as a Canadian, I can think of less problematic cultural artifacts and historical moments we might alternatively celebrate), when such patriotic clamor is so easily exploited by the profiteering of the character's major shareholders. Should varied and conflicting cultural authorities invoke Pooh's image, or tell a story about his origins for nationalistic purposes, chastising their efforts for staking an "undeserved" claim in the character's ownership is a misplaced criticism. No one can truly "own" or control Pooh's image, save the major shareholders who hold its rights and whose pockets are lined by "licensing" the image to as many culture machines as it wishes.

To an extent, the variety of claims to cultural origin is unsurprising considering the character's international popularity. Beginning in 1998, "Pooh Friendship Day" is now an annual celebration in New York, with similar events taking place in Canada, China, and Japan. The 1998 "Pooh and Friends 100 Acre Holiday" in Osaka, for example, drew over three hundred thousand people in a single month.[34] However, comments made by spokespersons for the Disney Company only contribute to the Pooh schism or, more specifically, the character's removal from a cultural context. John Singh, a publicist for the Consumer Products Division, claims that "Pooh belongs to everybody. He can be anything you want him to be."[35] Singh's comments are yet another example of the company's erasure of context and an alienation of its product from uncommodified cultural meaning. Pooh becomes an empty signifier—Disney Pooh, Classic Pooh, Hanukkah Pooh, Samurai Pooh—it's all the same animal. Removed from the confines of specificity, the character may be claimed by any party asserting ownership. Moreover, Disney has a direct financial interest in the various assignations of the bear's meaning, as well as the multiple claims to ownership. The wider its identity, the greater the profit margins.

But does Pooh really "belong to everybody"? The Disney Company is notorious for its ferocious protection of trademarked characters and iconography. Detection of "unauthorized" use results in assured litigation, as the owners of three separate day care centers in Orlando, Florida, discovered when they decorated their walls with trademarked Disney characters without permission in 1989.[36] Prevention of profit loss is the company's main concern, though the company is also within its legal rights to pursue litigation against public criticism it finds libelous. Lawsuits, then, represent more than a means to secure income, and "Disney becomes anecdotal of the tensions between cultural critique and institutional containment of resistance."[37] Not only is critical enunciation muffled by corporate intimidation, but such tensions speak of an even more fundamental conflict. Susan Willis states that

> the individual's right to imagine and to give expression to unique ways of seeing is at stake in struggles against private property. Mickey Mouse, notwithstanding his corporate copyright, exists in our common culture. . . . If culture is held as private property, then there can be only one correct version of Mickey Mouse, whose logo-like image is the cancellation of creativity. But the multiplicity of quirky versions of Mickey Mouse that children draw can stand as a question to us as adults: Who, indeed, owns Mickey Mouse?[38]

Substitute the Bear for the Mouse, and the issue remains the same. "Classic Pooh" may be an extension of the "way of seeing" Pooh, but to emblazon the Disney corporate logo on such merchandise is still an assertion of unilateral control.

By ostensibly returning to the character's origins in its development of a new line of merchandise, the company extends its reach over an alternative vision of the character, colonizing the work at its very source and tightening the range of imaginative ownership. Who owns Winnie the Pooh? The answer inevitably remains "Disney," Shepard versions or no Shepard versions. Control over the character's potentially myriad meanings is not in the company's interest and is not the issue at stake; Disney is concerned only with controlling its material production and distribution. Customers are "free" to manipulate the product in whatever way they wish, but this is certainly an illusory freedom at best. For in making Pooh "be anything you want him to be," consumers are allowed only to construct their choice of a signified from the material signifer that is purchased or rented from Disney. And the maintenance of this control limits and potentially impoverishes the culture(s) to which the character "belongs."

Disney's inscription of "Classic Pooh" into its canon is an assertion of creative power (or, rather, power over creativity, if you prefer Willis's account). There seems to be little question over whether Disney "is giving rise to new forms of imagination, expression, and collectivity, or whether [Disney] is merely perfecting techniques of total subjection and domination."[39] The company's domineering efforts to maximize profits through incorporation are not isolated strategies but are symptomatic of increasing global consumerism. In the cutthroat business of producing profitable entertainment culture, it would appear that Disney is perpetually haunted by the ghost of lost Oswald the Lucky Rabbit revenues from the late 1920s.[40] Through a continual commitment to total marketing, the company is able to secure profits from multiple fronts. A recognizable product line is essential as the toy industry "sell[s] directly to children by tapping their imaginations in playthings inspired by characters in the mass media."[41] Nostalgia also remains a bankable commodity since "Disney toys manage symbolically to bridge the gap between the 'traditional' and the newer mass culture, despite in fact being themselves absolutely typical of the latter in terms of global marketing and profitability."[42] "Classic Pooh" is both an old friend and an item to be acquired to satisfy the kollector's kraze. He is a success story in the age of multiple target markets and wide age-bracket appeal.

Pooh's primary appeal is to children but is not, of course, limited to them. The gentle simplicity and unabashed sentimentality that characterize the stories are associated with the still-popular post-Edwardian conceptions of inherent childhood "innocence." Ubiquitous subscription to childish naïveté proves advantageous for the corporation to inscribe the identity of "consumer" on such a tabula rasa. "In amusement society, the visual fantasies of marketing impinge on childhood to socialize and appropriate desire, condition emotional satisfactions, and establish identities through consumption."[43] In children's establishment of microcommunities through the use of consumer products ("Let's play Pooh bear!"), we see realized "Disney's attempt to turn children into consumers and to construct commodification as a defining principle of children's culture."[44] The films' role is vital to such a process. Continuing the Disney tradition of synergistic coadvertisements for a variety of products, *Many Adventures* is part of "a new marketplace of culture to which children [have] unprecedented access."[45] Films are used to plug the merchandise and vice versa while children's "freedom of choice as consumers blur[s] traditional distinctions between child and adult culture."[46] These distinctions are further broken down when "Classic Pooh" becomes a collector's fad among adults. While the bear of very little brain helps the kiddies develop into zombie shoppers of equally singular intellect, their already indoctrinated parents snap up Pooh's porcelain likeness in a frenzied, bourgeois accumulation of goods.

If Marxist theories are to be credited, then Pooh's corporate fragmentation and subsequent adoption by the much-maligned middle class can lead only to his alienation from his means of production. It is no accident that the labels that read "Disney Presents" on Pooh merchandise are much more prominent than those that read "Made in Taiwan." And it is also rare to discuss Disney labor practices these days without hearing mutterings of "sweatshops," although the company continues to protest these associations vehemently. However, the obfuscation of labor by the corporation's capitalistic practices does not end with a denial of the materiality of manufacturing; Pooh is also alienated from the historical materiality of his original source.

Although a plush toy's tag may read "Copyright Milne/Shepard," the huge, unmistakable Disney trademark dwarfs the credit. How close, then, is "Classic Pooh" to a historical meaning proper? Moreover, is it possible to discuss issues of adaptation and subsequent merchandising in the context of a "meaning proper"? One risks the elitism of an Ann Thwaite by arguing that Disney removed Pooh from his original aura by its appropriations and is now attempting to capitalize on the said truncated aura as well. Aggrandizing the ineffability of the aura is commonplace, especially when using adjectives like "superior" to describe the original. Walter Benjamin's discussions of a work's "aura" did not extend to the merchandising of plush toys, but one can infer that a manufactured Pooh is literally the means by which the consumer satisfies the urge to "get hold of an object at very close range by way of its likeness, its reproduction."[47]

However, it is quite a leap in logic to assume that in "belonging to everybody," Pooh's aura is eradicated by Disney. Instead, the artwork's "transcendent" aura becomes so much raw material for the manufacturing of a "synthetic" aura—a new, commercial quality reinforced by a rationalized hierarchy of class and exploitable in the marketplace. "Classic" Pooh's mass production is not necessarily the "mark of a perception whose 'sense of the universal equality of things' has increased to such a degree that it extracts it even from a unique object by means of reproduction."[48] More likely, it is the mark of a perception whose sense of a universal *hierarchy* supports and is supported by social distinctions as marked by price and taste.[49] Who was the "original" Pooh? A black bear from White River? An English swan? Christopher Milne's stuffed toy, Edward? A children's character by a New Brunswick writer? An ink drawing by E. H. Shepard? Not only are the character's literal origins murky, but the project of locating a transcendent (and superior), "authentic" bear is misguided. "Classic" is not a euphemism for "original," nor is "original" a synonym of "superior."

While discussions of an artwork's aura often move toward the realm of the mystical, the manufacturing of a "Classic Pooh" offers a more concrete problematic beyond the metaphysics of "authenticity." The creation of a schizoid Pooh may represent an erasure of history. Once the character assumes multiple incarnations, becoming a sign without a referent, it becomes increasingly divorced from its material origins. It is not Pooh's "authenticity" that is lost in the schism; it is the character's connection to its original authors. Such obfuscation is unsurprising when one considers the great amount of work performed by many Disney animators on numerous major animated films that went uncredited in the films themselves. The opening credits of *Many Adventures* are typically rather sketchy. Although the film combines the first three short features into a single package, there is no distinction between the episodes, and the film's opening credits do not specify who originally worked on which short. One suspects that the re-release simply uses the credits for *Honey Tree* and discards the other remaining original shorts, *Winnie the Pooh and the Blustery Day* and *Tigger Too*. These twenty-five-minute shorts were compiled into *The Many Adventures of Winnie the Pooh*.

Keeping in line with tradition, Disney manages to bury Shepard effectively with "Classic Pooh." While the "Classic" manifestation superficially appears to be an accrediting of Shepard's work, Disney (naturally) does not publicize its evocations of the source material, nor does it promote the original works. Part of the reason can be attributed to economics. Naturally, Disney would be loath to split potential revenues with Dutton's Children's Books. For its part, Dutton denies the existence of a "Classic Pooh." There is the original, and then there is "that other Pooh."[50] To ignore Pooh's division, however, is foolishly to turn a blind eye to Disney's economic and conceptual encroachment. The company released an abundance of its own Pooh storybooks in 1999, which would certainly eat into Dutton's own profits.[51]

However, Disney's strategies of appropriation have other material consequences beyond its alterations of a rival's sales figures. By creating "Classic Pooh," Disney completely incorporates the character by manufacturing and subsequently licensing its "historical aura." While the autonomous existence of such an aura is questionable, as mentioned earlier, its corporate (re)production has certainly proved profitable for the Disney Company. And yet this manufactured historicity, or authenticity, is generated at the expense of other, smaller corporations and further alienates the product from its origins. Because no matter how much "Classic Pooh" resembles Shepard's drawings, it is not Shepard's Pooh; it is Disney's animal—legally, conceptually, authentically—forever and ever amen (or at least while the copyright still holds). "Classic

Pooh" exists in order to credit the original, and to legitimize Disney's versions of the Milne and Shepard stories for a mass audience. The popularity of Milne and Shepard's Pooh is authenticated only via Disney's "Classic" version, and this schism is itself part of the company's larger strategies of decontextualization, alienation, and the perpetuation of commodity fetishism. Although Disney requires the appearance of product differentiation in the form of a bifurcated Pooh to feed and develop a wider market, its "Classic" product engulfs its source material during the very process of accreditation. Looking through a mirror darkly, this Pooh is the reflection, which, in an unexpected turn, renders the *subject* "other" and begins to colonize. You are not looking at two animals. There is only one animal. There has never been more than one animal. . . .

Postscript

On March 4, 2001, Disney paid an estimated $340 to $350 million to the Milne Estate for the rights to the royalty stream generated by Milne's characters, as well as all future use of the characters in any media. These rights, however, do not include the U.S. and Canadian rights, which are currently held by the Slesinger family, who reside in Beverly Hills. In 1991, the Slesingers initiated a lawsuit against Disney for lost royalties on the character dating back to 1983—especially lost revenue generated from media products (videotapes, DVDs, and computer software). They are presently seeking $700 million in compensatory damages and an unspecified amount of punitive damages. Disney could also stand to lose the entire franchise itself should breach of contract or fraud be proven in the event of a trial.

In an interesting move on November 6, 2002, the company prompted Milne's granddaughters, Clare Milne and Minette Hunt, to exercise their heirs' privileges and recapture the North American rights to Pooh from the Slesingers. Naturally, the English heirs would then have reconveyed the merchandising rights to Disney. Sadly (for Disney), the federal courts ruled against the heirs in May 2003. However, the Slesingers' temporary victory was short-lived. On March 29, 2004, Florida state courts dismissed the plaintiff's thirteen-year-old suit with prejudice due to the alleged illegality of the means by which the family had obtained the evidence needed for their suit—internal documents that Disney had attempted to conceal. So, while Disney's North American merchandising rights for Pooh remain secure for now, the Slesingers are currently seeking an appeal.[52] Evidently, contestation over the ownership and control of this silly old bear appears to be interminable.

Acknowledgment

This study is dedicated to Mark Langer, who showed me new ways to get my hands dirty during his remarkable graduate course on the Disney Company at Carleton University.

Notes

1. The Walt Disney Company, *Disney Store Online,* October 1, 1999, http://www.store. disney.com.
2. Vanessa Gisquet and Aude Lagorce, "Top Earning Fictional Characters," *Forbes,* September 25, 2003, http://www.forbes.com/2003/09/25/cx_al_0926fictionalintro. html.
3. Ibid.
4. Justin Valentin, "History," *Just Pooh,* http:// www.just-pooh.com/history.html.
5. Mary MacNamara, "Disney Strikes Honey of a Deal with Pooh Products," *Los Angeles Times,* December 27, 1998, D6.
6. For a more in-depth account of the controversy (which includes the company's alleged pressure to sack New York freelance reporter Nikki Finke for apparently grossly exaggerating the profits Disney stands to lose if the Slesingers terminate their contract with the company), see Joe Shea, "The Pooh Files," *Multinational Monitor,* March 20, 2002, http://www.monitor.net/monitor/0203a/pooh6.html.
7. S. M. Fjellman, *Vinyl Leaves: Walt Disney World and America* (Boulder, Colo.: Westview Press, 1992), 157.
8. David Buckingham, "Dissin' Disney: Critical Perspectives on Children's Media Culture," *Media, Culture & Society* 19, no. 2 (1997): 285.
9. Case in point: a children's theater troupe, in which I was once employed, had difficulty mounting a successful production of *Snow White.* Children frequently remarked that the various actors playing the heroine could not possibly be an authentic Snow. "That's not her dress," they would complain. After purchasing the yellow, red, and blue puffy-sleeved nightmare associated with Disney's Snow White, the show went on to become an audience favorite. Many tykes, in fact expressed a feverish desire to take the gown home with them.
10. Jack Zipes, "Breaking the Disney Spell," in *From Mouse to Mermaid: The Politics of Film, Gender, and Culture,* ed. Elizabeth Bell, Lynda Haas, and Laura Sells (Bloomington: Indiana University Press, 1995), 40.
11. Leonard Maltin, *The Disney Films* (New York: Crown Publishers, 1973), 23.
12. *The Many Adventures of Winnie the Pooh,* directed by John Lounsberry and Wolfgang Reitherman (1968; Buena Vista Pictures, 1993).
13. Maltin, *The Disney Films,* 276. Italics mine.

14. The makers of the video documentary have not done their homework, as Shepard's drawings of Winnie were *not* originally modeled after Christopher Robin Milne's bear; the artist chose to immortalize his own son's stuffed animal, "Growler," whose roly-poly figure Winnie more closely resembles.

15. Ann Thwaite, *The Brilliant Career of Winnie-the-Pooh: The Story of A. A. Milne and His Writing for Children* (London: Methuen, 1992), 162.

16. Brian McFarlane, *Novel to Film: An Introduction to the Theory of Adaptation* (Oxford: Clarendon Press, 1996), 8.

17. Ibid., 9.

18. Thwaite, *Brilliant Career,* 164.

19. Iain Smith and Jerry LeBlanc, "Massacre in 100 Aker Wood: Or How Disney the Walt Said Pooh to Winnie," (London) *Daily Mail,* April 16, 1966, E2.

20. George Bluestone, *Novels into Film* (Berkeley: University of California Press, 1971), 62.

21. David Sapsted, "Pooh Sticks Bridge Is Falling Down, but Disney Is Going to Help Re-build It," *National Post* (Canada), October 21, 1999, A14.

22. Ann Thwaite, *A. A. Milne, His Life* (London: Faber, 1990), 212.

23. Angela Milne, quoted in Thwaite, *Brilliant Career,* 166.

24. Ibid., 167.

25. Thwaite, *A. A. Milne,* 485. Italics mine.

26. Thwaite, *Brilliant Career,* 163.

27. Ibid.

28. Justin Valentin, "British Want Pooh Back Home!" *Just Pooh,* February 5, 1998, http://www. just-pooh.com/newsarchives.html.

29. Quoted in Justin Valentin, "Winnie the Pooh Will Stay in New York," *Just Pooh,* March 22, 1998, http://www. just-pooh.com/newsarchives.html.

30. In 2001, the city of Winnipeg purchased Shepard's only oil painting of Winnie to commemorate the bear's rather tenuous connection with Manitoba's capital.

31. If the makers of the CBC Heritage Moment had discovered that little Graham Shepard's stuffed teddy, "Growler," met his demise in Montreal (worried to death in Minette Shepard's garden by a Scottish terrier), doubtlessly they would have celebrated the bear's "Canadian" life cycle coming full circle. For further details, see Peter Dennis, "A Short History of Pooh and Winnie," *Pooh Corner,* http://www.pooh-corner.com/pooh.html.

32. Christopher Robin Milne has referred to these episodes at the London Zoo in several interviews and mentions them in his memoirs, which are likely the source of the documentary's information.

33. R. Kilpatrick, "Winnie the Pooh and the Canadian Connection," *Queen's Quarterly* 105, no. 4 (1998): 626 and 625.

34. The Walt Disney Company, "Disney Consumer Products," *Disney Annual 1998 Report,* http://www.disneyinternational.com/AnnualReport/consumer.htm.

35. MacNamara, "Disney Strikes Honey of a Deal," D6.

36. Paul Richter, "Disney's Tough Tactics," *Los Angeles Times,* July 8, 1990, D1.

37. Elizabeth Bell, Lynda Haas, and Laura Sells, "Introduction: Walt's in the Movies," in *From Mouse to Mermaid,* 14.

38. Susan Willis, "Critical Vantage Points on Disney's Work," *South Atlantic Quarterly* 92, no. 1 (1993): 6.

39. Miriam Hansen, "Of Mice and Ducks: Benjamin and Adorno on Disney," *South Atlantic Quarterly* 92, no. 1 (1993): 28.

40. Oswald was the first Disney character to generate a small line of merchandise, but Walt was not able to maintain the rights to the rabbit. In the process of trying to negotiate a more lucrative deal for his creation, he was forced to relinquish the copyright to Oswald's distributor, Charles Minntz of Universal Studios. According to Alan Bryman, Disney learned a valuable lesson in synergy and "thereafter, he zealously guarded his rights in this regard." See Alan Bryman, "The Disneyization of Society," *Sociological Review* 47, no. 1 (1999): 36.

41. Gary Cross, *Kids' Stuff: Toys and the Changing World of American Childhood* (Cambridge, Mass.: Harvard University Press, 1997), 10.

42. Dan Fleming, *Powerplay: Toys as Popular Culture* (Manchester: Manchester University Press, 1996), 37.

43. Lauren Langman, "Neon Cages: Shopping for Subjectivity," in *Lifestyle Shopping: The Subject of Consumption,* ed. Rob Sheilds (London: Routledge, 1992), 57.

44. H. A. Giroux, "Animating Youth: The Disneyfication of Children's Culture," *Socialist Review* 24, no. 3 (1994): 33.

45. Richard deCordova, "The Mickey in Macy's Window: Childhood, Consumerism, and Disney Animation," in *Disney Discourse: Producing the Magic Kingdom,* ed. Eric Smoodin (New York: Routledge, 1994), 209.

46. Ibid., 209–210.

47. Walter Benjamin, "The Work of Art in the Age of Mechanical Reproduction." 1935. Rpt. in *Film Theory and Criticism: Introductory Readings.* 4th ed. Ed. Gerald Mast, Marshall Cohen, and Leo Braudy (Oxford: Oxford University Press, 1992), 669.

48. Ibid.

49. My thanks to Mike Budd for this insightful comment.

50. MacNamara, "Disney Strikes Honey of a Deal," D6.

51. The Walt Disney Company, "Disney Consumer Products," *Disney Annual 1999 Report,* http://www.disneyinternational.com/AnnualReport/consumer.htm.

52. For a detailed account of the convoluted but dramatic lawsuit, see Joe Shea, "The Pooh Files," *Multinational Monitor,* March 20, 2002, http://www.monitor.net/monitor/0203a/.

8

Truer Than Life: Disney's Animal Kingdom

Scott Hermanson

In 1998, the Disney empire gained a new colony in central Florida when it opened its fourth major theme park at Walt Disney World. Animal Kingdom represents Disney's foray into the zoological sciences, integrating live animals alongside its more typical rides and attractions. As an entertainment company whose major stars are anthropomorphized animals, Disney has a substantial reputation for animating metal and plastic into lifelike automatons. The conjoining of this reputation with the presence of live animals conjured up all manner of bizarre scenarios. Would tigers roam the 100 Acre Wood with Tigger? Would visitors see a real baby elephant flying across its pen? Would grizzlies appear to sing "The Bear Necessities," tooth and nail in the service of song and dance? How and where would Disney draw the line that separated reality from fantasy? Exactly how would Disney differentiate its new park from typical metropolitan zoos? Even more crucial, how would Animal Kingdom differ from Busch Gardens and Sea World, its major competitors in the business of animal-oriented theme parks? Such a theme park would seemingly have to acknowledge wildlife's precarious position in an increasingly degraded ecology, potentially leading Disney into areas of contested political issues. The fascination of seeing live exotic animals would have to be balanced by a sensitive treatment of their often-depressing condition in the world outside protective zoo walls. By injecting live animals into its theme-park formula, Disney simultaneously ran the risk of injecting contentious environmental politics.

Animal Kingdom is larger in size but similar in approach to its predecessors: the Magic Kingdom, Epcot, and Disney-MGM Studios. The various attractions include simulated rides inside darkened theaters, 3-D movies, Broadway-style shows, and water rides intermixed with elaborate environments that hold exotic animals. At times, the park can resemble a traditional zoo, with crowds of people pressed up against glass to stare at a sleeping tiger. Yet Disney's park goes well beyond more typical zoos in creating habitats where animals appear to be in their natural surroundings. In traditional zoos, visitors encounter a familiar, comfortable presentation of exotic animals. Limitations of money, space and specimens confine wild-animal presentation to a relatively standard model. Bars or fences surround the animal: visitors observe the animal from a distance just beyond the barrier. Invested in that caged animal are the associations of exotic nature transmitted to the visitor. The experience of a wild, strange nature—the inaccessible wilderness of the savannah, the jungle, the ocean depths, or the skies—is contained, caged in that animal as much as the animal is caged in its pen. This metonymical relationship to nature is as far as most zoos go. Some of the more progressive and more flush zoological parks attempt to create more elaborate environments for their specimens, disguising cages and pens so that they appear as natural barriers or allowing compatible animals to occupy the same pens. But these re-creations are rarely exercised on a large, parkwide scale. Their rarity is confirmed by marketing that labels them as exceptional attractions. More generally, wild nature is presented in small, monadic bits.

In Animal Kingdom, Disney presents a zoo expanded in acreage and wealth, and the company attempts to change the quality of a zoo itself. Nature at Animal Kingdom no longer seems confined behind the eyes of the caged beast, no longer transmitted across an almost insurmountable distance only hinted at by the moat and bars separating visitor from animal. Instead, the expensive entry fee to Animal Kingdom purchases more than a glimpse of a far-off world, a longing for an exotic world. The forty-eight-dollar ticket attempts to purchase satisfaction of that desire.

Yet as Disney has multiple types of visitors, satisfaction of that desire must take multiple routes. Primarily, Animal Kingdom appeals to the seasoned Disney World tourist through its elaborate presentation of spectacle. Disney takes the exotic, wild essence hinted at in the eyes of the typical zoo animal and through plastic, fiberglass, narrative, costume, plants, and scenery creates a complete exotic world—an African village with nearby safari, an Asian marketplace with exotic birds and bats, a paleontological dig with real dinosaur bones. Such spectacle appeals to the youngest of Disney visitors who can immerse themselves in the 360-degree cartoon, playing their part as jungle biologist or paleontologist digging in the sand for bones, and it also appeals to the adult visitors who can marvel at the immense resources, attention to detail, and elaborate narratives that Disney constructs to make the experience as seamless as possible. Amid this spectacle, Disney also tries to appeal to the knowledgeable, perhaps cynical visitor who comes equipped with an educated eye toward animal rights, environmental pollution, and sustainable ecological practices. For these visitors, the park underscores nearly all of its attractions with scientific explanations of animal habitat and behavior, environmental problems, and paleontological puzzles. Of course these stereotypes of Disney visitors are never so clearly defined. Even the most critical of visitors will probably succumb to moments of guilty pleasure at being swept up in some elaborate re-creation. And the most avid Disneyphile will likely pause at some point to question some internal contradiction that cannot be hidden under Technicolor paint and snappy dialogue. The park succeeds for most visitors because it thoroughly embraces the role that nature plays outside the park boundaries. Outside the gates of Animal Kingdom, we've relegated nature to that which has no contact with humans—what Jennifer Price labels "Nature as a Place Apart."[1] In contemporary culture, nature already exhibits the qualities of a theme park, a fantasyland where we escape the rigors and frustration of modern life. Animal Kingdom merely conventionalizes and commodifies this relationship in the easily understood genre of theme park. The contradictions that would seemingly tear apart the fantasy of Animal Kingdom—the ludicrousness of a hyper-consumerist theme park spouting ecological messages—are no more troublesome for the typical Disney tourist than the contradictions of the Sierra Club member driving an SUV. In both cases, questions that should be raised are effaced by an economy that transforms ecological destruction into its opposite through elaborate and very effective green-coded images. Animal Kingdom is merely the hyperactive extension of our contemporary construction of nature.

Animal Kingdom's geography is similar to that of its Magic Kingdom predecessor. The park is laid out in a spoke-and-wheel configuration with its island center circled by Discovery River and four "lands" that girdle the visually dominant hub. Africa, Asia, Camp Minnie-Mickey, and DinoLand U.S.A. surround the island of Safari Village and its fourteen-story Tree of Life in the same way Frontierland, Tomorrowland, and Fantasyland surround Cinderella's Castle. And as Main Street U.S.A. funnels crowds away from the entrance, Animal Kingdom relies on its Oasis—a series of trails that meander around small animal pens, over streams, and under water-falls—to disperse crowds as they enter the park. The difference between Magic Kingdom's Main Street and Animal Kingdom's Oasis is telling. The former heightens the excitement of arrival as visitors are condensed into a hyper-consumer fantasyland of candy stores, souvenir shops, ice-cream parlors, and flower stands. In the distance, Cinderella's Castle draws the crowds into the different lands of the park. Animal Kingdom's Oasis, however, orchestrates an entirely different emotional pitch. Free of rides, restaurants, and, amazingly enough, gift shops, the Oasis is a dense, simulated jungle interspersed with exhibits of smaller animals such as parrots and anteaters. Unlike the visitors on Main Street, visitors here are hidden from one another, and no visual monument pulls them toward the center of the park. Curiously understated, the Oasis in many ways seems to disarm our defenses, our skepticism. The absence of shops, lines, and loud distractions serves to reassure the visitor that Animal Kingdom is about nature, allowing guests to decompress after the often frantic obstacle course of parking the car, riding a tram, purchasing tickets, renting a stroller or wheelchair, and all the other tiny frustrations of embarking on a day of fantasy. The Oasis convinces us that we are indeed away from modern life, away from all its artifices and unrealities. We have crossed the boundary into real nature, as evidenced by the real live animals lounging in the Oasis pens. And whereas even the least sophisticated visitor in Magic Kingdom can recognize the constructions of the mythical western Frontierland or the patriotic Liberty Square, even the most skeptical of visitors in Animal Kingdom may lose their self-awareness in the presence of nature's reality.

The Oasis leads to Safari Village and the Tree of Life. The Tree of Life is Animal Kingdom's centerpiece, and it's a showstopper. The gigantic, fourteen-story sculptural work depicts a baobab tree with intricately carved animals on its trunk and branches. The Tree houses a theater showing *It's Tough to Be a Bug,* Disney's 3-D film featuring characters from *A Bug's Life.* Surrounding the Tree of Life is a garden with smaller, traditional animal exhibits, and along the outer edges of the island are the bulk of Animal Kingdom's shops and restaurants. Crossing the various bridges from Safari Village and its Tree of Life, one arrives at the various "lands" of Animal Kingdom: Camp Minnie-Mickey, DinoLand U.S.A., Africa, and Asia. All these lands contain some rides, a show or two, and plenty of gift shops.

Moving clockwise from the entrance to Safari Village, we first encounter the land of Camp Minnie-Mickey. If the Oasis reassures visitors that they will indeed encounter authentic nature, Camp Minnie-Mickey begins to define the human relationship to nature. The bridge across Discovery River leads to an Adirondack-style campground, created especially for the younger visitors to Animal Kingdom. It features the *Festival of the Lion King* production, a lavish song, dance, and acrobatic celebration with the characters from the movie *The Lion King*. Camp Minnie-Mickey is also where guests can meet the traditional Disney characters for pictures and cuddly embraces. Besides Mickey and Minnie, the characters one finds are predictably anthropomorphic animals: Chip 'n' Dale, Winnie the Pooh, and Tigger.

Camp Minnie-Mickey is apparently the only locale in Animal Kingdom where a guest can see the "live" version of these characters. Disney clearly has recognized that a bouncing Tigger juxtaposed alongside real tigers would undercut the elaborate context created for the encounters with live animals (and, for that matter, the elaborate context created for Tigger). So Mickey and his pals are ghettoized in a secluded corner of the park, reposed in shady tree-lined paths, quietly greeting toddlers. This confinement of a certain strain of imagination is necessary because Animal Kingdom relies on a stronger sense of verisimilitude to achieve its fantasy. In the other parks, the absolute fantasy easily encompasses giant cartoon characters come to life. Everything is gleefully fake, a remarkable fantasy. Even the "France," the "Italy," and the other countries of Epcot, despite the real-world counterparts they aim to simulate, are rearranged, stylized representations of the originals. In Animal Kingdom, nature—especially animals—equates with absolute reality. The most important structural material holding up Animal Kingdom's world is a palpable sense of reality—something, in other words, that Disney has apparently not created.

The third major attraction of Camp Minnie-Mickey is *Pocahontas and Her Forest Friends* at Grandmother Willow's Grove. This show features an actress portraying Pocahontas, an audio-animatronic tree (Grandmother Willow), and numerous small, live animals that help Pocahontas learn about the forest. As the show opens, Pocahontas frolics through the forest scenery, enjoying the beauty of nature. The bucolic setting is quickly marred by the sounds of chain saws in the distance.[2] "The forest is in trouble, Grandmother Willow," Pocahontas tells her foliage friends. What follows is her quest to understand the prophecy of the forest, to discover that "one creature has the ability to save the forest." The attraction delights children as they squeal and gasp at numerous live animals appearing onstage to help Pocahontas learn about the forest ecology. As creatures such as a snake, a skunk, and a porcupine teach her that "we must respect nature or she will turn against us," Pocahontas comes closer to learning that individual animals cannot save the forest. But each animal reminds her of a trait that can help the forest. Slowly Pocahontas realizes that the only creatures who can save the forest are the humans who are destroying it. The show ends with Pocahontas celebrating the interconnectedness of the forest. "We are all connected in a circle, a hoop that never ends," she sings, and white doves are released into the air.3

The environmental message of *Pocahontas and Her Forest Friends,* that we are both curse and blessing on the environment, will be repeated with variations throughout the park. In this setting, geared toward the least sophisticated of Disney's guests, we receive the environmental message in its purest form: the direct, intimate contact with nature will teach us that the earth is our responsibility, under our stewardship. In Grandmother Willow's Grove, the forest literally speaks to the human, as the large willow tree reveals a face that talks to Pocahontas. As Grandmother Willow actually teaches Pocahontas how to save her environment, Disney visitors are expected to learn that nature knows best and that the best way to learn what nature knows is to immerse ourselves in the language of the forest. Learning to exist responsibly with nature requires that we overlook or ignore all the mediating influences between nature and us; nature will then gladly and easily tell us what is right. No forestry specialist or ecologist teaches Pocahontas the keys to saving the forest. Rather, the direct contact with the animals, trees, and land provide all the instruction needed. Though we will not get such an unmediated connection in the other lands of Animal Kingdom, the goal and the message remains the same. Nature, if we allow ourselves to listen, will teach us how to take care of her. Pocahontas learns this from her furry friends, and finds her role in the ecology of the forest. By listening closely, observing the actions of the forest creatures, and obeying her senses, Pocahontas has the direct contact with the physical environment that allows her to discern the best relationship between humans and the environment. Identifying with the Indian princess, we become savior and protector of the wild things of life.

This conceit, that the way to stem environmental destruction requires unmediated interaction with the physical environment, is one of the driving forces behind the park's aesthetic. Implicit in Pocahontas's lesson is the idea that nature is an absolute—a pure, unadulterated, authentic force that stands in contrast to the artificial, compromised world of humans. In effect, the meanings we associate with nature are so invested with authenticity that we equate nature with reality. All that is not nature stands as somehow artificial, not real. In Animal Kingdom, we must continuously negotiate this boundary, but we seemingly have little trouble discerning what qualifies as real nature compared to the elaborate creations of Disney. We easily separate the two in part because contemporary culture repeatedly demarcates this boundary in television commercials, movies, magazine advertisements, and nature shows, placing our encounters with nature in opposition to industrial, urban life. But we also discern the real from the artificial in Animal Kingdom because Disney goes to extensive lengths to present aspects of the park as "real" nature, installing signposts both literal (the educational plaques that instruct us in animal behavior and ecological practices) and metaphorical (the absence of identifiable human elements, the strict fidelity to a natural habitat). This quest for realism in presentation is a pure by-product of a naive empiricist stance toward nature present in contemporary culture, the belief that there surely is an easily recognizable nature, one quite comprehensible through our senses alone. The pursuit of fidelity and accuracy in realistic habitats merely reflects a certain reductive understanding of nature: we know nature when we see it, so let's make this park look like nature. The elevation of nature as the repository of truth in *Pocahontas and Her Forest Friends* explains how realistic habitats and live animals exist within the cartoon fantasy of a Disney World park. For the most part, the Disney theme parks playfully present their virtual reality to very successful ends. Visitors embrace the simulation of places that never were. But Animal Kingdom cannot rely solely on the absolute fake. Or rather, it chooses not to. Instead, Disney creates a parkwide narrative whereby nature is the repository of authenticity. Therefore, for its visitors to feel they have experienced that authentic connection, Disney must present, not a simulation, but a construction of reality that argues at every moment, at every turn, for its unassailable reality. As such, Animal Kingdom presents two narratives that exist in creative tension with each other. The park must enact nature's authenticity in one narrative populated by live animals, while creating its traditional fantasy reality in another narrative of ersatz lands and cartoon characters.

Animal Kingdom excessively touts its attention to detail in presenting a realistic environment for its animal inhabitants. The health and well-being of the animals dictate a certain fidelity to re-creating a native environment, but Disney goes far beyond supplying home cooking for its nonhuman performers. The "backstories" create a narrative that works overtime to convince guests that they are in a distinct historical place. Artificially aged exteriors, simulated posters and advertisements, even graffiti support the fictional narrative of each Disney land. Melody Malmberg tells us in *The Making of Disney's Animal Kingdom Theme Park* that "in a Disney theme park, story is paramount, and sometimes the story is not fantasy but reality."4 The Imagineers "create authentic-looking, authentic-feeling, authentic-sounding spaces . . . to form the physical basis for a willing suspension of disbelief—in other words, a surrender to the environment of the park."5 That surrender is part enjoyment—the transportation to another world—but it also is a necessity for Disney's environmental message to be most effective. The realist aesthetic of Animal Kingdom propagates the illusion that we are very near an unmediated connection with nature. We can "surrender to the environment" and hear the voice of nature free from all human interferences.

This voice, however, is a composite of "nature" sound and image bites that inundate us, a multimedia collage far from the pure instruction suggested by Pocahontas's lesson. In *The Culture of Nature*, Alexander Wilson argues that since the 1950s, when multiple transportation and communication technologies penetrated the natural world, people have begun "to experience nature as something manipulated, altered, composed by humans."[6] We can see this change dramatically presented in nature shows and films. In these films, despite editing, technology, and in some cases physical coercion of animals, the heavily scripted and controlled narrative is presented as spontaneous and with seemingly minimal mediation. Nature is nonetheless represented through artifice: compressed and accelerated in time, its remote aspects made to seem accessible, and often invested with human qualities. The move toward realism in zoos reflects this same dynamic. In all cases, the seemingly unmediated glimpse of nature corresponds not directly to exotic habitats but indirectly, through the heavily manipulated "nature" depicted on screen and in other media. In fact, Animal Kingdom's version of nature is directly influenced by Disney and other nature films made earlier in the past century.[7] We can trace a direct link from the depiction of nature in the Disney films of the 1950s and 1960s to the narratives of Animal Kingdom. Because our understanding of nature, especially exotic and remote nature, is inextricably linked with photographic and electronic images of nature, what we will accept as unmediated is that which most closely matches those images. The realism of Animal Kingdom is the realism of the Discovery Channel or National Geographic. As those electronic presentations of nature distort both time and space in order to construct nature inside a screen, so Animal Kingdom also distorts both temporality and geography by bringing exotic animals to Orlando and positioning them in "spontaneous" view. The human construction of this nature cannot be hidden, but it does not need to be. Disney presumes it will fade from our perception because the heavily constructed nature of Disney's re-creations accurately presents the nature represented on Animal Planet or at an IMAX theater. The central Florida landscape is remade to look like images of conventionalized Africa and Asia. Native plants perform the roles of African jungle. Redirected streams become misty Asian waterfalls. As the one aspect of exotic lands that cannot be imported—like animals or people or artifacts—the exotic landscapes are portrayed by an elaborately costumed Florida topography. In other words, for the majority of Disney visitors who will never visit the Serengeti or an Asian jungle, the nature they see in Animal Kingdom looks just like it does on TV.

Directly across the park from Camp Minnie-Mickey, passing again through Safari Village, a bridge crossing leads to the Kingdom of Anandapur ("place of all delights") in the land of Asia. The land of Asia and its next-door neighbor, Africa, define Animal Kingdom more than the others. Asia, recently opened in 1999, features tigers, bats, and Komodo dragons along with the Kali River Rapids thrill ride. Africa has gorillas, hippos, and Kilimanjaro Safari, the signature ride through Disney's African savannah. These two "continents," their enormous diversity radically reduced, highlight the most charismatic animals of the park and contain the bulk of the park's acreage. Africa alone, at 110 acres, is bigger than the entire Magic Kingdom.8 In these two lands, Disney devotes immense resources both in acreage and in presentation to simulate an intimate, exotic encounter with all the touchstones of veracity.

Asia and Africa lend their names to the two central lands for obvious reasons. They are the home habitats for the bulk of exotic wildlife found in American zoos. In addition, they offer a multitude of cultural signposts around which Disney can create something more than just artful cages and pens. Both continents have been key sites of colonial power and mythmaking that Disney exploits. These landscapes, Africa especially, are laden with Western stereotypes of unexplored and untamed lands. Disney has exploited such conceptions before. In the Magic Kingdom, Jungle Cruise's great white explorer shtick still draws in crowds. Things have changed, at least on the surface, and in the more progressive Animal Kingdom, Stanley and Livingston have been replaced by Dian Fosse and Jane Goodall. Still, there are underlying similarities between Jungle Cruise and Animal Kingdom, despite the latter's superficial sensitivity to environmental and cultural politics. Though the twenty-seven years between Jungle Cruise and the opening of Animal Kingdom may have given us a more realistic and truthful picture of the "dark continent" and the "mysterious East," for many of the park's visitors, and apparently for its designers, Africa and Asia still represent an antithesis to Western civilization. At the opening of Jungle Cruise in 1971, the West could still be nostalgic for the great unexplored, unconquered reaches of Africa and Asia. In the present, the themes of conquering and exploring are submerged as the two continents are enshrined as the unspoiled purity that has, unlike the West, escaped interment under a corrupt society. Yet those stereotypes never fully disappear, and in the generic "Africa" and "Asia," Disney constructs a landscape that relies on nostalgic myths and mediated images in patterns similar to the primitive Jungle Cruise. IMAX showings of the Serengeti have replaced the dispatches of lone journalists, but the results are similar.

Many of the stories that Disney presents in Animal Kingdom are enactments of this purity corrupted. Disney's strength as an entertainer lies in its narratives, its ability to produce an emotional connection with a pure hero and an equally potent repugnance for a corrupt villain. Environmental problems, however, rarely follow the simple plotlines of fairy tales. Reducing these issues to storybook level must have presented the Imagineers with a strong challenge. Producing simple and concrete villains is not easily accomplished within real and complex environmental relations. The destruction of an ecological system can rarely be executed by one person, and although corporations certainly can do serious environmental damage, there are certain problems with presenting a business as villain. Some offenders (such as Exxon, Kodak, General Electric) are Disney partners. Other situations are too complex to encompass in a twelve-minute attraction.[9] Predictably, Disney's narratives tend to be reductive.

In Asia's Kali River Rapids attraction, however, Disney does come close to addressing the complexities of an environmental catastrophe. The story of Kali River Rapids begins while waiting in line. Guests inch their way through a mocking re-creation of a third world bazaar catering to Western tourists. After passing a fake temple and a shrine filled with chattering birds, the line for Kali River Rapids winds through an Asian junk shop, filled with birdcages, beads, and knickknacks. Signs offer "spesial [sic] prices for tourists." The prelude updates the low-grade, pathetic colonial racism of the older Jungle Cruise. Disney's bazaar seems to mock poorer versions of its own brand of hyper-consumerism and first world entertainment for failing to live up to the excessive heights of Disney marketing. The somewhat smug tone has the unfortunate result of undercutting the mild critique of greed that follows.

When guests reach the ride itself, they encounter what may be the least puffy of Disney's softball attacks on environmental destruction. The narrative of this white-water rafting trip is that of an unauthorized excursion down a river decimated by the business of logging. Guests are positioned as ecotourists, paying a locally run expedition company for the privilege of riding an untamed river. Destructive logging practices are apparent in broadcast sounds of chain-saws and flyers for conservation meetings encountered in line. "The conflict between population explosion and traditional respect for animals and wild places was always borne in upon the Imagineers," Malmberg tells us. "Dramatizing it without simplifying it was the challenge."[10] As guests wait in line for the rafting trip, a video shows scenes of a generic, rural Asian village whose traditional way of life is being destroyed by illegal logging practices. The logging is described as illegal, though the events depicted are characteristic of legal operations as well. However, by placing this particular company outside the law, Disney makes its corporate villain a bit more threatening to the rafters yet manages to avoid a more serious critique about normalcy in everyday corporate practices. This mildly scary trip supposedly visits the out-law world of renegade capitalism, when, in fact, it merely reflects the results of typical Western exploitation. The Kali River Rapids attraction re-creates the capitalist struggles over how to benefit monetarily from the forests and remote areas of the Asian landscape. The video provides a context within which to understand the destroyed forest and the detrimental effects on culture as well as the landscape. Instead of an isolated, ahistorical scene of destruction, we are given reasons for the events we are about to see, a village dependent on West-ern tourism and threatened by corporate irresponsibility.

After a pleasant and scenic beginning, the rafting ride plunges into night-marish visions of burned-out forests, charred stumps, and vicious flames. The ride makes good use of the frightening environment to underscore the physi-cal thrills of riding the rapids. The excitement and awe that accompany the splash and dip of white-water rafting are doubled by the awesome spectacle of a ravenous lumber company out of control. With startling pyrotechnics and dismal dioramas, Disney is doing its best to create a monster out of an abstract corporation. Kali River Rapids is a long way from the Magic Kingdom's Splash Mountain. Yet there is something unseemly about well-off tourists, be they ecotourists or Disney guests, joyriding amid scenes of such destruction. We are positioned as ecotourists, but those of the worst kind: the exploitive, rave-nous spectacle-hunters who seek out exotic locales like new cable channels, consuming a people's tragedy for our enjoyment.

Disney's ecotourism becomes neocolonialist kitsch. The very concept of ecotourism—that leisured consumerism and exotic adventure from the wealthy West can save endangered areas—rests on an unhealthy dependence on global capitalism to save the very things it destroys. Disney tries to separate bad capitalism (illegal logging practices) from good (its own warmhearted merchandise shop), but the rafting story never seems to escape its whirlpool of exploitation. Kali River Rapids elaborately re-creates the trappings of a floun-dering neocolonial economy desperate for anything that will bring in the sav-ing American dollar, be it exploitive forestry techniques or Western tourists. The ride begins with a shop bowing and scraping to the wealthy Western eco-tourist and then reveals the devastation wrought by a company willing to sac-rifice safety and sound environmental practices in order to continue to accu-mulate that wealth. Unintentionally, the ride is an accurate commentary on the collision of international capital and third world labor made all the more acute by the plaintive, crude conservation notices to "Speak up to save our for-ests" plastered around the shop. Beyond the flawed critique of destructive log-ging practices, the ride endorses an economic system that thrives on—indeed helps produce—the desperation of third world nations to slip through the back door of capitalism. Disney itself has a less than stellar record of treating its workers in foreign countries.[11] The sweatshop conditions of some of its subcontractors are products of the globalized capitalism dramatized in Kali River Rapids. And the parallel extends further: the voyeuristic wealthy eco-tourists in Disney's fantasy—its consumers—likely own stock in companies that practice the same exploitation that Animal Kingdom purports to criticize. Such exploitation leads to offshore sweatshops, ecological nightmares in northern Mexican *maquiladoras,* and, ironically, industrial logging.

Kali River Rapids exemplifies how Disney co-opts environmentalism toward its entertainment ends. The tepid ecological critique of Kali River Rapids has little to do with social and environmental justice. Rather, the corporate ecology lite adds entertainment value to the ride by engaging—albeit on a very superficial level—the noble desires of people to protect the less fortunate and preserve the beauty of nature. Visitors are meant to feel righteous anger and heroic for standing on the side of good. Fun and conservation are "balanced" by converting environmental action into another brand for Disney to market. Every aspect of the park, from souvenirs to trash cans to the paint on the walls, is marketed on the strength of its connection to nature and animals. As *The Safari Style Book* on the shelves of Africa's Mombasa Marketplace reveals, environmentalism at Animal Kingdom is quite in vogue. Animal Kingdom is sharply decked out in the fashions of ecology, and it eagerly encourages its guests to adopt the same fashions. Malmberg tells us that "the Merchandise team decided that everything on sale in the park would reflect the human love of all animals,"[12] and as a result, jewelry, clothes, and trinkets rely partially on a love of nature for their attractiveness. Buying things is fun, but Disney makes it environmentally sound by connecting it to the conservation messages of the park.

With our bag of green goodies in hand, we can head out into the village of Harambé and the land of Africa. Harambé, which means "coming together" according to Disney's Animal Kingdom guide, is a conventionalized representation of a present-day East Kenyan coastal town. The fake town is an extraordinary construction, perhaps the best-realized environment in Animal Kingdom. All the structures, from the bridge over Discovery River to the walls of the ersatz Hotel Burudjka, have been artificially aged. Faded letters on the side of a wall advertise "Tusker House Restaurant—Best Food in East Africa," a real restaurant for Disney guests. The hyperreality of the village has the overall effect of stylized reality—reality enhanced. In the village itself, we recognize the artifice, and Disney appeals to our self-awareness by including subtle details like faded handbills and trompe l'oeil paintings that reward scrutiny. Harambé doesn't purport to be a faithful translation of a real place but is rather an absolute simulation, where the details are constructed to draw attention to the simulation, not to disguise it.

As the showcase attraction at Animal Kingdom, the Kilimanjaro Safari ride is magnificent in its realization of an African savannah. Once again we are given a conventionalized and synthetic reproduction of African wildness. However, where the close attention to detail in Harambé village enhanced the playful virtual reality of the fantasy, the realist aesthetic inside the safari attraction works to obscure the construction of this reality. Disney invests just as much effort in re-creating a stylized African savannah as it does in re-creating an East Kenyan village. Yet the difference between the realism of the safari and the realism of the village lies in Disney's use of our self-awareness. In the village, we are encouraged to participate in the construction by acknowledging that Disney is the storyteller, but in the safari, Disney seduces us into seeing the simulated landscape as an authentic experience of reality—there *is* no story, simply what is, is. Again, nature is equated with reality, the equation enhanced by the presence of verifiably real animals. Disney's use of nature works to disarm our skepticism about the creation of this reality, and at our most skeptical, we are persuaded to accept the safari as a re-creation of reality rather than a simulation of a fantasy.

Herded onto large trucks, guests are driven into a re-creation of the African plains. This eighteen-minute ride through the fictional Harambé Wildlife Reserve offers amazingly close-up views of giraffes, hippopotamuses, cheetahs, and lions, all of which appear to be unencumbered by any cages or restraints. In fact, some of the less dangerous animals are free to roam to such an extent that occasionally they will obstinately block the vehicle's path, halting the ride until a keeper arrives to urge them along. With no cages, fences, or barriers in sight, the landscape suggests a wilderness that a traditional zoo rarely summons. The ride presents an illusion of complete immersion in the natural world. In planning the park, Disney employees traveled to Africa to research their safari ride. "The Imagineers knew that the safari component needed to be authentic," Malmberg writes,[13] because Disney felt that Africa itself would be the standard by which the park was judged. But when the Imagineers found the safari parks of East Africa to be too familiar, Kilimanjaro Safari was pushed beyond authentic. "The team was struck by the 'theme park-ness' of Africa," says Malmberg, and then she quotes a project writer: "[T]he tourists' Africa is a theme park—just not a particularly well-run one. . . . We knew the experience we could provide in the Animal Kingdom would be as good as or better than that."[14] Overseas, the Imagineers found that their idealized image of a wild Africa had been corrupted and manipulated, tainted by the pursuit of money. But in Animal Kingdom, they could re-create, not an authentic repro-duction of a contemporary Kenyan preserve, but the *image* of Africa handed down from books, pictures, and film, where the untamed wilderness still ex-ists. Kilimanjaro Safari "improves" on the reality of its model by adapting the safari experience, not to the reality of the model, but to the mediated impres-sion of Africa we receive, the vast, untouched Serengeti. Alexander Wilson de-scribes the standardization of those culturally valorized scenic places:

> [C]ertain elements have to be rearranged to meet tourist expectations. In the game preserves of East Africa for example, the elephants or lions must be visible and uncontained when the sight seers go by in their tour buses, and preferably the beasts will be eating other animals. But we don't want other buses full of tourists angling for good photos crowding the scene and causing a distraction.[15]

Confined to smaller and smaller areas and with their numbers shrinking, the exotic animals have become even rarer spectacles. In the real Africa, Disney planners found themselves in a traffic jam as up to forty vehicles closed in on a leopard, but in Animal Kingdom, animals are always on display: the spectacle is always present, always reliable. Through control of landscaping and sched-ules, vistas are preserved, and the presence of other guests in safari vehicles is barely noticeable.

Of the safari attraction, Disney proclaims, "This is no ordinary safari. We have a story to tell,"[16] and, like most Disney attractions, the story needs a hero and a villain. The villain in this ride is the poacher. The story line of the ride suggests that this savannah is crucial to the local economy and that poachers are threatening both animals and businesses.[17] From the beginning of the wait in line, visitors are warned that poachers have been seen in the Harambé Wildlife Reserve. At nearly every turn in the endless, snaking queue, we are encouraged to keep a lookout for poachers and report anything suspicious to the authorities. Thus by the time we board our safari jeep, we are prepared to identify the villain when he shows his face. Which, of course, he soon does. The ride is narrated through a staged communication between a live guide and the recorded voice of the director of the Harambé Wildlife Reserve. The director warns the guide that there has been a poacher spotted in the reserve and we should keep an eye open for him. Eventually the director spots the poacher, and we are marshaled into service to catch him. We exit the reserve and a brief, hectic chase traps the poacher and overturns his jeep. The ride fin-ishes as we pass by the culprit held at gunpoint by a reserve ranger.

The narrative follows the villain-threat and happy-resolution formula typi-cal of the park's attractions. This is, of course, the main reason the threat to the animals is embodied in the persona of the poacher. He's singular, definable, and represents a genuine threat present in wild animal preserves. The Kilimanjaro Safari attraction is so focused on the poacher as the central character of the ride that one half expects to see Poacher shirts and boxer shorts alongside Cruella de Ville earrings and Captain Hook back scratchers at the Mombasa Marketplace gift shop. Unfortunately, this reliance on the poacher as the main or only threat minimizes the complexities of the real threat to the African savannah. Poaching is a significant problem in wild animal preserves, but Disney's portrayal diminishes the convoluted social and economic conditions that lead Africans to kill animals for their commodity value. Poaching is a problem rooted in socially constructed scarcity, not simply individual greed. Unlike the story of Kali River Rapids, Kilimanjaro Safari offers little context for understanding poaching. The greater evil does not lie in the poacher himself but in the created conditions that often force people to kill for scarce luxury items—ivory, pelts, horns—to scratch out a living. In the line for the attraction, Disney does offer a video that addresses the encroaching spread of civilization into wilderness areas. Two wild rhinos are filmed with an urban skyline in the background, depicting the uneasy juxtaposition of Africa's wild landscape with its increasing urban landscape. However, the video fails to make a connection between this conflict over space and the accompanying social issues that result in poaching. Instead, horrific images of poached carcasses further inflame our hatred of the poacher. One wonders just how much the enjoyment of Kilimanjaro Safari is related to underlying class definitions of poaching and preservation. Do we as wild preserve tourists revel in our aristocratic game preserve while we punish the lowly peasant who would dare poach on our enjoyment? Disney's environmental plot boils down to the level of the organism, ignoring the species in order to depict one man against one animal.

In one instance, however, Disney does foreground the species over the organism in Animal Kingdom. Disney must delicately balance its need to make its guests feel good about themselves against the truth that humans are responsible for the plight of the animals. Usually, Disney contrives to have it both ways. *Flights of Wonder* presents a standard bird showcase similar to those at Busch Gardens and other zoos. Various birds perform tricks derived from their natural behavior. Much of the show consists of large, beautiful birds flying over the heads of the audience, and the occasional raptor catching a tossed object. Amid the athletic and comic displays of exotic birds, the show's hosts feed bits of environmental pabulum to the audience. *Flights of Wonder* uses a common environmental trope for its bad guy. Here, the evil is abstracted to a faceless "people" and nameless "civilizations"—addressed on the level of species rather than particular people or civilizations. "Man" has worked to destroy the birds' habitats and poison them with chemicals, and "civilization" is slowly eroding the birds' ability to exist. Andrew Ross shows the danger of this view of humans as a blight upon the landscape: "The species is therefore addressed as a collective 'we,' or, at best as 'divisions of the human family.' Consequently, there is little room for exposes of the agencies—corporations, governments, large-landowners—primarily responsible for the ecological crisis."18 Humans become the invasive element in the purity of nature. It's an emotional plot device that Disney uses frequently to demonstrate the bad relations between humans and animals. The poacher certainly stands as one element of this invasion. Another example of faceless humans taking the blame occurs in Asia's Maharajah Jungle Trek, where we encounter tigers roaming an abandoned hunting lodge, a reinscription of purity after the ugly human element has been removed, presumably forced to turn tail and run. In this conception of nature, humans are at worst destructive invaders of nature and at best token reminders of third world authenticity like the authentic Kenyan guide or the Indians working Anandapur Ice Cream. The reduction of complex issues results in mindless storybook confrontations that offer nothing but bumper-sticker environmental messages.

Disney has trouble fitting real, social human beings into its ecological narrative. Forced to use abstractions so as not to offend a customer, Disney never accomplishes a smooth fit of humans within its nature. Such a failure is symptomatic of Disney's alienation from any genuine integration with the natural world. The narrative moves from the third-person abstraction of evil humans to a first-person plural abstraction when it wants to tap into the feelgood activism. Yet even this apparent switch to the personal still refuses to address anyone specifically. Where a faceless "they" have perpetrated a crime against the environment, it is an equally anonymous "we" who fix it. And no matter how apathetic or ignorant we are as environmentalists, Disney's narrative lets us feel very good about "our" efforts to ban DDT, to save falcons and pelicans, and to help right the wrongs of civilization. Disney promotes us as having the ability to change the world, but never asks us to do much. The perky bird trainer in the *Flights of Wonder* show brightly tells us that we can recycle and reuse, never telling us to refuse. The company has no problems with pushing our activism buttons so long as the message doesn't conjure up any guilt when it comes time to purchase a new pair of mouse ears. We might thoughtfully discard our plastic water bottle in the proper recycling vessel, but Disney does not expect our environmental conscience to reach any higher. Nothing at Animal Kingdom ever questions the wisdom or necessity of buying worthless trinkets at inflated prices simply for a souvenir of our experiences with nature.

A giant brontosaurus skeleton frames the entrance to DinoLand U.S.A., the final land of Animal Kingdom. Among the attractions are the Cretaceous Trail, filled with plants and animals that have survived from the last period when dinosaurs were present, and the Boneyard, a McDonald's playland on steroids, with slides, ladders, rope bridges, and a pretend fossil bed. On the more serious side there is a working fossil preparation lab where guests can view paleontologists cleaning and preparing dinosaur fossils. Most recently the lab, in cooperation with Chicago's Field Museum of Natural History, prepared a *Tyrannosaurus rex* skeleton.

Unlike the immediate, intimate connection with the animals of Africa and Asia, the "love" of creatures in DinoLand U.S.A. is not driven by proximity. Instead, the connection with these beasts comes through an intellectual bridge, reaching through the past via scientific discovery. In Africa and Asia, the awe of exotic and ferocious beasts is created by strenuous verisimilitude and an intimate relation with the living creatures. At DinoLand U.S.A., the awe emerges intertwined with the powerful presence of big science. We connect with the animals through the mediation of paleontology. The unique Disney touch on this highly scientific discourse is to make academia a theme. The fictional dig operates under the auspices of the equally fictional Dino Institute, a scientific society devoted to the study and discovery of dinosaurs. At every turn of DinoLand's paths we encounter the props of postgraduate scholarship, tenured research, and the scientific life of the mind. Playing on popular notions of graduate school, DinoLand U.S.A. is awash in the goofy high jinks of graduate student paleontologists and the laughable attempts at control by their professors. The nerdish behavior of scientists is made appealing by the crazy rebelliousness of students. As Malmberg puts it, "the students are pranksters, while the professors are voices of authority."[19] The story line even carries into the authentic workings at the Fossil Preparation Lab. Juxtaposed with the day-to-day detritus of a working lab—the dust, dirt, tools, and equipment along with real, working scientists—is an Imagineer's conception of graduate student life. Little dinosaur doodles comment on the map of the *T. rex* skeleton. A poster of the rock group Kiss hangs on the back wall. A Frisbee can be seen among the books. In the same manner as the real animals in the Kilimanjaro Safari, the Fossil Preparation Lab introduces an element of authenticity amid the simulation of the Dino Institute. Unlike Harambé, however, the fossil lab does not quite blend seamlessly with the virtual reality of the Dino Institute, in part because the preparation of fossils is not exactly riveting entertainment for most people. A more revealing cause of the lab's discontinuity is that the real scientists have no direct connection to nature, and therefore the presentation of authenticity seems awkward in the virtual reality of DinoLand U.S.A. Nature always authenticates itself. As Jennifer Price notes, "Nature circumnavigates questions . . . it is a reprieve from irony and self-awareness."[20] The Fossil Preparation Lab attempts to escape irony and self-awareness through the straightforward presentation of reality. But despite occupying the same dramatic role as Nature in Disney's Africa, Science as presented in the Fossil Preparation Lab does not create the same performance.

The Dino Institute's backstory—its fictional history and context—evokes a nonprofit organization comparable to such giants as the National Geographic Society or the Audubon Society. In a particularly clever way to divert attention from crass commercialization, McDonald's sponsors, not Animal Kingdom's DinoLand U.S.A., but the fictional Dino Institute. The narrative has McDonald's providing a substantial "grant" to the institute for the study of dinosaurs, allowing the golden arches to appear all over DinoLand U.S.A. without breaking the story line. We even see a very formal and austere plaque of recognition in the lobby of the Dino Institute's headquarters. Corporate sponsorship is thus reconstructed as benign, more stewardship than commercialism. Instead of merely including corporate sponsorship in its attractions, a practice that would divert attention away from the simulation to extrapark concerns about money and the interrelations between Disney and other businesses, Disney writes the sponsorship into the story line. In doing so, Disney reinforces the simulation—most large museums and nonprofits benefit from and publicize corporate giving—but also plays to the visitor's self-awareness that this is an elaborate simulation. The effect is to undercut any cynicism toward Disney's selling out its creation for a profit.

The simulation of philanthropy pervades the expensive rotunda of the institute. In addition to the McDonald's plaque of recognition, this large circular room contains numerous museum-quality exhibits, including a reconstructed *Tyrannosaurus rex,* that give the waiting room the feel of a heavily endowed organization. Big business appropriates big science at the Dino Institute. In this rotunda, we are given a preliminary presentation about the life and extinction of dinosaurs. Disney wants to appropriate the prestige, legitimacy, and cultural capital of museums, so it mimics their institutional style. Using paintings on the walls, voice-overs, and lights, the show seems typical of any contemporary natural history museum. But the subdued theatrics are a setup for the technological wonders that follow.

The lobby of the institute also functions as the waiting area for the only genuine thrill ride in Animal Kingdom, Countdown to Extinction. The preliminary show closes with an austere institutional voice telling us, "Mother Nature reinvents the animal after the mass extinction." Countdown to Extinction then proceeds to mock such simplistic ideas of natural history in a technology-driven, high-speed manipulation of the natural processes just described. In a second holding pen just before boarding the ride, we are introduced to Dr. Grant Seeker, another young scientist rebelling against the control of his elder mentors. He ridicules the "quaint and antiquated" bones and paintings of the rotunda, preferring the science and technology that will allow us to see the real thing. Seeker prepares us to travel back in time to see and capture an iguanodon just moments before a meteor strikes the earth, triggering the mass extinction. Seeker calls the time-traveling device the perfect blend of science and technology, yet refuses to reveal how the vehicle works. "How do we do it? That's proprietary," he says, using business terminology to sidestep a more convoluted story line. Seeker's rebelliousness is still contained by an unbreakable narrative of corporate propriety. Countdown to Extinction exhibits big science in the service of big business.

The time-travel adventure is nearly a colossal failure. We are chased by menacing dinosaurs, nearly lose contact with the present, and just barely escape being obliterated by a meteor. The thrills are the product of an amazing number of technological effects that produce terrifyingly loud dinosaurs and a whiplash journey through the darkened attraction. And we do succeed in capturing our pet iguanodon for the juvenile doctor. Though Malmberg, in her description of DinoLand U.S.A., suggests that technology should pale in the shadow of nature, it is technology that seems to win out on all fronts. Countdown to Extinction lauds technology's ability to accomplish the miraculous and turn a profit as well. Far from suggesting that our overreliance on technology may create problems, Countdown to Extinction argues that our awe of technology is justified and, further, that this technology-worship shapes our understanding of nature. Like Disney World generally, it exploits the postmodern ability to suspend disbelief while concurrently marveling at the technological effects that help construct that suspension. The awe generated by a supposedly attacking dinosaur is not a respect for the immensity of nature but is rather the opposite, an awe in the face of technology's ability to transport us to a remarkably believable representation of another time and space. We are in awe of the simulated, not the real. By celebrating nature and reality manipulated by technology, the techno-industrial set of the Dino Institute's time travel sketches a terror more deadly than a raging carnosaur. Countdown to Extinction teaches us that advanced science knows no "natural" boundaries.

The ride reinforces a technological solution to ecological problems—in this case, extinction. One of the most potent arguments for environmental reform is the cry "Extinction is forever." Countdown to Extinction, while clearly a fantasy, plays on our belief that technology will eventually ride to the rescue.

By the time we've lost the last elephant, we will be so technically advanced that we can simply travel back in time to retrieve a breeding pair. On a more general level, if time travel is a far-fetched idea, we still feel that a solution to our problems is not a matter of structural change but simply a matter of time and Yankee ingenuity. We may not come up with time travel, but don't worry, we'll think of something.

Though DinoLand U.S.A., Africa, Asia, and Camp Minnie-Mickey are the four main lands of Animal Kingdom, there is another section of the park that falls outside the realm of any actual land. In a remote corner of the park sits Conservation Station, a section devoted primarily to educational entertainment. Here is where Disney sets aside its fantastic stories to create a more informative and educational atmosphere. Compared to the traditional Disney theme park, this section inverts many of the themes of fantasy and escape. For this reason, it would seem, Conservation Station is inaccessible to guests except by riding the Wildlife Express train just outside Kilimanjaro Safari. Guests board the train in Harambé, at a station constructed of wood pillars, thatched roofs, and faded crumbling stucco, all consistent with the palette and fabric of the fictional town. Soon, the storybook world of pretend is left behind, and Animal Kingdom takes a turn toward the functional. In a park where one's gaze is always directed at perfection and fantasy, the real world of labor intrudes as the train travels behind the scenes of Animal Kingdom. Instead of cartoon vehicles or horse-drawn carriages, we get pickups and forklifts. The train passes along the unadorned metal fence line of the African savannah, a view unseen while on Kilimanjaro Safari. This is followed by a look at the evening housing for the elephants. No elaborate facades or architectural flourishes conceal these buildings. Industrial steel and concrete, parking lots, and cages are all on display. Briefly, postmodern pastiche and facade take a backseat to unadorned functionalism. When guests disembark at Conservation Station, the architecture indicates that their journey has been much further than the mere few acres the train has traveled. Here, though the buildings are still adorned with festive, bright primary colors, wrought iron, and colorful banners, there is no hint of any fictional backstory for our narrative pleasure. Conservation Station presents "reality," another variation on the desire for an unmediated connection with the animals.

Yet transformation to "reality" at Conservation Station is itself a facade. Despite the apparent lack of a narrative framework, this section tells a story as much as Disney's Africa and Asia do. Conservation Station is Animal Kingdom's story about itself. Here, amidst veterinarians, computers, cameras, and petting zoos, guests are told the story of Disney's commitment to conservation and the well-being of its animal stars. Conservation Station is Disney's most intensive effort to script and broadcast the "reality" of animals in Animal Kingdom. Here are a petting zoo with exotic breeds of goats, sheep, and pigs; various computer-enhanced looks at animals and conservation; and picture windows onto the examination and surgical rooms of the veterinary hospital. We can actually see "behind the scenes" of Disney's production. Famous for the hidden utility corridors under Magic Kingdom, Disney would seem to have adopted here a new strategy to appeal to those guests intrigued by the mechanics behind the magic. Animal Kingdom reveals its access roads and mechanical equipment to those educated, environmentally aware visitors most likely to view the park's ecology with a critical eye. The unveiling signifies a commitment to authenticity in Disney's presentation of its collections. Disney is quite aware that its environmentally sophisticated visitors will be sensitive to any exploitation of its animals. When a few animals died before the opening of the park, such scrutiny only confirmed that the spotlight on Disney is very bright.[21] Disney's reputation as a wealthy innovator calls not just for exceptional entertainment but also for a high degree of advancement over traditional zookeeping, and Conservation Station demonstrates that commitment. We are shown the wires and pulleys as a way of underscoring the serious educational component of Animal Kingdom. Rather than sweeping everyone away with the magic, Disney romances those visitors most likely to view its simulations skeptically—those sensible, concerned environmentalists who would most object to real animals and ecological messages being subsumed in a simulated fantasy. The hard facticity of veterinary science and state-of-the-art housing facilities lends credence to the environmental rhetoric that is part of our enjoyment.

Yet we have to consider that even this seemingly unfiltered view is a display under the control of Disney. The highly specialized veterinary exhibits, the computer terminal filled with facts, and the surveillance cameras on the animals' habitats are more seduction than education. They are informative to a degree, especially if one is fortunate enough to observe an actual operation by the vets, but even in this instance there is no demonstrable connection between a medical procedure on an individual animal and environmental science. Conservation Station makes the same reduction from species to organism as Kilimanjaro Safari, using an emotional connection in place of a logical concern for ecosystems. Despite its name, Conservation Station is not focused on conservation. Rather it uses an image of science to reinforce an emotional connection.

At Conservation Station, Disney uses an image of science to underscore its parkwide claim that guests are experiencing an authentic re-creation of nature, revisiting the importance of science first seen in DinoLand U.S.A. Disney employs a peculiar use of the sober realism of science to make the fantasy that much more legitimate. Unlike the science at Fossil Preparation Lab, science at Conservation Station works successfully to authenticate the constructions of reality in Animal Kingdom. Because nature is accorded an absolute reality in and of itself, the science of Conservation Station reinforces the idea that the landscapes we have seen in Animal Kingdom are nature and not a product of simulation. As with the magician who reveals nothing up his sleeve, the glimpse behind the scenes reveals that Disney truly has made the African savannah appear in central Florida. Or if not a true conjuring act, the scientific weight behind the re-creations makes them true habitats. Conservation Station definitively draws the line between real and artifice, putting the animals and their habitats clearly on the side of the real. Its magic is to change Animal Kingdom from just a theme park about animals into an ecologically informed utopia. It provides the politically correct window dressing for Disney's fantastic nature ride.

In the end, Conservation Station accomplishes a number of goals for Disney. It presents the park as more than a simple zoo. Under Conservation Station's scientific whitewashing, the park becomes a scientific experiment, with animals closely studied as though Animal Kingdom were an outpost for biological fieldwork. Similarly, Conservation Station reinforces the authenticity, exoticism, and reality of the animals of Animal Kingdom. Seeing their pens, learning about their diet, and witnessing their healing reminds us that these animals are real—a necessary step in the epitome of authentic re-creation. Finally, it reinforces Disney's role as the master storyteller by giving us a seemingly unmediated glimpse of the immense apparatus needed to create the "story" outside the walls of Conservation Station.

In effect, the verisimilitude of Animal Kingdom's nature is marketed as a brand, one that promotes the park's extensive line of merchandise, 90 percent of which is themed to attractions and characters within the park.[22] In discussing Animal Kingdom's merchandise, Malmberg tells us that "every piece has a story, every piece tells a story, and every piece contributes to the story,"[23] and that story relies on the livestock of the park. Living animals lend, by association, their authenticity to everything else in the park, including the staff. For the lands of Africa and Asia, Disney has recruited workers from these continents to staff food carts, serve as guides in the safari and on the animal trails, and perform as entertainers. The Kenyan drummer and the Indonesian fruit vendor carry the same Animal Kingdom brand recognition as the giraffe and fruit bat native to their countries. Alexander Wilson, again discussing the standardization of African safaris, notes, "Native human communities, moreover, might or might not be an acceptable component of the safari experience. If they are acceptable they're perhaps best presented in traditional, that is, archaic dress."[24] In Animal Kingdom, some people are dressed in "archaic" clothing, namely, those who are artists and performers. Sometimes, however, the attempt at fantasy fails. A native of South Africa working at the park occasionally encountered guests who refused to believe he was African. Despite his accent and insistence, they could not overlook his white skin. He was perceived as fake because he did not conform to the image of Africa. Essentially, his product did not match its marketing.

As these workers are reduced to symbolic representatives of generic indigenous cultures, so too do the animals succumb to the branding of nature. Taken from one context and inserted into another—no matter how accurately that context re-creates their original one—the animals are stripped of their distinctiveness, becoming mere coded indications of wild "nature." Despite all of Disney's efforts at promoting the impression of a direct encounter with authentic animals, the notion of an unmediated contact with nature is quite ridiculous at Disney World, even with—or because of—all of the company's ingenuity and resources. Modernity, especially in its manifestations of industrialization and consumer capitalism, has almost completely colonized the natural world so that most meanings associated with nature are attached only through the use of increasingly alienating mediators. Expecting Disney to provide an unmediated experience is far-fetched because contemporary culture places nature further and further apart as the anticivilization. The meanings associated with nature necessarily must come to us scripted and manipulated because we have decreed that the human has virtually no place in authentic nature. And for tourist attractions that traffic in associations with nature, even the authentic must, as Wilson says, "be rearranged to meet tourist expectations."[25] In many respects, Animal Kingdom's simulated authenticity transcends the mere accurate re-creation of habitat. It ironically mirrors and thus extends the Disneyfication of all nature as entertainment. Our gaze is always directed, framing nature in much the same way nature is framed by a TV console.

In Animal Kingdom, Disney capitalizes on the public's desire for the stable, secure return to innocence that nature represents. Disney achieves this by layering an environmentalist sheen over the romantic portrayal of exotic lands, distant enough to enthrall us but juxtaposed with enough green rhetoric to alleviate any guilt at escapism. Every aspect of Animal Kingdom is not only expected to amuse and excite but also designed to convince guests that, despite their artificial surroundings, they are immersed in nature. The unbleached eco-tint of snack-stand paper products and the leopard-skin mouse ears inform us that even the most minor of acts at Animal Kingdom is an act in nature. Nevertheless, what Animal Kingdom presents is not a nature-friendly park but a nature-themed park. Nature, here, is the aesthetic principle but not the moral or political guide for the park.

How could it be otherwise with such an undertaking? Animal Kingdom's environmental message does not reflect its own practice. True environmentalism, almost by definition, must be a challenge to industrial capitalism. As a consequence, Animal Kingdom must severely dilute its environmental message so as not to draw attention to the contradictions inherent in the very existence of a conservation theme park. Its rhetoric, therefore, is not descriptive or realist but rather performative, uttered to produce the ideal consumer of its eco-friendly facade. Animal Kingdom presents, not an ecologically progressive environment, but a landscape of consumption that disguises every act of commercialism as a gift to nature. The theme park itself, however, is hardly a light footprint on the environment. The vast scale of resources devoted to the more or less mindless entertainment and crazed consumerism of Disney World is only the most obvious of practices unfriendly to nature. More deceptively, Disney exploits the lukewarm but ever-present desire of its visitors for happy animals and a healthy planet in much the same way nature-themed catalogs pressure readers to save the environment. They both redirect the broader, communal desire to improve the environment into a personal, orgiastic desire to accumulate. In *Reading Zoos,* Randy Malamud describes the strategy: "The green marketing approach combines a few items that are actually ecologically beneficial with a great deal of other flotsam, ecokitsch, tailored to the design aesthetic—yet with little discernible difference from any other consumer products—of people who fancy themselves environmentalists."[26] Disney masterfully employs this approach. Its environmental message leans heavily on the park's status as progressive, saving endangered animals from extinction and educating the masses about sound ecological practices. At Animal Kingdom, Mickey Mouse safari hats and Tree of Life snow globes become totems for genuine environmental action. Disney pulls out of context those meanings Animal Kingdom encourages us to ascribe to nature and reinscribes them into the consumerist ideology it wants to pursue, namely, the commodification of nature. This consumerism positions nature as a brand, one that is easily marketable as the antidote to modern life. But nature at Disney World reinforces the dominant trends of modern life: branding, commodification, and entertainment. In linking this obsession for nature to souvenir hunting, Disney not only commodifies nature; it co-opts environmentalism's countercultural impulse.

Behind all the signs of environmentalism, there are few connections to strong environmentally sound practices. Disney boasts of its "attitude and commitment to our environment,"[27] trumpeting its conservation initiatives with the Nature Conservancy, its immense horticultural programs throughout the company, and even its mass transit capabilities. And to give Disney its due, it does make an effort to integrate environmental practices into its operations, especially when they are clearly profitable or reflect well in the eyes of the public. More often than not, however, Disney's environmental practices are merely coincidental, happy side effects arising from different motives. One publicity pamphlet notes, "Our Guests are encouraged to use our mass transit systems, such as the monorails, ferry boats and an extensive bus fleet, to decrease the amount of fossil fuels used."28 The "green" spin placed on Disney's transit options disguises the fact that this system is designed to completely control guests' experience, down to the very ways they approach the resort. For a park like the Magic Kingdom, "encouraged" is a euphemism for "required." Aside from the monorail, ferryboats, and bus fleets, there is no other way to reach the park.29 Disney wants guests under its direction for as much of their vacation as possible. As for Disney's commitment to reducing the amount of fossil fuels used, the acres of parking lots and Walt Disney World's deliberate isolation from Orlando and its hotels suggest otherwise.

Even its work with a respected environmental organization is fundamentally tainted. Disney's collaboration with the Nature Conservancy is primarily the result of an environmental mitigation agreement with county, state, and federal government officials that gives Disney a near-blanket approval for twenty years of development rights on its property.30 The Disney Wilderness Preserve, now at 12,000 acres, was established in 1992 with the Disney purchase of the 8,500-acre Walker Ranch. Disney then donated the preserve to the Nature Conservancy to offset the wetland destruction that accompanied the building of Celebration, a new town southwest of Disney World developed by the company. In addition, the construction of Celebration allowed by this land mitigation deal secured freeway interchanges and development permits that one Disney vice president labeled "an economic development area that's probably unmatched currently anywhere in the country."31 The good inherent in the preserve is more than offset by the impending development in the northern part of the county. Although Celebration, with its walkable streets, high density, and mixed-use zoning, is in many ways an environmentally sound neighborhood, the political repercussions originating in its creation will no doubt lead to more suburban sprawl, with its accompanying congestion, pollution, and aesthetic blight on the Orlando landscape.

The Walt Disney World resort proclaims that an environmental awareness dictates many of its practices in its parks and resorts. The Disney term for its earth-friendly attitude is "Environmentality," with Jiminy Cricket as the conscience mascot of the program. Concocting a neologism is appropriate for

Disney's commitment to the environment. "Environmentality" is not quite environmental and relies mostly on the appearance of environmental concern. Malmberg writes, "The Walt Disney Company realizes one of the greatest contributions it can make to global conservation is raising awareness,"[32] which is a particularly easy and unproductive way of claiming an environmental commitment. Such an emphasis on perception and attitudes depoliticizes the problem, allowing Disney to assume an environmental stance without engaging in any action that might prove contentious. Celebrating the beauty and importance of animals and bemoaning their fate engender very little disagreement. But this uncontroversial environmentalism accomplishes little. It easily and safely overlooks the political and historical causes and, worse, suggests that increasing awareness is a positive step toward rectifying ecological damage, when in fact it does no such thing. It may even inhibit action as guests leave Animal Kingdom with warm feelings about their devotion to the planet, pleased with themselves that they have helped turn the tide of destruction. Such feelings may comfort them for their three-hundred-mile minivan journey back to their suburban sprawl.

Animal Kingdom's patently false environmentalism works primarily to increase revenue; though this is something not in and of itself an ecological danger, the terms on which nature is presented sacrifice the health of nature for the pursuit of profit. The very scarcity of the animals Disney exhibits as its star attractions is caused by the persistent encroachment of worldwide consumerism. The unquenchable desire for more goods, more land, more of everything has put unbearable pressure on those realms outside the capitalist system. The African savannah, the Asian jungle, and, not least, the wild spaces of America are systematically shrinking as a result of capitalism's incessant need for growth. At best, Disney offers us a zero-sum trade with some wild spaces being protected while development rages on. The consumerist project of Walt Disney World, its hard sell of commodities and its marketing of a world that is bigger and better than anything else, is part of the larger systematic destruction of habitat for the animals it claims to preserve. No matter what shade of green Disney chooses to cover Animal Kingdom, and no matter how many acres it donates to placate government watchdogs, it still remains on the wrong side of the ecological scale.

Disney presents its amusement park as an educational thrill ride that will teach its visitors about the importance of the environment without ever letting them leave the amniotic magic of Walt Disney World. It purports to give guests a renewed sense of respect for the planet and its inhabitants through its message of conservation. It trumpets its treatment of wild animals as the most progressive and enlightened worldwide. In nearly every instance, it fails to live up to these claims. What we find is an exceptionally well-designed zoo that is the equivalent of a Park Avenue address for its lucky inhabitants, but one whose conservation philosophy is repeatedly contradicted by its unstated but obvious goal of turning a profit. Its uplifting message doesn't renew or engage us in a respect for the planet but rather entices us to buy a piece of nature. Its commitment to education doesn't help us understand the complex relation of humans to the physical world but rather teaches us a simplistic and ultimately damaging lesson that environmentalism can be as much a commodity as anything else for sale at Walt Disney World.

Disney's "nature" purports to be an extraordinary replica of authentic habitats and locales where nature is purest, yet the fact that Disney is able to re-create so accurately an African savannah or an Asian jungle challenges our ideas of what can be labeled authentic. We know that no matter how faithful the reproduction, our experience with lions, elephants, and tigers in central Florida cannot be an authentic encounter with nature. Yet the reference points we have for an authentic nature are so overprocessed and the result of so much cultural baggage that what can be labeled authentic is hardly clear. Disney's theme park further twists and manipulates the markings of nature to the point that concepts of authentic and inauthentic are beside the point. Instead, we are overwhelmed by myriad details that signify nature but never seem to become natural. In the absence of cages and borders, we seem to be enveloped completely in a system, but that system isn't exactly nature, nor does it feel like civilization either. Because of its hyperextension of "nature" into every single facet of the amusement park, Animal Kingdom isn't an authentic representation of animals in a re-created environment but a near-perfect Technicolor simulation of our media-soaked creation of nature. As Disney excels at perpetuating capital's penetration and colonization of nature, it succeeds in blurring the boundaries between the real and the simulation, confirming that nature is a social construction rather than an absolute.

Notes

1. Jennifer Price, *Flight Maps: Adventures with Nature in Modern America* (New York: Basic Books, 1999), xxi.
2. The sound of chain saws seems to be the default aural indicator of environmental damage. It also makes an appearance at Kali River Rapids, the site of indiscriminate logging.
3. If chain saws signal destruction, then a small flock of doves signals redemption. Besides Pocahontas's birds, a small flock also closes the show at the *Flights of Wonder* bird show and exhibition.

4. Melody Malmberg, *The Making of Disney's Animal Kingdom Theme Park* (New York: Hyperion, 1998), 107.

5. Ibid.

6. Alexander Wilson, *The Culture of Nature: North American Landscape from Disney to the Exxon Valdez* (Toronto: Between the Lines, 1991), 108.

7. See Margaret J. King, "The Audience in the Wilderness: The Disney Nature Films," *Journal of Popular Film and Television* 24.2 (1996): 60–68.

8. Stephen Birnbaum, *Birnbaum's Walt Disney World: The Official Guide,* ed. Jill Safro (New York: Hyperion, 1998), 170.

9. In Tomorrowland at Magic Kingdom, Disney does treat us to a fairly cynical, satiric stab at corporate culture. The Extraterrestrial Alien Encounter features the slimy and amoral Chairman of X-S Technologies. The ride is rooted in a portrayal of arrogant science combined with unrestrained greed that is often at the heart of ecological problems. Yet it is difficult to imagine a similar approach in Animal Kingdom. Alien Encounter's narrative, coupled with its truly frightening and intense presentation, seems out of place in the benign fantasy world of Walt Disney. Such sharp criticism, even in jest, would be even more jarring in the context of the easy environmentalism of Animal Kingdom.

10. Malmberg, *Animal Kingdom,* 176.

11. See Andrew Ross, ed., *No Sweat: Fashion, Free Trade, and the Rights of Garment Workers* (New York: Verso, 1997).

12. Malmberg, *Animal Kingdom,* 160.

13. Ibid., 18.

14. Ibid.

15. Wilson, *Culture of Nature,* 48.

16. Malmberg, *Animal Kingdom,* 70.

17. Despite assurances from Malmberg that the ride would show the townspeople managing the savannah, that economic aspect is not made clear. Knowing this in advance, a guest might see the connection of the savannah to a local economy, but the average visitor, distracted by the spectacle of the ride, will not likely deduce that the simulated Harambé Reserve is a critical component of the local economy. Or at least this attuned guest missed any strong connection. Such concerns take a backseat to the emotions aroused by the plight of an elephant attacked by poachers.

18. Andrew Ross, *The Chicago Gangster Theory of Life: Nature's Debt to Society* (New York: Verso, 1994), 184.

19. Malmberg, *Animal Kingdom,* 74.

20. Price, *Flight Maps,* 253.

21. The deaths in early 1998 of four cheetah cubs, two otters, two West African crowned cranes, a white rhinoceros, and a black rhinoceros brought closer attention from the U.S. Department of Agriculture and some unpleasant media exposure. By most accounts, the deaths were deemed accidental or the fault of previous owners, and Disney weathered the storm. See Mike Clark, "Some Creatures in New Disney Park Meet Unhappy Endings," *Los Angeles Times,* 12 April 1998, A1+.

22. See Malmberg, *Animal Kingdom,* 160.

23. Ibid., 161.

24. Wilson, *Culture of Nature,* 48.

25. Ibid.

26. Randy Malamud, *Reading Zoos: Representations of Animals and Captivity* (New York: New York University Press, 1998), 95.

27. *Environmentality* pamphlet (Disney 2000), 2.

28. Ibid., 4.

29. The ferryboat is an especially specious example. Unlike the monorail, which at least can transport guests from the Magic Kingdom to Epcot, the boat's sole purpose is to ferry guests from the ticket counter to the park's entrance. Following these standards, one could lump the Wildlife Express train and the submarines at 20,000 Leagues Under the Sea into the myriad mass transit options at Disney.

30. See Andrew Ross, *The Celebration Chronicles: Life, Liberty, and the Pursuit of Property Value in Disney's New Town* (New York: Ballantine, 1999), 280.

31. Ibid., 281.

32. Malmberg, *Animal Kingdom,* 170.

Part V

Urban Planning and Themed Environments

9

Saying No to Disney: Disney's Demise in Four American Cities

Stacy Warren

What happens when the imagineering logic of Walt Disney World
becomes the logic of the real world?[1]

What is more universally reviled among cultural critics today than Disney? From virtually every theoretical position—whether neo-Marxist, postmodern, deconstructionist, postcolonial—it is almost taken for granted that anything the company does will result in a blandly homogenized sugary-sweet facade masking the ruthless and fundamentally undemocratic corporate activities and policies that are its underpinning, all willingly swallowed by a politically gullible public. As Disney sensibilities seep more frequently and visibly into the real world, Disney's critics seem to be getting more testy. And with good reason. Disney's impact is global, and following Disney's involvement with the "rehabilitation" of its complete antithesis, Times Square, in the mid-1990s, it becomes clear that no space is immune from the Disney effect. Additionally, it is not just the Disney Company involved in this type of development; numerous other developers emulate the apparent successes of the Disney method. Indeed it is a troubling situation. Critics rightly articulate concern that the very design and construction of our everyday landscapes is being taken out of

231

local hands and put into the well-oiled jaws of multinational corporations who have the power and capital to impose pan-national Disney cultural economies on local ones. Disneyfied urban space offers perhaps the quintessential example of the replacement of public space with private simulations of it. But what often escapes attention are the many times that Disneyfied plans flounder, unbuilt or grudgingly transformed, under the weight of organized protest, impulsive acts of resistance, and that unwieldy and inefficient mechanism known as democracy. The hegemonic dynamic between Disney's world and the real world offers an excellent opportunity to compare the theoretical and the empirical, and explore the actual dimensions of Disney development as they affect both private and public spaces.

In this chapter, I examine the trajectories of Disney's increased involvement in the planning and design of the real world that led the company toward Times Square and beyond. My interest, however, is as much on what has *not* happened as on what has. Disney's development plans have by no means been uncontested. Some were shelved entirely, and others transformed by resistance and surrounded by clouds of controversy. Thus my goals in this paper are threefold. First, I develop a time line of Disney's development activities both on Disney property and off in order to establish the sometimes breathtaking scope of Disney's agenda. Second, I focus on four case studies to examine the struggles that Disney encounters with real-world citizens. By carefully tracking Disney's activities in Seattle (1985–1989), Long Beach (1990–1991), Anaheim (1991–1995), and Haymarket, Virginia (1993–1994), we can develop a comprehensive understanding of how Disney developments are planned and constructed, and how they can come unraveled. Finally, I situate the everyday contours of Disney development, and resistance to it, in the context of broader discourse concerning the planning and development of the so-called postmodern city.

A Time Line of Disney Projects

Walt Disney's interest in urban planning is well documented and has reached almost mythic proportions. The famous 1965 Florida press conference in which he unveiled his ideas for his experimental city EPCOT revealed to the world that Disney was at heart not just a theme-park developer but also an urban planner who dabbled in the utopian. Disney's urban model was often attributed to his dislike of the chaos that surrounded Disneyland in Anaheim.[2] The more observant also noted that his approach was decidedly totalitarian in nature; in his insightful examination of Walt Disney's desire to create a private government on his vast Florida property, Richard Foglesong quotes a Disney executive who refers to Walt's kingdom as an "experimental absolute monarchy."[3]

Since Walt Disney's death in 1966, the company has continued this expansion of empire. Disney officially made the transition to bona fide urban consultant long before Times Square came along, with a lot less fanfare.[4] The Disney Development Company was formed in 1984 as the corporate arm (some might say strong-arm) that would handle real estate development, both on and off Disney property. During the late 1980s, Disney was hired by a handful of cities to participate in minor facilities development and design consultancy—an airport expansion here, a museum there—that primarily involved non-Disney property. In the early 1990s, a series of in-house Disney projects overseen by the Disney Development Company (and its subsequent transformations under the guises of Walt Disney Imagineering and Disney Regional Entertainment) were located closer to and often squarely within cities. Some were designed to be stand-alone entertainment complexes in downtown sites, and some were planned to be much broader in scope, including hotels and commercial, industrial, and residential space.[5]

Table 1 illustrates the scope and longevity of Disney's involvement in real world development. While the theme parks represent the largest and most comprehensive developments to date, equally important are the numerous smaller urban contributions, both successes and failures. Taken as a whole, these indicate that Disney has long been inserting itself into urban space with varying degrees of success.

Table 1.
Time Line of Disney's Development Projects and Related Event

Year	Development	Comments
1938	Burbank Studios*	Movie studios (51 acres), San Fernando
1955	Disneyland	Theme park (160 acres), Anaheim
1962	Seattle World's Fair*	Design and management consultant for the fair
1964	New York World's Fair*	Developed attractions for the fair
1964	Walt Disney World (WDW)	Disney begins buying land for Orlando park
1971	Walt Disney World	The Florida theme park officially opens
1975	Walt Disney Village	Retail and resort area opens on WDW property
1981	Houston Airport*	Disney installs PeopleMover at airport
1982	EPCOT	EPCOT opens at WDW
1983	Tokyo Disneyland	Japanese theme park opens (Disney partial owner)
1984	Arvida Real Estate*	Disney purchases Florida real estate company

Table 1. *(continued)*

Year	Development	Comments
1984	Managerial change	Disney Development Co. created
1985	Seattle Center*	Disney begins negotiations to be consultant
1987	Disney Store*	First Disney Store opens in Glendale, Calif.
1988	Gene Autry Museum*	Disney oversees exhibit design for museum
1989	Disney-MGM Studios	Opens at Walt Disney World
1989	Seattle Center*	Disney proposal for Seattle Center rejected
1991	Long Beach*	Failed attempt to buy theme park
1991	WESTCOT*	Expansion into Anaheim announced
1992	Houston Space Center*	Disney participates in design of tourist attraction
1992	Euro Disney	Disney park located in Paris opens
1993	Los Angeles Airport*	Disney participates in terminal redesign
1993	Disney's America	Failed attempt to build Virginia theme park
1994	Celebration	Construction begins on Disney-planned community
1995	Times Square* (TS)	Disney buys theater, participates in TS redesign
1995	California Adventure	New Anaheim park announced, WESTCOT gone
1996	Managerial change	Disney Development Co. merges with WD Imagineering
1996	Managerial change	Disney Regional Entertainment created
1996	Las Vegas*	Disney installs monorail at Bally-MGM
1996	Celebration	First residents move to Disney community
1997	Downtown Disney	First retail zone opens in WDW
1997	Club Disney*	Two children's play zones open in L.A. region
1998	Disney Quest	First electronic play zone opens in WDW
1998	ESPN Zone*	First sports zone opens in downtown Baltimore
1998	Animal Kingdom	Opens at Walt Disney World
1999	Disney Quest*	Entertainment complex opens in Chicago
1999	Club Disney*	All Club Disneys closed
1999	ESPN Zone*	New openings in Chicago, Times Square
1999	Hong Kong Disneyland	Plans for Chinese theme park announced
2000	ESPN Zone*	New openings in Atlanta and Washington, D.C.
2000	Disney Quest*	Failed attempt to locate in Philadelphia
2001	Disney Quest*	Chicago location closed
2001	ESPN Zones*	New openings in Las Vegas, Denver, and Disneyland
2001	California Adventure	Theme park adjacent to Disneyland opens
2001	Anaheim	Third Gate Disneyland expansion announced
2002	Disney Studios Paris	Opens at Disneyland Paris
2003	Hong Kong Disneyland	Groundbreaking for Chinese theme park

* Indicates non-theme-park development.

Disney as Urban Planner: Four Case Studies

In order to ask what Disney's invasion of public space means on a broader level, it is first necessary to examine more precisely where, how, and among whom it has occurred. Here I present four case studies that situate these questions in actual lived space—one non-theme–park development, two hybrid theme park-urban commercial developments, and one traditional theme park. At first glance, each proposed project would have seemed to be a guaranteed success: as I explain below, the economic climate was ripe for commercial development, and local governments were eager to encourage entertainment-related projects. And who, as we shall often hear, knew entertainment better than Disney? Yet by the mid- to late 1980s, the terrain of commercial urban development was becoming trickier to negotiate than it may have appeared on the surface, and Disney, as we shall see, for a variety of reasons remained steadfastly ill equipped to deal with it. After first providing a brief outline of the broader context of contemporary land development and urban planning practices within which Disney would have to operate, I then turn to the details of the four case studies themselves.

A Brief Overview of Recent Planning Practices

The latter part of the twentieth century was a disconcerting time for many urban planners. The seemingly infallible planning model they had been taught in school—the rational, objective planner who had the power to impose great civic ideas upon the landscape—was coming under theoretical attack. Even worse, in practice it was just not working anymore. Shopping center developers like Victor Gruen and James Rouse replaced public works czars like Robert Moses as the prime movers in shaping the urban and suburban landscape. Commercial real estate priorities increasingly governed land use as federal urban funding dried up in the 1970s. Festival marketplaces, downtown atriums, themed entertainment zones, and the like replaced housing, public facilities, and freeway interchanges as showpiece urban projects. Cities actively competed for the biggest developers they could attract through strategies such as public/private partnerships, tax incentives, impact fee waivers, infrastructure improvements, and other concessions typical of the sort Disney was granted by the Florida state government in the 1960s.[6]

During the 1980s, however, cities across the United States were reevaluating their willingness to subsidize developers while receiving little in return.[7] Attention turned to regulatory mechanisms such as impact fees, job creation programs, day care provisions, and other social amenities for which the developer would be responsible as part of the negotiated agreement.[8] Cities became more demanding, and deals struck from the early 1990s onward were marked by developer concessions that were occasionally startlingly generous, more often modest, but always there.[9] As planners became more adept at navigating the complicated web of federal, state, and local agencies, private developers, lawyers, environmentalists, and other citizens—each with their own mandates and funding situation—they came to see themselves less as plan makers than as negotiators and mediators trying to achieve consensus among the many potentially adversarial players.[10]

The shift in planning roles paralleled a shift in planning theory. Two planning-theory changes are of particular interest here. First, as Fainstein comments, "planners now spoke in the same language as investment bankers, property brokers, and budget analysts."[11] Planning schools incorporated economics and real estate classes into their curricula; planners learned to think like developers. At the same time, a postmodern interest in planning discourse as role playing and storytelling emerged.[12] "Consensus building begins," Innes and Booher instruct, "with something like a storytelling phase that lays out the setting, the drama, and the characteristics of the players."[13] Similarly, Throgmorton comments that the most successful planning is presented as stories that "incorporate the literary techniques of plot, point of view, character, and use of tropes, weaving conflict and crisis together in a compelling manner."[14]

In other words, the new generation of planners who would encounter Disney in the late 1980s and 1990s were categorically different from their predecessors who had dealt with Disney in the 1960s; the uneven power relations that had characterized earlier city-developer relationships had been publicly exposed. Though it is debatable that the balance of power had truly shifted, what is significant for this argument is that the rhetorical strategies had—both sides publicly acknowledged that they needed to communicate successfully on some level, because one could not survive without the other. Far from seeing themselves as eager servants of developers' whims, planners of the 1990s were more likely to feel their role was to navigate the multiple discursive narratives they encountered, provide a stimulating environment for development, and yet, importantly, still protect the interests of the citizens they represented by extracting developer concessions in turn. The Disney Company, however, apparently had undergone no such transformation from the 1960s to the 1990s. Closer examination of its experiences in four American cities reveals that Disney consistently expected that its powers as developer should be absolute, expectations that were embedded into day-to-day operations in what I call the Disney Planning Storyboard.

The Disney Planning Storyboard (DPS)

Reading through the mundane details of each case, one is struck by a sense of déjà vu. One sees over a ten-year period different Disney faces reciting almost verbatim the same stock Disney statements and responses—the same demands of local officials, the same platitudes when dealing with the public, the same wounded statements of surprise when faced with resistance. Indeed, Disney's approach to planning in the real world seems carefully scripted in advance, as would be a Disney cartoon or attraction at a Disney theme park. I argue that this is not coincidence; the same underlying principles appear to shape Disney's production philosophy, whether the final product is a cartoon, a theme park, urban space, or the very process of urban land development itself.

Numerous observers have remarked on Disney's penchant for the all-controlling, all-enveloping narrative story line especially as it contributes to the unique landscapes created at Disney's theme parks, and they credit Disney's narrative design skills to the studio's long-standing experience with filmmaking and animation. In particular, a Disney innovation dating back to the 1930s—the storyboard—is pinpointed as a watershed breakthrough that gave Disney's cartoons and films, and later theme parks, their hallmark tight organization and logical flow. The storyboard—literally a piece of corkboard onto which cartoonists would pin individual scenes—allowed animators to plan and visualize a sequential order for their ideas.[15] Significantly, the advent of the storyboard also signaled a fundamental change in the creative process. Animators from the period describe a transition from a democratic, if somewhat chaotic, atmosphere where everyone helped out, there was little concern for structured preparation, and no rigid division of labor, to a highly structured environment where every scene was centrally planned and numerous tasks assigned to unskilled laborers; in his biography of Walt Disney, Christopher Finch notes that "Disney himself must have been delighted by this innovation. The storyboard enabled him to participate even more closely in the development of his cartoons, allowing him to . . . see at a glance exactly what needed to be done."[16]

Now, five decades later, Disney seems to have come up with a new version of a Disney storyboard, this time applied to both the process and the design of its development activities. Disney representatives utilize what appears to be a scripted narrative that defines and organizes personalities, dialogue, design standards, political demands, and expected outcomes in a manner reminiscent of the animation storyboard. The contours of what I call the "Disney Planning Storyboard" (DPS) crystallized during the 1960s as the company successfully extracted remarkable concessions from the state of Florida.[17] The DPS as applied from 1985 to 1994 appears to have frozen in time many of the assumptions that Disney staff brought to the Walt Disney World negotiations—for example, that city officials are so desperate to attract capital they will cheerfully overlook social consequences; that state funding exists primarily to support private business; and that a private business has no ethical responsibility to give anything back to the community beyond simply gracing it with the company's presence. In exactly the same sense that the original animation storyboard gave Walt Disney the ability to know "exactly what needed to be done," the DPS likewise places Disney employees as the sole experts in planning matters. What is especially striking about the four implementations of the DPS we are about to examine is the at times almost complete disconnection with more recent planning tropes, strategies, or even etiquette. At a time when most developers strive for consensus, willingly offer some degree of concessions, and at least appear to listen to the public, Disney instead clings resolutely to the parameters of its planning storyboard—even in the face of unmistakable failure. I now turn to the details of Disney developments in Seattle, Anaheim, Long Beach, and Haymarket, Virginia, to demonstrate how this has been the case.

The Disney Planning Storyboard in Seattle

Between 1985 and 1989, the Disney Company was hired to serve as urban planning consultant in its first high-profile project in a non-theme-park context. The client was the city of Seattle, and the focal point was Seattle Center, the city's publicly owned and aging seventy-four-acre civic center and former World's Fair grounds. Once the centerpiece of an ambitious redevelopment project that used the 1962 Century 21 Exposition as a vehicle to impose a more suburban, middle-class landscape on the lower-class, industrial neighborhood—a vision designed in the late 1950s with input from the Disney company itself—Seattle Center had never lived up to its promise. Who better than Disney could the city turn to for help?[18] The timing was fortunate. The Disney Development Company had been created the year before, in 1984, and already had begun dabbling in a few other minor—and apparently uncontested—off-site projects.[19] Seattle Center would be its first major urban project, involving at least the site itself and potentially some rehabilitation of the surrounding neighborhood. Three Disney Development Company employees were assigned to head the project. Their Imagineering background gave them a uniquely Disney set of urban planning skills: two of them had extensive Tomorrowland design experience, and the third had worked with EPCOT's Corporate Computer Timesharing system.[20]

The Disney effort was spearheaded in 1985 by a local pro-growth coalition including the director of Seattle Center and the mayor. With great fanfare they announced their intentions to bring Disney to Seattle because, as Mayor Charles Royer declared, when it came to "helping cities create excellent people places, [Disney is] probably the best in the world."[21] Disney's role was to be strictly as urban planning consultant and not theme park developer. As such, Disney for the first time would experience full-scale urban development in the absence of the notorious sweetheart deals that previously had insulated the company from various local, regional, and state planning regulations and practices such as in Orlando.[22] The company would discover that planning in the "real world" occupied a rockier sort of terrain.

Friction began almost instantly. Since Seattle Center was public property, Seattle City Council was required to authorize formal negotiations with the company before further plans could be made. City Council was not enthusiastic about the idea. The mayor's exuberant call to pursue Disney was seen as inappropriate in light of the recent establishment (with the mayor's support) of a local advisory commission to study and recommend changes concerning Seattle Center. Council members were concerned that Disney's involvement would usurp these local voices.

Face-to-face meetings with Disney staff during their first Seattle site visit heightened council members' concerns. One Disney Imagineer announced that Disney's first priority was to look over the entire site and consider what buildings and activities to retain and what new images to create—implying that a sizable portion of Seattle Center might be bulldozed.[23] An informal comment by another Imagineer more explicitly summarized Disney's tone: "nice town—we can do something with it."[24] Disney critics on the City Council—which after Disney's first visit to Seattle numbered eight of nine—were leery of spending what now was revealed to be $400,000 to hire an outside consultant who publicly stated that "we will not enter competitive bidding because it is our belief that there aren't people who are competitive with us."[25] Council members were openly offended by Disney's tone and further incensed by the company's demand that it be granted right of first refusal; as council member Norm Rice summarized, Disney "should have a public process that is above board."[26] The council voted against authorizing further negotiations with Disney. Disney staff returned to California and issued a statement of explanation rather unrelated to the proceedings, proclaiming "the many people concerned about Seattle Center didn't seem to have a clear direction in what they want, and we don't want to force our services on them."[27]

This was not, however, to be the last of Disney in Seattle. The mayor and his business coalition redoubled their lobbying efforts and spent nearly a year actively persuading council members, business and arts groups, neighborhood councils, and the media of Disney's invaluable services.[28] Disney representatives revisited the city, this time appearing more inclined toward compromise and, not insignificantly, giving the distinct impression that Disney was considering financing any redevelopment that would occur.[29] The final effect was that, by July 1987, council voted five-four in favor of authorizing the Disney project.

The official contract stipulated that the Disney Company would receive $475,000 for the development of three alternative plans for Seattle Center's redevelopment, and called for a public process that required extensive meetings with a city-appointed local advisory group and the general public *before* Disney generated the three plans. Disney, for its part, initially appeared to dive enthusiastically into its own Disney Planning Storyboard version of public process: it undertook telephone surveys,[30] user interviews, focus groups, and on-site participant observation to determine "the place Seattle Center held in the minds of the public."[31] Questions focused exclusively on Seattle Center's physical design and programmed activities; no attempt was made to assess neighborhood impact, parking and traffic, safety, and other community issues. Disney used this information to prepare three sets of blueprints, which it presented to the city in spring 1988.

The unveiling of the three plans provoked criticism from almost every angle. The plans were given the unimaginative titles Plan A, Plan B, and Plan C by Disney Imagineers; their design, according to many complaints, was equally unimaginative. Little distinguished one plan from the next. All appeared to be springboards for Disney to bulldoze many beloved buildings and fountains in order to impose the same mediocre new plan on Seattle Center. Advisory board members described the new plans with words such as "peculiar," "functionless," "boring," and "curious lack of imagineering on their part." Local critics further noted the plans seemed to exclude population segments such as senior citizens and ethnic groups who were adequately served by the existing center.[32] Surveying the overall product Disney presented, original Seattle Center architect Paul Thiry denounced the plans as a travesty of his vision; many Seattle residents agreed.[33]

Equally problematic was the realization that Disney's design process held little room for true public input. Local citizens complained that public meetings had devolved into slick Disney-run shows, where Disney talked and the public listened. Audience questions were answered in what was perceived to be patronizing, evasive fashion. The most sustained critical commentary was voiced by the Disney Study Advisory Group (whose formation had been stipulated as part of the initial contract to ensure public participation in the process). Working with Disney behind the scenes, the advisory group observed Disney's attitude toward local input in the numerous everyday minor events that comprised the bulk of the actual planning process. The advisory group reported a plethora of disturbing incidents, such as Disney's arrogance in proposing the demolition of a building that was not owned by the city without first contacting the owners, Disney's refusal to work with local transportation authorities on solutions to Seattle Center's traffic morass, and Disney's inability to envision anything other than a white, middle-class use of the site.[34] Direct attempts to confront Disney representatives on these issues were most often dismissed with the vague assurance that they would be addressed "later." The advisory group concluded that Disney's message was clearly "we know best," and issued a harsh criticism of the entire planning process.[35]

In short, most constituents were displeased with Disney's efforts. The general tone can be best summed up in the words of Dale P. Rothlind, who signed himself "Disgruntled Citizen" in a letter to the mayor: "I am very nearly dumbstruck by the sheer nerve of these people."[36] Acting in a similar vein, the Seattle City Council officially declared that Disney had not fulfilled the conditions of the contract and refused to accept any of the plans. Instead, council passed a resolution that requested "further refinement and analysis" of virtually all design elements in Plan B. The resolution also stipulated that Disney would be expected to coordinate with local city planners and traffic engineers concerning Seattle Center and surrounding areas and engage in genuine public discussion with the Disney Study Advisory Group, community groups, and "other interested citizens."[37] Finally, the revamped Disney plan would be subject to an Environmental Impact Statement review.

Four months later, version two of the Disney plan was unveiled. Yet in the eyes of most observers, the results of the supposedly civically enlightened Disney team were suspiciously reminiscent of the earlier plans. The architectural rhetoric was slightly different—now Disney spoke of "community integration" and "site unification," and made token efforts to retain more original buildings and evoke local images. But the only change that truly caught people's attention was the new price tag. Whereas a few months earlier Disney had tentatively proposed that Plans A, B, or C might cost the city of Seattle around $75 million to complete, the updated financial commitment had climbed to $335 million—for which, Disney finally clarified, it expected Seattle to be wholly responsible.

Seattle residents—and, significantly, those in positions of power—felt even greater antipathy toward Disney and the latest plan. "For that amount of money," stated advisory group member Norm Johnston, "we should have got a better job"; council member Jane Noland commented: "this development has breached faith with what we asked for. . . . To say I am disappointed is putting it very, very lightly."[38] Numerous citizens complained to the mayor's office, often echoing the message articulated by local architect Richard Haag that "the tactic of bypassing public input does not work."[39] The image of Seattle Center surrounded by a fence and admission booths was, in council member Jane Noland's words, "the unthinkable."[40] That Disney had devised a plan that would force the city into a position where an admission fee would be virtually unavoidable symbolized the true private and exclusionary nature of Disney's so-called public-planning venture. A local reporter summed up the general conclusion that Disney was no more than a slick private entity that turned the "bumbling public partner into a sucker."[41]

In the end, it was the required Environmental Impact Statement (EIS) process that proved to be the death knell for Disney's involvement in Seattle. While Disney was pursuing the stock Disney Planning Storyboard line regarding environmental impact statements and trying to convince the council to waive the requirement, the council already had shifted its interest beyond the Disney plan. The EIS process called for three alternative plans to be reviewed. In a move that was widely applauded, the council suggested that all three plans be drafted locally, using the Disney plan only as "a planning tool."[42] Three unsolicited local plans were submitted to council in addition to the Disney plan and the three local ones the council had commissioned. On June 5, 1989, council resolved to allow five plans into the formal EIS process. The Disney plan was not one of them. Thus, Disney's involvement with the city of Seattle officially came to an end. A half million dollars were spent, and the primary outcome was Seattle's conviction that their own local architects and planners could do a better job than Disney.

And so Disney concluded its first extended foray into urban planning beyond theme-park walls. As a consequence, one single change was applied to the Disney Planning Storyboard. Significantly, this change affected not so much how but *where* it would be applied. Never again would Disney allow itself to be placed in a position where it had relatively less power than a governmental structure or the citizenry at large. The DPS had evolved in settings where Disney had full control as a private developer within broader governmental structures eager to grant concessions and waivers. In Seattle, the DPS simply did not work. In fact, to the contrary, its inflexibility appeared to give the opposition an even stronger foothold. Rather than try to co-opt resistance into the narrative, the DPS scarcely even recognized it, leaving the company with no effective way to diffuse criticism. As we shall see in the next three case studies, each time Disney applies the DPS without further modification, the possibility for resistance grows.

The Disney Planning Storyboard in Long Beach and Anaheim

In 1989, at about the same time as Disney's demise in Seattle, a relatively minor real estate transaction in southern California set into motion Disney's next two urban development projects. Disney's acquisition of new properties in both Anaheim and Long Beach renewed the company's interest in redesigning urban spaces, and introduced a new twist to the Disney Planning Storyboard. Rather than first choosing a location and then attempting to convince the appropriate authorities to agree to its demands, Disney borrowed a tactic that had worked splendidly to its advantage in finding a site for Euro Disney. In the spirit of so-called "friendly competition," Disney pitted the two potential locations against each other and let each voluntarily come up with the more Disney-friendly concession package. Since the ensuing experiences of neither Long Beach nor Anaheim can be fully understood in isolation from each other, I treat them together.

As per the DPS, Disney began its work in secret. Company representatives started with Long Beach first, holding private meetings with city officials and port authorities. Within a few months, rumors of a new theme park plus development project began to fly; Disney observer and speculator Jim Hill surmises that Disney let the rumors work to its favor, and might itself have promulgated some of them.[43] Reportedly, Disney hoped that "unofficial" news of a Long Beach project would so dismay Anaheim officials that they would promise Disney anything to win the company back.

In August 1990, rumors of a possible Disneyland expansion in Anaheim began to circulate also. The timing of these rumors was also somewhat suspicious, coming precisely as Disney released design details of the Long Beach project to the media. Finally, Disney issued the public statement that "while it wants to build both, the Walt Disney Company can only build one of these parks in the 1990s. The company will build first in the city that provides us with the best support package."[44]

Design details for both projects affirmed that Disney was not merely envisioning another theme park in either location. In Long Beach, at stake was a three-billion-dollar redevelopment of a 350-acre, fairly run-down portion of the waterfront. "Port Disney" was to include the theme-park anchor "Disney-Sea" (which recently has been resurrected in a Japanese version for Tokyo Disneyland), five resort hotels, specialty shops, waterfront dining and entertainment, a new marina, a cruise ship port, shuttles, water taxis, maybe even a monorail, and an ominously named Future Research Center. The local site posed two vexing conditions that ultimately helped play a role in the demise of the project: (1) over half of the proposed acreage was at the time underwater and would need to be filled in, requiring zoning and environmental approvals at both local and state levels; and (2) the California Coastal Commission required that a portion of all waterfront development must be accessible to the nonpaying tourist, thus eliminating the possibility of the classic walled Disney compound.[45] Disney's Long Beach endeavor was nothing short of an urban redevelopment project encompassing all the usual local, regional, and state agencies. The question for Disney would be how much of the "regulatory maze," as the governor of Virginia would later call it, the company could sidestep.

Details of the Anaheim project were released in May 1991, during which time Disney had quietly purchased an additional twenty-three acres adjacent to existing Disneyland property.[46] More than just an expansion of Disneyland, the plan would bring Disney design into the city streets (the proposed boundaries even extended into a few land parcels that Disney did not own, which came as startling news to some of the current landowners). The "new themed urban resort," as Disney officials referred to it, was to be called WESTCOT. It would include a theme park where, according to promotional material, one could "take a cruise around the world, ride a Chinese dragon roller coaster, shop along the Champs Élysées, climb an Egyptian pyramid, and splash down the roaring rapids of the Congo River—all in one day and without ever leaving Anaheim."[47] The real centerpiece of the plan would be the newly developed hotel and retail space surrounding the park. As the master plan noted, by 1991 "Disneyland [was] the only green space in an area of busy streets, parking lots, and extensive commercial development." The master plan proposed a "Garden District . . . an extensively landscaped system of walkways, thoroughfares, streetscapes, and promenades . . . reminiscent of the landscaped avenues of Beverly Hills and Santa Barbara in the 1930s. The Disneyland Resort . . . will be the cornerstone of the City's plan to rejuvenate the Commercial Recreation Area."[48]

Once plans for both sites were made public, two diametrically opposed processes were set into motion. On the one hand, officials in both cities, keenly aware of the competitive atmosphere Disney had fostered, behaved much like their predecessors thirty years earlier in Florida: they scrambled to come up with the better package while publicly acknowledging the financial sacrifices the cities themselves were willing to carry. Anaheim, for instance, offered Disney one billion dollars' worth of street widening, tree planting, and public improvements. Long Beach came up with $880 million in local highway improvements and pledged to support Disney in its attempts to gain waivers from environmental and rezoning regulations.[49] On the other hand, however, with the same energy that city officials exhibited in trying to please Disney, a number of local, regional, and state organizations began to protest Disney's plans. The resistance took different forms in the two locations. In Long Beach, statewide environmental groups voiced the loudest opposition. In Anaheim, concerned home owners within the city organized the most effective anti-Disney campaign. While the tactics differed, the overall effect was the same—resistance in Anaheim and Long Beach eventually encouraged Disney to drop its plans in both cities. I next briefly outline the forms of resistance Disney encountered in order to establish the breadth of tactics utilized.

In Long Beach, concern focused specifically on Disney's plans to fill in 256 acres of San Pedro Bay. Environmentalists across the state protested that such an act could severely threaten the ecosystem, and eventually the state of California and the California Coastal Commission refused to allow the coastline zoning variance that Disney had requested. State-level support had been a central part of the DPS, given Disney's experiences with the Florida state government. Consequently, it is not surprising that once the California state decision was handed down in fall 1991, Disney lost interest in the Long Beach project. By Christmas, Disney formally announced its decision not to pursue Port Disney. Almost by default, Anaheim had won the competition. Yet while Anaheim city officials were breathing a collective sigh of relief, city residents were gearing up for a protracted battle with the Mouse.

Local Anaheim residents, after observing the Disney Planning Storyboard swing into action with pep rallies complete with marching bands, cheerleaders, and extensive media coverage, reached the limits of their tolerance during the public hearing process hosted by the Anaheim Planning Commission during spring 1992. Much as we have seen in Seattle, hearing attendees reported that city officials appeared to have lost control of the proceedings as Disney turned what was to be a forum for serious debate into an opportunity to instruct Anaheim residents why Disney knew best. Again, incisive planning questions were dismissed with patronizing answers. For instance, a question about the provision of adequate schools for the families of the projected 17,500 new employees was met with a resounding endorsement of WESTCOT's educational aspects and the possibility for school field trips.[50] Anaheim residents refused to accept Disney's version of urban development as readily as their city officials appeared to be doing. One group of families, for example, sued Disney over its unwillingness to contribute to the educational infrastructure that would be needed should WESTCOT be built.[51] On a broader level, the community support group Anaheim HOME (Homeowners for Maintaining the Environment) formed in spring 1992. For the next three years, its estimated 1,600 members fought to regain local control of the development of their own city through media exposure and by tactics such as picketing in the Disneyland parking lot and uncovering a decades-old practice of free Disneyland passes for all city employees.[52]

In June 1995, Disney announced that WESTCOT could not be built as initially planned and would be dramatically scaled back into an attraction called Disney's California Adventure. Though Disney press releases cited internal financial and managerial pressures unrelated to Anaheim such as Euro Disney's economic problems and Eisner's heart surgery, organized opposition from Anaheim citizens had clearly played a role. The ways in which original WESTCOT plans were scaled back are revealing. They let us see how Disney, as after its Seattle experience, further restricted the types of environments in which it would consider development in order to avoid changing the DPS. The notion of weaving a "themed urban resort" into existing city streets as part of a grander renewal plan was eliminated. Instead, Disney's California Adventure would be a much smaller and almost antiurban affair, basically not much more than a theme park with limited hotel and retail space. The mission was no longer to create a livable urban setting; rather, the new version was to offer simulacra of famous California sites such as San Francisco, the Central Valley, the beaches, and Hollywood, in the hopes that visitors would never feel the need to leave Disney property.[53] All retail space was subsumed under the stock "Downtown Disney" package, which means that the only portion of the entire design meant to represent city streets was, in the end, reduced to a commodified package. Finally, in the aftermath of WESTCOT's demise, Disney attempted a managerial change that, though later reversed, reveals its commitment to the spirit of the Disney Planning Storyboard. Instead of utilizing the Imagineers for all theme-park design, as traditionally had been done, Disney management initially announced that all design and construction for Disney's California Adventure would instead be overseen by the Disney Development Company because it had a better reputation for meeting deadlines and controlling costs. The announcement generated such a vicious backlash among Imagineers that Eisner himself stepped in to cancel the transfer of power.[54] One year later, however, the Disney Development Company would be merged with Walt Disney Imagineers to create a single development unit. Though the unit now retains the name "Walt Disney Imagineering," one senses that the underlying message behind this managerial change comes straight from the Disney Planning Storyboard: urban development, whether within theme-park walls or beyond, works best as an efficient and ruthless enterprise. We have seen that this attitude in the real worlds of Seattle, Long Beach, and Anaheim proved highly fractious. And in our final case study, Virginia, things will go from bad to worse.

The Disney Planning Storyboard in Virginia

Unlike the three previous development attempts outlined above, the historically themed "Disney's America" at first promised to be a much less contentious project. It was to be a theme park in the traditional Disney vein, located on a large tract of ex-urban land outside of Washington, D.C. All development would occur within Disney property. It appeared to be a perfect candidate for the Disney Planning Storyboard. Ironically, the Virginia project generated far more resistance that anything Disney had witnessed before, and was the first truly to elevate both the discourse and the practice of resistance from local to national levels. The DPS was completely inadequate to deal with it.

The project began much as its Florida counterpart Walt Disney World had three decades earlier. In the spring of 1993, the Disney Company anonymously purchased an option to buy three thousand acres owned by Exxon in Haymarket, Virginia, approximately thirty-five miles west of Washington, D.C., and less than five miles from Manassas National Battlefield Park, a Civil War site.[55] Significantly, since the purchase had occurred anonymously, no local or state officials were as yet involved in the impending development. Exxon already had won zoning approval for large mixed-used development, so Disney could easily proceed with its plans behind the DPS veil of secrecy. By November 1993, though, rumors leaked to the press prompted Disney to officially announce Disney's America.[56]

In Michael Eisner's own words, the theme park would "be built around a small number of emotionally stirring, heart-wrenching stories based on important themes in American history."[57] Promotional material gushed about historical attractions such as antique steam trains chugging through simulated nineteenth-century towns, a miniature version of Ellis Island, a simulated Depression-era family farm, and a Lewis and Clark white-water raft ride.[58] In addition to the theme park proper, the entire complex would include a water park, campgrounds, a zoo, a twenty-seven-hole golf course, a stadium, an airstrip for vintage air shows, a battlefield reenactment, 1,340 hotel rooms, 2,500 residential units to include houses, condominiums, and apartments, and two million square feet of commercial space. The theme park would occupy only 405 of 3,006 acres.

This seemingly standard Disney project, however, in fact presented multiple points of friction. First, given that the existing population of Haymarket, a one-stoplight town at the time, was 483 people, Disney in essence proposed the development of a new and much larger community that would exist entirely within privately controlled space.[59] Second, the surrounding land that would be affected was far from undeveloped. To the contrary, though not heavily populated it had deep regional and national significance. Not only was the area home to an affluent population that historian Mike Wallace characterizes as "Virginia gentry, suburban squires, and Washington power brokers"—including as residents Senator John Warner, ambassador to France Pamela Harriman, Jacqueline Onassis, and Alice Mills DuPont—but it also struck a national chord as a Civil War site.[60] Consequently, the Disney Planning Storyboard would be employed against an unprecedented assembly of constituents.

Officials and business leaders at the state, regional, and local levels initially were supportive of the Disney theme park. The most vocal critic was the County Board of Supervisor's representative in whose district the project would be built. Generally, officials at all levels saw Disney as an economic boon whose development inconveniences would be outweighed by the revenue generated. Newly elected governor George Allen made the Disney theme park a primary goal of his administration and vowed to help Disney navigate the "federal regulatory maze" and any other barriers that might be in its way.[61]

Disney's interactions with public officials at first proceeded according to Disney Planning Storyboard lines. After a high-energy press conference to announce the project, Disney presented its set of political demands to the appropriate authorities in Prince William County, the North Virginia regional area, and the state of Virginia. The requests adhered to the familiar contours of the DPS, and for the most part in these early stages Disney was granted what it requested. For example, Disney representatives asked the state of Virginia to finance the major portion of highway improvements deemed necessary to build the new park ($153 million was approved by the state General Assembly); they lobbied the state to waive a full Environmental Impact Statement (though the waiver was not granted, the regional Transportation Planning Board agreed to sanction all Disney-related projected highway improvements as meeting federal pollution limits by 1999);[62] and they requested that Prince William County offer a substantial reduction in rezoning fees (the county agreed to reduce Disney's total fee of $621,540 by two-thirds, based on a new category of "large-scale zoning request" fabricated for the occasion).[63]

From this point onward, however, the process grew more complicated as events required that Disney deal with the growing number of players who all felt they should have a voice in determining the outcome of the contested three thousand acres. Repeatedly, Disney appeared to treat the complex of local, regional, and national constituents as minor nuisances who could be brushed aside with slick multimedia presentations and Disney pixie dust—a strategy that again, as in Seattle, Long Beach, and Anaheim, would paradoxically further empower the company's critics.[64]

Relations with local government grew strained as it became apparent to Prince William County planners that Disney expected to be treated deferentially and to bypass the normal regulatory process. Disney refused to participate in routine presubmission meetings to discuss its rezoning application, claiming it did not need any assistance from the county. The ensuing skirmish that would take place over its application was reminiscent of its experiences with Plans A, B, and C in Seattle. County staff members felt that the Disney application was so poorly conceived and vaguely worded that they dedicated months of labor to sorting out the zoning issues and doggedly pressing Disney to be more responsive. Disney was asked to submit a total of five versions of the application before county officials were satisfied that Disney had successfully addressed solid planning issues and not merely presented splashy propaganda.[65] In spite of the lengthy struggle, the Prince William County Planning Commission voted seven to one to authorize Disney to proceed to the next step, perhaps giving Disney the false sense that resistance was now behind it.

It was not. As Michael Eisner would later recall, the company felt completely blindsided by the next level of opposition, which he likened to finding oneself suddenly the captain of the *Exxon Valdez*.[66] Two main lines of attack developed, one more concerned with the *where* of the project and the other more concerned with the *what*.[67] The Piedmont Environmental Council was a well-established and well-funded environmental preservation group with over twenty years of experience opposing new development plans in the region. It represented concerns regarding the loss of farmland, forests, watersheds, and local histories in the face of Disney and the encroaching sprawl they felt would accompany its theme park.[68] The Protect Historic America group was formed in response to the proposed themes in the new park, and enlisted nationally known historians and media personalities to argue against the Disneyfication of American historical narratives. Though ostensibly not as concerned with the urban and suburban impact of the project as with its symbolic messages, the issues raised by this group served to reinforce the notion that this particular location was of almost sacred importance to Americans in general. These two groups employed tactics that placed the debate on the national agenda, including nationally placed advertisements and editorials, mass mailings, lobbying, shrewdly timed threats of legal action, and, ultimately, a place on the agenda of the U.S. Senate's Energy and Natural Resources Subcommittee on Public Lands, National Parks, and Forests.[69] From "disgruntled citizens" in Seattle to congressional scrutiny in Virginia, resistance to Disney was growing more potent. Finally, in September 1994, with the deadline rapidly approaching on its option to purchase the land, Eisner announced that Disney would not pursue the Virginia project further.

The demise of Disney's America is often linked in the public eye to the tremendous amount of negative publicity generated, primarily through the media, concerning the historical aspects of the project. Close assessment of the way the Disney Planning Storyboard played out here reveals that other forms of resistance were equally effective. For a company that prefers to act anonymously and strike quickly, traditional regulatory planning structures again acted as deceptively powerful deterrents. Even when most officials involved were generally on Disney's side, Disney's stubborn belief that it was above standard treatment unnecessarily slowed the process down by at least six months and made enemies of former allies. Further, the threat of lawsuit—a tactic that surfaced in both Long Beach and Anaheim and was used frequently by various environmental representatives here—proved especially bothersome to Disney. For a fourth time, Disney decided that urban development that was to proceed in an environlment that included various governmental structures, activist groups, and private citizens—in other words, within the pure messiness of democracy—was not worth the trouble.

Critical Analysis of Disney Development

Careful examination of Disney's demise in four separate locations invites questions as to the broader theoretical significance of Disney-like development. What are the implications of the privatization of public space? And what are the implications when such attempts fail? What avenues of public debate are available and utilized to determine how the takeover occurs? Why and under what conditions does public debate make a difference? In order to answer these questions, it is first useful to revisit a recent Disney project that did *not* fail, Times Square.

Although the Virginia episode had elevated resistance to Disney to national levels, by the following year the Times Square redevelopment (chronologically Disney's next urban project) presented a very different image in the public eye: Disney's naturalness as an urban developer, as possibly the only antidote to the horrible state of New York's public streets.[70] Times Square, on the surface at least, appeared to signal the triumphant return of the Disney Planning Storyboard as a successful development tool. Disney played the role of demanding private developer to the hilt, including relentless haggling, threatened drop-dead dates, and several "fits of pique." The city acquiesced to most of Disney's demands, granting low-interest loans, subsidies, and other concessions that were generous enough to raise the hackles of other Times Square developers.[71] The final product generally was praised as a vast improvement over the old

Times Square, although numerous critical observers directly connected Disney's perceived success in Times Square with "the triumph of private ownership over public space" and lamented an apparent lack of public protest.[72] In other words, the Disney Planning Storyboard at last seemed to work, and the controversy and resistance that had marked Disney's forays into urban space over the last decade diminished to nonthreatening levels.

In light of this apparent turnaround in Disney's planning fortunes, two entwined yet ultimately distinct theoretical issues must be addressed—Disney as a symbol of the privatization of public space, and Disney's Planning Storyboard as a symbol of the decline of public discourse. While the former has received ample attention in the literature, the latter—potentially just as significant—has been scarcely addressed. After briefly reviewing general denunciations of Disneyfied private space, I turn to the DPS to interrogate its role in urban transformations.

The privatization of public space has been of intense concern among urban scholars and others for several decades; from the early 1960s onward commentators have looked directly to the Disney Company as a leading force in the process. Some of the most splendidly polemical attacks on the Disneyfication of space—and hence the most widely quoted—come from European analysts of postmodernism, such as Jean Baudrillard, Umberto Eco, and Louis Marin, as well as from the American Fredric Jameson. The observations they make are riveting—Marin's conclusion that Disneyland is an "empty abyss" of capitalist exploitation "tantamount to a shipwreck or loss of consciousness," for example, is intensified by assertions about actual urban space such as Baudrillard's comment that the Disney abyss has reached the real world with cities becoming "nothing more than a network of endless, unreal circulation."[73]

Urban theorists such as Michael Sorkin, Edward Soja, and Sharon Zukin bring a more concrete understanding of urban process to their analyses of Disney space.[74] All reach a similar conclusion, which in the end is not unlike what European cultural critics surmised from afar: the privatized Disney city is about simulacra, placelessness, and control. Sorkin's three salient characteristics of what he calls a new "ageographical" city—the elimination of ties to local physical and cultural geographies; our obsession with security and surveillance; and the supremacy of simulations—often have been used as evidence that our public spaces are being transformed into private theme parks.[75] Soja similarly looks at Los Angeles and sees "a gigantic agglomeration of theme parks, a lifespace comprised of Disneyworlds [sic]."[76] Zukin hones in on the cultural power of these landscapes of consumption, noting that "Disney's market-oriented landscape evokes a strong sense of place" that, in its comfortable, conflict-free way, borders on a "utopian dream."[77] The Disney way appears to guarantee attractive, inviting spaces that also promise a healthy cash flow. In this "utopian dream," however, who benefits from that cash flow is less often considered, nor are the broader implications of a primarily low-wage, no-benefits service sector economy. Those who have delved more deeply into what might be called the "Disney economy" all confirm how themed spaces in many ways conceal the real relations underneath, whether examined in terms of the daily operations of Walt Disney World's infrastructure, such as in Richard Foglesong's work, as symbolic referents influencing business improvement districts in other cities, as Sharon Zukin has explored, or as manifest within the boundaries of Disney's real town, Celebration, as Andrew Ross discovered.[78]

A third wave of Disney-related research helps situate Disney's urban activities within the context of the entertainment industry, which itself has followed in Disney's footsteps and begun infiltrating urban and suburban space.[79] Fainstein and Judd note that "the constant transformation of the urban landscape to accommodate tourists has become a permanent feature of the political economy of cities"; following postmodern trends, these themed environments "owe more to Disneyland . . . than to urban history or culture."[80] As Hannigan summarizes, locally designed and maintained public space is replaced with "an infrastructure of casinos, megaplex cinemas, themed restaurants, simulation theatres, interactive theme rides, and virtual reality arcades."[81] Local ties are nearly imperceptible; each space is visibly branded, like cattle, with the corporate owner's logo, and invisibly sustained by the global connections that buttress the activities of late capitalism—to sweatshop workers in Malaysia who produce the goods sold, to financial institutions in the Cayman Islands that handle the electronic banking, to the petroleum rigs in the Persian Gulf that provide the energy. Thus, the privatization of public space quite consistently manifests itself as a new generation of fantasy spaces embedded in transnational relations of power. Almost every major city has a Nike Town, a Hard Rock Café, and the like; more elaborate developments like Universal's City Walk or the Grove in Los Angeles offer to the paying public complete immersion in a private urban dreamscape.

The very profusion of these privatized spaces, however, raises a perplexing question. All of these privately developed spaces were built within the same existing democratic structures that so aggravated the Disney Company in its ventures. Each developer had to navigate successfully a gauntlet of planners, environmentalists, lawyers, citizens, and others in order to win approval to complete its projects. Most urban theory, while offering many other valuable insights into the privatization process, remains silent on the actual day-to-day interactions that construct our cities. Did everyone involved eagerly acquiesce to the developers' wishes? Did anyone protest the privatization of their world—or even notice? Has the Disney Planning Storyboard, like the Disney version of urban space, also seeped into the real world? Again, a closer look at Disney's experiences in Times Square can be instructive.

Alexander Reichl offers a valuable starting point when he observes that Disney's success in Times Square had as much to do with the specific urban narratives that had grown around the redesign of the New York site as with the Disney Company itself. Drawing on Robert Beauregard's work on cities as narrative objects, Reichl demonstrates that already surrounding Times Square was a powerful set of perceptions and representations that informed people what the problems were, and how best to solve them.[82] Disney was successful because it fit the script; it encountered an audience willing to play out the development process as proscribed by the Disney Planning Storyboard.[83] Lynn Sagalyn's monumental documentation of the minutiae of nearly three decades of Times Square redevelopment—of which Disney occupied merely a few months by comparison—further suggests that internal squabbling (which apparently did not warrant much press coverage at the time) underlay Disney's seemingly uncontested presence in New York.[84] The successful implementation of the Disney Planning Storyboard was in part pure serendipity, hinging on the fact that the particular grouping of Times Square redevelopers who happened to be at the financial and political forefront in the mid-1990s proved amenable to Disney's way of development.

Reichl and Sagalyn remind us that as Disney (or any private developer) takes over public space, it is always a participant in a broader public process that it does not single-handedly control. While that broader public discourse continues increasingly to privilege private development as an urban solution, it does not always support the Disney Planning Storyboard as the appropriate way to achieve this. Earlier in this chapter, I reviewed current trends in planning theory that seek to empower planners with tools to outstrategize DPS-style developers. A brief survey of recent development projects suggests that such strategies also work in practice: few private developers assume a position of untouchable arrogance, and few communities allow new developments to progress unchallenged. Most current projects involve complicated negotiations that provide tangible social benefits for the local public: in their examination of four recent shopping developments in southern California, for example, Kotin and Peiser found that in all cases a substantial portion of benefits was directed back into public revenue streams; similarly, Sagalyn reported approximately fifty million dollars in developer obligations stemming from a deal for a Los Angeles entertainment complex.[85] Community groups often take an active role in the negotiations, whether invited or not: announcement of a new Wal-Mart, for example, almost certainly generates local protest, and even the deceptively "anticorporate" Starbucks coffee chain has been the target of local disapproval.[86]

This general pattern of negotiation, resistance, and compromise thus more accurately depicts the development climate across North America than the relatively rare Disney-friendly atmosphere that Disney representatives encountered in New York. In fact, while the expansion of entertainment giants and other private developers across our cities continues unabated, Disney's specific efforts to colonize urban space since Times Square have met with mixed results. The Disney Regional Entertainment division was gutted in 2000 in the messy aftermath of attempts to locate Disney Quest indoor entertainment complexes and Club Disney family play centers in major urban settings.[87] Some, such as the Philadelphia Disney Quest, were never built, because city officials would never agree to Disney's demands.[88] Others were closed a few years into their operation. At the time of this writing, only the ESPN Zone sports bars remain open on off-site property. Significantly, Disney's only major U.S. project announced at this time is the "third gate" Disneyland expansion in Anaheim. Vaguely reminiscent of WESTCOT plans, this expansion will bring Disney representatives together with known allies in the Anaheim city government to create the right regulatory atmosphere—zoning changes, traffic updates, etcetera—for further Disney expansion. And as with WESTCOT, the Anaheim HOME community group is again gearing up for battle.[89] As an important point of comparison, however, and possibly indicative of longer-range globalization of the Disney Planning Storyboard, Disney is currently in the middle of construction of Hong Kong Disneyland, a project carried out with the full cooperation of and approximately twenty-two billion dollars in subsidies from the Chinese government.[90]

In the end, it is by tracing Disney's planning failures in four North American locations that we can gain fresh insight into the implications of the privatization of public space. Privatization is not a monolithic cultural and economic expression that has flowed across North America like lava. Each new Disney project, NikeTown, or Planet Hollywood is a hegemonic possibility inserted into the urban fabric and experienced by actual people. It represents at once the loss of public space, the commodification of cultural expression, and the imposition of corporate will—and the grounds upon which these conditions can be contested. Zukin encourages us to listen to the "little voices of autobiography that make up the local hegemonies of urban landscapes"; in this chapter I have attempted to do just that in Seattle, Long Beach, Anaheim, and Virginia.[91] Each of the four locations hosted great debates about Disney shaped by the local culture and geography, and each managed to retain some level of local control over the development proceedings. It may be the abstract global conditions of late capitalism that put cities in a position where they feel the need to attract private developers to remain competitive, but the tangible local conditions and democratic traditions are what empower local residents (and interested regional and national parties) to insert themselves into the public discourse and rewrite the Disney Planning Storyboard.

Notes

1. Edward Relph, "Postmodern Geography," *Canadian Geographer* 35, no.1 (1991): 104.
2. See Randy Bright's otherwise glowing review of all matters relating to Disneyland, *Disneyland: Inside Story* (New York: Harry N. Abrams, 1987), for a revealing discussion of the strategies Disney used to finalize site locations for his southern California properties.
3. Richard Foglesong, *Married to the Mouse: Walt Disney World and Orlando* (New Haven, Conn.: Yale University Press, 2001), 59.
4. Because of Walt Disney's own interest in urban design issues, in large part spurred by his loathing of the sort of uncontrolled sprawl he saw enveloping first his Burbank and then more spectacularly his Anaheim property, almost every development decision Walt made could arguably be seen as an urban-planning move. His actions regarding the planning and design of Walt Disney World in Florida as well as his original vision of EPCOT as working utopian city provide an excellent basis for understanding Walt's planning objectives. For overviews of Walt Disney World and EPCOT planning, see for example Richard Foglesong, "Walt Disney World and Orlando: Deregulation as a Strategy for Tourism," in *The Tourist City*, ed. Dennis Judd and Susan Fainstein (New Haven, Conn.: The Yale University Press, 1999), 89–106; Michael Harrington, "To the Disney Station," *Harper's*, January 1979, 35–44; and John Taylor, *Storming the Magic Kingdom* (New York: Ballantine Books, 1987). Additionally, the Disney Company was involved as consultants in the planning for at least two World's Fairs (Seattle 1962 and New York 1964). The planned community of Celebration epitomizes more recent planning endeavors (see Andrew Ross, *The Celebration Chronicles: Life, Liberty, and the Pursuit of Property Values in Disney's New Town* (New York: Ballantine, 1999), and Douglas Franz and Catherine Collins, *Celebration U.S.A.: Living in Disney's Brave New Town* (New York: Henry Holt and Company, 1999).
5. John Hannigan, *Fantasy City: Pleasure and Profit in the Postmodern City* (New York: Routledge, 1999), and Saskia Sassen and Frank Roost, "The City: Strategic Site for the Global Entertainment Industry," in *The Tourist City*, 143–154, provide excellent overviews of the increasingly urbanized nature of entertainment developments.
6. General discussions of city-developer packages can be found in Todd Swanstrom, "Semi-sovereign Cities: The Politics of Urban Development," in, *The Politics of Urban America* (2nd ed.), ed. Dennis Judd and Paul Kantor (Boston: Allyn and Bacon, 1998), 272–288; Paul Kantor and H. V. Savitch, "Can Politicians Bargain with Business? A Theoretical and Comparative Perspective on Urban Development," in ibid., 288–306, and Susan S. Fainstein, *The City Builders: Property Development in New York and Lon-*

don, 1980—2000 (2nd edition revised) (Lawrence: University of Kansas Press, 2001) (see especially chapter 5: "Economic Development Planning Strategies"). Susan Fainstein and Michael Neuman, "Does Planning Need the Plan," *Journal of the American Planning Association* 64, no. 2 (1998): 209-220 provides overviews of planning theory as it has changed throughout the twentieth century.

7. Rachel Weber, "Do Better Contracts Make Better Economic Development Incentives?" *Journal of the American Planning Association* 68, no.1 (2002): 43-55. Weber points out that perceived corporate arrogance was at least in part driving this backlash: when firms such as GM, Volkswagen, and Playskool either dramatically downsized or pulled out entirely from sites where they had recently received financial incentives, cities reacted more aggressively than in the past. The city of Yonkers, New York, for example, took Otis Elevator to court for breach of contract. That the courts sided with Otis only further convinced cities of the need to protect their own interests.

8. Fainstein, *City Builders;* Lynne B. Sagalyn, "Negotiating for Public Benefits: The Bargaining Calculus of Public-Private Development," *Urban Studies* 34, no.12 (1997): 1955-1970; Allen Kotin and Richard Peiser, "Public-Private Joint Ventures for High Volume Retailers: Who Benefits?" *Urban Studies* 34, no. 12 (1997): 1971-1986.

9. Weber, "Better Contracts"; Kotin and Peiser, "Public-Private."

10. Judith Innes, "Challenges and Creativity in Post-modern Planning," in *The Profession of City Planning,* ed. Lloyd Rodwin and Bishwapriya Sanyal (New Brunswick, N.J.: Center of Urban Policy Research, 2000), 31-35.

11. Fainstein, *City Builders,* 99.

12. Judith E. Innes and David E. Booher, "Consensus Building as Role Playing and Bricolage," *Journal of the American Planning Association* 65, no.1 (1999): 9-26; Dowell Myers and Alicia Kitsuse, "Constructing the Future in Planning: A Survey of Theories and Tools," *Journal of Planning Education and Research* 19, no. 3 (2000): 221-231. Citation is from p. 229.

13. Innes and Booher, "Consensus Building," 17.

14. James Throgmorton, quoted in Myers and Kitsuse, "Constructing the Future in Planning," 229.

15. Christopher Finch, *Walt Disney: From Mickey Mouse to the Magic Kingdoms* (New York: Harry N. Abrams, 1973), 82-84; John Canemaker, *Paper Dreams: The Art and Artists of Disney Storyboards* (New York: Hyperion Press, 1999), 3-5.

16. Finch, *Walt Disney,* 84. For more discussion of the history of the storyboard and its impacts, see also John Canemaker's *Paper Dreams* and David M. Boje, "Stories of the Storytelling Organization: A Postmodern Analysis of Disney as "Tamara-Land," *Academy of Management Journal* 38, no. 4 (1999): 997-1035.

17. For details on Disney's Florida negotiations, see Foglesong, *Married to the Mouse.*

18. Stacy Warren, "The Disneyfication of the Metropolis and Popular Resistance in Seattle," *Journal of Urban Affairs* 16, no. 2 (1994): 89-107. Unless otherwise cited, references from the Seattle section come from this work and Warren's unpublished Ph.D. thesis, "The City as Theme Park and the Theme Park as City" (Ph.D. diss., University of British Columbia, 1993).

19. Ted Kenney, "Disney Disengages," *Seattle Weekly,* June 22, 1988, 9, and Terry Tang, "Sending Walt Disney to Never Never Land," *Seattle Weekly* September 24–30, 1988, 22–24; Marc Borrelli, "Encounter at the Theme Building," LaughingPlace.Com, http://www.laughingplace.com/News-PID503190-503191.asp.

20. "Biography: Gordon Hoopes," "Biography: Juliann Juras," and "Biography: Vance Ablott," Box 2, Norman J. Johnston Papers, Acc. 1648-4-88-35, University of Washington Libraries.

21. Charles Royer, quoted in "Royer Seeks Approval on Disney Plan," *Seattle Times,* March 5, 1987, F2. Royer also hoped that his connection with a Disney project would further his own political aspirations, as outlined in Warren, "The City as Theme Park and the Theme Park as City." Several years later Virginia governor George Allen would express the same sentiments in the context of his support for Disney's America.

22. Foglesong, "Walt Disney World and Orlando."

23. "Disney Refuses to Compete to Renovate Center," *Seattle Times,* September 12, 1986, G4.

24. Unnamed Imagineer, quoted in Tang, "Sending Walt Disney to Never Never Land," 24.

25. Patrick Scanlon, quoted in "Disney Refuses to Compete to Renovate Center," G4.

26. Ibid.

27. Disney spokesperson Paul Goldman, quoted in Tang, "Sending Walt Disney to Never Never Land," 22.

28. "Seattle Center Wants New Look for Next 25 Years," *Seattle Times,* January 25, 1987, F3.

29. "Fair Memories," *Seattle Times,* April 21, 1987, E1.

30. Demographic data supplied by the Disney Company relating to the phone surveys suggest that the overwhelmingly white, predominantly middle-class sample population interviewed (N = 824) more closely resembled profiles of Disney theme-park guests, not Seattle residents.

31. Walt Disney Imagineering, "Seattle Center Development Study: Phase III Site Design Concept" (1988), 5.

32. Disney Study Advisory Group member Norman Johnston made these comments in Norman Johnston, "Comments on Seattle Center Phase II Interim Report," May 18, 1988, Benson Papers, Local Government Information Center, Seattle, 1.

33. "Everybody Has a Plan for Seattle Center," *Seattle Times,* June 5, 1988, D1.

34. David Sprague to Julianne Juras, Box 2, Norman J. Johnston Papers, Acc. 1648-4-88-35, University of Washington Libraries, April 19, 1988.

35. "Minutes of the Disney Study Advisory Group," Box 2, Norman J. Johnston Papers, Acc. 1648-4-88-35, University of Washington Libraries, March 28, 1988.

36. Dale P. Rothlind to Charles Royer, Box 2, Norman J. Johnston Papers, Acc. 1648-4-88-35, University of Washington Libraries, August 16, 1988.

37. "Resolution #27803," City of Seattle, May 26, 1988.

38. "Disney's Projected Ride-Park Admission Fee Disappoints Nolan," *Seattle Times,* August 2, 1988, C4; "Bickering Continues over Disney's Center Plan," *Seattle Times,* August 8, 1988, B1.

39. Richard Haag to Charles Royer, Box 2, Norman J. Johnston Papers, Acc. 1648-4-88-35, University of Washington Libraries, May 27, 1988.

40. "Disney's Center Called a Plan Fit for a King," *Seattle Times,* August 16, 1988, B1.

41. David Brewster, "Two Weeks to Catch a Victory at Seattle Center," *Seattle Weekly,* July 12, 1989, 2.

42. "Seattle Center: Master Plan Draft Environmental Impact Statement," City of Seattle, 1990. Brewster, "Two Weeks to Catch a Victory at Seattle Center."

43. Jim Hill, "The Road to Adventure," MousePlanet, April 3, 2000, http://www.mouseplanet.com/jim/apr0300.htm.

44. Unnamed Disney representative, quoted in Hill, "Road to Adventure."

45. Faye Fiore, "Disney Unveils Plans," *Los Angeles Times,* August 1, 1990, B1.

46. Hill, "Road to Adventure." Jeff Rowe, "Disney Outlines $3 Billion Project," *The Orange County Register,* May 9, 1991, http://www.disneyphenom.com/site/California/Westcot/3billion.html.

47. "Westcot: Preliminary Master Plan," August 1, 2000, http://www.wed.simplenet.com/westcot.

48. *Disneyland Newsletter,* Spring 1991, http://www.wed.simplenet.com/ westcot.

49. Hill, "Road to Adventure."

50. Ibid.

51. Mike Wallace, *Mickey Mouse History and Other Essays on American Memory* (Philadelphia: Temple University Press, 1996), xxx.

52. Hill, "Road to Adventure."

53. Ibid.

54. Ibid.

55. Mike Wallace, "Disney's America," in *Mickey Mouse History,* 159–176.

56. Michael Eisner, *Work in Progress* (New York: Random House, 1998), 4. His autobiography is a treasure trove of heavily propagandized Disney information offered in a wonderfully genuine voice.

57. Ibid., 1, 2.

58. Richard Moe and Carter Wilkie, *Changing Places* (New York: Henry Holt and Company, 1997), 8.

59. Ibid., 4, and Michael P. Brooks, "Getting Goofy in Virginia: The Politics of Disneyfication," *American Planning Association National Conference Proceedings* (1997), http://www.asu.edu/caed/proceedings97/brooks.html, provide a detailed account of Disney's dealings in Haymarket.

60. Wallace, *Mickey Mouse History,* 166. Brooks, "Getting Goofy in Virginia," 7, provides a comprehensive list of the power elite who at the time of the Disney proposal owned land in the nine-county area surrounding the proposed site.

61. George Allen, quoted in Brooks, "Getting Goofy in Virginia," 5.

62. Brooks, "Getting Goofy in Virginia," 16.

63. Ibid., 19.

64. I focus my remarks primarily on Disney's reaction to issues surrounding the location of the theme park, where I maintain Disney simply applied the standard DPS as usual.

There is intriguing evidence, however, that the company was more open-minded in terms of theme-park content (another arena in which Disney traditionally utilizes the same tropes). Michael Eisner himself has argued that, in direct response to previous criticisms, Disney attempted to be sensitive to contemporary concerns regarding historical representation, going so far as to include alternative voices such as that of Maya Angelou in the designs (Eisner, *Work in Progress,* 10).

65. Brooks, "Getting Goofy in Virginia,"17–20.

66. Eisner, *Work in Progress,* 9.

67. Mike Wallace brings out this useful distinction in his essay "Disney's America" in *Mickey Mouse History,* 159–176.

68. Brooks, "Getting Goofy in Virginia," 7.

69. Wallace, *Mickey Mouse History,* 167; Brooks, "Getting Goofy in Virginia," 13.

70. Three sources provide excellent overviews of Disney's role in Times Square. Alexander J. Reichl offers cultural analysis of the Times Square redevelopment process from the 1980s through the Disney denouement of the mid-1990s in his book *Reconstructing Times Square* (Lawrence: University Press of Kansas, 1999); Susan S. Fainstein in *The City Builders* (especially pages 118–137) uses Times Square as one of several case studies in which she examines broader processes underlying contemporary property development in New York and London; and Lynn B. Sagalyn, *Times Square Roulette: Remaking the City Icon* (Cambridge, Mass.: The MIT Press, 2001), documents in great detail the numerous, sometimes intersecting redevelopment efforts that have been attempted in Times Square since the 1970s.

71. Reichl, *Reconstructing Times Square,* 158.

72. Joshua Wolf Shenk, "Hidden Kingdom," *The American Prospect* 6, no. 21 (1995): 84. Reichl and Sagalyn more accurately discuss the protests that did occur beyond general media attention.

73. Louis Marin, *Utopics: Spatial Play* (Atlantic Highlands, N.J.: Humanities Press, 1984), 240, and Jean Baudrillard, *Simulations* (New York: Semiotext(e), 1983), 26. Umberto Eco's most famous attack on Disney can be found in his book *Travels in Hyperreality* (San Diego: Harcourt Brace Jovanovich, 1984).

74. Edward Soja, *Postmodern Geographies* (London: Verso, 1989); Michael Sorkin, ed., *Variations on a Theme Park* (New York: The Noonday Press, 1992); and Sharon Zukin, *Landscapes of Power: From Detroit to Disneyworld* (Berkeley: University of California Press, 1991).

75. Sorkin, *Variations on a Theme Park,* 231.

76. Soja, *Postmodern Geographies,* 246–247.

77. Zukin, *Landscapes of Power,* 231.

78. Richard E. Foglesong, *Married to the Mouse;* Sharon Zukin, *The Cultures of Cities* (Cambridge, Mass.: Blackwell, 1995) (see especially pp. 65–69); Ross, *Celebration Chronicles.*

79. Sassen and Roost, "The City," 147. Shenk further notes that before it was bought out by Viacom, Blockbuster Entertainment had won the authority to collect taxes and condemn land on 2,500 acres in southern Florida ("Hidden Kingdom," 7).

80. Judd and Fainstein, *Tourist City*, 6–7.

81. Hannigan, *Fantasy City*, 1.

82. Robert Beauregard, "Representing Urban Decline: Postwar Cities as Narrative Objects," *Urban Affairs Quarterly* 29, no. 2 (1993): 187–202.

83. Though Disney's Celebration—as residential space—remains outside the boundaries of my essay, it is useful to point out that the apparent acquiescence of Celebration residents to Disney Planning Storyboard strictures likewise works only when the nature of the regulations falls within an agreed-upon urban narrative. The extended struggle over the Celebration School, for example, provides an excellent example of how the Disney Planning Storyboard will completely break down as soon as an implicit boundary is overstepped—in this case, when parents were informed they could not control their children's education. See Andrew Ross's *Celebration Chronicles* for full details.

84. Sagalyn, *Times Square Roulette*.

85. Kotin and Peiser, "Public-Private," 1984; Sagalyn, "Negotiating for Public Benefits," 1962.

86. Looking only at resistance to "big box" developments such as Wal-Mart, the Web site www.sprawl-busters.com identifies 195 communities that have successfully fought off developers as of January 2004. See also the Web site http://www.newrules.org for updated lists of ongoing community struggles.

87. "The Stinger Report #2," http://www.casbox.com/Stinger/Sting2.html.

88. Susan Warner, "2001 Opening Set at DisneyQuest," *Philadelphia Inquirer*, October 7, 1999, http://gop2000.philly.com/news/99/Oct/disney100799.asp.

89. "Disney's Third Park Advances," *Los Angeles Daily News*, July 12, 2001, http://dailynews.com/news/articles/0701/12/new11.asp. Company promotional quote from its Web site http://www.thirdthemepark.com.

90. "Hong Kong Disneyland: An Asset for the Future," Hong Kong Commissioner for Tourism Official Website, http://www.info.gov.hk/disneyland/indexe.htm.

91. Zukin, *Cultures of Cities*, 288.

10

Synergy City: How Times Square and Celebration Are Integrated into Disney's Marketing Cycle

Frank Roost

The Walt Disney Company is a key player in two of the most important developments in urban planning currently under way in the United States. On the one hand, Disney is building the town of Celebration in Florida, a residential community that is designed to be extended step by step and will eventually house twenty thousand residents. With this project, the company has become a major force in the promotion of neotraditional communities—a relatively new kind of residential development that is likely to become one of the most profitable businesses in the American real estate industry over the next few decades. On the other hand, Disney has become the driving force in New York City's Times Square redevelopment, one of the country's most comprehensive inner-city planning projects and the best-known example of entertainment-driven urban redevelopment.

With these investments, the Walt Disney Company has demonstrated once more its capacity to adapt public space for private consumer uses and its understanding of the values of U.S. middle-class suburbanites, deriving from its theme park experience. Over the past two decades, a Disney-style simulation of urbanity was a key element in the transformation of many American cities for the requirements of financial-service-industry firms and employees,[1] as historicizing tourist attractions,[2] and as sanitized consumer areas of shopping mall-like uniformity.[3]

The most important consequences of this kind of urban planning are the related economic and social changes. Entertainment-industry-dominated projects represent not only a significant transformation of those cities' economic basis,[4] but also a substantial change in their social structure, because they lead to a homogenization of the cities' culture and are often coupled with the exclusion of nonconforming uses and persons.[5]

However, the introduction of a theme-park-like atmosphere and a homogenization of culture is just one side of the Walt Disney Company's growing influence on American cities. Another remarkable aspect of Disney's urban planning projects is their integration into the company's multimedia marketing strategies in a way that has hitherto been known only in theme parks. Disney's urban entertainment facilities primarily attract customers who have consumed other company products, are designed to foster brand loyalty in the future, and represent a new part of an ever-expanding cycle of entertainment consumption that is systematically planned and managed by the firm's marketing specialists.

In this chapter, I describe why these urban planning projects' striking popularity is not just the coincidental success of an ambitious media firm trying to expand its business but in large part the result of Disney's extensive and systematic use of in-house cross-promotion or synergy—a key marketing strategy that had previously been employed mostly for the promotion of movies, TV shows, toys, or theme parks and is now being utilized in the urban planning realm.

The Concept of Synergy

Like all major media corporations, the Walt Disney Company is today involved in fields as diverse as movie, television, music, and print media production; it owns TV and radio networks and stations; it operates theme parks and manages sports teams; and it has expanded into new businesses such as Internet services and computer games. This way, the company can use one media product to promote another, for instance by introducing a new song as part of a movie sound track, by promoting the broadcasting of a sports event with articles in a magazine, or by selling computer games featuring popular cartoon characters. In most cases such promotional activities are supposed to work in both directions, for example, when a successful movie is followed by a spin-off television series and then in turn this TV program is used to advertise another movie produced for the same target group. With this kind of mutual advertising, media firms like Disney are trying to generate a never-ending cycle of consumption.

Given the broad range of Disney's activities, there is a huge potential for the use of such marketing methods, which are known in the industry as in-house cross-promotion, which is called synergy within the Walt Disney Company.6 For decades, the concept of synergy has been a key to Disney's economic success, it has been employed even more intensively since Michael Eisner became CEO, and it is used more thoroughly and comprehensively than in any other media company. The ongoing diversification of the company is mainly a consequence of this strategy. Disney's major investments during the 1990s, such as the acquisitions of the ABC network or the Internet content provider Starwave, are largely a result of management's aspirations to foster the company's ability for synergistic marketing.

In addition to pioneering synergy, branding, and merchandising beginning in the 1930s, Walt Disney also developed the idea of synergy between media consumption and theme park visits in the 1950s. The producer of animated films used the popularity of his famous cartoon characters for a weekly show on ABC that served as an advertisement for his theme park. In turn, visiting Disneyland helped secure customers' brand loyalty to the Disney trademark for the future.7 This strategy of cross-promotion among different entertainment products that included consumers' trips to a specific site of consumption was developed further over the decades and has become a basis for the Walt Disney Company's rapid growth. In recent years, urban entertainment destinations (such as themed restaurants, merchandising stores, and musical theaters) have been included in this synergistic marketing concept, too. This so-called location-based entertainment sector has become an integral part of the Disney marketing scheme, since it represents another way to exploit the value of the media company's brand identities.8

Synergy at Work

Considering the broad range of the Walt Disney Company's activities, it is understandable that the firm is regarded as "uniquely positioned to fulfill virtually any marketing option, on any scale, almost anywhere in the world."9 Indeed Disney offers an immense potential for both cross-promotional campaigns in cooperation with other companies and in-house cross-promotion marketing strategies—and the firm's management knows how to use this potential intensively. Cross-promotion—marketing activities carried out in cooperation by two different companies using the popularity of their brand names to promote one another's—is today a major profit source for Disney. The entertainment giant has a number of long-term agreements with so-called marketing partners, which cooperate with Disney for cross-promotional campaigns on a regular basis. For example, Kodak is paying Disney for being chosen as the "official film brand" of Disney's theme parks. The cooperation is advantageous for both partners, since photos taken in Disney theme parks account for 5 percent of all Kodak processing in the United States.[10] A three-part deal among Disney, McDonald's, and Coca-Cola works in a similar way. Considering that such alliances now account for 18 percent of the revenues of America's biggest companies, and that the three brands are all among the best known in the world, this arrangement is a marketing instrument of major influence.[11] Coca-Cola and Disney have had their marketing alliance in place since 1985. While Disney made the beverage company the sole provider of soft drinks in its theme parks, Coca-Cola has helped the media firm to get a stronger foothold in overseas markets, where the soda giant already had more marketing experience. The formal ten-year alliance of McDonald's and Disney, in effect since 1997, is even more comprehensive. An important part of the agreement is the promotional tie-ins with Disney movies, in which the fast-food chain gives away toys that feature Disney cartoon characters to their youngest customers whenever Disney releases a new animated movie. The prospect of receiving Disney toys helps to attract more families to the McDonald's restaurants—and in turn the children who have received the toys are likely to go and see the new Disney movie.

Another common form of cross-promotion is product placement—advertising through a product's appearance in a movie or TV show. Putting these half-concealed commercials into its movies is a regular part of Disney's business, as it is for all major media companies. Already in the 1980s and early 1990s, film studios routinely received up to $250,000 for introducing brand products into a film.[12] In recent years, cross-promotional deals of this kind have become even more profitable. In 1998, Disney's subsidiary Miramax Films introduced the movie *The Faculty* in cooperation with the Tommy Hilfiger Jeans Corp. The latter spent $10 million for a campaign promoting the movie in exchange for an agreement that the film's stars would appear in the campaign and the movie in Hilfiger clothes, thereby "blurring the line between advertising and the content of films."[13]

This kind of product placement has already become such an important source of profit for movie producers that in the United States the two largest media companies, Disney and Time Warner, have forced movie theaters to abandon traditional premovie advertisements because these would dilute the attractiveness of the "hidden" commercials in movies.[14] But there are also cases in which Disney has been the paying partner in cross-promotional deals.

For example, in the early 1990s Disney paid U.S. TV networks for airing *Movie News*. Designed to look like a program, in fact this was an infomercial for movies produced by some of Disney's subsidiaries. The consequence of such marketing strategies is a deliberate blurring of the distinction between program and advertisement, leaving the audience unsure whether they are viewing news and entertainment or a kind of commercial.[15]

This problem of a fading difference between programming and advertising is becoming even more widespread since Disney has bought several TV and radio stations, giving the firm control of conception, production, distribution, and advertisement of multiple media products. The centralization of power offers the media giant endless opportunities for including product placement and commercials for its own commodities in the programs without having to pay any extra charges.[16] Aware of this potential, the firm's management is determined to implement in-house cross-promotion and has taken several measures to institutionalize this marketing synergy at the core of the company's business. In recent years, CEO Michael Eisner has founded a special synergy department at corporate headquarters that works exclusively on concepts for in-house cross-promotion, has introduced weekly meetings of the company's top management aimed at elaborating such companywide projects, and has created the position of senior vice president of corporate synergy for the top executive who continuously checks the effectiveness of these efforts.[17] High-ranking Disney managers even attend weeklong meetings on every aspect of the company, which Eisner calls "synergy boot camps."[18] As a Disney spokesperson puts it: "It's a unique attribute of the Disney company, the ability to create synergy between divisions . . . and we do it aggressively . . . We actually have people in every division that are responsible for the synergy relationships of the company and every division has that."[19]

A case that illustrates the performance of Disney's synergy specialists is the promotional campaign based on the popularity of actor Tim Allen, which *Time* magazine considered in 1994 as the year's "most brilliant example of multimedia Hollywood marketing."[20] Allen rapidly became a star after Disney's management chose him to be the main character of ABC's situation comedy *Home Improvement,* about the everyday life of a suburban family. The show became one of the most successful TV series of the 1990s in the United States and brought in about $400 million for Disney. In consequence, Allen's popularity was used to promote other Disney subsidiaries, too. Soon after the TV show had become a big success, the Disney-owned publisher Hyperion released a comic-ironic autobiography of Allen—which became a best seller immediately. In the same year, Disney also produced a movie starring Allen, titled *The Santa Clause.* The movie relied on Allen's popularity with suburban families and, in an effort to ensure that parents and children could go and see it together, was brought onto the market at Thanksgiving. As expected, the movie was also a success and became 1994's Thanksgiving box office hit, turning Allen into the year's "number one" in all major media: star of the most popular TV show, author of a best-selling book, and star of the season's most successful movie.[21]

This is just one of many cases of Disney synergy at work, and the company's cross-promotional effort becomes even clearer if the extremely popular theme parks are taken into account. One example is the way Disney uses its media to advertise its theme parks and, reciprocally, uses theme park attractions to advertise new movies—even before they are released. In 1998, Disney supported the opening of its new Animal Kingdom theme park at Walt Disney World in Orlando with a massive campaign on its own ABC television network, watched by twenty million viewers at peak times. In turn, the first visitors to the new theme park were then subjected to a promotional event for a new Disney movie. For this purpose, a short film named *It's Tough to Be a Bug* was shown to people who visited Animal Kingdom, intensively advertising the characters of Disney's new animated feature, *A Bug's Life,* to four million people prior to the movie's premiere.[22] In other cases, even program plots have been changed to promote Disney's theme parks: "After its merger with ABC in 1995, Disney began more fully to explore the synergistic potential of television. A number of ABC programs, such as *Roseanne,* began to integrate family trips to Disney World into their plots."[23]

As the examples indicate, the Walt Disney Company is extraordinarily successful in putting in-house cross-promotion into practice, because, in the words of a media industry consultant, "Synergy is not a theoretical credo at Disney; it is the company's distinguishing *modus operandi.*"[24] The Walt Disney Company now uses the same multimedia marketing scheme for its expansion into the urban planning business. For that purpose, the popularity of Tim Allen and other media stars or cartoon characters is employed once more. Disney uses movies and TV shows featuring these celebrities to present half-concealed advertisements for its planning projects in Times Square and Celebration to millions of viewers and potential customers.

Times Square: Simulating Urban Diversity

An Icon of Urban Culture

For more than a century the area around Times Square, located at Broadway and Forty-second Street, has been New York's most important entertainment district. Theaters, bars, and restaurants are clustered here, but throughout the twentieth century, the district was also a hub of prostitution, and during the era of Prohibition, Times Square was well known for a large number of "speakeasies.[25] Nevertheless, the popularity of the district's legitimate businesses grew over the decades, especially after numerous large movie theaters opened in the 1920s. But the district's golden age ended in the postwar era, when the introduction of television and the suburbanization of New York City's middle class brought dramatic changes. With their traditional customers staying at home, the live performances in the old theaters were replaced with movies, many of which were pornographic. The area became known for a large number of prostitutes and drug dealers, and as New York's population of homeless grew, many of them stayed in the district. With this concentration of marginalized groups, Forty-second Street, traditionally an icon of urban culture, also became a symbol of the economic decline and social problems of American cities in the 1970s.

In an attempt to change this specific character of Times Square and to transform the district into a prime office location, New York City's administration and New York State's Urban Development Corporation (UDC) began to prepare a large-scale redevelopment project in 1981. Developers were found who were willing to build four skyscrapers on Forty-second Street, designed by the architects Philip Johnson and John Burgee. But as the planning review process took its course, inhabitants and owners of the sites filed lawsuits that delayed the project's implementation. After their objections were eventually overruled, condemnation of the sites began, and by the end of 1992 more than two hundred small businesses had been closed. But by then New York City's real estate market had collapsed, so that the UDC had to allow the developers to postpone construction of the office towers until market conditions improved. As a result, four blocks in the heart of Manhattan stood empty for years, prepared for redevelopment.

Disney Takes Over Broadway

Trying to find ideas for an intermediate use of the vacant buildings, the UDC in 1993 commissioned architect Robert A. M. Stern, who had already designed several hotels and office buildings for the Walt Disney Company, has been a member of the firm's board of directors since 1992, and is known as a close friend of Disney CEO Michael Eisner. Stern devised a new plan, named "42nd Street Now!" consisting of three major elements: restoration of the historic theaters on Forty-second Street, construction of a hotel and entertainment complex on Eighth Avenue, and renovation of the empty buildings around Times Square for intermediate use of their ground floors to be financed by the developers. Stern suggested renting those shops to tourism-oriented businesses—such as restaurants, bars, "music/video stores, . . . tourist super stores, . . . typically New York or American hard-goods and clothing stores, . . . [and] memorabilia stores."[26]

At the same time that Stern was publishing his plans for Times Square, the Walt Disney Company was preparing its first Broadway musical, *Beauty and the Beast*. In 1993 a tryout of the musical took place in Houston, Texas, and since 1994 it has been shown permanently at a theater near Times Square. Considering the musical's success on Broadway and Robert Stern's close ties to the entertainment corporation, it is not surprising that the Walt Disney Company turned out to be the key provider of entertainment in the projects Stern had suggested. In 1996, a huge Disney Store opened on the site where the architect had proposed to build video stores, tourist superstores, typically American hard-goods stores, and memorabilia stores. In the same year the company also began the renovation of the historic New Amsterdam Theatre, where the musical *The Lion King* has been performed continually since 1997. Like *Beauty and the Beast,* this play is a stage version of a Disney animated feature with the same name, and therefore can expect recognition by millions of potential customers who have already seen the cartoon version.[27]

The planning process of the third key project on Forty-second Street—the construction of a hotel and entertainment center—was also affected by Disney. During the UDC's competition for this site, the media firm cooperated with the developer Tishman Speyer by allowing Tishman Speyer to designate Disney and its subsidiary ESPN as the project's entertainment anchors. This kind of assistance turned out to be the decisive factor, since the team of Disney Development Company, Tishman Speyer, and the Miami-based architectural firm Arquitectonica won the competition because the jury thought that their concept was economically the most viable.[28] Ironically, the cooperation didn't last very long. Disney withdrew, and Tishman Speyer finished the project on its own. But as an alternative, two Disney subsidiaries realized their own projects on Times Square in 1997: ESPN opened a sports-themed restaurant on Forty-second Street, while ABC started construction of a Times Square studio for its TV show *Good Morning America* just a few blocks away.

With the Walt Disney Company as a major investor, the UDC was able to find other companies willing to build more entertainment facilities on Forty-second Street. Therefore Disney's investments can be seen as the defining moment for Forty-second Street redevelopment or, as Mayor Rudolph Giuliani referred to it,"the turning point in the revival of Times Square."[29] Thus, Disney has become the driving force in one of the most important urban redevelopment projects in the United States of the 1990s, and can present itself as an important definer of urban culture. Trying to popularize this new "urban" corporate image and to advertise new products at the same time, Disney also uses its entertainment facilities in Manhattan for promotional events. A first experiment had already been successful in 1995, when Disney premiered its animated feature *Pocahontas* with an open-air event in Central Park—a promotional campaign that supported not only the movie's but also Disney's overall popularity in New York.30 Since Disney built the entertainment facilities on Forty-second Street, the company had used Manhattan's urban space even more intensively for the promotion of its products. In June 1997, Disney celebrated the release of its animated feature *Hercules* with a series of events that took a whole weekend:

> The *Hercules* World Premiere Weekend in New York included a wide range of events scattered around the city, which were promoted widely and covered extensively by the media. During the entire weekend, "The Hercules Forum of Fun at Chelsea Piers" (sponsored by Chevrolet) featured live performances, interactive games, and animation demonstrations. . . . On Saturday, jugglers, dancers, and other entertainers were featured outside the New Amsterdam Theater (owned by Disney), where the "Heroes from Around the World" ceremony was held. The event featured Disney's chief honcho, Michael Eisner, plus New York Mayor Rudolph W. Giuliani, Robin Roberts of ABC sports and ESPN, and a group of "world-class athletes known for their Herculean efforts." The world premiere of the film was followed by "The Hercules Electrical Parade," a 1⅞ mile extravaganza which started on 42nd Street and continued up Fifth Avenue to 66th Street. . . . The festivities continued on Sunday with a "Hercules Breakfast with the Champions"—a news conference hosted by Robin Roberts and held at New York's Essex House Hotel, honoring five U.S. Olympic gold medal Decathlon winners. . . , who received hero proclamation certificates from the City of New York. . . . The finale was the kick-off for "The Hercules Summer Spectacular" at the New Amsterdam Theater—a 12-day exclusive New York engagement of the film before its release, including a live stage show featuring a full orchestra and a cast of Disney characters. The Manhattan premiere party and parade were covered live on E! and also received extensive coverage by other media outlets.31

But it is not only the sheer size of Disney's activities in New York that adds a new dimension to the use of urban public space for promotional purposes. Probably the most inventive element of this campaign is the company's employment of organizational know-how and design elements deriving from similar festivities in Disney theme parks. The nighttime parade through Midtown Manhattan was to some extent similar to Disneyland's "Main Street Electrical Parade" and featured floats that had previously been used only for parades inside Disneyland and Disney World.[32] Disney was even able to convince the city to shut off hundreds of streetlights along the parade's route. In addition, the company's management asked about five thousand businesses along Forty-second Street and Fifth Avenue to turn off their lights during the night of the parade so that the event would look more impressive.[33] This way, the media company was able to claim New York City's center as a location for the promotion of one of its movies—and Manhattan's public space was integrated into Disney's marketing strategy using elements from its theme parks.

Cultural Homogenization

Before officially announcing its investment on Forty-second Street, Disney bargained hard and secured a $26 million low-interest loan from state funds for the renovation of the New Amsterdam Theatre—a perk that other Broadway theater owners have historically been denied. In effect, the company had to invest only $8 million of its own money.[34] In addition to those financial concessions, Disney demanded the social transformation of Times Square. With the condemnation and relocation of small businesses along Forty-second Street, the city's administration had already started to change the area's social structure. But for Times Square's establishment as a family-friendly entertainment destination, the exclusion of nonconforming uses had to be intensified. During the negotiations between Disney and the city's administration, Michael Eisner and Mayor Rudolph Giuliani got together at Times Square. In the meeting, Eisner expressed his reservations about bringing Disney's family-style entertainment facilities to an area known for its high concentration of adult entertainment. Those doubts were wiped out by the mayor, who promised Eisner more than once that by the time the theater opened, the sex shops would be gone.[35]

Them Mayor proposed new adult entertainment regulations, discussed intensively in previous years. Trying to prohibit adult entertainment was impossible because of constitutional questions. Also, banishing those facilities only from Manhattan didn't seem to be an option, since politicians from the outer boroughs feared that adult entertainment could then be relocated into their districts. As a compromise, the Department of City Planning developed a set of regulations to forbid the *concentration* of adult entertainment. In this way it was possible to reduce the number of sex-related businesses in the Times Square area—as the only district with an extreme concentration of adult entertainment—and to prevent at the same time new concentrations in other parts of the city. The new regulations made sure that those businesses would be barred from operating within five hundred feet of residential zones, churches, schools, or one another.[36] As a consequence, the number of sex-related businesses in the Times Square district was reduced dramatically. Only 3 of the more than 114 adult entertainment facilities existing in the area before redevelopment were allowed to stay.[37]

In an effort to stop those measures, some of the sex shop owners instituted court action, delaying the implementation of the new adult entertainment regulations for a while. But in July 1997 the case was finally settled when the appellate division of the New York State Supreme Court ruled that choosing a location for their businesses was not protected by the constitutional right of free speech, as the shop owners had claimed.[38] Thus, as Giuliani had promised, most sex shops around Times Square were facing relocation when Disney finished the renovation of the New Amsterdam Theatre and opened *The Lion King* on Forty-second Street. The Times Square area, which had already been the city's hub for sex-related businesses even before the first theater in the district was opened, and where all kinds of amusement had coexisted with the big business of live musical shows, radio programming, and movie production for more than a century,[39] was turned into a district reserved for "legitimate" entertainment. A district that had always been known for typical urban inconsistencies and heterogeneities finally became a homogeneous family-friendly amusement zone for suburban tourists.

This process of social transformation has been backed and enhanced by the activities of the Times Square Business Improvement District (BID), a non-profit organization financed by mandatory assessments on all local property owners. The Times Square BID supports the redevelopment through activities such as hiring guards to provide additional security in the area and paying workers to preserve the area's cleanliness by removing graffiti or sweeping sidewalks.[40] The Times Square BID encompasses not only the actual entertainment district but also the western part of Midtown Manhattan's office cluster. Financed for the most part by large corporations, retailers, and hotels, the BID's first and foremost goal is to make the district more attractive for office clerks, shoppers, and tourists. Individuals who do not belong to one of these groups will hardly benefit from the BID's activities. Instead, they probably will be controlled more intensively by the BID's security forces patrolling day and night. Guards are instructed to focus their attention on minor offenses such as shoplifting, gambling, unauthorized theater ticket vending, and selling counterfeit T-shirts. If they witness one of these offenses, they are advised to inform the police and hold the suspect until the officers arrive.[41]

After being taken into custody, the suspect has to cope with another control measure developed by Times Square's property owners. Unlike suspects arrested in other parts of Manhattan, those seized in the entertainment district are brought straight to the Midtown Community Court—a law court with the exclusive task of dealing with minor offenses committed in the Times Square area. It has been established in public-private partnership through a cooperation of the city and the BID, and is financed with the support of the local business community. In most cases the penalties imposed on the offenders by the Midtown Community Court are so-called community services, carried out in cooperation with the Times Square BID. In practice, this means the delinquent must join the BID's cleaning crew and has to sweep sidewalks for several days.[42] With this measure, the local business and property owners were able to include even the legal system in their efforts to expel marginalized groups from the entertainment district.

The Times Square BID claims that the homeless can benefit from its activities, too, since they have the opportunity to work and earn money. But civil rights groups have accused New York's BIDs of mistreating the homeless by forcing them into underpaid labor.[43] Considering the way BIDs are financed and managed, their aim is, of course, to satisfy the local business community. Hence, their activities result inevitably in a reorganization of public space that reflects the anticipated requirements of consumers and tries to drive out nonconforming persons. This is evident in the redevelopment of Times Square, where the Walt Disney Company's demands during the negotiations, the UDC's planning activities, the city's regulations, and the BID's activities have all contributed to the exclusion of marginalized groups—in order to create a homogeneous atmosphere that satisfies consuming tourists.

To criticize this cultural homogenization, of course, is not to glorify every aspect of Times Square's character before redevelopment. Because of frequent reports of prostitution, drug trafficking, and related street crime, many visitors felt unpleasant, while others accepted such problems as common for red-light districts and understood Times Square's character as an expression of urban diversity. In any case, the district has experienced a dramatic social transformation, and this was a demand of the investing corporations, above all the Walt Disney Company. Considering that Disney's decision to renovate the New Amsterdam Theatre was the linchpin for Times Square redevelopment, and given that Eisner was expecting that all adult entertainment would be closed on Forty-second Street, it is obvious that the exclusion of nonconforming persons and uses from the district and the related cultural homogenization wasn't just a side effect of Disney's involvement but rather its precondition.

Reinterpretation of the Entertainment District

Despite disagreements about this transformation of Forty-second Street into a publicly and privately controlled, family-friendly setting, Disney tried to present its version of Times Square as the appropriate solution. For this purpose, the company used a strategy M. Christine Boyer described as the tourist industry's attempt "to justify a particular aspect of the present by emphasizing a related aspect of the past."[44] The key element of this effort was the explicit reference to the district's history in Robert A. M. Stern's "42nd Street Now!" plan. In an attempt to justify the replacement of the sex-related uses with musical theaters and other new entertainment facilities, Stern's report stressed Times Square's historical role as a symbol for the spirit of "the individual entrepreneur," epitomized by the traditional Broadway producer.[45] Therefore his guidelines asked for a design reminiscent of Times Square's heyday in the 1920s and required a lively streetscape, colorful architecture, and a large number of illuminated signs. The irony is that despite the suggestion of the design guidelines, the redevelopment has brought problems to traditional individual Broadway producers because the concentration of large media corporations in the area has caused production and marketing costs to rise sharply, making it difficult for smaller producers to find individual investors prepared to take the great financial risks involved in producing musicals.[46]

This obscuring of one aspect of the area's past while emphasizing another was also the underlying concept in other parts of Stern's plan. While Times Square's effervescent look throughout the century was described in detail and recognized as a feature to be preserved for the future, the area's traditional character as a red-light district was hardly mentioned. Consequently, Stern's recommendations consisted for the most part of design guidelines, including a detailed description of the required illuminated signs as architectural elements intended to reflect the area's traditional appearance. Proclaiming these design codes, the redevelopment, which is aimed at changing the very special character of the area, at the same time tries to preserve the unique look of the district.

On the whole, Stern's report reduced Times Square to a symbol of the American entertainment industry's tradition, while the area's historical function as a place of social inconsistencies and a niche for marginalized persons was almost ignored. In a few sentences, the study was getting nearer the truth, mentioning Times Square's diverse social structure in the 1920s. In an effort to recall that structure, the study recommended once more a large number of neon signs on all new buildings because these design elements were perceived as "visually compelling and essentially democratic, they draw people regardless of their economic or social background."[47] But this open-mindedness was meant only for the activities of large media corporations, because just a few months later the city's *Adult Entertainment Study* suggested banning the large signs used by sex-related businesses, arguing that they would offend most passersby.[48] In opposition to what the design report suggests, Times Square's exceptional appearance is no longer the expression of an unconventional mix of uses and an extremely diverse social structure. Instead, it is a marketing and design gimmick introduced by the city's and Disney's planners in order to provide visitors with a vague feeling of authentic urban diversity and excitement while they visit an urban space that has actually been sanitized for suburban tourist families.

This use of history, embedded in the design of a project, is also a characteristic element of the company's theme parks, since "Disney's fantasy both restored and invented collective memory."[49] Disneyland's imaginative historical re-creations, such as those in Adventureland, Fantasyland, or Frontierland, represent key elements of America's past by transforming them into an idealized and easily recognizable image. In a similar way, Times Square is now brought into a simplified form and adjusted for visual consumption by emphasizing its traditional appearance. The key element of this process is the highly selective appropriation of history, as it is reflected in a description of the company's strategy by one of the theme park designers: "What we create is a 'Disney realism,' sort of Utopian in nature, where we carefully program out all the negative, unwanted elements and program in the positive elements."[50] And just as all unwanted elements are removed from the scenery in Disneyland, nonconforming businesses and persons are now excluded from Times Square.

From early on, Disneyland's popularity has been based for the most part on design elements that give visitors the feeling of experiencing a kind of adventure combined with a rigid organization that guarantees cleanliness and promises safety.[51] In a similar way, stimulation and protection are simultaneously provided at Forty-second Street, as design elements suggesting urban diversity (like the neon lights and the lively streetscape) are combined with measures that demonstrate the district's orderliness (like private security guards and cleaning staff). This way, Disney is able to simulate urban diversity for suburban tourists and to organize this space like a privately controlled shopping mall environment. With its entertainment facilities at Times Square, Disney starts to offer this "riskless risk,"[52] hitherto found only in theme parks, now also in cities—enabling the media firm to tap into the growing market of suburbanites' tourism to urban destinations.

Considering that Times Square epitomizes the glorious past of America's cities as well as their current problems, Disney's investment on Forty-second Street has the ability to support the company's future business, too. The area's redevelopment has become one of the most prominent examples of entertainment-driven urban planning, and this helps the entertainment giant to present its subsidiary Disney Development Corporation (DDC) as a company that is well prepared to redevelop America's declining inner cities in an economically successful way. And finally, Disney's appropriation of the famous entertainment district can help to foster the overall popularity of the company's brand. The Walt Disney Company, which has always celebrated its founder's economic success as an outstanding example of the American dream, can present itself more than ever as an essential part of American culture.

Celebration: Reinventing the American Small Town

Urban Planning Experiments in Florida

Disney's activities in the field of urban planning aren't limited to urban entertainment destinations. While investing in New York, the company is also building a residential community named Celebration, adjacent to the huge Walt Disney World resort complex near Orlando. Construction began in 1995, first residents moved in by the end of 1996, and by 2002 Celebration had six thousand of a projected twenty thousand residents.

The idea of building a town of this size completely planned, organized, and controlled by the Walt Disney Company is much older. In the 1960s Walt Disney wanted to build a community for twenty thousand people on a part of the more than twenty-eight thousand acres in central Florida he had acquired for his second theme park. The model city with the programmatic name Experimental Prototype Community of Tomorrow—EPCOT—was supposed to serve as an example of modernist urban planning and a showcase for technological progress. Disney envisioned a community with an air-conditioned city center lying under a fifty-acre glass roof, connected with surrounding residential areas by means of a monorail system.[53] In addition to this unusual design and transportation concept, Disney also had a political vision. He wanted his company to control all social, educational, and cultural institutions—and tried to secure this hegemony by limiting representative local government and citizens' participation in the planning process. Disney's desire to control every aspect of his city is also reflected in one of his descriptions of the planned city: "In EPCOT there will be no slum areas because we won't let them develop. There will be no landowners and therefore no voting control. People will rent houses instead of buying them, and at modest rentals. There will be no retirees. Everyone must be employed. One of our requirements is that the people who live in EPCOT must help to keep it alive."[54] Furthermore, Disney wanted to ban all pets from his city, and he even planned to enforce a strict dress code on residents, who would also have faced expulsion for drunkenness or unmarried cohabitation.[55] However, after Disney died in 1966, his successors were concerned about the legal responsibilities involved in such a comprehensive project. Eventually, they just built the Epcot theme park with surrounding resort colonies instead of a new town—and Disney's paternalistic dream remained unrealized.

Twenty years later, the economic success of Disney's theme parks had turned Orlando into one of the nation's fastest-growing metropolitan areas,[56] and with the increased demand for housing the idea to build a residential community on the vast Disney area in central Florida was revived. In 1984, Disney acquired Arvida, Florida's largest developer, which had already built many gated communities with near-identical houses surrounding a golf course. In the first stages of the planning process for its new town near Orlando, the Walt Disney Company considered letting its subsidiary Arvida build one of those standardized suburbs.[57] But Disney sold its subsidiary after a few years, and Arvida's plans weren't implemented.[58] Instead, a number of different architects were commissioned to find ideas for the development of the future town, among them Elisabeth Plater-Zyberk and Andres Duany, founding partners of the Miami-based firm Arquitectonica. The couple is well known for its proposals for so-called neotraditional communities. With this relatively new kind of residential development, architects try to reproduce the atmosphere of historic small towns, using a traditional architecture and an urban design pattern that reflects the spatial structure of a slowly grown historic town. Disney CEO Michael Eisner was quite impressed by those proposals and suggested a neotraditional master plan for the new town.[59] As architect for the future city, Eisner chose his friend Robert A. M. Stern.

Stern's plan tried to avoid the typical car-oriented pattern of lining up suburban single-family homes and introduced several urban design innovations that are supposed to re-create some of the qualities of historic cities: First of all, Celebration has a small, relatively dense city center consisting of multistory buildings with commercial uses in the ground floors and apartments in the upper levels. The residential areas, too, look more diverse than in most other new residential communities and offer homes in different sizes, such as town houses, cottages, and estate homes. And finally, with several parks, playgrounds, and thoroughly designed squares as well as a grid of narrow streets instead of the usual cul-de-sac pattern, the town is also exceptionally pedestrian-friendly.

Disney's Influence on New Urbanism

With these urban design features, Celebration is the largest development built in accordance with the ideas of so-called New Urbanism. Although there is no official cooperation between the Walt Disney Company and the Congress for the New Urbanism (CNU)—the lobbying group in which its supporters are organized—Celebration is well known among architects and urban planners as one of the most prominent examples of a New Urbanist community. CNU claims that constructing neotraditional communities with an architecture reminiscent of historic cities is the only way to overcome the currently predominantly car-oriented pattern of suburban development. With a good public relations strategy, CNU members have been able to spread their ideas, and New Urbanism has become one of the most debated subjects among architects and urban planners in the United States.

The first New Urbanist project was the resort community Seaside on Florida's Gulf Coast. Built in the late 1980s, it is well known to a broad public from the 1998 movie *The Truman Show,* starring Jim Carrey. Renamed "Seahaven" in the movie, Seaside played a community where everything looks perfect but in fact is simulated. Designed by Duany and Plater-Zyberk, Seaside is supposed to re-create the atmosphere of a traditional seaside resort and consists mainly of white, Victorian-style houses built along three main streets and around a town square. Shortly after Seaside was built, and before the Walt Disney Company utilized the CNU's concepts for its own purposes, Sharon Zukin remarked that the artificial small-town harmony of this new residential community was based on design principles developed in Disney's theme parks, and modeled on the socially harmonious elaboration of Disneyland's Main Street, U.S.A.[60] When Andres Duany confirmed in an interview with the renowned *Harvard Design Magazine* that the expression "neotraditional," used by New Urbanists to describe their architecture, was adopted from Disney's marketing vocabulary, the influence of Disney's theme park experience on New Urbanism became even clearer. According to Duany, the word "neotraditional" was used for the first time in 1985, when Disney commissioned the Stanford Research Institute to study the baby boomer generation's consumption preferences. The marketing specialists used the term neotraditional to describe the kind of goods this target group would prefer: products that combined modern and traditional elements in a very efficient way, for example, a clock with a Victorian design but modern technology inside.[61]

This description also shows that neotraditional communities like Celebration are planned primarily for those Americans who have spent most of their lives in suburbia. Having grown up with postwar single-family homes, highways, and shopping centers, their experience with traditional urban environments is sometimes very limited. But while their perceptions of today's urban environments may be harmed by stereotypes about the cities' social and economic problems, their positive images of "historic" small-town places are likely to derive from experiences in Disney's theme parks. Few places have influenced the collective memory of America's middle class in the past decades to the extent that Disneyland did. At the moment when the majority of the middle class was leaving the cities for the suburbs, Disney started to offer Disneyland's Main Street, U.S.A. in 1955, an idealized image of the now historic urban era. In this sense, Main Street, U.S.A. has become over the years what its name suggested from the very beginning: a kind of collective American main street for suburbanites who spend their leisure time in shopping malls and whose perceptions about the social character and the physical appearance of traditional main streets derive primarily from TV shows and theme park visits.

Main Street, U.S.A. is, of course, only a cinematic version of small-town America that actually never had such a harmonic look.[62] But Disney's selective view of the city was projecting the desires of the middle class, and with Main Street, U.S.A. he turned these collective dreams into a visible and visitable tourist attraction.[63] The Walt Disney Company is well aware of this competence and tries to employ it, especially since New Urbanism's popularity has led to a reinvention of the main street and to a growing number of potential home buyers in neotraditional developments. Having produced with its mock-up Main Street, U.S.A. the country's most popular variation on the theme "Main Street," Disney now offers with Celebration yet another variation on this theme. Thus, the design of the media firm's new town is in many ways a copy of a copy. In Celebration, Disney's idealized theme park version of a small town, Main Street, U.S.A., was replicated once more to become the architectural setting for a "real" city where people actually live.

Designing Small-Town Harmony

Not only the overall urban design concept but also the details of the architecture are a part of Disney's efforts to re-create a harmonious old-town atmosphere.

Disney requires Celebration's inhabitants to follow strict design guidelines when they build their new homes. For this purpose a *Celebration Pattern Book* has been developed in which possible ground plans, facade elements, roof forms, windows, shutters, and combinations of colors are scrupulously described. Future residents must decide among six historical architectural types: Classical, Victorian, Coastal, Mediterranean, French, and Colonial Revival. Once they pick one of these six styles residents can select among different architectural components shown in the pattern book and combine these elements according to their taste.

The pattern book, of course, isn't an invention of the Walt Disney Company but a marketing instrument that has been used by the American building industry since the nineteenth century. However, in the past, pattern books were used mostly for the assembly of individual homes or a row of houses, rarely for the construction of a complete town. Yet Disney insists on the six styles, which go well together and which are all based on traditional southeastern architecture, in order to create a picturesque small-town atmosphere that combines both a certain variety and an overall harmony. In doing so Disney tries to simulate the typical look of authentic historic cities with their distinctive buildings that nonetheless make a good match. In this way, urban diversity, with all its complex and contradictory social implications, is replaced in Celebration with a diversity of architectural elements—bringing Disney one step closer to its objective of creating an easily marketable, socially homogeneous residential community that nevertheless is perceived by potential home buyers as a place with traditional small-town qualities.

The architecture of Celebration's public buildings serves this purpose, too. Analogous to Zukin's description of Disneyland's imaginative historical recreations as a "multidimensional collage of the American landscape,"[64] Celebration's public buildings could be described as a kind of multidimensional collage of the American small town, since they are arranged as a display of easily recognizable traditional small-town elements. A good example of this use of symbols is the mock-up historical water tower that Disney has built at Celebration's entrance. It doesn't have any technical function, but it serves as an advertisement that can be seen from a great distance and at the same time helps to symbolize the supposed historical small-town character of Celebration.

The importance of such symbols for Celebration's marketing concept is also reflected by the fact that Disney commissioned for the other public buildings prominent architects from all over the world who are known for their postmodern style. The local bank was designed by Robert Venturi; the preview center was built in accordance with a blueprint made by the late Charles Moore; Michael Graves planned the tiny post office with its oversized entrance rotunda; the movie theater was built by Cesar Pelli in a 1930s Art Deco style; and an office complex near the town was designed by Italian star-architect Aldo Rossi. Furthermore, a building called "Town Hall" was designed by the doyen of postmodern architecture, Philip Johnson, who gave the building a representative entrance area with dozens of columns, playing with images of the classicist architecture typical of buildings that house democratic institutions.

Corporate Management as Government

However, the name "Town Hall" for Johnson's building is confusing and misleading, since it implies that the building is the seat of a mayor or city council—but in Disney's town there is neither a mayor nor a city council. Celebration is unincorporated, and its services are provided by, and authority delegated to, Osceola County.[65] In addition, the Celebration Company, a fully owned Disney subsidiary, manages most everyday affairs. The only possibilities for Celebration's inhabitants to participate in the governance of their community on the local level are two community associations, but their authority is limited to the management of neighborhood amenities and common areas, they have no law enforcement powers, and their decisions can be overruled by Disney's veto.[66] A further restraint on the town's democratic self-organization is the rules of conduct imposed by Disney on all residents. The most important of these rules is that residents must stay at least nine months per year in Celebration. While this rule was drawn up to prevent Celebration from becoming a resort community empty for most of the year (as with Seaside), most other regulations are designed to avoid anything that has the potential to disturb Celebration's idyllic appearance. Therefore, it is forbidden to change the look of a building or front yard, glaze the porch, dry laundry in the yard, leave a broken-down car outside, or let a garden "spoil" the neighborhood's appearance.[67] Also the kinds and the maximum amounts of different kinds of plants in the front yard are regulated. Precise percentages are decreed for the mix of grass, hedges, shrubs, and trees.[68] The side of all window coverings visible from the street must be white or off-white, residents may hold only one garage sale per year, and they may post only one political sign, measuring no more than eighteen by twenty-four inches, in their yard for no more than forty-five days before an election.[69] Those who dare to ignore these regulations can expect a warning from Disney staff, nicknamed "porch police."[70]

A case that reflected the unpleasant consequences of the company's extensive control of Celebration was the dispute about the educational approach Disney had chosen for the town's school. In an effort to develop a school that would help to bring forth the students' creative potential and personal skills required in a postmodern information society, Disney's management decided to apply a very progressive educational philosophy. This included new methods such as learning groups with students of different ages instead of traditional classes, learning projects that incorporated several disciplines instead of a fixed time for each subject, and detailed assessments to measure a student's progress instead of grades. But the Walt Disney Company had underestimated how conservative its customers were, and those residents who had moved to Celebration because they expected Disney to guarantee a traditional system of values were disappointed. Nonetheless, the company wasn't willing to compromise, so that ironically those people who were most confident about Disney were the first to experience the consequences of the lack of democratic self-government in Celebration. A few families tried to organize resistance, but since they were anxious about the company's reaction, they decided to meet secretly at a place outside Celebration. When they finally decided to bring their demands before the public, Disney's management made clear that this nonconforming behavior would not be tolerated. As a result, some of the families decided to move out of town, but even then they could feel the company's power once more: Disney offered them help selling their houses, but only in return for a promise not to disclose to any third party their reasons for leaving.[70]

The City as a Branded Product

Although these conflicts indicate a disturbingly far-reaching corporate rule, Celebration's social and political organization is far from unique. In fact, some of the regulations that are enforced in Celebration aren't unusual for a residential development of this size.[72] In many recently built subdivisions all over America, developers and home owners implement complex legal arrangements to protect themselves from any uncertainty that might harm their property value.[73] Considering that these so-called common-interest developments are today America's fastest-growing form of housing development, it becomes clear that Celebration's social and political organization is not entirely Disney's creation but, to a large degree, a mixture of existing trends in the real estate industry adapted and transformed into a more authoritarian Disney-specific practice.

Nonetheless, Disney's efforts to limit democratic self-government in Celebration are still very remarkable given the high aspirations for the development of New Urbanist communities and, more important, the company's immense ambitions. With its launching of Celebration, Disney wanted nothing less than to build a "prototype for the millennium,"[74] and Disney's CEO Michael Eisner wants Celebration to become a town that "will set up a system of how to develop communities. I hope in fifty years they say 'Thank God for Celebration.'"[75] Hence, the most remarkable aspect of Celebration isn't the fact that is a common-interest development but rather the notion that despite being only a common-interest development, it is described and sold by Disney's management, architects, staff, and salespersons as a model town based on the traditional American ideals of community and neighborhood. This contradiction was described by Russ Rymer: "Considering that subdivisions generally are not self-ruled, the arrangements would not seem notable, except that other subdivisions don't claim descent from the American charter."[76] And indeed, average developers trying to protect the property value of their investment with a complex legal system that included design codes and rules of conduct would hardly call their project a prototype for the millennium. Moreover, they would neither dare to call the city manager's office "town hall" if there was no mayor or city council who resided in it nor commission one of the world's most famous architects to design it. But for the Walt Disney Company, the central democratic function of such a building is—in the words of a Disney manager—"an aesthetic."[77] In this way the company is trying nothing less than to replace deep-rooted ideals, such as a common responsibility for neighborhood and community concerns—inextricably linked with the concept of democratic self-government—with a merely symbolic sense of neighborhood and community. However, this rather vague sense of community, produced primarily by the exploitation of architectural symbols of small-town harmony and a corresponding sales promotion, seems to be one of the reasons for Celebration's popularity. Residents get the illusion that they can combine two incompatible elements: the cultural and aesthetic quality of an authentic city with the safety and homogeneity of a planned residential development.

Furthermore, and not really surprisingly, the Walt Disney Company used its famous brand name to increase the value of Celebration. The entertainment firm's unique image as a family-friendly and trustworthy company is, of course, a major advantage that helps to sell homes to customers expecting a pleasant environment for their children. Considering this image, Celebration's commercial success is understandable. Especially in the first phase, when demand exceeded supply three to one, many potential customers were interested in buying a home in Celebration simply because they were convinced that every Disney product would be just perfect.[78]

Altogether Disney's decision to expand into the residential development business turns out to be less adventurous than it might seem at a first glance, since the company had economic, political, and marketing-related reasons to build Celebration. The project was an economic success because it made profitable use of a remote part of the company's huge central Florida property that couldn't be used for tourist purposes as it was separated from the theme parks by large highways.[79] In addition, building Celebration served Disney in the political realm at a time when the company was negotiating intensively with Metro–Orlando area counties over growth management issues. The greater part of Disney's central Florida property and all of Disney's tourist attractions are located in Orange County, whereas the remote part of Disney's property where Celebration was built is located in Osceola County. Since Orange County was complaining about Disney-stimulated overdevelopment while Osceola politicians wanted more taxable development in their county, building Celebration strengthened Disney's bargaining position as it helped to appease Osceola County politicians and reminded Orange County that Disney could go elsewhere.[80] And finally, Celebration also opened up a new way to diversify the company's business because it made use of the Disney brand name's value in yet another part of the economy. After the corporation has internationalized its business, diversified into all kinds of media, and established a huge merchandising machinery that encompasses almost every imaginable product from computer games to underwear, it now goes one step further and offers its primary target group, the white suburban middle class, another product with the Disney brand: a complete town to live in. Considering that the Disney brand name puts a 15 to 30 percent surcharge on every house in Celebration (compared with similar real estate in other nearby developments), it becomes clear that this can be quite a profitable business.[81] "What is remarkable is Michael Eisner's clear statement: When Disney builds it costs fifteen percent more than is normally calculated for comparable buildings. Disney invests this fifteen percent into the design."[82] In this way the architectural and organizational expertise developed in the company's theme parks can now be exploited in the real estate industry as well, sold profitably once more—and possibly sold over and over again in many more neotraditional communities to be built in the next fifty years.

Drawing Customers

It is not only Disney's knowledge in the field of producing neotraditional design and neatly organized space with theme-park-like qualities that has turned Celebration and Times Square into an economic success for Disney. In addition, the company uses the full range of its multimedia power to advertise its projects—introducing methods into urban planning that have been known hitherto only in the marketing of media products and theme parks.

The Walt Disney Company had already begun to use its media-marketing experience and its brand image to enhance the success of its urban planning projects in 1984 when it bought Arvida, Florida's leading residential developer, for $200 million. Driven by a desire to combine the developer's knowledge with its own strength as one of Florida's largest private landowners, Disney's management hoped that Arvida would help to generate more profits from the vast territory surrounding the theme parks near Orlando. To complete this kind of synergy, Disney would in turn use its marketing machinery to help sell the projects of its new subsidiary. Armed with this strategy, Arvida began in 1985 to develop the largest project in its history, a $2 billion residential community called Weston located in suburban Broward County, twenty miles north of Miami. Before this, Arvida had hesitated to start this huge project, which was designed as a family-oriented community for sixty thousand inhabitants, including commercial uses, industrial areas, and a pedestrian-oriented main street.[83] But with the support of Disney, the project became a hit. Backed by its marketing and theme park experience, Disney organized preview shows (called "hometown fairs") featuring family games, shows, and Disney characters that were usually displayed only in the Magic Kingdom. Thanks to Mickey Mouse's popularity and the company's image, thousands of families attended the shows on several weekends in May 1985, and accordingly Weston became a success from the very beginning. In a description of the marketing strategy, Roger E. Hall, then president of the Disney Development Company, stated that with this kind of support it was "the Disney connection that helped sell Weston."[84]

At the same time Disney's CEO, Michael Eisner, started another undertaking that had the capacity to influence Arvida's performance. In spring 1985, he began negotiations with a small television production company, Witt, Thomas, and Harris, which had developed a concept for a new TV program called the *Golden Girls*. Witt, Thomas, and Harris were looking for a "deficit-financing" studio, and Eisner was willing to take this role. He made sure that Disney's subsidiary Touchstone would launch the show in the NBC network. To make the deal more appealing for the network, Disney paid every week $120,000 of the production costs that NBC wasn't compensating. Also, Eisner agreed to pay the producers and actors percentages, so that in the end Disney would make only a little money even if the show became a hit.[85] The reason for taking this risk seems to be that Eisner recognized the program's synergistic potential. *Golden Girls* was a show about four older women from different American states moving to Florida after their retirement and having a great time together in their new home near Miami. Since retiring senior citizens constituted one of the biggest and most affluent group of home buyers in Florida, the show had the potential to build Arvida's business. During 1985–1986 *Golden Girls* was the top-rated show in the United States, and with this success the idea of moving to the Sunshine State was brought closer to millions of older viewers throughout the country. For years, the show could function every week as a kind of continuous advertisement for a retirement in Florida, but an advertisement free of charge for the state's leading developer, Arvida. It seems likely that the entertainment giant's efforts were successful. When Disney sold Arvida in 1986, just two years after acquiring it, the media firm had already doubled the invested money and charged $400 million for its subsidiary.

In the 1990s, Disney has used methods of this kind to promote its newest theme parks and urban planning projects. One of these measures is to employ movies for the promotion of Disney entertainment facilities by inserting scenes that foster the viewer's desire to visit these locations. This technique has been used since 1994 in Europe in order to attract more customers to Disney's theme park near Paris. In the first few years, the park attracted fewer visitors than expected. But it has recently become much more successful, mainly because of changes in the marketing concept. Disney increased its efforts to attract those travelers who were already considering a trip to Paris. Given the large number of tourists visiting the French capital, the company tries to tap into this market and to convince potential customers to combine their stay in Paris with a visit to the theme park. In accordance with this new marketing concept, advertising campaigns have been revised, and even the name of the park was changed from EuroDisney to Disneyland Paris.[86] In order to support this new marketing strategy, Disney cooperated with the French company TF 1, which released the movie *Un indien dans la ville* (An Indian in the City) at the same time. It was seen by eight million people during that season in France alone, and attracted parents and children alike with a simple story: a boy is raised by his mother in a remote tropical village, gets to visit his father in the French capital, and is confronted with modern everyday life. More important for Disney, the filmmakers portrayed Paris as a wonderful possible destination for families. They included a key scene, in which one of the main characters is walking through the city, in order to show the company's name on a Disney Store among the city's major tourist attractions. This way, the idea of a trip to Paris could be connected to the brand name Disney in the minds of some viewers, helping to enlarge the number of potential customers for Disneyland Paris.

A few years later, the Walt Disney Company tried to use the same strategy for the marketing of its Times Square project. In 1997, Disney's subsidiary Touchstone Pictures produced an American version of the movie, this time set in New York and called *Jungle2Jungle*. With this film, Disney wanted to attract customers to its newly opened Times Square entertainment facilities in the same way the French version had been used to try to draw customers to Disneyland Paris. For this purpose, the movie had to pull in as many families as possible, and accordingly it was brought out around Thanksgiving so that whole families would go to see the film together. In addition, it combined the child-pleasing plot with the baby boomer generation's star Tim Allen so that fathers would also attend. What the assembled families saw was a movie that depicted New York City and its sights in a way the city's tourist board couldn't have improved on. Among the scenes depicting icons of Manhattan, one sequence had no relevance for the story but showed the "little Indian" walking along Times Square. If only a few percent of the millions of *Jungle2Jungle* viewers remembered this indirect advertisement, they were more likely to make a family trip to New York in the following months and to spend some time at the now family-friendly tourist destination Times Square. This way, the media firm could draw more visitors to the area and enlarge the number of potential customers for its newly opened Disney Store, ESPN restaurant, and musical theater on Forty-second Street.

Mutual Advertising

Using media products to draw visitors to Disney's entertainment centers in New York City is one way the company's in-house cross-promotion works. But synergy is supposed to function in both directions, and therefore Disney's tourist destinations in turn serve as sites for the promotion of other media products. Similar to the way the theme parks have been integrated in both directions into the marketing cycle for decades—being attractive for customers who have consumed other Disney products before and simultaneously securing visitors' brand loyalty for the future—nowadays also Disney's media are used to advertise its tourist destinations in Manhattan as well as vice versa.

The large Disney Store on Forty-second Street is a good example of the way the company's synergy specialists tried to use Times Square to promote new Disney products. For this purpose, large "Times Square–typical" billboards were attached to the building, displaying advertisements for products of different Disney subsidiaries. Those billboards were changed on a regular basis, with the intention that visitors to the district would be prepared for upcoming media events like a movie premiere or a new TV series.

In the case of the promotional campaign for products starring Tim Allen,

Disney tried to close the marketing cycle with an advertisement to those Tim Allen fans who actually went to Times Square after seeing *Jungle2Jungle*. In the weeks after the release of the movie, the company put up a huge sign promoting Allen's new book *I'm Not Really Here*.[87] By doing so, Disney was able to advertise this new product to visiting Tim Allen fans, and some of those who did not notice the message in New York probably brought it back home unawares. With an estimated 100 million pictures taken at Times Square per year, there is no other man made attraction in the United States where tourists make more photos.[88] Considering this, there is a good chance that some New York visitors get their idea to buy a new Disney product on an occasion when they don't expect it at all: while looking at their photo album with the pictures of their trip to Times Square.

In a similar way, Disney uses its new $75 million *Good Morning America* studio on Forty-fourth Street, where ABC has produced its popular live TV show since 1999. The show can now profit from the special appeal of Times Square and probably attracts more viewers than it used to in its old studio, but like the billboard-stacked Disney Store on Forty-second Street, it is also an example of reciprocal synergy. ABC and Disney officials consider the large investment "in no way related to any budget-tightening moves and . . . in any event *Good Morning America* does not have to take in additional millions in the coming years to justify Disney's investment."[89] Cost was not an issue for this project because, as a Disney manager put it, "It's part of the overall corporate strategy.[90] Because of this dominance of synergy, a much more important aspect for Disney's planners than the cost was to build the studio with a large window so that ABC's stars would sit in front of a background showing Times Square. For this purpose, they even decided to put the studio in the second floor, although it meant a hurdle for another element of the show, the interaction between selected tourists and the show's hosts.[91] But the way the studio was built, Disney is able to advertise the destination Times Square to viewers all over the country every morning. And if they actually come, they are subjected to another Disney promotion. The studio's facade has large electric signs forming colorful bands that get the passerby's attention even in the neon-lit Times Square. On those bands are shown flashy computer-animated advertisements for Disney's several TV channels—alternating between commercials for ABC, ESPN, Lifetime, or the Disney Channel. In addition, a 585-square-foot video screen displays ABC's program as well as short ads for other Disney products like books or movies—exposing thousands of tourists to the company's products every day in intensive synergy at the "Crossroads of the World."

Influencing Public Opinion

Besides the integration of urban planning projects into its synergistic marketing cycle, the Walt Disney Company also uses its media power to manipulate public opinion about these projects through reports on its own various media divisions. A good example was the opening ceremony for the ABC studio on Times Square on September 13th, 1999. New York's mayor Rudolph Giuliani was invited, and since he was campaigning for U.S. senator at that time, he was especially eager for publicity. Considering Giuliani's reputation as a police-supporting hard-liner, the redevelopment of Times Square served him as a good example of the results of his "zero-tolerance" policy. Hence he welcomed Disney's involvement with the redevelopment of Forty-second Street and paid tribute to the company on many occasions, including public appearances in Disney character-costumes as the Lion King or Beast (from the Disney films *The Lion King* and *Beauty and the Beast*) to help lighten his image.

For the studio's opening, Giuliani had closed off part of Broadway, and ABC's investment at Times Square was honored with a parade by the New York Police Department's (NYPD) Band, NYPD Highway Patrol Motor Bikes, and NYPD Mounted Police Unit. After this demonstration of the connection between Times Square's new status as an intensively guarded tourist destination and the Disney company's presence, Giuliani was interviewed by ABC's hosts. In the interview, Times Square's change from a red-light district to a mainstream-oriented entertainment area was described as resulting from Giuliani's anticrime policy, with the mayor stating that he considered the Times Square redevelopment an achievement that would help him to be elected senator. The show then ended with a performance of Broadway singers and dancers, who were, of course, members of Disney's stage casts and advertised the company's musicals. In this manner, urban redevelopment, politics, police presence, and media coverage contributed to one another's success. A clean, NYPD-controlled Times Square, marked by the Disney brand as a family-friendly tourist destination, symbolized the new, clean, and protected New York, and served as a political promotion of the "zero-tolerance" strategy. In turn, the city's new image emphasized its attractiveness for potential customers from the suburbs and other states, contributing to the pool of paying Disney customers.

Critical viewers might not be surprised by such a lack of neutrality in the news. But the Walt Disney Company also uses films to justify its urban planning projects where few might expect it. A good example is the use of story elements playing with motives related to Disney's involvement at Times Square in Disney's animated feature *A Bug's Life* in 1998. In this film, some creepy cartoon characters, all insects, are shown living in "the city," an easily recognizable representation of Times Square, made of garbage. Although such a depiction of Times Square as a kind of junkyard filled with strange creatures, with all its racist implications and class prejudices, could appear in a non-Disney film, this instance is different for Disney. Considering the company's synergistic approach to all economic activities, it is unlikely that Times Square's appearance in *A Bug's Life* at the same time that Forty-second Street's cultural homogenization was being criticized in the independent media was just a coincidence. Instead it seems to be a part of Disney's corporate strategy to persuade the public that Times Square's former character was so dirty that it needed Disney to clean it up.

Disney's repeated use of this strategy becomes evident in the cartoon *Hercules*, which was also used to justify Times Square redevelopment. For this purpose, the story of Disney's activities in Times Square—the tale of a neglected district, the arrival of somebody who is "cleaning up," the opening of a merchandising store, and, eventually, the parade to celebrate this investment—was transformed into a story about the ancient hero, who acts in a similar way. In the central part of Disney's cartoon, the demigod Hercules comes into the city of Thebes, which is presented as New York's ancient counterpart. To make sure that all viewers get this message, Thebes is described as "The Big Olive," and a cartoon character uses the famous phrase: "If you can make it there, you can make it anywhere." After this introduction of the city, the hero Hercules goes to the central square, which is surrounded by high buildings, where his friend complains that "the city is a dangerous place," with people who are "wackos" and "nuts." After this, Hercules runs into some mentally retarded people and meets a seller of counterfeit watches (for which Times Square used to be well known). But he also meets some working citizens, who are complaining about the "crime rate" and dirt in the city. After a sequence in which Hercules wins the fight against the Hydra, the hero comes back to the city, where he is celebrated by the residents with a parade on the city's streets—and the opening of a "Hercules Store." With these allusions, Disney describes its own role at Times Square as a "heroic" activity that's worth celebrating.

At the same time, the film also includes an ironic portrayal of Disney's own merchandising and tie-in efforts, symbolized in the movie by "Herculade" soda and "Air Herc" shoes, appearing together with the "Hercules Store" in the aforementioned scenes. This kidding about the company's own merchandising methods (as was done earlier in other extensively promoted movies like *Jurassic Park,* which featured its own merchandise) is a kind of self-ironic confession about the huge merchandising business that Disney built around the movie itself. The *Hercules* merchandising was bigger than ever: it included more than six thousand different products as well as promotional campaigns all over the world featured by tie-in partners like McDonald's, Nestlé, Choice Hotels International Inc., Quaker Oats, and General Motors Corp. But in this case, Disney went too far and it seems that the calculated commercialism was one of the reasons why the movie wasn't as big a success as previous Disney releases. Despite the company's tongue-in-cheek apology for the advertising campaign's bulk and dullness, the movie's box office revenues were disappointing compared with those for *Pocahontas* or *The Lion King*.[92] Nevertheless, it is quite unlikely that *Hercules* failed to generate any profits for Disney, especially if all merchandising and spin-off products (TV series, video games, etc.) are taken into account.[93]

Mildly satirizing commodification, *Hercules* also served as a tool that helped to justify Disney's role in the Times Square redevelopment. By incorporating a popular argument against Disney's presence in New York—the notion that Times Square would become too commercial—into its own movie, Disney changes the implications of the scenes showing Hercules' activities in Thebes/New York into a doubly twisted message. Now the scenes' underlying message isn't just bluntly advocating that Disney's presence would be in every sense perfect for New York City. Instead, it implies that the Disneyfication of a city could indeed mean a commercialization of urban space but that this would still be better than the supposed only alternative—a crime-ridden and dirt-filled neglected city waiting endlessly for heroic investors like Disney to come and save it.

Persuading Viewers Subconsciously

A trickier aspect of Disney's multimedia promotion methods is the employment of pictures that are shown in a movie so briefly that they cannot be recognized consciously but can nevertheless influence a potential customer's behavior. However, despite rumors and urban legends about the content of such brief messages, this method is not related to sexual or violent stimuli.[94] Instead this marketing method is linked to research about the recognition of briefly shown (up to a few seconds) geometric or abstract forms. It is based on the work of psychologist Robert Zajonc, who found that "mere repeated exposure of the individual to a stimulus object enhances the attitude toward it."[95] This so-called mere exposure effect, defined as the increase in positive affect that results from the repeated presentation of stimuli, is today well documented and is the foundation for numerous other psychological research projects.[96] The "mere exposure effect" has also become a standard marketing term, and knowledge about this effect is the reason why advertisers believe that the repeated brief presentation of a corporate logo—for example, as part of a very short advertising message ("brought to you by . . .")—is an effective marketing tool that results in a more positive attitude toward the presented logo, brand, or product.

Zajonc later also found that the described affective reactions to stimuli can also occur in the absence of recognition memory, and that preferences for certain objects "can develop even when the exposures are so degraded that recognition is precluded."[97] In the marketing realm, these findings were interpreted as useful because they mean that the "subliminal presentation of a stimulus may produce a positive affective response to that stimulus."[98] For the actual use of the described effect in advertising, this means that consumer attitudes may be affected by subliminal advertising "for image creation, preference, or some other objective short of actual purchase."[99] For the individual consumer, this would mean that it is possible that he or she can be exposed repeatedly to an image of a corporate logo or product so briefly each time that the image does not exceed the threshold of conscious recognition—but it can nevertheless have the effect that if this logo or picture is seen again later, the person will show a positive emotional reaction to it without knowing why.

It seems that Disney is now using this effect as part of a long-term promotional campaign for its city of Celebration. For this purpose, once more the popularity of Tim Allen is being employed. For years, he has been the star of Disney's TV series *Home Improvement,* which attracts the attention of suburban families by depicting Allen's fictional life as a father and TV-show host (Tim "The Toolman" Taylor). As a white baby boomer middle-class media-industry employee with a house, a garden, and strict family values, the popular character also represents a typical customer of Celebration, and thus offered great potential for Disney's synergy specialists. Hence, when a new set of episodes was produced in the late 1990s, the new episodes were used to support the popularity of Celebration, too. In earlier episodes, the show's opening credits had consisted of a collage of typical suburban homes of the postwar era. However, the opening credits shown in the new set of episodes, released after the decision to build Celebration, consist of an animation showing a bundle of letters and abstract forms that are moving around quickly. Only when seen frame by frame is it possible to recognize what this animation was designed for. Several times, and for just fractions of a second, pictures of architectural elements and different houses are shown—and these are the six types of homes that are used in Celebration and depicted in the *Celebration Pattern Book.* Although the pictures are shown too briefly to be consciously recognized, it is probable that most viewers will memorize them after having seen ten or more episodes of *Home Improvement.* Thus, the Walt Disney Company is already preparing for the future growth of its Celebration project. When Disney expands its city over the next twenty years (as planned), or should Disney build even more cities of the same kind, the company can be sure that millions of potential customers will already be familiar with the offered types of houses and will show "a positive affective response." The firm's sales agents will, of course, argue that Celebration looks so recognizable and cozy because it is modeled on the ideal of a typical small American town. But the truth is that to many buyers this city seems familiar because they have been exposed to images of Celebration through "hidden persuasion" for many years prior to their decision to live in a Disney city.

Promoting Neotraditionalism

The newest and fastest-growing medium, the Internet, is also used by Disney for its ingenious marketing campaigns, and the company's synergy specialists are starting to use this medium for the advertisement of Celebration, too. In 1998, Disney's Internet service ABC.com introduced a webpage that was trying to build on the success of the movie *The Truman Show*. As mentioned before, the neotraditional town of Seaside, Florida, had been used as a location for this movie. The film was produced by Disney's competitor Paramount and was mildly critical of the media industry's power. But the Disney marketing experts used the popularity of the movie to promote the idea of New Urbanism among those viewers who liked Seaside's Disneyesque appearance even though the neotraditional town was depicted in *The Truman Show* as a too-good-to-be-true environment. Customers using ABC.com's homepage in the summer of 1998 found themselves being asked whether they were impressed by the city they had seen in the movie. They then could click to get more "information" about this subject and were linked to a webpage designed by Disney's Internet content provider Starwave.[100] There customers could read an "article," written by an ABC journalist, praising the advantages of neotraditionalism, "reporting" about the Disney Development Company's activities in Celebration, and offering links to the homepages of other promoters of New Urbanism.

In a little pseudodemocratic electronic guest book for user comments on this webpage, ironically, one patron criticized the article as "paid journalism." Although a laudable example of small resistance, this comment shows that the intensity of Disney's use of media power and the regularity of the disguise of promotion-as-journalism are still underestimated. This critique is one that would have been appropriate if a journalist wrote a flattering article to get an extra benefit from a developer, as was perhaps common practice at other media companies ten years ago. But now, in the Disney case, such criticism is insufficient since the ABC journalist, the Internet specialist Starwave, and the Celebration Company are all part of one media giant, the Walt Disney Company. Within this conglomerate there is no need to pay for a positive report. Instead this kind of reporting is the company's modus operandi. The different units are all linked into the same net of corporate synergy that is continuously working toward the creation of a never-ending cycle of consumption and recreation in which various media, urban entertainment centers and neotraditional towns are completely integrated.

Conclusion

With its Times Square and Celebration projects, the Walt Disney Company has brought the commercialization of urban culture to a new level. But Disney's projects are not only problematic for their site-specific effects—their homogenization of previously diverse urban areas or the rigid organization of a neotraditional community that derives from theme park experience. What differentiates Disney's urban planning projects is that they are completely integrated into the company's synergistic multimedia marketing schemes in a way previously applied only to media products and theme parks.

Disney not only uses its movies and TV shows to attract customers to Times Square but in turn then employs this location to promote other new media products, thereby introducing the reciprocal marketing system hitherto used only in media and theme parks into the urban realm. At the same time, the company uses its numerous media to influence public opinion about its urban planning projects. And finally, Disney even attempts to attract potential customers for its neotraditional town Celebration with a kind of subliminal message, introducing this form of hidden persuasion into the real estate business. The employment of these marketing techniques in the field of urban planning marks a new dimension of the increasing commercialization of American cities, and is a good example of the Walt Disney Company's growing influence on ever more aspects of our daily lives in cities and suburbs.

Notes

1. Susan S. Fainstein, *The City Builders: Property, Politics, and Planning in London and New York* (Cambridge, Mass.: Blackwell, 1994), 170–217.

2. M. Christine Boyer, "Cities for Sale: Merchandising History at South Street Seaport," in *Variations on a Theme Park: The New American City and the End of Public Space,* ed. Michael Sorkin (New York: Hill and Wang, 1992), 181–204.

3. Michael Sorkin, "Introduction," in *Variations on a Theme Park,* xi–xv.

4. Saskia Sassen and Frank Roost, "The City: Strategic Site for the Global Entertainment Industry," in *The Tourist City,* ed. Susan S. Fainstein and Donald Judd (New Haven, Conn.: Yale University Press, 1999), 43–151.

5. Frank Roost, "Recreating the City as Entertainment Center: The Global Media Industry's Strategies for the Redevelopment of Times Square and Potsdamer Platz," *Journal of Urban Technology* 5, no. 3 (1998): 1–21.

6. Matthew P. McAllister, *The Commercialization of American Culture: New Advertising, Control, and Democracy* (New York: Sage, 1995), 68–69.

7. Sharon Zukin, *Landscapes of Power: From Detroit to Disney World* (Berkeley/Los Angeles: University of California Press, 1991), 222–224.

8. Raymond E. Braun, "Exploring the Urban Entertainment Center Universe," *Urban Land* 4, supplement, no. 8 (1995): 11–17.

9. Joe Mandese, "Is It Magic Kingdom or an Evil Empire? For Marketers, It All Depends on How Disney Handles 'Dominance,'" *Advertising Age* 66, no. 31 (1995): 2.

10. Michael J. Wolf, *The Entertainment Economy: How Mega-Media Forces Are Transforming Our Lives* (New York: Times Books/Random House, 1999), 221–252.

11. *Economist,* "The Science of Alliance," April 4, 1998, 71.

12. Leo Bogart, *Commercial Culture: The Media System and the Public Interest* (Oxford: Oxford University Press, 1995), 72.

13. Bruce Orwall, "Miramax Films Plans to Introduce Movie in a Hilfiger Ad Campaign," *Wall Street Journal,* May 7, 1998, B 10.

14. McAllister, *The Commercialization of American Culture,* 68–69.

15. Paul Farhi, "Disney Blurs the Line between Ballyhoo and Broadcasting," *Washington Post,* July 5, 1994, E1–E2.

16. A related aspect is, of course, the question of how this multimedia power influences news and other information programs. Although Disney claims that its different divisions are allowed to conduct investigative journalism without constraints, at least one incident has become public in which an ABC TV report on Disney's problems with pedophiles in its theme parks was postponed. Lawrie Mifflin, "An ABC News Reporter Tests the Boundaries of Investigating Disney and Finds Them," *New York Times,* October 19, 1998, C8.

17. Wolf, *The Entertainment Economy,* 221–252.

18. Quoted in Suzy Wetlaufer, "Common Sense and Conflict: An Interview with Disney's Michael Eisner," *Harvard Business Review* 78, no. 1 (2000): 120.

19. Quoted in James Zoltak, "Aggressive Marketing, Disney Synergy Keys to Disneyland's Banner '95 Season," *Amusement Business* 108, no. 2 (1996): 5.

20. Richard Zoglin, "Tim at the Top: With a No. 1 Movie, a No. 1 TV Show and a No. 1 Book, Tim Allen Is Having an Unbeatable Year," *Time* 144, no. 24 (1994), 76.

21. Ibid., 76–81.

22. *Economist,* "Size Does Matter," May 23, 1998, 61.
23. Jeff Smith, *The Sounds of Commerce: Marketing Popular Film Music* (New York: Columbia University Press, 1998), 193.
24. Wolf, *The Entertainment Economy,* 232.
25. William R. Taylor, "Broadway: The Place That Words Built," in *Inventing Times Square,* ed. William R. Taylor (Baltimore: Johns Hopkins University Press, 1991), 212–231.
26. New York State Urban Development Corporation, *42nd Street Now! Executive Summary* (New York, 1993), 14.
27. Three years later, Disney started to show a third Broadway musical. Since March 2000 *Aida,* a contemporary musical based on Verdi's opera and composed by Elton John and Tim Rice, has been performed in the Palace Theater near Times Square.
28. Jayne Merkel, "Fireworks on 42nd Street: Too Much about Economics, Too Little about Architecture," *Competitions* 5, no. 3 (May 1995): 45.
29. Quoted in Bruce Weber, "Disney Unveils Restored New Amsterdam Theater," *New York Times,* April 3, 1997, B3.
30. Karen Schoemer, "Disney Beats the Drums: A Park Spectacle Launches 'Pocahontas,'" *Newsweek,* June 19, 1995, 26.
31. Janet Wasko, *Understanding Disney: The Manufacture of Fantasy* (Cambridge, UK: Polity Press, 2001), 78–79.
32. Matthew Purdy, "Disney Parade About to Turn Midtown Goofy," *New York Times,* June 13, 1997, B1–B7.
33. Douglas Martin, "Its Greeks Bearing Glitz, Disney Parades a Hero," *New York Times,* June 15, 1997, Metro sec., 27.
34. Alex Witchel, "Is Disney the Newest Broadway Baby?" *New York Times,* April 17, 1994, sec. 2, 1.
35. Quoted in Bruce Weber, "Disney Unveils Restored New Amsterdam Theater," *New York Times,* April 3, 1997, B3.
36. Frank Bruni, "Some Sex-shops Vow to Fight City's New Rules," *New York Times,* October 22, 1995, B8.
37. Tom Redburn, "Putting Sex in Its Place," *New York Times,* September 12, 1994, B1–B3.
38. David Firestone, "X-Rated Businesses Lose Appeal of Law Forcing Them to Shut Doors or Move," *New York Times,* July 11, 1997, B3.
39. Timothy J. Gilfoyle, "Policing of Sexuality," in *Inventing Times Square,* 297–314.
40. Times Square Business Improvement District, *Times Square: Crossroads of the World,* company brochure (New York, 1995).
41. Gretchen Dykstra, "The Times Square Business Improvement District and Its Role in Changing the Face of Times Square," in *Sex, Scams, and Street Life: The Sociology of New York City's Times Square,* ed. Robert P. McNamara (Westport, Conn.: Praeger, 1995), 75–81.
42. John Feinblatt and Michele Sviridoff, "The Midtown Community Court Experiment," in *Sex, Scams, and Street Life,* 83–96.
43. Sharon Zukin, *The Cultures of Cities* (Cambridge, Mass: Blackwell Publishers, 1995), 33.
44. Boyer, "Cities for Sale," 199.

45. New York State Urban Development Corporation, *42nd Street Now!* 6.

46. Rick Lyman, "Where Love Outranks Power and Profit," *New York Times,* May 27, 1997, C11.

47. New York State Urban Development Corporation, *42nd Street Now!* 19.

48. New York City Department of City Planning, *Adult Entertainment Study* (New York, 1994), 48.

49. Zukin, *Landscapes of Power,* 221.

50. Quoted in ibid., 222.

51. Michael Sorkin, "See You in Disneyland," in *Variations on a Theme Park,* 205–232.

52. Russell Nye, "Eight Ways of Looking at an Amusement Park," *Journal of Popular Culture* 15: 63–75, quoted in Hannigan John Hannigan, *Fantasy City: Pleasure and Profit in the Postmodern Metropolis* (London: Routledge, 1998), 71.

53. Karal Ann Marling, "Imagineering Disney's Theme Parks," in *Designing Disney's Theme Parks: The Architecture of Reassurance,* ed. Karal Ann Marling (New York/Paris: Flammarion, 1997), 29–178.

54. Quoted in Bob Thomas, *Walt Disney: An American Original* (New York: Simon and Schuster, 1976), 349.

55. Deyan Sudjic, *The 100 Mile City* (San Diego: Harcourt Brace, 1992), 210.

56. Richard Foglesong, "Walt Disney World and Orlando" in *The Tourist City,* 89–106.

57. Russ Rymer, "Back to the Future: Disney Reinvents the Company Town," *Harper's,* October 1996, 65–78.

58. Nevertheless, a loose cooperation connects the two companies, and Arvida was chosen in 2002 as the developer of Celebration's next extension of six hundred single-family homes and condominiums to be built on 160 acres at the southern edge of the town.

59. Ruth Eckdish Knack, "Once Upon a Town: Lots of Hype and Disney Dollars Could Put New Urbanism on the Map," *Planning* 62, no. 3 (March 1996): 10–13.

60. Zukin, *Landscapes of Power,* 265.

61. "Urban or Suburban?" *Harvard Design Magazine,* Winter/Spring 1997, 47–63.

62. Zukin, *The Cultures of Cities,* 56–57.

63. Zukin, *Landscapes of Power,* 222.

64. Ibid., 223.

65. Rymer, "Back to the Future," 75.

66. Ibid.

67. *Economist,* "It's a Small Town After All," November 25, 1995, 27–28.

68. Andrew Ross, *The Celebration Chronicles: Life, Liberty, and the Pursuit of Property Value in Disney's New Town* (New York: Ballantine Books, 1999), 88.

69. Douglas Frantz and Catherine Collins, *Celebration, U.S.A.: Living in Disney's Brave New Town* (New York: Henry Holt, 1999), 155.

70. Quoted in Frantz and Collins, *Celebration, U.S.A.,* 179.

71. Ibid., 135.

72. It should also be acknowledged that Celebration has no entrance gate or guard, unlike most other new residential communities in central Florida. However, this was hardly necessary since the town's geographical situation secures a certain exclusivity.

Celebration is enclosed on the north and west by highways and a golf club and in the south and east by protected wetlands. Access to the town is limited to three roads.

73. Evan McKenzie, *Privatopia: Homeowner Associations and the Rise of Residential Private Government* (New Haven, Conn.: Yale University Press, 1994), 56–78.

74. Quoted in Beth Dunlop, "Designs on the Future," *Architectural Record* 1 (1996): 64.

75. Quoted in Rymer, "Back to the Future," 66.

76. Ibid., 75.

77. Ibid.

78. Ibid., 68.

79. In fact the swampland on which Celebration is built is located so far away from Disney's tourist attractions and was originally perceived as so unlikely to be developed that the company used it as a dumping ground for alligators cleared out of Lake Buena Vista when the foundations of Disney World were being excavated (Ross, *The Celebration Chronicles,* 13).

80. Richard Foglesong, *Married to the Mouse: Walt Disney World and Orlando* (New Haven, Conn.: Yale University Press, 2001), 146–152.

81. Ross, *The Celebration Chronicles,* 30

82. Quoted in Dietmar Steiner, "A Diary of Disney's Celebration," *Domus* 787 (November 1996): 52.

83. Charles Lockwood, "Weston, a Jewel of a Community," *Urban Land* 4, no. 8 (April 1997): 55–58.

84. Quoted in Terri Thompson, "Housing Gets the Disney Testament," *Business Week,* June 3, 1985, 72.

85. Ron Grover, *The Disney Touch: How a Daring Management Team Revived an Entertainment Empire* (Chicago: Irwin Professional Publications, 1991), 220.

86. Bruce Crumley, "Disneyland Paris Hawks Adult Appeal," *Advertising Age* 65, no. 45 (October 24, 1994): 2.

87. This sign can be observed in a photo printed in the *New York Times* shortly thereafter (Andrew Jacobs, "After Years of Sleaze and Decay, the Great White Way 'Suddenly' Looked White Hot," *New York Times,* December 29, 1996, sec. 13, 6).

88. Alastair Gordon, "Der Neonkrieg," *Geo Special New York,* Geo Special No. 5, 1999, 56–60.

89. Bill Carter, "Part ABC Studio, Part Disney Billboard," *New York Times,* September 18, 1999, Business sec. 1+4.

90. Quoted in ibid., 4.

91. Ibid.

92. Wasko, *Understanding Disney,* 80.

93. Ibid., 81.

94. The Walt Disney Company has repeatedly been the subject of rumors concerning subliminal messages supposedly hidden in its movies. However, in all the reported cases, the company's management blamed practical joking by unidentified individual animators for the incidents (Richard Roeper, *Urban Legends* [Franklin Lakes, N.J.: Career Press, 1999]). This is a very reasonable explanation, because a closer look indicates how

unlikely it is that such measures are systematically planned and conducted. Sexual or emotional stimulation through subliminal messages seems to be impossible, and serious research has not found any significant use of these stimuli for marketing purposes (Sid C. Dudley, "Subliminal Advertising: What is the Controversy About?" *Akron Business and Economic Review* 18, no. 2 [1987]: 6–18). As a result this practice is widely denied by most people in the media and advertising realm (Martha Rogers and Christine A. Seiler, "The Answer Is No: A National Survey of Advertising Practitioners and Their Clients about Whether They Use Subliminal Advertising," *Journal of Advertising Research* 34, no. 2 [1994]: 36–45). Consequently, it appears that subliminal messages with sexual content aren't systematically used as a part of Disney's corporate strategy.

95. Robert B. Zajonc, "Attitudinal Effects of Mere Exposure," *Journal of Personality and Social Psychology,* monograph supplement 9, no. 2, part 2 (1968): 1.

96. John G. Seamon and others, "The Mere Exposure Effect Is Based on Implicit Memory: Effects of Stimulus Type, Encoding Conditions, and Number of Exposures on Recognition and Affect Judgements," *Journal of Experimental Psychology: Learning, Memory, and Cognition* 21, no. 3 (1995): 711–721.

97. Robert B. Zajonc and William Raft Kunst-Wilson, "Affective Discrimination of Stimuli That Cannot Be Recognized," *Science* 207 (February 1980): 557–558.

98. Timothy E. Moore, "Subliminal Advertising," *Journal of Marketing* 46 (1982): 43.

99. Kathryn T. Theus, "Subliminal Advertising and the Psychology of Processing Unconscious Stimuli: A Review of Research," *Psychology & Marketing* 11, no. 3 (May/June 1994): 282.

100. The webpage, www.abcnews.com/sections/living/DailyNews/nightline_newurban_ 980731.html, was kept in ABC.com's "health & living" section for more than two years (including the user comment).

11

Disneyfication, the Stadium, and the Politics of Ambiance

Greg Siegel

Introduction

In his essay "Gentrification, the Frontier, and the Restructuring of Urban Space," Neil Smith distinguishes between the fact of urban gentrification and the particular form it assumes in a given historical and geographical context.[1] If the term "gentrification" is understood to designate not only the residential rehabilitation and consequent colonization of low-income neighborhoods by well-heeled investors but also the broader social, spatial, and economic restructuring of the city in the interest and as an expression of capital, then the *fact* of urban gentrification has been readily apparent and relatively constant in the United States since the end of World War II. As regards the *form* taken by urban gentrification in the last half century, however, nothing so sweeping can be rightly asserted. The specific character and composition, as well as the scope and scale, of gentrification varies from city to city—and within the same city, from district to district—depending on the complex interplay of innumerable local and global contingencies. Yet to say that the process of gentrification is always asymmetrical and locally inflected is not to deny the possibility of structural commonalities and pattern similarities—in a word, trends—existing within and across urban formations at a particular historical moment.

According to a number of sociologists, geographers, urbanologists, and architecture critics, the last quarter century has witnessed the emergence and proliferation of a new mode of urban development, in which fantastic scenography effaces architectural authenticity, rampant consumerism vitiates genuine community, commercial iconography obscures social history, and private police forces—trained in paramilitary tactics, armed with high-powered weaponry, and equipped with sophisticated surveillance apparatus—ensure socioeconomic homogeneity. In such "urbanoid environments"—Paul Goldberger's term for "places that purport to offer some degree of urban experience in an entertaining, sealed-off, private environment"—services, recreation, and consumption have been exponentially expanded, even as crime, poverty, and homelessness have been apparently (but by no means actually) eradicated.[2] Within these cocoon-like confines, visitors behold what David Harvey calls "an architecture of play and pleasure, of spectacle and commodification, emphasizing fiction and fantasy."[3] Welcome to the Disneyfication of downtown.

This last statement requires clarification. The term "Disneyfication," as Alan Bryman points out, has been invoked to describe, explain, and critique a range of disparate phenomena, including the peculiar method, initiated by Walt Disney and perpetuated by his successors, by which an original text, once acquired by a Disney-owned film studio, is simplified, bowdlerized, and homogenized, thereby rendering it immediately identifiable as a Disney production.[4] As employed in this essay, however, the term is used to refer to the aforementioned mode of urban development, in which a circumscribed space is strategically sanitized and spectacularized for maximal and manifold consumption. More specifically, "Disneyfication" denotes the aggregate of transformative logics and procedures by which a particular site or landscape is materially refashioned and symbolically reinscribed in such a way that the resulting site or landscape is conceptually, perceptually, and functionally redolent of the Disney theme parks. Thus, for present purposes, the term does not refer to the actual intentions, operations, or enterprises of the multinational entertainment corporation The Walt Disney Company, even if, as Saskia Sassen and Frank Roost have shown, that corporation has been the prime mover in the redevelopment of particular urban districts, most famously (and controversially) the area around Times Square and Forty-second Street in New York City.[5] "Disneyfication," rather, specifies the conception, construction, coordination, cross-promotion, and control of all the economic and experiential elements—architecture and landscape, goods and services, sights and sounds, players and performances—in an enclosed, entertainment- and consumption-oriented environment.

Another point that needs to be stressed is that Disneyfication is always a selectively applied, unevenly distributed process. It is important, therefore, to take notice of the geographical boundaries, as well as the social consequences, that typically attend this peculiar mode of urban "revitalization." Strictly speaking, cities do not undergo Disneyfication; only certain sectors of cities do. Now, this qualification is hardly surprising, for, as mentioned previously, the nature and extent of urban gentrification within a given city varies from district to district. Disneyfied districts, however, are noteworthy not simply because they are distinct and distinctive urban territories (the same could be said for any number of city sectors) but because they are so evidently *incongruous* urban territories, so culturally, aesthetically, and economically out of place. As Goldberger's definition of urbanoid environments suggests, the process of Disneyfication, at least within urban settings, tends to result in the formation of solipsistic and fortified enclaves devoted to high-concept, high-roller consumption. Susan S. Fainstein and David Gladstone, following *City of Quartz* author Mike Davis, talk about this phenomenon in terms of the "militarization and privatization of urban space":

> Tourism promoters have reacted to the geographic proximity of tourist districts and impoverished, high-crime areas by constructing defensible spaces. Rather than being woven into the existing urban fabric, hotel and convention facilities, sports stadiums, restaurant districts, and downtown shopping malls are cordoned off and designed to cosset the affluent visitor while simultaneously warding off the threatening native. Private police, video surveillance, and architectural design all work to keep undesirables out of touristic "compounds" and "reserves."[6]

Like Disneyland and Disney World, these "compounds" constitute demarcated dreamscapes of carefree consumption for members of the leisure class, protected playgrounds of spectacle and splurge operating as though they were light-years away from the dangerous and "dirty boulevards" that besiege them.

Significantly, the rise of what John Hannigan calls the "contemporary theme park city" represents a strategic response to decades of urban deindustrialization, disinvestment, and deterioration.[7] Beginning in the 1970s, urban economies—and the laborers that motored them—reeled from a double-barreled assault: the exportation of industrial production to the Far East and Latin America, on the one hand, and the implementation of "corporate downsizing," on the other. To this already bleak equation were added the lingering effects of the post–World War II "white-flight" syndrome, as well as the abject failures, fiscal and social, of the federally funded urban-renewal projects of the 1950s and 1960s. Inevitably, by the end of the 1970s, cities across America were engaged in a desperate bid for survival. In this "postindustrial" milieu, the establishment of an urban infrastructure and marketing machine geared toward entertainment and excursion seemed to offer a viable solution, since, as Fainstein and Dennis R. Judd observe, "tourism is an industry with few barriers to entry and the potential for large returns to investment."8 In order to attract new infusions of cash and capital—the former from tourists, business travelers, and suburban day-trippers, the latter from private investors and multinational corporations—city governments across North America, in conjunction with commercial real-estate developers and high-profile entertainment companies, have been repurposing their infrastructures and repackaging their identities as safe, clean, and "fun for the whole family."

The Stadium Boom

Not incidentally, newly constructed or renovated sports stadiums have been integrally involved in this metropolitan makeover.9 For many urban politicians, planners, and "growth strategists," a state-of-the-art stadium constitutes an indispensable ingredient in the elixir of downtown recovery and revitalization, one that justifies the expenditure of tens of millions or, in some cases, hundreds of millions of taxpayer dollars.10 Hannigan explains: "In formulating strategies designed to return downtown areas to prominence, urban planners, civic leaders and real estate developers [call for] . . . heavy investment in flagship destination projects: such as convention centers, aquariums, professional sports complexes, casinos, museums, redeveloped waterfronts and entertainment districts."11 Once these "special activity generators" are in place, Hannigan adds, they "can be aggressively marketed as part of a city's reimaging efforts."12 According to this line of reasoning, a newly constructed or renovated stadium, while not necessarily paying for itself in the strict sense, redounds to the city's long-term benefit inasmuch as it serves as an "image enhancer," a sign of social vibrancy and economic vitality so prominent and persuasive it is capable of luring private capital, trade conventions, affluent tourists, suburban shoppers, and new residents to the downtown area.13

There are sound reasons for challenging the premises on which this claim rests, including the notion that whatever benefits private capital benefits the wider community, as well as the semiotic sleight of hand that blurs the distinction between stadium-as-*symbol*-of-urban-prosperity (the order of mythology) and stadium-as-*index*-of-urban-prosperity (the order of causality). Nevertheless, since the mid-1980s, there has been an unprecedented boom in stadium construction and renovation in the United States and Canada.[14] In the years spanning 1988 to 1998, a total of thirty-two new stadiums were erected, while another twelve were substantially refurbished.[15] In 1999, eleven new stadiums (worth $2.5 billion) opened for business, the most ever to debut in a single year.[16] And according to economist Raymond J. Keating, the trend is showing no signs of abating any time soon:

> Looking to the [second half] of 1999 and the next several years, considering what is already agreed to and what various teams and cities are seeking or proposing, [a] conservative estimate indicates that at least $13.5 billion will be spent on new ballparks, stadiums, and arenas for major league teams. Taxpayers are expected to pay more than $9 billion of that amount (in nominal terms).[17]

Keating's policy analysis represents a recent installment in more than a decade's worth of sober inquiry into the pros and cons of publicly subsidized stadiums. Journals of economics, sports business, and urban studies have been crowded with articles on the stadium-financing controversy in recent years, as have metropolitan newspapers and mass-circulation magazines. Entire books have even been written on the subject, most notably Michael N. Danielson's *Home Team: Professional Sports and the American Metropolis,* Mark S. Rosentraub's *Major League Losers: The Real Cost of Sports and Who's Paying for Them,* and Joanna Cagan and Neil deMause's *Field of Schemes: How the Great Stadium Swindle Turns Public Money into Private Profit,* the titles of which leave little doubt as to the authors' take on the matter.[18]

Newly constructed or renovated stadiums have attracted the attention of critics and commentators for other reasons as well. According to stadium architect Rod Sheard, we are presently in the midst of a

> revolution in sport, the "entertainment" revolution, when sports are having to accept that they are now big business, competing for our leisure time along with the many other forms of entertainment. This is producing [a] generation of stadia . . . designed for as wide a range of events and audience as possible. Entertainment is the aim and "service" is the method.[19]

William Johnson, vice president of Ellerbe Becket, one of the leading sports-architecture firms in the United States, concurs, observing that today's stadiums are engineered to be "complete entertainment environments."[20] In his article "Baseball's Big Hit—Intimate, Luxury Parks Designed for the Sybarite in You," journalist David Conrads notes that "video kiosks, gourmet food, luxury suites, learning centers, meeting rooms [and] retractable roofs . . . are becoming standard equipment in new baseball stadiums."21 And architecture theorist Michael K. Hays insists that the current crop of high-tech sports venues "signals architecture's entry into the contemporary culture of entertainment and communication."22 Taken together, these comments suggest that the sporting event in itself is thought to be insufficiently entertaining in an era of richly diversified, highly mediatized leisure consumption. They also imply that newly constructed or renovated stadiums, reconceived and reconfigured as Disneyfied pleasure domes, are well equipped to respond to this "crisis."

Amusement Alternatives

Until the late 1980s, the stadium promised and provided the sports spectator entertainment in the form of a monolithic attraction: the game. The Disneyfied stadium, by contrast, offers a wide variety of amusement alternatives, including (depending on the venue) shopping malls, full-service restaurants, sports-history museums, batting and pitching cages, fitness clubs, sports-memorabilia exhibits, food courts, video-game arcades, merry-go-rounds and Ferris wheels, picnic spots, multiplex movie theaters, children's play areas, virtual-reality displays, swimming pools and hot tubs, pedestrian plazas, learning centers, miniature golf, and "interactive touch-screen kiosks with team histories, player interviews, archival videos, and season schedules."23

The existence and nature of these "adjacent attractions" underscore the link between the Disneyfied stadium and Hannigan's contemporary theme-park city.24 Like that of Disneyfied urban territories, the "affective ambiance" of the Disneyfied stadium is at once reassuring and spectacular, engendering a sense of security while delivering "wholesome" recreation in the form of multisensory stimulation and polymorphous consumption.25 On the one hand, the Disneyfied stadium registers and reiterates what Hannigan calls "a longstanding cultural contradiction in American society between the middle-class desire for experience and their [sic] parallel reluctance to take risks, especially those which involve contact with the 'lower orders' in cities."26 On the other hand, it seeks to satiate that desire for experience by eliminating "negative" cues in the immediate environment, by engaging the senses as much and as often as possible, and by staging escapist events and encounters.27 For B. Joseph Pine and James H. Gilmore, authors of *The Experience Economy: Work Is Theatre & Every Business a Stage,* such "theatrical" tricks of the trade, particularly when deployed in concert (as they are in the Disneyfied stadium), can help turn a "plain space" into a "distinctive place," thus encouraging "guests to *spend more time* engaged in the offering."[28] No longer a one-dimensional venue doomed to remain vacant for the better part of the day, week, and year, the stadium has been recast as a functionally heterogeneous entertainment *destination*—a term, Michael Sorkin reminds us, frequently invoked by travel agents to emphasize the definitive "thereness" of the Disney theme parks.[29]

The stadium as a site of touristic fascination? How else to explain the fact that many newly constructed or renovated stadiums offer—and charge a fee for—guided tours of the premises? Or that "more than one third of [Sky-Dome] patrons come from outside Metropolitan Toronto"?[30] Or that a number of stadium restaurants are open for business during the off-season? Or that the concourses at the MCI Center in Washington, D.C., are open daily to the general public and provide information, accessible via computer kiosks, about the district's history, geography, and visitor attractions?[31] Video-game arcades, shopping malls, multiplex movie theaters, children's play areas, sports-history museums—these attractions, while auxiliary, are not accidental in any sense of the word. Rather, they are concrete manifestations of sophisticated marketing techniques aimed at conventional middle-class families. They are also markers of a radical rearticulation of traditional meanings and practices of "nonproductive" family togetherness: not the socializing and sharing of event and experience in bounded space and time, but rather their privatizing and sundering into myriad, concurrent, mutually exclusive moments. Glorifying a future of intrafamilial atomism and alienation that is already upon us, Sheard prophesizes that "tomorrow's stadia will be places of entertainment for the family, where sport is the focus but not the complete picture. It will be possible for five members of a family to arrive and leave together but in the intervening period experience five different activities."[32] Insofar as it functions as a destination of diversified diversions for customers of all ages (but not of all classes), the Disneyfied stadium is both a metonym for and a microcosm of the Disneyfied district that contains and conditions it.

The introduction of amusement alternatives into the space of the stadium is by no means a value-neutral affair; its effects are not simply additive but fundamentally transformative. Ringing the stadium interior like so many stationary satellites, adjacent attractions remap the material geometries and symbolic economies of the spectator-sports landscape. To be precise, they effectively attenuate the centripetal orientation, or centralizing tendencies, of the sporting event, siphoning off and redirecting to the perimeter—that is, to the newly expanded concourses—a substantial portion of its sensorial stimuli, affective appeals, and libidinal intensities. Stadium architect Frank Scicchitano explains: "Outside of the seating bowl, the concourse—traditionally more about operations, circulation and 'check the box' design than experience creation—is evolving into . . . a variety of environments intended for gathering or supporting sub-venue events."³³ This radial redistribution, this peripheralization of the stadium's spatial dynamics, works to reorder the attentional priorities and revise the participatory routines—the traditional rhythms and rituals—of sports spectatorship, inviting the stadiumgoer, like the mallgoer, to adopt, in Anne Friedberg's words, "the perceptual mode of flânerie while instrumentalizing it for consumer objectives."³⁴ Just as the utilitarian stadium has been repackaged as a tourist destination, so has the sedentary spectator been reconstituted as a corridor cruiser, a peripatetic sightseer and shopper, a circulating subject—or "guest," as Pine and Gilmore, following Disney, would have it—for whom the provision of an array of amusement alternatives affirms the bounty of contemporary capitalism even as it facilitates the dream of self-actualization through "consumer choice."³⁵ Scicchitano declares:

> Sports facilities are evolving into places that offer varied experiences for small, diversified "micro-classes" with multiple levels of engagement and exclusivity. . . . In order to give a maximum amount of choice to spectators who have more ways than ever to spend their entertainment dollars, it is imperative that the design of sports facilities . . . focus on the diversity of spectator experience at all levels.³⁶

Although the sporting event still occupies center stage in a topographical sense, the universality of its magnetism, the irresistibility of its allure, can no longer be taken for granted. In the Disneyfied stadium, the game continues to serve as an architectural and experiential anchor, to be sure, but it is now one attraction among many, as much a controlling *theme* as it is the main event.

From Multitheming to Monotheming

Of course, the Disneyfied stadium is not themed to the same degree or in the same fashion as the Disney parks. Perhaps the most obvious difference, in this respect, is that the Disneyfied stadium is singly, not multiply, themed. Whereas Disneyland and Disney World use several different themes (drawn from nature, geography, folklore, history, and children's literature, by way of Disney movies and television shows) to physically delimit and conceptually/perceptually define their semiautonomous subregions, the Disneyfied stadium uses a single, locally inflected theme—spectator sports in general, the home team in particular—to integrate its attractions, organize its address, and regulate its ambiance. In the Disney parks, multitheming accomplishes two critical objectives—objectives that at first blush seem to be mutually canceling but on closer inspection prove to be mutually reinforcing: it encourages visitors to keep moving and to stay longer. The multithemed environment keeps visitors on the move—and from exiting the park—by offering them the opportunity to continually reexperience, through and as serialized simulation, the touristic frisson of entering an exotic locale and the consumerist satisfaction of expending one. In this way, multitheming delivers a preemptive strike against atmospheric homogeneity, experiential monotony, and, ultimately, economic inefficiency.

That the Disneyfied stadium uses monotheming, rather than multitheming, to much the same end speaks volumes about the differing spatial dimensions, social customs, and institutional histories of the amusement park and the sports stadium. Compared with the size and scale of Disneyland or Disney World, the stadium is a Lilliputian land. More pronounced still does this disparity become when considered in terms of the area allocated for visitor activities: modern sports spectators are seldom, if ever, allowed to access or occupy the playing field, which takes up a substantial share of the stadium's usable space.[37] Such spatial constraints make multitheming a less practicable option for stadium architects and design consultants. It is also a less culturally warranted one. Theming enabled Disney to differentiate his product from "grimy," garden-variety amusement parks (this point will be elaborated shortly). In the Disneyfied stadium, however, theming is not so much a means of external differentiation as it is a means of internal unification. Disneyland's multithemed environment responded to the problem of how to distinguish its collection of rides and attractions from its competitors' collections of rides and attractions. The Disneyfied stadium's monothemed environment, by contrast, responds to the problem of how to assimilate its attractions to the cultural conventions of sports spectatorship, to the structural codes of stadium architecture, and to the place-based (if corporately mediated) identifications and aspirations of regional residents. In the Disneyfied stadium, the theme of spectator sports is abstracted from the sporting event, emblazoned with the icons and insignia—the trademarked totems—of the home team, and projected, in turn, onto the stadium's attractions, imparting to them, and to the stadium surroundings in general, a measure of semiotic coherence.

It is useful to recall, in this connection, that a theme, as deployed in Disneyland and Disney World, is more than a principle of semiotic coherence; it is an instrument of social control and a catalyst for consumer desire. More than a few Disney biographers, historians, and critics have noted that Disney and his cadre of "imagineers" took pains to distinguish Disneyland, a bourgeois theme park "designed to provide edifying adventures for baby-boom families," from "sleazy," turn-of-the-century amusement parks designed to dispense cheap thrills to the urban masses.[38] According to Christopher Anderson,

> Disney assured the public that any amusement experienced in his park would be tempered by middle-class educational values. Disneyland wouldn't be another park trading in the temporal gratifications of the flesh; instead, it would be a popular monument to human knowledge, a "permanent world's fair" built around familiar Disney characters and a number of unifying social goals, including educating the public about history and science.[39]

Besides offering Disney a socially sanctioned means of disciplining "the unruly pleasures of the amusement park," theming proved an enormously profitable means of organizing, interrelating, and administering milieu and merchandise.[40] Disneyland might not have been the first commercial venture to feature themed attractions (several of Coney Island's rides and exhibits bore exotic or erotic motifs), but it was the first to feature a wholly themed environment.[41] For Susan G. Davis, "the concept of the 'themed environment,' the fully designed, highly coordinated 'land' with all services, performances and concessions designed and provided in house, was arguably the most important Disney contribution to the industry."[42] Disney's entrepreneurial genius, in other words, lay in the realization that his park could be exploited as a site for the minutely managed sale and "synergy" of goods, services, and experiences, all themed to his company's proprietary images and texts. "Total merchandising," Disney's term for this style of cross-promotional dynamism, this "strategy of seamless market expansion,"[43] ensured that "products aimed at baby boom families and stamped with the Disney imprint—movies, amusement park rides, books, comic books, clothing, toys, TV programs, and more—would weave a vast commercial web, a tangle of advertising and entertainment in which each Disney product, from the movie *Snow White & the Seven Dwarfs* (1937) to a ride on Disneyland's Matterhorn, promoted all Disney products."[44]

Because commercial advertising has long adorned the visible surfaces and rippled the acoustical spaces of professional sports venues, it would be easy to dismiss the Disneyfied stadium's consumerist landscape as merely a latter-day extension and embodiment of time-tested promotional practices in the world of sports business.[45] To do so, however, would be to overlook, not only the qualitative differences between the atmospheric operations of the Disneyfied stadium and those of its formal precursors, but also their disparate political-economic underpinnings. While the stadium, in its modern capitalist incar-

nation, has always been a locus of commercial penetration, the Disneyfied stadium, like the Disney theme parks, is a locus of "hyper-commercial interpenetration," a source of synergistic opportunities whose emergence as a distinct
technocultural form in the late 1980s is inextricably tied to the contemporane-
ous convergence of the sports, media, and entertainment industries.[46]

From the perspective of political economy, the story of these industries—
beginning in the 1980s, accelerating in the 1990s, and continuing apace in the
first decade of the twenty-first century—is the story of multinational corporate mergers, buyouts, and takeovers, of vertical and horizontal integration
through ownership concentration and market consolidation. Mark Crispin
Miller maintains that the rise of the modern media cartel "represents the grand
convergence of the previously disparate U.S. culture industries—many of
them vertically monopolized already—into one global superindustry providing most of our imaginary 'content.'"[47] In an era of cross-industrial, cross-
national conglomeration, when major media firms such as the Walt Disney
Company, News Corporation, AOL Time Warner, Cablevision Systems Corporation, Tribune Company, and Comcast Corporation all wholly or partly
own professional sports franchises, spectator sports—the venues, the games,
the teams, the athletes—are indeed conceptualized and operationalized as entertainment "content."[48] Just as Disneyland boosted the brand recognition
and enhanced the exchange value of Disney commodities (emblems, characters, narratives) by providing a context, at once "magical" and material, in
which they could be advertised, merchandised, and experienced, so the Disneyfied stadium, with its monothemed amusement alternatives, multiple
points of sale for licensed merchandise, and myriad promotional surfaces and
spaces—from players' jerseys to playing field to public-address system, from
conventional signage to cutting-edge interfaces—feeds the cultural capital and
fuels the commercial synergies of global media conglomerates.[49]

The State-of-the-Art Scoreboard

There is another attraction that participates in the Disneyfication of the stadium: the large-screen video display.[50] Whether suspended as an octagonal
gondola above the playing field (as in basketball and hockey) or rearing up as
an optoelectronic billboard alongside it (as in baseball and football), the large-
screen video display is a diversion of a different order. Unlike the Disneyfied
stadium's other amusement alternatives, the large-screen video display is most
often accessed—that is, visually apprehended—from the comfort of one's seat.
Because its "rewards"—to borrow Yi-Fu Tuan's term for "the distinctive

sensory-aesthetic experiences that visitors to Disneyland can expect"—are available from every seat in the house, this real-time moving-image technology does not beckon the stadiumgoer to stroll the commodious concourses as do the attractions on the perimeter.[51]

Yet it furnishes a certain mobility nonetheless. Through the use of zooming close-ups, multiple angles, instant replays, and slow-motion effects, the large-screen video display confers on the sports spectator a visually/virtually mediated mobility. Tuan argues that, for visitors who use them, Disneyland's rides, in addition to producing kinesthetic sensations, transform the visual landscape into an impressionistic panorama:

> A landscape may . . . function as a spectacle if riders, rushing along, see it for only a few seconds and it is gone. That flash of color and form, unavailable for prolonged viewing, is what makes it a spectacle, as sword fights and fireworks, too quick in their individual movements to be considered a stable composition, are spectacles.[52]

Disneyland's rides generate spectacle through machinic mobilization; the Disneyfied stadium's large-screen video display generates (virtual) mobilization—a flash of color and form, a feeling of rushing along—through machinic spectacle. In so doing, the large-screen video display, like the Disneyfied stadium's peripherally positioned attractions, works to restructure the stadiumgoer's attentional practices and affective investments—in this case, by inducing and sustaining a novel mode of sports spectatorship, in which immediate, relatively stationary views of the game alternate with mediated, virtually mobilized ones.[53]

Sheard and fellow stadium architect Geraint John have this to say about the large-screen video display:

> In addition to attracting and pleasing audiences, thus increasing gate revenue, pre-programmed entertainment sequences on big video screens can also usefully slow down the rate at which people enter and leave the stadium. Keeping a proportion of the audience in their seats after the final whistle, instead of rushing for the exits, makes for a safer stadium. It can also make for a more profitable one if people are persuaded by entertaining video programs to arrive earlier than they otherwise would do, and to stay longer, using stadium restaurants and other facilities before and after the game.[54]

This quotation brings together, in striking fashion, the large-screen video display's role in the establishment of the stadium as a media-saturated, recreationally varied destination and its possibilities as an apparatus of behavioral manipulation and management, conditioning the comportment, orchestrating the movement, and charting the itineraries of bodies within the space of the stadium in such a way that "going with the flow" appears to be a matter of individual volition.

In many Disneyfied stadiums, the large-screen video display is incorporated into a larger, more elaborate, and increasingly ornate scoreboard ensemble. Once conceived and received as a simple and straightforward alphanumeric display, possessing an equally simple and straightforward informational function, the scoreboard has become an attraction unto itself. Journalist Jeff Houck describes the situation at Comerica Park in Detroit:

> In what seems like a Cold War–style escalation among professional teams, the Tigers have their own larger-than-life scoreboard in left-center field. There are three components to the 202-foot wide structure: a full motion color video screen, a black-and-white board for the linescore and statistics and a color matrix board for messages and graphics. The scoreboard, the largest in baseball, is hooked up to a $1.2 million control room. The Tigers can show replays, create their own graphics, show fans in the stands and synchronize the boards with the sound speakers, lighting and a computer-controlled water fountain that sends choreographed jets of colored water 120 feet into the air.[55]

"Designed as both a visually dynamic form and a piece of 'performance sculpture,'" the scoreboard at Miami's AmericanAirlines Arena has been touted as "a new icon for the city":[56]

> A central feature of the bowl is the scoreboard; as much artwork as information provider, this Medusa-like anemone—appropriately named "Turn Up the Heat," flashes, changes colors and appears to explode, emitting smoke and firing off pyrotechnics. The tentacles support scoreboards, LED screens and strobelights and are the creation of artist Christopher Janney. . . . The Medusa is also interactive—fans will be able to affect the pulse and brightness of the lighting by increasing the volume of their cheers.[57]

At the MCI Center, the scoreboard converts spectatorial subjectivity into its own specular object, commemorating it and commodifying it at the same time:

> Mounted on the scoreboard is a digital photo image system. . . . With this system a photo of every spectator in the arena will be taken and sent to a processing

system which combines them with replicas of the event ticket and either a limited edition photo of a famed athlete or a panoramic shot of the event itself. Though each photo is of a block of seats rather than an individual, the blocks are small enough so that each spectator can be seen clearly. Because they are taken digitally, they can be sold during the event itself through vendors visiting each section of seats.[58]

Whether owing to its mediatization (video screens, matrix boards, digital cameras), its aestheticization ("choreographed," "sculpture," "artwork"), its spectacularization (hydraulics, pyrotechnics, stroboscopics), or some combination thereof, the state-of-the-art scoreboard contributes to the Disneyfication of the stadium by providing the sports spectator another source of perceptual pleasure as well as another incentive to programmed participation.

As with other artifacts and applications of electronic exhibitionism (homemade videos, reality-TV shows, personal webcams), the MCI Center's scoreboard entices audiences to enjoy the production and products of self-exposure and spontaneous celebrity, to delight in the actions and projections of their own likenesses, to objectify the virtual performativity and, finally, the very facticity of their own iconicity. Of course, it also dramatizes, and in effect domesticates, the panoptic dimensions of the Disneyfied stadium, as such self-exposure forms the smiling face of surveillance. Although in the Disneyfied stadium, as in nearly all places of mass public and semipublic assembly in technologized societies, cameras are trained on bodies and physiognomies more for crowd control (closed-circuit surveillance) and, increasingly, for biometric identification (cybernetic surveillance) than for audience amusement, these strategies of power are complementary, not contradictory.[59] The slippery reversibility and constitutive reciprocality of self-exposure and surveillance, the automatic photographic capture of "every spectator in the arena" for fun, for sale, *and* for identification, is neither ironical nor paradoxical. Rather, it embodies the dual nature of what Tony Bennett calls "the exhibitionary complex." For Bennett, the peculiarity of the exhibitionary complex as a political rationality and disciplinary apparatus—that is, as an ensemble of power/ knowledge relations and techniques—consists in the way it imbricates the principles of the panopticon with those of the panorama, forming a machinery of vision that regulates spectator-subjects by rendering them visible to themselves, "by making the crowd itself the ultimate spectacle."[60] Gridded with countless, crisscrossing lines of observation, inspection, and detection, shot through with intersecting and overlapping planes of performance, with kaleidoscopic, constantly shifting sights and screenings, the Disneyfied stadium plays to both the panoptic and the panoramic impulses of contemporary stadiumgoers by playing up and playing out the vertiginous possibilities of seeing, being seen, seeing oneself seeing, and seeing oneself being seen.

Amenities and Appearances

Unlike its architectural antecedents, which, by and large, were no-frills affairs, the Disneyfied stadium offers amenities galore. Consider the recent regeneration of the stadium concession stand. Prior to the late 1980s, concession stands traditionally served fast-food fixes: hot dogs and hamburgers, roasted peanuts and soft pretzels, domestic beer and soda pop. Since then, however, the quantity and "quality" of menu items, like the prices affixed to them, have increased sharply, as have the quantity and "quality" of concession stands themselves. To be sure, concession stands now offer a veritable cornucopia of foods and beverages, including (depending on the venue) deli sandwiches, Caesar salads, fajitas, turkey bratwursts, imported ales, burritos, frozen yogurt, pasta primavera, chardonnay, fruit smoothies, chicken wings, sushi, veggie dogs, jalapeno sausages, cheese-cake, fish tacos, egg rolls, cappuccino, baked potatoes, crab cakes, microbrews, bison burgers, clam chowder, pierogies, meatball subs, and shrimp cocktail.

According to journalist Janice Matsumoto,

> Even though hot dogs, nachos, popcorn and beer are perennial ballpark favorites, guests want choices, and are willing to pay for that privilege. "Customer expectations have been raised so high for the entire industry that when they go to a stadium, their idea is, if we're going to pay that much to see a game, the food had better match up," says Carmen Torzon, vice president of operations for Spartanburg, S.C.–based Volume Services America. "Customers want variety and the ability to buy high-end food."[61]

On the one hand, the Disneyfied stadium's eclectic (and comparatively exotic) eatables, like its adjacent attractions, demonstrate a dual commitment: to a particular marketing methodology, in which the diversification of goods and services is valorized in the name of consumer choice, and to a no less particular affective ambiance, in which, to quote Liza Cartmell, an executive of a company that oversees dining and retail operations in thirteen major-league baseball stadiums, "off-the-field fun—including new and innovative food—is part of the overall experience."[62] On the other hand, if, as Sharon Zukin contends, "Gourmet food—specifically, the kind of reflexive consumption beyond the level of need that used to be called gastronomy—suggests an organization of consumption structurally similar to the deep palate of gentrification," then the appreciable "upscaling" of stadium cuisine marks a historic shift in the cultural politics and socioeconomic relations of spectator sports, much as the Disneyfication of downtown marks a historic shift in the cultural politics and socioeconomic relations of the city.[63]

In addition to dishing up all manner of fashionable fare, the Disneyfied stadium's concession stands (and concourses) come equipped with prominently placed television monitors tuned to the "live" sporting event, so that queuing (or ambling) customers need not worry about missing a moment of the action. Here we glimpse yet another means by which the Disneyfied stadium renders seductive the prospect of circumambulatory consumption: the pervasion of real-time representations of the game throughout the concessions and concourses ("Blink your eyes and you might think you're at Circuit City," quips journalist Kevin Paul Dupont) means that the usual disincentive to leaving one's seat is virtually nullified—nullified, in fact, through virtualization.[64] In many Disneyfied stadiums, moreover, an auditory version of this amenity can be found in the restrooms, where ceiling speakers transmit the local radio broadcast of the game.

The restrooms are noteworthy for other reasons as well. Pre-Disneyfied stadiums, like other public and semipublic facilities built before the 1980s, contained an equal number of men's and women's restrooms (and often not enough of either). The Disneyfied stadium, by contrast, contains between twice and thrice as many women's restrooms as men's (and more of each), exemplifying an eagerness to accommodate the practical needs of women, much as the presence of diaper-changing tables, in men's and women's restrooms, exemplifies an eagerness to do the same for families with young children. Dennis Robinson, executive vice president and chief operating officer for business operations of the New Jersey Sports and Exposition Authority, comments on the received relationship between hygienic norms, culinary niceties, and what baseball historian Brian J. Neilson refers to as "the feminization—or at least gender neutralization—of previously 'male' spaces" such as the sports stadium:[65]

> Bathrooms are an issue we deal with every day. We have a commitment from the president on down about the bathrooms in our places [sports venues]. We installed changing tables in the bathrooms, we've put more stalls in there, we have conveniences, we have attendants in our bathrooms throughout every event; they are constantly cleaned during every event. . . . We have a commitment to the needs of women. We have also increased the variety of items that are in the concession stands. Now you have grilled chicken sandwiches, you don't have just the pizza and the beer and the popcorn. We have salads that you can take to your seats. These types of things appeal particularly to women.

Traditionally, I guess, these spaces have been coded as male, but as more and more women become more and more interested in sports, people like us are going to move more and more to appeal to them.[66]

In contrast to earlier generations of stadiums, which functioned primarily as "men's cultural centers," and in conformity with the Disney theme parks, where the nuclear family is ritualistically reaffirmed (in the form of the family vacation) and ideologically enshrined (in the service of turning a profit), the Disneyfied stadium, as Robinson's remarks illustrate, calculatedly caters to the cultural priorities and preferences of conventional middle-class families.[67]

The middle-class family, however, is not the only demographic group the Disneyfied stadium targets. Although it first appeared in the 1960s, the sky-box—an amenity-intensive, spatially partitioned, and socially segregated luxury suite for corporate executives and wealthy season-ticket holders—did not become an obligatory aspect of stadium architecture until the 1980s. Since then, the skybox has replicated with virulent efficiency. Besides incorporating multiple tiers of luxury suites, the Disneyfied stadium allocates several sections of lavishly appointed "premium seats" for privileged patrons, who, like the skybox set, can afford to pay handsomely for creature comforts and conveniences.[68] Interestingly, it is not so much their nearness to the playing field that makes luxury suites and premium seats desirable (they are, in fact, relatively removed from the action), but rather the sorts of services they tender, most of which involve the use of new media technologies. At the Xcel Energy Center in St. Paul, Minnesota, "interactive flat-panel computer screens [and] high-speed data hookups" enable skybox occupants to access "game-day previews, stats, player profiles and league highlights . . . with the click of a mouse."[69] Meanwhile, at New York City's recently refurbished Madison Square Garden,

fans in one of 557 ChoiceSeats installed [in 1999] can tap a computer screen in front of their seats and order food for delivery . . . call up photos, scouting reports and statistics for any player, see a graphical representation of the position, type and speed of every play, view replays from different camera angles, follow scores of other games and even watch the regular live TV broadcast of the game in front of them—just like at home. If they choose, fans in the smart seats can shop for official team merchandise, vote for All-Star selections and play a trivia game or bingo.[70]

And each luxury suite at General Motors Place in Vancouver furnishes two television monitors capable of receiving seventy-seven channels, some of which carry "dry feeds" (unedited signals) from the stadium's own dedicated cameras, allowing suite holders to view the sporting event from various vantage points.[71]

Once again the Disneyfied stadium confronts us with the appearance of heterogeneous plenitude: more and different things to do, more and different things to engage, more and different things (and ways) to watch. In the latter case, significantly, the appearance of heterogeneous plenitude is synonymous with the plenitude of heterogeneous appearances. Insofar as they are involved in the endless reproduction of apparent abundance—in the inexorable flow of visual representations, in the split-second stream of statistical data—luxury suites and premium seats are functionally akin to the large-scale video display. But whereas the large-screen video display offers sports spectators an ever-renewing choice between immediate and mediated views of the game, the aptly named ChoiceSeats (and other brands of "smart seats") offer the fortunate few a seemingly infinite range of iconographic and informational options—including, paradoxically, the "option" to work.

Indeed, for many skybox occupants, the game is but a backdrop for business, a curious state of affairs that instantiates Sorkin's compelling claim: "One of the main effects of Disneyfication is the substitution of recreation for work, the production of leisure according to the routines of industry. Now, one of the products of postindustrialism is not simply the liberation of vast amounts of problematic leisure time, it's the reinvention of labor as spectacle"—and, it might be added, of spectacle as labor.[72] Replete with the latest information and communication technologies—laptop computers, broadband Internet connections, fax machines, laser printers, multimedia jacks, flatbed scanners, even videoconferencing equipment—the Disneyfied stadium's luxury suites serve as an "office away from the office" for the movers and shakers of corporate capital, a Janus-faced place where elite executives and middle managers can, or must, labor amid the trappings of leisure, and vice versa.[73] If, as Neilson suggests, structural alterations and technical innovations such as floodlights, artificial turf, domed roofs, and, most recently, retractable roofs signify the technorationalist desire to condition and control the natural surroundings in spectator sports, then the skybox signifies and reifies the technocapitalist desire to do the same for the social surroundings.[74] But today the skybox signifies—and stages—something else as well: the corporate class's celebration and fetishization of its own technologization, and of the global reach—anywhere, anytime, in an instant—such technologization affords. In the cultural economy of the Disneyfied stadium, social status and monetary muscle are measured and expressed less in terms of physical proximity and presence (the ability to obtain front-row seats) and more in terms of visual mastery and virtual mobility (the authority to access luxury-suite technologies).

Conclusion

According to Max Frankel, Disney World

> demonstrates that it's not Mickey's message that brings the crowds. It is the wondrous technology by which the Disney inventors charm and frighten, delight and transport. The kids who are flown to Orlando's plantation of fantasy may still heed the story lines of the rides and exhibits. But the adults who spend a year's savings on the journey worship the technology itself, the magical animations and animatronics that bring robots to life and turn life into a multimedia performance.[75]

The Disney theme parks, like the nineteenth- and early twentieth-century world's fairs and international expositions on which they were principally modeled, pinned the promise of an American utopia on the machines of modern industry, those quintessential emblems and supposed agents of technical and scientific advancement, of economic efficiency and abundance, of social progress and civilization. The Disneyfied stadium, like the socially, spatially, and economically restructured city in which it is situated and on which it depends, renews and revises that promise, tethering the dream of the good life to the consumption of high-tech amusements and amenities, and to the command and control of information capital—one a middle-class compulsion, one a corporate-class megalomania, both putative testaments to the greater glory of the postindustrial economy.

Acknowledgment

I am grateful to Mike Budd for his helpful comments on earlier drafts of this essay.

Notes

1. Neil Smith, "Gentrification, the Frontier, and the Restructuring of Urban Space," in *Gentrification of the City,* ed. Neil Smith and Peter Williams (Boston: Allen & Unwin, 1986), 22.
2. Paul Goldberger, "The Rise of the Private City," in *Breaking Away: The Future of Cities,* ed. Julia Vitullo-Martin (New York: Twentieth Century Fund Press, 1996), 140.

3. David Harvey, "The Urban Face of Capital," in *Our Changing Cities,* ed. John Fraser Hart (Baltimore: Johns Hopkins University Press), 60.

4. Alan Bryman, "The Disneyization of Society," *Sociological Review* 47, no. 1 (1999): 26–27.

5. Saskia Sassen and Frank Roost, "The City: Strategic Site for the Global Entertainment Industry," in *The Tourist City,* ed. Dennis R. Judd and Susan S. Fainstein (New Haven, Conn.: Yale University Press, 1999), 150–153.

6. Susan S. Fainstein and David Gladstone, "Evaluating Urban Tourism," in *The Tourist City,* 26–27.

7. John Hannigan, *Fantasy City: Pleasure and Profit in the Postmodern Metropolis* (London: Routledge, 1998), 81.

8. Susan S. Fainstein and Dennis R. Judd, "Global Forces, Local Strategies, and Urban Tourism," in *The Tourist City,* 2.

9. In this essay, the term "stadium" is used generically; no distinctions are drawn between the terms "stadium," "arena," "ballpark," and the like.

10. Architecture critic and stadium design consultant John Pastier ("The Sporting Life," *Architectural Record,* August 1999, 113) asserts that "sometimes, rather than sparking revitalization, a stadium or arena will supply what [architecture firm] HOK Sport's Earl Santee calls 'a missing piece' of the downtown matrix. Houston's Enron Field [now named Minute Maid Park] . . . is one example; he says, 'it's not so much a catalyst as a precedent-setter showing that the neighborhood is a good area to develop in.'"

11. Hannigan, *Fantasy City,* 51.

12. Ibid., 56. Karl B. Raitz ,"The Theater of Sport: A Landscape Perspective," in *The Theater of Sport,* ed. Karl B. Raitz (Baltimore: Johns Hopkins University Press, 1995), 4–5, writes: "Even in a large city, the distinctive size and shape of a stadium makes it a landmark. It is not only the site of periodic athletic competitions but often a source of civic pride and a symbol of victory and accomplishment. Therefore, it represents success. In the off-season it serves as a navigational marker and . . . may also symbolize the city itself. This is the kind of symbol that can be successfully exploited in advertising photography."

13. Kimberley S. Schimmel, "Growth Politics, Urban Development, and Sports Stadium Construction in the United States: A Case Study," in *The Stadium and the City,* ed. John Bale and Olof Moen (Keele, UK: Keele University Press, 1995), 131. Research conducted by independent economists has demonstrated, time and again, that publicly subsidized stadiums are, at best, break-even propositions and, at worst, backbreaking boondoggles. Contrary to the rosy rhetoric of civic officials and sports-industry boosters, not only is a newly constructed or renovated stadium unlikely to be an "economic engine"; it has the very real potential of being an economic drain. See Raymond J. Keating, "Sports Pork: The Costly Relationship between Major League Sports and Government," *Policy Analysis* 339 (April 5, 1999): 17–18, http://www.cato.org/pubs/pas/pa339.pdf.

14. Robert A. Baade, "What Explains the Stadium Construction Boom," *Real Estate Issues* 21, no. 3 (1996): 5–11.

15. Keating, "Sports Pork," 14–15.

16. Eric Mitchell, "Stadium Construction Boom Could End in U.S.," *Washington Business Journal,* July 2, 1999, 15.

17. Keating, "Sports Pork," 1.

18. Although the ongoing expansions of Major League Baseball, the National Football League, the National Hockey League, and the National Basketball Association have contributed to the recent spike in stadium construction, most of the structures built in the last few decades were designed to replace existing facilities, many of which had been servicing one or more professional teams for decades. (Before it was demolished in 1991, Chicago's Comisky Park had been home to the White Sox baseball team for eighty-one years.) Nevertheless, during the 1980s, in city after city, it was decided and declared, first by team owners, then by municipal politicians and other civic officials, that the older stadiums were hopelessly "obsolete." Even a sizable contingent of sports journalists, many of whom, as self-identified traditionalists, initially supported the preservation and continued use of the existing buildings, eventually attested to their obsolescence. These claims of obsolescence, however, did not—and do not today—hinge primarily on concerns over a stadium's structural soundness or the creeping cost of its maintenance and repair. Instead, they refer to the comparative economic inefficiency of the older venue. For team owners, an obsolete stadium is a stadium drowning in sluggish streams of revenue. One means of opening the financial floodgates, of course, is to build a stadium with an increased seating capacity in the hope of selling more tickets. Yet the majority of the stadiums erected in the last few decades possess a seating capacity no greater, and in some cases actually less, than those they were designed to replace. The way to turn a trickle into a torrent, it seems, has nothing to do with the sheer quantity of paying customers and everything to do with their social "quality." It became apparent to sports industrialists, beginning in the 1980s, that the key to boosting stadium revenue and maximizing profit margins lay in the provision of diversified attractions and upgraded accommodations.

19. Rod Sheard, "Stadia and Arena through the Ages," in *Stadia, Arenas and Grandstands: Design, Construction and Operation,* ed. P. D. Thompson, J. J. A. Tolloczko, and J. N. Clarke (London: E & FN Spon-Routledge, 1998), xviii.

20. Quoted in David Conrads, "Baseball's Big Hit—Intimate, Luxury Parks Designed for the Sybarite in You," *Christian Science Monitor,* May 9, 1997, 10.

21. Conrads, "Baseball's Big Hit," 10.

22. Michael K. Hays, "All-Stars: Top-Seeded Designers Invade the Turf of Pro Stadium Specialists," *Architecture* 87, no. 11 (1998): 116.

23. Ellen Lampert-Greaux, "CoreStates Center," *TCI: Theatre Crafts International,* May 1997, 43.

24. The term "adjacent attractions" comes from Margaret Crawford, "The World in a Shopping Mall," in *Variations on a Theme Park: The New American City and the End of Public Space,* ed. Michael Sorkin (New York: Hill and Wang, 1992), 14–17.

25. The term "affective ambiance" comes from Hannigan, *Fantasy City,* 74.

26. Ibid., 7.

27. B. Joseph Pine and James H. Gilmore, *The Experience Economy: Work Is Theatre & Every Business a Stage* (Boston: Harvard Business School Press, 1999), 46–61.

28. Ibid., 42.

29. Michael Sorkin, "See You in Disneyland," in *Variations on a Theme Park,* 215.

30. Bruce Kidd, "Toronto's SkyDome: The World's Greatest Entertainment Centre," in *The Stadium and the City,* 184.

31. *Amusement Business,* "MCI Center: Showcasing the Link Between Technology and Entertainment," December 22, 1997, MasterFILE Premier (online database).

32. Sheard, "Stadia and Arena through the Ages," xix.

33. Frank Scicchitano, "Features Galore," *Panstadia International Quarterly Report* 6, no. 2 (1999), http://www.panstadia.com/vol6/62-054.htm.

34. Anne Friedberg, *Window Shopping: Cinema and the Postmodern* (Berkeley: University of California Press, 1993), 112.

35. Accentuating the positive, Mark Gottdiener (*The Theming of America: Dreams, Visions, and Commercial Spaces* [Boulder, Colo.: Westview, 1997], 7) claims that "when [shoppers] enter the commercial realms of consumption, as in a visit to a mall, the themed retailing environment actualizes their *consumer selves.* . . . [Consumers] *self-actualize* within the commercial milieu by seeking through the market ways of satisfying desires and pursuing personal fulfillment that express deeply-held images of the self."

36. Scicchitano, "Features Galore." For Brian J. Neilson ("Baseball," in *The Theater of Sport,* 65), "such a design imperative, far from meriting praise, epitomizes and confirms the rise of the imperial and universalizing entertainment culture, which posits no hierarchy of cultural values but offers an unlimited horizontal choice of 'leisure options.' The corollary of such flattening is that all choices—a movie, a video game, a baseball game—are equal and neutral, attached to no history or values external to themselves, subject only to the criterion of diversion, of 'fun.'"

37. John Bale, *Sport, Space and the City* (London: Routledge, 1993), 9–19, reminds us that in premodern Europe, a sport such as football (soccer) was only a folk game, "much more a form of play and carnival than of seriousness" (p. 11). Its enabling terrain was equally informal and ad hoc. "No specialized sites existed for football; it was played, not simply *in* places usually used for other activities, but also *while* other activities were going on" (p. 13). The playing field was unmarked, uneven, and unbounded, allowing for fluid and frequent interactions between players and spectators. In contrast to these Dionysian circumstances, the sports landscape of late- eighteenth and nineteenth centuries, including and especially the modern stadium, adhered to an Apollonian agenda of codification, confinement, and control. The playing field had become specialized, standardized, and rationalized, its territorial parameters and internal zones clearly demarcated and officially monitored. By the same token, the spatial segregation of players and spectators was now strictly enforced, as was the class segregation—the bourgeoisie here, the proletariat there—of the crowd itself. For patrons with deep pockets, the modern stadium's terraces, grandstands, and pavilions offered superior sight lines, protection from the elements, and, not least, a measure of social insulation.

38. Christopher Anderson, *Hollywood TV: The Studio System in the Fifties* (Austin: University of Texas Press, 1994), 149.

39. Ibid., 149–150.

40. Ibid., 150.

41. Bryman, "The Disneyization of Society," 32.

42. Susan G. Davis, "The Theme Park: Global Industry and Cultural Form," *Media, Culture & Society* 18 (1996): 403.

43. Janet Wasko, "The Magical-Market World of Disney," *Monthly Review,* April 2001, http://www.findarticles.com/p/articles/mi_m1132/is_11_52/ai_74410355.

44. Anderson, *Hollywood TV,* 134.

45. "The first [advertising] signs appeared in ballparks (and on the walls of adjacent buildings) by the turn of the [twentieth] century" (Neilson, "Baseball," 51).

46. The term "hyper-commercial interpenetration" comes from Davis, "The Theme Park," 408.

47. Mark Crispin Miller, "What's Wrong with This Picture?" *The Nation,* January 7, 2002, http://www.thenation.com/doc.mhtml?i=20020107&s=miller.

48. For an instructive discussion of the synergistic opportunities available to sports-team-owning media conglomerates, see Jeremy Howell, "Luring Teams, Building Ballparks," in *Baseball and the American Dream: Race, Class, Gender, and the National Pastime,* ed. Robert Elias (Armonk, N.Y.: M. E. Sharpe, 2001), 207–213.

49. The selling of "naming rights" is arguably the most conspicuous means by which the Disneyfied stadium attempts to amplify the brand recognition and augment the cultural capital of corporations—in this case, by articulating together the nominal signifiers of private capital, the architecture of municipal pride and power, the historical associations and geographical orientations of local inhabitants, and the topophiliac intensities and home-team allegiances of sports spectators. In May of 2000, journalist Lynn Graebner ("Companies Spend Big Bucks on Naming Rights," *Business Journal,* May 26, 2000, http://www.findarticles.com/cf_0/m5024/5_18/62873874) reported that "companies vying to get professional sports stadiums named after them are investing hundreds of millions of dollars for the exposure. . . . In 1998, there were three such naming-rights deals worth $25 million. Today, there are fifty-five, with a total contract value of $2.5 billion."

50. Sony's JumboTron, Mitsubishi's Diamond Vision, Panasonic's Astrovision, SACO's SmartVision, and Daktronics's ProStar are well known makes/models.

51. Yi-Fu Tuan, "Disneyland: It's Place in World Culture," in *Designing Disney's Theme Parks: The Architecture of Reassurance,* ed. Karal Ann Marling (Montreal: Canadian Centre for Architecture, 1997), 196.

52. Ibid., 196.

53. Greg Siegel, "Double Vision: Large-Screen Video Display and Live Sports Spectacle," *Television & New Media* 3, no. 1 (2002).

54. Geraint John and Rod Sheard, *Stadia: A Design and Development Guide,* 2nd ed. (Oxford: Architectural Press, 1997), 203.

55. Jeff Houck, "Technical Foul: Technology Invades the Ballpark," FoxSportsBiz.com, July 20, 2000, http://www.foxsports.com/business/bites/20072ostadium_tech1.sml.

56. PhenomenArts, Inc., "Turn Up the Heat," publicity sheet, 1998.

57. Peter Murray, *The AmericanAirlines Arena Miami Florida,* publicity booklet (London: Wordsearch, n.d.), 11.

58. *Amusement Business,* "MCI Center."

59. With respect to cybersurveillance, consider the controversial—and, according to many legal experts, unconstitutional—use of face-recognition software and digital-image databases at the 2001 Super Bowl in Tampa, Florida.

60. Tony Bennett, *The Birth of the Museum: History, Theory, Politics* (London: Routledge, 1995), 68.

61. Janice Matsumoto, "Home Plate Advantages," *Restaurants & Institutions,* June 1, 2001, http://www.findarticles.com/cf_0/m3191/14_111/75407369.

62. Quoted in *Business Wire,* "Quick! Take Us to the Ballpark! Fan Food Choices Abound at Baseball Stadiums," March 26, 2002, http://www.findarticles.com/p/articles/mi_m0EIN/is_2002_March_26/ai_8418160.

63. Sharon Zukin, *Landscapes of Power: From Detroit to Disney World* (Berkeley: University of California Press, 1991), 206.

64. Kevin Paul Dupont, "Providing the Inside Information: From Seats to Eats, This Will Tell You What's Afoot at Fleet," *Boston Globe,* October 5, 1995, 92.

65. Neilson, "Baseball," 65.

66. Quoted in *Making and Selling Culture,* ed. Richard Ohmann (Hanover, N.H.: Wesleyan University Press, 1996), 155.

67. The term "men's cultural centers" comes from John Bale, *Landscapes of Modern Sport* (London: Leicester University Press, 1994), 174. The relationship between "the family vacation" and the Disney theme parks is explored in Susan Willis, "The Family Vacation," in *Inside the Mouse: Work and Play at Disney World,* ed. The Project on Disney (Durham, N.C.: Duke University Press, 1995), 49–53.

68. Scicchitano ("Features Galore") estimates that "about eighteen percent of seats in arenas and stadiums are considered 'premium seats' and are the primary source of facility revenue. The trend is [for] this ratio to increase in the future."

69. Susan E. Peterson, "Technology Scores Big at Xcel Energy Center," *Star Tribune,* Metro Edition, September 17, 2000, 1D.

70. Houck, "Technical Foul."

71. Gary Coffey, "No Shortage of Technology Among GM Place Offerings," *Amusement Business,* September 11, 1995, 23. It is worth noting that affluent patrons and corporate executives are not the only ones reaping the benefits of the Disneyfied stadium's technologically advanced amenities: athletes, managers, and journalists, too, enjoy their share of privileges and perquisites. Imparting fresh sense to the idiom "home-field advantage," San Francisco's Pacific Bell Park boasts a state-of-the-art video-coaching system, with a five-terabyte database outputted to a 750-DVD jukebox, allowing players and coaches to call up video segments of previous games and burn customized DVDs for analytical and archival purposes (Stephanie Sanborn, "Technology Hits a Home Run at Giants' Pac Bell Park," *InfoWorld,* May 15, 2000, 67). And at the Xcel Energy Center, "radio and TV reporters [are] able to broadcast on-the-spot interviews

from almost every location in the arena, thanks to a network of phone terminals that can be converted quickly to high-speed connections. In the press box, there are multiple phone lines and data lines at each seat, and the [home team] plans to set up an intranet system to provide electronic game notes and stats to reporters" (Peterson, "Technology Scores Big").

72. Sorkin, "See You in Disneyland," 228.

73. The labor of luxury-suite holders is one thing; that of the Disneyfied stadium's employees is quite another. Bryman ("The Disneyization of Society," 40) notes that "the ever-smiling Disney theme park employee has become a stereotype of modern culture. Their demeanor coupled with the distinctive Disney language is designed among other things to convey the impression that the employees are having fun too and therefore not engaging in real work." Baltimore's Ravens Stadium renders explicit the link between Disneyfied labor (in Bryman's sense) and the Disneyfied stadium. Journalist Scott Wilson ("Baltimore's New Stadium Is 'Beautiful, Just Beautiful,'" *Washington Post,* Final Edition, August 9, 1998, D07) reports that Ravens Stadium "represents the latest evolution of the customer-service era in professional sports. The ushers wear pressed khaki pants and purple ties. Elevator operators use 'sir' and 'ma'am' liberally, trained to do so during daylong etiquette class and two days of rehearsal before the debut game. Ravens owner Art Modell even spent $160,000 to send staff to Disney World for training in the finer points of crowd pleasing."

74. Neilson, "Baseball," 63. Not incidentally, in "convertible" stadiums such as SkyDome, Phoenix's Bank One Ballpark*f*, Seattle's SAFECO Field, and Houston's Minute Maid Park (nee Enron Field), the retractable roof—the literalization of the stadium-as-machine metaphor—is promoted (and presumably experienced) as a spectacular attraction, a technological wonder without equal.

75. Max Frankel, "Machinations: Billions for the Medium, Nothing for the Message," *New York Times Magazine,* May 11, 1997, 24.

CONTRIBUTORS

LEE ARTZ is Associate Professor in the Department of Communication and Creative Arts at Purdue University Calumet. His most recent books are *Bring 'Em On! Media and Power in the U.S. War on Iraq* and *The Globalization of Corporate Media Hegemony*, both with Yahya Kamalipour.

MIKE BUDD is Professor of Communication at Florida Atlantic University, where he teaches courses in film and media studies. He is the coauthor (with Steve Craig and Clay Steinman) of *Consuming Environments: Television and Commercial Culture* and the editor of *The Cabinet of Dr. Caligari: Texts, Contexts, Histories*.

SEAN GRIFFIN is Assistant Professor in the Division of Cinema-Television at Southern Methodist University. He is the author of *Tinker Belles and Evil Queens: The Walt Disney Company from the Inside Out* and the coauthor (with Harry Benshoff) of *America on Film: Representing Race, Class, Gender and Sexuality at the Movies*.

DICK HEBDIGE has written extensively on contemporary art, design and music, the media, and critical theory. He is Professor in the Departments of Art and Film Studies and Director of the Interdisciplinary Humanities Center at UC Santa Barbara. His books include *Subculture: The Meaning of Style* and *Hiding in the Light: On Images and Things*.

SCOTT HERMANSON is an assistant professor at Dana College in Blair, Nebraska. He writes and teaches about postmodernism, nature, and American literature.

RADHA JHAPPAN is Associate Professor of Political Science at Carleton University. She has published in the areas of indigenous peoples' politics and law, Canadian sociopolitical history, constitutional law and politics, the Charter of Rights and Freedoms, race and gender in feminist theory, and feminist legal theory and litigation strategies.

MAX KIRSCH is Associate Professor of Anthropology at Florida Atlantic University and the UNESCO Chair in Human and Cultural Rights. He is the author of *In the*

Wake of the Giant: Multinational Restructuring and Uneven Development in a New England Community and *Queer Theory and Social Change.*

FRANK ROOST has studied the global media industry's influence on urban planning as a visiting researcher at the United Nations Institute for Advanced Studies in Tokyo and at the Universidad de Buenos Aires. He teaches architecture and sociology at Technische Universitaet Berlin.

GREG SIEGEL is a Ph.D. candidate in Media and Cultural Studies in the Department of Communication Studies at the University of North Carolina, Chapel Hill.

DAIVA STASIULIS is Professor of Sociology at Carleton University and Co-Director of the Research Centre on the Study of Children, Sexuality and Popular Culture. She has published extensively on citizenship, race and migration, feminism and difference.

AARON TAYLOR is a lecturer in Film Studies at the University of Western Ontario and has written for *The Canadian Journal of Film Studies, Cineaction,* and *The Journal of Popular Culture.* He deeply regrets Walt Disney World's decision to replace the sublime lunacy offered by Mr. Toad's Wild Ride with The Many Adventures of Winnie the Pooh.

STACY WARREN is Professor of Geography at Eastern Washington University and a long-standing Disney scholar. Her research has focused on the impact of Disney development on urban and suburban space in increasingly global settings, and most recently investigates the Disney theme park experience from the perspective of its seasonal employees.

MAURYA WICKSTROM teaches theatre at the City University of New York: College of Staten Island and the Graduate Center. Her book *Performing Consumers: Theatrical Identifications in Corporate Cultures* is forthcoming from Routledge.

SUSAN WILLIS is coauthor (with Karen Klugman, Jane Kuenz and Shelton Waldrep) of *Inside the Mouse: Work and Play at Disney World;* her most recent book is *Portents of the Real: A Primer for Post-9/11 America.* Her work aims to reveal the contradictions of capitalism in everyday life.

INDEX

Commodification *(continued)*
    alibi, 111–13; of nature, 24–25, 201, 213,
    220–21, 222–23, 225; overview of, 18–20;
    and theme park experience, 15; of Winnie
    the Pooh, 23–24, 181–95; and worker ex-
    ploitation, 4–5
Commodity fetishism: appropriation of art
    by, 9; art as alibi for, 111–13, 117–18;
    Disney's contribution to, 4; vs. empathy
    with humans, 119–20; in *Lion King* stage
    production, 110, 112–13; and mimesis, 99–
    100, 104–9, 114–15; overview of, 18–20;
    and Roy Disney vs. Eisner, 115–20
Common-interest development, Celebration
    as, 281–82
CompuWho? 134, 135
Concession stands in sports stadiums, Dis-
    neyfication of, 313–16
Concourses, sports stadium, 305–6
Congress for the New Urbanism (CNU), 277
Conner, Leland, 163
Conrads, David, 303–4
Conservation narrative, 54–57, 67. *See also*
    Environmental issues
Conservation Station, 56–57, 59, 218–20
Consumer capitalism: and commodification
    of sports stadiums, 29–30; and consumers
    as low-wage workers, 6; and cultural stud-
    ies, 13; Disney's support for, 4, 95; and en-
    vironmental hypocrisies, 222–23, 224; and
    failure of moral outrage over Disney, 10–
    11; and Gay Days phenomenon, 125–26;
    gays and lesbians as target market, 22,
    140–45, 146–47; and in-house cross-
    promotion, 263; integration of culture in-
    dustries into, 17; power structures in, 12;
    vs. social reform as road to acceptance,
    140; and sophistication of teen consumers,
    102; theming as promoter of, 307. *See also*
    Commodification
Control issues: and alienation of public insti-
    tutions, 6; and animated feature develop-
    ment, 81; in animation themes, 86; in Cel-
    ebration project, 280–81; consequences for
    opposition to corporate power, 41; and
    Disney's contradictions, 3; Disney's obses-
    sion with, 2; vs. early Disney creative free-
    dom, 39; and power of fantasy, 12; and
    trademark protection, 5, 191; and urban

planning, 232, 237, 242, 251, 271–72, 275–
    76; and Winnie the Pooh, 182–95
Copyright control, excessive, 5, 191
Corporate culture, Disney's: and appropria-
    tion of high art, 112; arrogance of, 27;
    Eisner's transformation of, 131; and
    government of Celebration, 280–81; in-
    vestment in mimetic experience, 118; and
    manipulation of image and ideology, 15–
    18; narrative message vs. selling goals, 38–
    40; overview of issues, 4–5; and Pop art,
    44–45. *See also* Control issues
Corporate narratives, 208–9, 216–17
Corporatism and Eisner's shift in Disney, 115
Countdown to Extinction ride, 66, 216–18
Counterculture, 1960s/1970s, 41, 48, 127
Courtship and romance narratives, 84, 86,
    128, 161, 168–71
Creativity, Disney's repression of animator, 79
Critical analysis of Disney: cultural reluctance
    to engage in, 78; current foci of, 11–15; de-
    velopment of, 7–11; social taboos against,
    2, 12; spectrum of, 41–42
Cross-promotion: and corporate influence on
    public opinion, 288–90; with Disney part-
    ners, 263–64; media to real estate, 284–85,
    289–90; synergistic, 28–29, 47–48, 262–
    66, 284; and themed environments, 308–
    9; Times Square, 286–87
Cultural differences, homogenization of: and
    exile of marginalized social groups, 267,
    270; as hallmark of Disneyfication, 40; for
    tourism, 268; and urban spaces, 270–73,
    274, 282, 300. *See also* Celebration, Flor-
    ida; Urban planning
Cultural relativism in *Pocahontas,* 152–53, 156–
    57, 161–64
Cultural studies, origins of, 11
Culture capital, Disney's, 19
Culture of Nature, The (Wilson), 206
Customization of narrative to demographic
    audience, 25

Davis, Mike, 300
Davis, Susan G., 308
Death and extinction narrative, 66–70
Debidour, V. H., 64–65
DeBord, Guy, 13
Democracy: Celebration's lack of, 280–82;

Merchandising: and cross-promotion partnerships, 264, 289–90; decline in Disney, 49n2; and extended life of Disney influences, 81; as integral part of spatial experience, 14; and live theater productions, 28; and mimetic experience, 102–3, 105; as money-making enterprise, 76; and product integration, 39–40; and sweatshop manufacturing, 4–5, 210; and Winnie the Pooh, 181–95. *See also* Stores, Disney

Mere exposure effect, 290–91

Miami Beach, Florida, as gay vacation mecca, 141

Mickey Mouse, 77, 182, 191

Mickey Mouse clubs, 102–3

Middle class: and appeal of simulated small-town environment, 278; and branding of Celebration, 283; defensible urban spaces for, 300–301; sports stadiums as entertainment for, 304, 305; theme parks as designed for, 308

Midtown Community Court, 29, 272

Miller, Mark Crispin, 309

Milne, A. A., 23, 181, 185, 188

Milne, Clare, 195

Milne Estate, 195

Mimesis: in Animal Kingdom, 69–70; art as alibi for commodity fetishism, 111–13; and commodity fetishism, 104–9; digital, 47; introduction of, 100–104; and magical capitalism, 109–11; overview of, 19–20; and primitivism in *Lion King,* 113–15; Roy Disney's investment in, 115–20

Mimesis and Alterity (Taussig), 100–101

Miramax film studio, 264

Mitchell, George, 116

Mobility, virtual, in sports stadium environment, 310

Modernity: and alienation from nature, 221; vs. pop culture, 44–45; vs. primitive fetishism, 114–15

Mole rats, naked. *See* Naked mole rats

Monogamy, Disney's narrative support for, 42

Monotheming vs. multitheming and sports stadiums, 306–9

Monsters, Inc.: departure from stereotypes in, 89; naturalization of hierarchies in, 79, 85, 87, 88; nonelite characters in, 91

Moore, Charles, 279

Morakami, Takashi, 47

Moral issues, 10–11, 45, 80, 89. *See also* Good vs. evil

Moses, Robert, 235

Movie industry and cross-promotion, 264, 285–86

Movie News, 265

Mulan, 85, 87, 89

Mullen, Jim, 6

Multitheming vs. monotheming and sports stadiums, 306–9

Naked mole rats, 56

Naming of sports stadiums, corporate, 321n49

Narratives vs. business plan for Disney, 37–38. *See also* Animation narratives; Themed environments

Narrator as character in Winnie the Pooh films, 186–87

National Organization of Women (NOW), 128

Native Americans, and conflicting messages in *Pocahontas,* 173–74nn12–13, 176n58. See also *Pocahontas*

Naturalization of hierarchies, Disney's promotion of, 18, 83–88

Nature: alienation from, 157, 221; commodification of, 24–25, 201, 213, 220–21, 222–23, 225; Disneyfication of, 60–66; humans as generic despoilers of, 213–14; media as source for perceptions of, 206, 212, 225; unmediated interaction with, 204–6, 211, 221; yielding vs. dominating relationship to, 111, 114. *See also* Animal Kingdom

Nature Conservancy, 223

Neilson, Brian J., 314–15, 316

Neocolonialism and ecotourism, 208–9

Neotraditionalism, promotion of, 261, 275–83, 292–93. *See also* Celebration, Florida

Never Never Land art exhibition, 37, 46–47

New Amsterdam Theatre, 28, 99, 270, 271

New Queer Cinema, 140

News as entertainment, 288–89, 292–93

New Urbanism, 277–78, 292. *See also* Celebration, Florida

New York City. *See* Times Square project

Niederman, Andrew, 44

Noland, Jane, 241–42

Nondiscrimination policy on sexual orientation, 131
Nonelite characters, passive stereotyping of, 83-84, 87-88, 91-93
NOW (National Organization of Women), 128

Oasis in Animal Kingdom, 201-2
O'Donnell, Rosie, 146
Odyssey Adventures travel agency, 133-34
"One Mighty Party" events at Disney/MGM Studios, 141
Orange County, Florida, 283
Orlando, Florida, 136-37, 139-40, 276. *See also* Walt Disney World
Osceola County, Florida, 280
Oswald the Lucky Rabbit, 192, 198n40
"Others," racialized, 151, 159, 170. See also *Pocahontas*
"Outside the brand" concept, 2, 10
Ovitz, Michael, 4

Paleontology, romanticization of, 215-16
Parents: animated characters' lack of, 42; lesbian and gay, 146. *See also* Children
Paternalism of Disney, 2
Peiser, Richard, 253
Pelli, Cesar, 280
Pentecost, James, 164, 171, 174n12
People with AIDS (PWAs), 130-31
Petrocelli, Daniel J., 182
Phillips, Mark, 17
Piedmont Environmental Council, 6, 249
Pietz, William, 110
Pine, B. Joseph, 304-5, 306
Pirates of the Caribbean display, toning down of sexuality in, 148n6
Pixar animation studio, 76, 79, 85, 94
Plater-Zyberk, Elisabeth, 276, 277
Pleasure Island at Disney World, 137-38
Pleasure without risk, 39, 81
Pocahontas: historical authenticity problems, 171-73; naturalization of hierarchies in, 84-85, 87, 88; New York City premiere of, 269; overview of stereotyping issues in, 22-23, 151-54; plot outlines, 154-56; racial textual strategies in, 156-71
Pocahontas, historical evidence vs. Disney fantasy, 161, 163-64, 170-71

Pocahontas and Her Forest Friends, 203-6
Pocahontas II: Journey to a New World, 22-23, 152, 155-56, 167
Politics: Disney's avoidance of, 59-60; and gay assimilation through recreation, 142-43, 146; Gay Days as, 126-29, 130; gay rights activism, 127, 147-48n4; political correctness vs. inaccuracies in *Pocahontas,* 172
Politics of forgetting, 173, 177n76
Pop art, 44-45
Popular culture: animation as effective distributor of, 75; and intellectual community, 8-9, 10-12
Port Disney project, 243-44, 245
Postcapitalist fetishism, 110
Postmodernism: and consumer mimesis, 99-100, 101-2; Disney as exemplar of decorative, 47; and embrace of commercialism, 9; and irony of merchandizing in *Hercules,* 39-40; and sports stadiums, 320n37
Power relations: and animation narratives, 88-90; and claim to whiteness, 151-52; and commodity fetishism, 106; in consumer capitalism, 12; as crux of Disney problems, 9, 11; and Disney's culture of domination, 16, 101; and reciprocity in mimesis, 105; and urban planning, 236. *See also* Control issues; Hierarchies, social
Powhatan Renape Nation, 172
Price, Jennifer, 201, 216
Primitivism in *Lion King,* 110, 111, 113-15, 121n24
Prince William County, Virginia, project, 5-6, 27, 247-50, 259n64
Private appropriation of public space: and big business control over science, 216; and Disneyfication, 6, 40, 93; and loss of reality's social complexity, 45; and Orlando's relationship to Disney World, 28; and theme parks as models for public spaces, 26-27; and urban gentrification, 299-302. *See also* Sports stadiums; Theme parks; Urban planning
Private parties at Disney theme parks, 21-22, 126-34
Production, means of, and Conservation Station, 218-19
Product placement, 49n3, 264, 265

Shepard, Ernest A., 182, 184–85, 189, 194, 197n14, 197n31
Shepard, Graham, 197
Shohat, Ella, 154
Short, Bill, 143
Shrek, 81
Siegel, Greg, 7, 29–30
Singh, John, 190
Skyboxes in sports stadiums, 315–16
Slesinger family, 182, 195
Smith, John: history vs. fantasy, 166–67, 173n11
Smith, Neil, 299
Smoodin, Eric, 15
Socialization, Disney animation's role in, 78, 80
Social structures, Disneyfication of, 214
Soja, Edward, 251
Sontag, Susan, 9
Sorkin, Michael, 251, 305
Southern Baptist Convention, boycott of Disney, 138, 139
Spiegel, Robert, 101–2
Spirituality and mimesis, 101
Sports stadiums: adjacent attractions, 304–6; and ambience emphasis, 319n18; amenities, 313–17; athlete/manager amenities in, 322–23n71; and corporate naming rights, 321n49; monotheming in, 306–9; overview of, 29–30; premodern vs. postmodern incarnations, 320n37; and public value of stadium, 302–4, 318n12–13; video displays and scoreboards, 309–13; and workers as cast members, 323n73
Stabiner, Karen, 143
Staged environments, artificiality of, 57–58
Stage versions of Disney animation. *See* Broadway plays
Stam, Robert, 154
Stannard, David, 161
Starbucks, local resistance to expansion of, 253
Stasiulis, Daiva, 22–23
Stereotyping, Disney, and primary vs. secondary animated characters, 83–84, 87–88. *See also* Heroes/heroines, Disney stereotypes; Villains, Disney stereotypes
Stern, Robert A. M., 267, 268, 273, 276
Stone, Lawrence, 161

Stonewall riots in Greenwich Village, 127, 147–48n4
Stores, Disney: decline of, 118–19; fundamentalist picketing of, 139; and mimesis, 103–4, 111; and mimetic experience, 105, 112–13; Times Square, 268, 286; and Winnie the Pooh merchandising, 182
Strong, Pauline Turner, 159
Subliminal advertising, 290–92, 297–98n94
Suburbanites, longing of for small-town ambience, 278
Surveillance: as entertainment, 312; as model for employee monitoring, 45
Swallow, Doug, 135, 138
Sweatshop labor, 4–5, 210
Sympathetic imagination vs. commodity fetishism, 119
Sympathetic magic. *See* Mimesis
Synergy projects, 28–29, 47–48, 262–66, 284. *See also* Cross-promotion

Taboos, animated social, 42
Tamarins, anthropomorphizing of, 61
Tao of Pooh (Hoff), 183
Tarzan, 86
Taussig, Michael, 100–101, 110–11
Taylor, Aaron, 23–24
Taylorization of leisure, 39
Taymor, Julie, 19, 99, 109, 110–11
Technology: and corporate class, 316–17; and manipulation of imagination, 66; and replacement of the real, 68; self-acting, 16, 217–18
Te of Piglet, The (Hoff), 183
Text as visual character in Winnie the Pooh films, 186
TF1, 285
Themed environments: alienation from local culture, 251–52; and commodification of nature, 24–25; as cultural homogenization devices, 47; as focus of cultural studies, 13–14; and urban renovations, 262, 301. *See also* Sports stadiums; Urban planning
Theme parks: Disneyland, 24, 126–34, 148n6, 278; Disney's America project, 5–6, 27, 247–50, 259n64; extension into public environment, 26; marketing synergy with other media products, 263; and synergetic marketing, 266, 270; and urban planning,

Walt Disney World: anthropological critique
of, 14–15; cultural studies on, 13; Gay Days
at, 134–45; mass transit at, 223, 227n29;
and Orlando, 28, 136–37, 139–40, 276;
Pleasure Island, 137–38; as worship of
technology, 317. *See also* Animal Kingdom
Ward, Annalee, 80
Warhol, Andy, 8–9, 44
Warner Brothers and Looney Tunes charac-
ters, 2, 104–5
Warren, Stacy, 6
Wasko, Janet, 2, 3, 17, 82
Wells, Frank, 6, 131
WESTCOT project, 244, 245–46
Western culture: Africa and Asia as antithesis
of, 207; and Disney's role in end of Cold
War, 49–50n5; vs. primitivism, 121n24;
and separation from mimesis, 114–15. *See
also* Colonialism, cultural
Weston, Florida, 284
Wetlands, Disney's mixed record on, 223
Whiteness, decentering of in *Pocahontas*, 22–
23, 151–54, 156–71
Wickstrom, Maurya, 18–20
Wildness narrative, 17, 54–57, 207, 210–14
Williams, Raymond, 13
Willis, Susan, 13, 191
Wilson, Alexander, 206, 220–21
Winer, Linda, 112

Winnie the Pooh, 23–24, 181–95
Winnie the Pooh and the Blustery Day, 183
Winnie the Pooh and the Honey Tree, 183
Witt, Thomas and Harris (television producers), 284
Workers: as animals, 69–70; animals as, 55,
57–60, 69, 205, 221; homosexual, 132, 135–
36, 136; international Animal Kingdom,
220–21; mimetic experience of, 107–8; as
protagonists in *Monsters, Inc.,* 88; reduc-
tions in, 131; toleration of gays at theme
parks, 127. *See also* Animators; Exploitation of workers
"Working at the Rat" (Kuenz), 13–14
Work persona, extension into home life, 45–
46

Xcel Energy Center, St. Paul, Minnesota, 315

Yielding vs. dominating relationship to nature, 111, 114
Young romantics narrative, 84, 86, 168–71

Zajonc, Robert, 290–91
Zane, Billy, 167
Zoos, metropolitan, vs. Animal Kingdom,
199–201, 206, 219
Zukin, Sharon, 251, 252, 254, 277, 279, 313